Luke

TEACH THE TEXT COMMENTARY SERIES

John H. Walton
Old Testament General Editor

Mark L. Strauss
New Testament General Editor

When complete, the TEACH THE TEXT COMMENTARY SERIES *will include the following volumes:*

Old Testament Volumes

New Testament Volumes

To see which titles are available, visit the series website at www.teachthetextseries.com.

TEACH the TEXT
COMMENTARY SERIES

Luke

R. T. France

Mark L. Strauss and John H. Walton
GENERAL EDITORS

Rosalie de Rosset
ASSOCIATE EDITOR

BakerBooks

a division of Baker Publishing Group
Grand Rapids, Michigan

© 2013 by R. T. France
Captions and Illustrating the Text sections © 2013 by Baker Publishing Group

Published by Baker Books
a division of Baker Publishing Group
P.O. Box 6287, Grand Rapids, MI 49516–6287
www.bakerbooks.com

Printed in the United States of America

Library of Congress Cataloging-in-Publication Data
France, R. T.
    Luke / R. T. France.
        pages cm. — (Teach the text commentary series)
    Includes bibliographical references and index.
    ISBN 978-0-8010-9235-0 (cloth : alk. paper)
    1. Bible. Luke—Commentaries. I. Title.
BS2595.53.L86 2013
226.4'07—dc23   2013012205

13 14 15 16 17 18 19   7 6 5 4 3 2 1

Contents

Welcome to the Teach the Text Commentary Series

Why another commentary series? That was the question the general editors posed when Baker Books asked us to produce this series. Is there something that we can offer to pastors and teachers that is not currently being offered by other commentary series, or that can be offered in a more helpful way? After carefully researching the needs of pastors who teach the text on a weekly basis, we concluded that yes, more can be done; this commentary is carefully designed to fill an important gap.

The technicality of modern commentaries often overwhelms readers with details that are tangential to the main purpose of the text. Discussions of source and redaction criticism, as well as detailed surveys of secondary literature, seem far removed from preaching and teaching the Word. Rather than wade through technical discussions, pastors often turn to devotional commentaries, which may contain exegetical weaknesses, misuse the Greek and Hebrew languages, and lack hermeneutical sophistication. There is a need for a commentary that utilizes the best of biblical scholarship but also presents the material in a clear, concise, attractive, and user-friendly format.

This commentary is designed for that purpose—to provide a ready reference for the exposition of the biblical text, giving easy access to information that a pastor needs to communicate the text effectively. To that end, the commentary is divided into carefully selected preaching units, each covered in six pages (with carefully regulated word counts both in the passage as a whole and in each subsection). Pastors and teachers engaged in weekly preparation thus know that they will be reading approximately the same amount of material on a week-by-week basis.

Each passage begins with a concise summary of the central message, or "Big Idea," of the passage and a list of its main themes. This is followed by a more detailed interpretation of the text, including the literary context of the passage, historical background material, and interpretive insights. While drawing on the best of biblical scholarship, this material is clear, concise, and to the point. Technical material is kept to a minimum, with endnotes pointing the reader to more detailed discussion and additional resources.

A second major focus of this commentary is on the preaching and teaching process itself. Few commentaries today help the pastor/teacher move from the meaning of the text to its effective communication. Our goal is to bridge this gap. In addition to interpreting the text in the "Understanding the Text" section, each six-page unit contains a "Teaching the Text" section and an "Illustrating the Text" section. The teaching section points to the key theological themes of the passage and ways to communicate these themes to today's audiences. The illustration section provides ideas and examples for retaining the interest of hearers and connecting the message to daily life.

The creative format of this commentary arises from our belief that the Bible is not just a record of God's dealings in the past but is the living Word of God, "alive and active" and "sharper than any double-edged sword" (Heb. 4:12). Our prayer is that this commentary will help to unleash that transforming power for the glory of God.

The General Editors

Introduction to the Teach the Text Commentary Series

This series is designed to provide a ready reference for teaching the biblical text, giving easy access to information that is needed to communicate a passage effectively. To that end, the commentary is carefully divided into units that are faithful to the biblical authors' ideas and of an appropriate length for teaching or preaching.

The following standard sections are offered in each unit.

1. *Big Idea*. For each unit the commentary identifies the primary theme, or "Big Idea," that drives both the passage and the commentary.
2. *Key Themes*. Together with the Big Idea, the commentary addresses in bullet-point fashion the key ideas presented in the passage.
3. *Understanding the Text*. This section focuses on the exegesis of the text and includes several sections.
   a. The Text in Context. Here the author gives a brief explanation of how the unit fits into the flow of the text around it, including reference to the rhetorical strategy of the book and the unit's contribution to the purpose of the book.
   b. Outline/Structure. For some literary genres (e.g., epistles), a brief exegetical outline may be provided to guide the reader through the structure and flow of the passage.
   c. Historical and Cultural Background. This section addresses historical and cultural background information that may illuminate a verse or passage.
   d. Interpretive Insights. This section provides information needed for a clear understanding of the passage. The intention of the author is to be highly selective and concise rather than exhaustive and expansive.
   e. Theological Insights. In this very brief section the commentary identifies a few carefully selected theological insights about the passage.

4. *Teaching the Text*. Under this second main heading the commentary offers guidance for teaching the text. In this section the author lays out the main themes and applications of the passage. These are linked carefully to the Big Idea and are represented in the Key Themes.

5. *Illustrating the Text*. Here the commentary provides suggestions of where useful illustrations may be found in fields such as literature, entertainment, history, or biography. They are intended to provide general ideas for illustrating the passage's key themes and so serve as a catalyst for effectively illustrating the text.

Abbreviations

General

ca.	circa
cf.	*confer*, compare
chap(s).	chapter(s)
e.g.	*exempli gratia*, for example
lit.	literally
v(v).	verse(s)

Ancient Text Types and Versions

LXX	Septuagint

Modern Versions

KJV	King James Version
NIV	New International Version
NRSV	New Revised Standard Version
REB	Revised English Bible
RSV	Revised Standard Version

Apocrypha and Septuagint

Sir.	Sirach
Tob.	Tobit

Dead Sea Scrolls

CD	*Damascus Document*
1Q28a (1QSa)	*Rule of the Congregation*
11Q19	*Temple*[a]

Mishnah and Talmud

b.	Babylonian Talmud
m.	Mishnah
'Abot	*'Abot*
Ber.	*Berakot*
Ketub.	*Ketubbot*
Mak.	*Makkot*
Pesah.	*Pesahim*
Sanh.	*Sanhedrin*
Shabb.	*Shabbat*
Yoma	*Yoma (= Kippurim)*

Apostolic Fathers

Did.	*Didache*

Greek and Latin Works

Eusebius

Hist. eccl.	*Ecclesiastical History (Historia ecclesiastica)*

Josephus

Ag. Ap.	*Against Apion (Contra Apionem)*
Ant.	*Jewish Antiquities (Antiquitates judaicae)*
Life	*The Life (Vita)*
J.W.	*Jewish War (Bellum judaicum)*

Philo

Embassy   *On the Embassy to Gaius (Lega-*
            tio ad Gaium)

Pliny the Younger

Ep.   *Epistles (Epistulae)*

Tacitus

Ann.   *Annals (Annales)*

Introduction to Luke

Luke-Acts: A Two-Volume Work

The traditional canonical order of the New Testament books divides Luke's work into two separate sections, the Gospel of Luke and the Acts of the Apostles. But Acts 1:1–2 makes the continuity clear, and the latter part of Luke 24 reads as if Luke's mind is already as much on his second volume as on completing his first. Luke 1:1–4 does not specify what he includes in "the things that have been fulfilled among us," but it seems likely that when Luke began his Gospel, he was already intending to cover the whole story up to his own time. Certainly by the time he got to the end of the Gospel, he was clearly planning to provide the mysterious Theophilus with a comprehensive account of the origins of Christianity. The division of this ambitious project into two books reflects the practical limits of a single scroll (Luke alone is already the longest "book" in the New Testament, with Acts a close second), though of course there is also a clear and convenient division into two periods: the period of Jesus's presence on earth and the period of his disciples' mission after his ascension.

Theophilus, to whom both volumes are explicitly addressed, is otherwise unknown. The title "most excellent" (Luke 1:3) suggests a person of high social standing (it is so used in Acts 23:26; 24:3; 26:25), and the verb translated "taught" in Luke 1:4 became in Christian usage a designation of the "catechesis," formal instruction in the faith, which often preceded baptism. So Theophilus may have been a high-ranking convert to Christianity. His Greek name may suggest a non-Jew, though the same name was borne also by Jews in the multilingual culture of Palestine. He is normally understood to be Luke's literary patron; such an address to a prominent figure was a recognized mode of launching a literary work, with no intention that the work was for his use alone.

Who Was Luke?

The only "Luke" we know from the New Testament was an associate of Paul, described as one of his "fellow workers" (Philem. 24; cf. 2 Tim. 4:11), and as "our dear friend Luke, the doctor" (Col. 4:14). It is unlikely that such a relatively obscure person would be credited with the authorship of these two important books unless his name was already firmly associated with them in Christian tradition, and no other name was ever proposed as author; most scholars accept the attribution.

A curious feature of Acts is that the narrative, normally in the third person, switches abruptly to the first person at several points, suggesting that the author himself was present during those parts of the story. These "we passages" cover Acts 16:10–17; 20:5–16; 21:1–18; 27:1–28:16, which would mean that the author joined Paul's group at Troas on the second missionary journey and accompanied them as far as Philippi, then rejoined the group for the latter part of the third journey, traveling with them from Philippi to Jerusalem, and finally went with Paul from Caesarea to Rome, on the journey with which Acts concludes. This would indicate that he spent a substantial time in Palestine during Paul's imprisonment, a period that he may well have used to research material for his history. If he then remained with Paul in Rome, this would fit the references to Luke's presence in Colossians, Philemon, and 2 Timothy.

None of this amounts to proof of Luke's authorship, but that seems the most adequate explanation of such data as we have. If, then, Luke was the author of Luke-Acts, these would probably be the only books of the New Testament written by a non-Jew, since Luke appears in the list of Paul's non-Jewish associates following Colossians

The most likely candidate for the author of the Gospel of Luke was trained as a physician and was Paul's associate and companion during several stages of Paul's missionary journeys. Shown here is an icon of Luke from a larger piece entitled *Christ and Twelve Apostles* taken from a nineteenth-century Orthodox church in the Antalya region of Turkey.

4:11. The "we passages" indicate a member who joined the group in the Greek rather than the Jewish world. The excellent Greek style and literary presentation of the work would suit a native Greek speaker, even though the author is clearly well informed about Jewish affairs and makes frequent and enthusiastic use of the Greek version of the Hebrew Scriptures (the Septuagint, abbreviated "LXX").

The Origin of the Work

We will look in more detail later at Luke's statement of intent in Luke 1:1–4, but it is clear that he did not write in a vacuum, at least as far as the first volume of his work was concerned. Others had already been drawing up accounts of the life and teaching of Jesus, and Luke is self-consciously adding to their number and aiming to improve on what they have been able to offer. He does not tell us who they were, but most scholars believe that the Gospel of Mark was one of them and was a major source of Luke's story. We will consider below the possibility that there were other, less substantial accounts in circulation in either written or oral form that have not survived but were available as sources for Luke.

The three Gospels of Mark, Matthew, and Luke share the same essential narrative structure (the more strikingly similar when it is compared with the very different outline of John's Gospel) of an extensive ministry in Galilee, followed by a decisive journey south to Jerusalem, after which the climactic events take place in that city. If, as most scholars believe, Mark is the earliest of the three, it seems likely that this scheme originated with him. At times Luke follows Mark's story quite closely, but he also has a lot of material (considerably more than Matthew) that is independent of Mark. In particular, the story of the journey to Jerusalem, which in Mark takes up just over two chapters, and in Matthew a little over four, accounts for nearly half of Luke's Gospel (Luke 9:51–19:44). Into this section

A ninth-century Greek manuscript of the Gospel of Luke

of the story he has packed a great deal of material unknown to Mark and (to a lesser extent) Matthew.

That there is a close literary relationship between Mark, Matthew, and Luke is obvious, but attempts to define the nature of that relationship continue to vary widely. At least it is clear that Luke's Gospel is very much more than simply a revised version of Mark, and that Luke has both a great deal of independent source material and his own distinctive approach to how the story of Jesus should be told. We will explore these issues further when we look at Luke 1:1–4 below.

The date at which Luke's Gospel was written is an intriguing puzzle. On the one hand, it is natural to assume that Acts was written after Luke, and the story of Acts finishes in AD 62 with Paul triumphantly spreading the gospel from his house arrest in Rome. It is almost certain that this period of relative freedom did not last, and that Paul was executed during the persecution of Christians in Rome by Nero in AD 64–65, yet Acts gives no hint of this drastic change or of the subsequent destruction of Jerusalem in AD 70. An obvious explanation of this startling silence ("the dog that did not bark") is that Acts was written before the Neronian persecution and the death of Paul. That would place the origin of Acts in the early 60s, and the Gospel therefore presumably a few years earlier.

On the other hand, it has long been traditional among scholars to speak of the 60s as the very earliest possible date for Mark, and, since Matthew and Luke are assumed to have had access to a completed version of Mark, to place both Matthew and Luke some time later; a date around AD 80 is widely favored. In particular, it is often taken for granted that passages such as Luke 19:43–44; 21:20–24, though ostensibly Jesus's words of prediction, reflect Luke's own knowledge of the Roman siege and capture of Jerusalem in AD 70.

The arguments are too complex to pursue here, but the reader should be aware that although the later date remains the most widely supported, there is a growing minority of scholars who argue that a date for at least the first draft, and possibly the finished version, of Luke's Gospel before AD 64/65 best fits the evidence, however inconvenient that may be for the conventional view of the relative dating of the Gospels. Such a proposal is particularly plausible if it is combined with a less rigidly "X copied Y" understanding of the nature of the literary relationship between Mark, Matthew, and Luke than mainstream scholarship has often been prepared to envisage.

Luke the Historian: Luke 1:1–4

Luke has provided a clear statement of intent at the beginning of his work, and a study of this preface tells us much about his purpose and method.

Many have undertaken to draw up an account of the things that have been fulfilled among us, just as they were handed down to us by those who from the first were eyewitnesses and servants of the word. With this in mind, since I myself have carefully investigated everything from the beginning, I too decided to write an orderly account for you, most excellent Theophilus, so that you may know the certainty of the things you have been taught.

Other ancient historians and authors of literary works of nonfiction made similar statements of intent, assuring their readers that their works could be trusted, and the formal style of Luke's opening words conforms to that Greco-Roman literary convention. But not all ancient historians seem to have delivered quite what they promised, and there has been much debate as to how far Luke was able to fulfill his stated ideal.

On the one hand, there are specific problems such as the Roman census referred to in 2:1–3 (see commentary there), or the fact that Luke's account of Jewish insurrections in Acts 5:36–37 differs in sequence from Josephus's account of the same events. Against this must be set the accuracy with which Acts reflects the changing political situations in different Roman provinces, as well as Luke's extraordinary ability to use the right technical terms for the various local officials.

On the other hand, some scholars emphasize Luke's lack of "objectivity," in that he writes as a Christian believer with the aim of commending the faith and its founder, and that he has no hesitation in presenting as factual history supernatural events that defy scientific explanation. On that basis, of course, none of the biblical writers can be allowed to be "objective" historians. But that is a question of philosophical presupposition rather than of historical method. That Luke writes as a committed believer in the risen Jesus is hardly likely to jeopardize his historical reliability for those whose worldview can accommodate God and miracle![1]

If we take Luke's opening words at face value, several clauses throw important light on his aims and methods as a historian.

1:1 *Many have undertaken to draw up an account.* Most scholars assume that early collections of Jesus's words and deeds were circulating orally among the Christian congregations for some time before our written Gospels appeared, but since Luke presents his work as in the same category as that of the "many," it appears that at least some of those earlier accounts already existed in written form. As mentioned above, Mark's Gospel should probably be understood to be one of these predecessors, and many scholars believe that Luke also used a written source or sources for much of the additional material that he shares with Matthew (the "Q" material), but "many" suggests that Luke had a larger pool of written as well as oral material to draw on, most of which did not survive except as incorporated into his own and the other Gospels.

1:2 *those who from the first were eyewitnesses and servants of the word.* Clearly, Luke does not include himself in this category, but he has had good firsthand material available. Note the requirement in Acts 1:21–22 that a member of the Twelve must have been part of the disciple group from the time of John's baptism until Jesus's ascension. They had seen and heard it all, and so now here was a rich fund of (presumably largely) oral tradition for Luke to draw on in addition to the written records compiled by the "many."[2]

1:3 *I myself have carefully investigated everything from the beginning.* Luke's work presents itself as a serious research project rather than a random collection of reminiscences. If Luke was in Palestine during the two years or so that Paul was in prison before his transfer to Rome (see above on the "we passages"), he had plenty of opportunity to pursue this research by contacting the eyewitnesses both in Jerusalem and in Galilee. The remarkable insights into the private world of Mary and her family in chapters 1–2 suggest that Mary herself may have been among those he interviewed (see on 2:19).

In speaking of "an orderly account," is there perhaps here a hint of criticism of some of Luke's predecessors' work as lacking in "order"? The early Christian writer

Luke gathered the information for his Gospel from eyewitnesses and earlier written sources, which may have included the Gospel of Mark. His account was probably transcribed using the common writing implements of this time period such as the bronze pen and inkpot from Roman Britain shown here.

Papias (early second century) indicates a similar criticism with regard to the Gospel of Mark, which, based as it was on Peter's ad hoc reminiscences and teaching, could not be blamed for being "not in order"; Papias also speaks by contrast of Matthew as having "put in order" the Gospel material available to him (Eusebius, *Hist. eccl.* 3.39.15–16). "Draw up" (*anatassomai*) in 1:1 also more literally means "put in order." The word that Luke uses in 1:3 is different (*kathexēs*, "in sequence"), but it suggests a similar concern that everything be properly organized. Readers often assume that he is referring especially to putting events in the right *chronological* order, but there are other types of "order"—thematic order, a satisfying literary structure, and so on. Luke is a sophisticated writer who knows how to tell a good story, and putting the elements of the story in chronological sequence may not always be the most effective way of presenting it. For instance, the dramatic scene in the synagogue at Nazareth with which he opens his account of Jesus's Galilean ministry (4:16–30) occurs later in the Gospels of Matthew and Mark, and it includes a reference to Jesus's previous activity in Capernaum (4:23) before Luke has recorded Jesus's first visit there. Luke has placed the incident in chapter 4 not necessarily because it happened first, but because it provides a vivid programmatic account of what Jesus's mission was to be all about. That is a more satisfying literary "order" than mere chronology.

1:4 *that you may know the certainty of the things you have been taught.* Perhaps all that Luke means is that he wants Theophilus to have the firm evidence to back up the teaching that he has received. But some have again detected here a note of criticism of Luke's predecessors. "Certainty" translates *asphaleia*, denoting that which is firmly founded and cannot be moved. Whatever weaknesses other accounts of Jesus may have had, Luke's record will not let the reader down. It is to be utterly reliable.

If, then, we take Luke at his word, he tells us that his aim is to write reliable, accurate history, set out in an acceptable literary form, and he went to considerable pains to ensure that he was as well informed as he could be.

Luke the Evangelist

But Luke is not just a chronicler of events. He is a man with a message. Much of what he wants his books to convey is, naturally, shared with the other Gospel writers and with his associate Paul. But in some ways his work stands out as distinctive from theirs.

Perhaps the best term to sum up Luke's essential message is "salvation."[3] In both the Gospel and Acts we meet many people whose lives are transformed by the grace of God, such as Zacchaeus, to whose house "salvation" has come, prompting Jesus to make his programmatic declaration "The Son of Man came to seek and to save the lost" (Luke 19:9–10).

Zacchaeus was a successful financier, but a social outcast. Others were "lost" in many different ways, and Luke's story is famous for its broad sympathy with the marginalized and the disadvantaged—the poor and the sick, the harassed and the demon-possessed, widows and bereaved parents, women and children, the social underworld of tax collectors and sinners, the Gentiles and even the Samaritans. To all, in their different needs, salvation and wholeness came through the ministry of Jesus, who came to proclaim "good news to the poor" (4:18), and Luke took delight in using their stories to illustrate the revolutionary ideals of the Magnificat (see 1:51–53), the dawning kingdom of God, in which the last will be first and the first last (13:30).

All this is, of course, in fulfillment (note the use of "fulfilled" in 1:1) of what God has promised, and Luke, no less than the other (Jewish) evangelists, delights to trace the fulfillment of Scripture in the events that he records, beginning with the remarkable concentration of scriptural material in Luke 1–2, and concluding with Jesus's definitive expositions of Scripture in Luke 24:25–27, 44–48.

Teaching the Text: Luke 1:1–4

Luke 1:1–4 can be taught as part of a message introducing a study of the Gospel of Luke. Since this is the only place in the four Gospels where an author explicitly refers to himself in the first person ("I") and identifies his purpose in writing (but see also the purpose statement in John 20:30–31), it serves as a natural introduction to the Gospel. The passage allows you to introduce (1) Luke the physician as the author, (2) Theophilus (and the community with which he is associated) as the recipient, (3) the likely occasion and situation to which Luke wrote, and (4) his purpose in writing. The passage also illustrates Luke's role as a storyteller, historian, and theologian. He is writing a "narrative" (= story), with features like characters, setting, and plot, so that it is important to read and follow the story through introduction, conflict, climax, and resolution. But it is also *history*. Luke has carefully researched and sought out eyewitnesses in order to produce an accurate and trustworthy historical narrative. It is not, however, just "bare history." It is theologically driven history, the account of the salvation *God* has accomplished through Jesus the Messiah, and what he continues to accomplish through his church (in Acts). All these important points—critical to an introduction to the Gospel of Luke—can be teased out in a sermon or lesson on 1:1–4. Be sure to stress Luke's emphasis on tracking the course of "salvation history"—that is, that Luke sees the events of Jesus's life, death, and resurrection, and the expansion of the church in Acts, as the climax of God's worldwide plan of redemption and the fulfillment of his promises made to the nation Israel.

A Special Child Promised

Big Idea *The promise of the birth of a special child shows that a new age is dawning: John the Baptist will prepare the people for the coming of the Lord.*

Understanding the Text

The Text in Context

We have considered Luke's introductory statement of intent (1:1–4) in the introduction ("Luke the Historian: Luke 1:1–4"), and I will not comment further on it here. The story then begins, to the reader's surprise, not with Jesus but with the promise of the birth of John the Baptist. The reader will be invited to compare the origins of the two men, both born by the special power of God, both heralded by the same angelic messenger, both named by the angel, and both called to fulfill a key role in the working out of God's purpose of deliverance for his people.

Chapters 1–2 (Luke's "infancy narrative") stand apart from the rest of the Gospel in that they do not derive from the same sources used by Matthew and Mark, and indeed they overlap with Matthew's opening chapters only in the minimal data of Jesus's birth to a virgin mother in Bethlehem in the time of King Herod, his parents' names, Joseph's Davidic descent, the angelic announcement of the name "Jesus," and the location of Jesus's childhood in Nazareth.

The focus on Mary and her family in these chapters (as opposed to the focus on Joseph in Matt. 1–2) suggests that they may originate in Mary's own reminiscences. They are full of the atmosphere of traditional Jewish piety and are notable for the sequence of psalm-like declarations by Mary, Zechariah, and Simeon (1:46–55, 68–79; 2:29–32), which, together with the angels' song in 2:14, locate the events of the Gospel firmly in the trajectory of prophetic fulfillment.

The prominence of John the Baptist in this introductory section (as indeed in the rest of the Gospel [3:1–20; 7:18–35; 9:7–9, 19; 16:16; 20:1–8]) warns us against the common tendency to treat him merely as a "warm-up act" before the main character comes on the stage. John himself is the fulfillment of prophecy, and his ministry begins the work of deliverance that Jesus will continue.

Historical and Cultural Background

Herod the Great (1:5) died probably in 4 BC; the births of John and Jesus are thus dated several years before the traditional beginning of the "Christian era."

By the first century there were several thousand priests, organized in twenty-four "divisions," each of which was allocated two weeks of temple duties in the year. Since there was only one temple and only two daily sacrifices, the privilege of offering incense was a rare one. As Luke points out (1:9), priests were chosen by lot (a practice similar to casting dice) to offer incense; according to Jewish tradition, only those who had not offered incense before were eligible to cast lots (*m. Tamid* 5:2). So this was Zechariah's big day, perhaps a once-in-a-lifetime event.

Interpretive Insights

1:6 *Both of them were righteous.* Readers of the Gospels sometimes gain the impression that Jewish religion at the time of Jesus was corrupt and superficial. But Luke introduces us to ordinary, pious people, faithfully following God's call to holy living. In the case of Zechariah and Elizabeth there was the added dimension that both came from priestly families. There is thus a direct continuity between Old Testament piety and the dawning age of salvation.

1:7 *Elizabeth was not able to conceive.* Throughout this chapter we are reminded of Hannah (1 Sam. 1) and her son Samuel, also born against natural expectation. A

special birth presages a special life in God's service. For God's preparation of his special servant even before birth, see Jeremiah 1:5.

1:9 *to go into the temple of the Lord and burn incense.* Incense was offered with both the morning and evening sacrifices each day, on the incense altar inside the sanctuary (the holy place behind the first curtain, not the most holy place, or holy of holies). Worshipers could watch the animal sacrifices on the great altar in the courtyard, but they could only wait while the chosen priest went into the sanctuary to burn incense and then came out to pronounce the priestly blessing (see 1:21).

1:11 *an angel of the Lord appeared to him.* The angel identifies himself in 1:19 as Gabriel, one of only two angels who are named in the Old Testament (Dan. 8:16; 9:21), the other being Michael (Dan. 10:13, 21; 12:1). These two are regularly included in later Jewish accounts of the four "archangels." Whereas Michael appears in Daniel as a warrior, Gabriel comes to reveal secret

John the Baptist and Jesus were born near the end of the reign of Herod the Great, who was appointed as King of Judea by the Romans and ruled Palestine from 27 BC until his death in 4 BC. Herod the Great was buried at the Herodium, one of his palace fortresses. This photo shows the remains of his tomb, which were discovered in 2007.

knowledge to the prophet. Gabriel will also declare God's purpose to Mary (1:26–27). He is not mentioned by name again in the New Testament, but in Matthew 1:20; 2:13, 19 an unnamed "angel of the Lord" guides Joseph in his dreams. Here Zechariah apparently is awake.

1:13 *you are to call him John.* Jesus's name likewise will be supernaturally revealed (1:31). This is a further indication that God has a special role for this child, and the name is symbolic. The name Jesus, a common Jewish name (the Greek form of Joshua), is explained in Matthew 1:21 as declaring his saving role. John, also a common name, is not explicitly interpreted in that way, but it represents the Hebrew Yohanan, meaning "God has been gracious," and 1:14–17 (and still more 1:68–79) will spell out how God's grace ("the tender mercy of our God" [1:78]) is to be exercised through John's ministry.

1:15 *He is never to take wine or other fermented drink.* John's ascetic lifestyle, which is described in Mark 1:6, is based on what looks like a lifelong Nazirite vow. Abstinence from alcohol was a key feature of the Nazirite life (Num. 6:1–21), but whereas this was normally understood to be a voluntary and temporary adult commitment, for John it was to be from birth and for life. In this he conforms to the image of Samson, another special child born to a supposedly barren mother (Judg. 13:2–7); compare also Samuel (1 Sam. 1:11). John's adherence to this ascetic model was to mark him out in distinction from Jesus, who, as Luke will later note, was known to enjoy eating and drinking wine (7:33–34).

1:17 *in the spirit and power of Elijah.* The return of Elijah was widely expected in Jewish circles as the prelude to God's coming to judgment. The angel's words closely echo the prophecy of Malachi 4:5–6 (cf. Mal. 3:1–5), but whereas Malachi places the primary emphasis on Elijah's role of family reconciliation in preparation for the "day of the Lord," the angel here speaks more broadly of John as "bringing people back to God," "turning the disobedient to the wisdom of the righteous," and "a people prepared for the Lord." John's mission was to bring about a comprehensive religious revival. His appearance signals the dawn of the new era that the prophets foretold.

Zechariah offered incense in the holy place while worshipers stood in the courtyard to watch and pray. Zechariah would have entered the temple building, shown here, which housed the holy place and the most holy place. This model is part of the 50:1 scale reproduction of the first-century AD city of Jerusalem now on display at the Israel Museum in Jerusalem.

1:20 *you will be silent and not able to speak.* For Zechariah's understandable "disbelief" in the face of such an extraordinary promise, compare the reaction of both Abraham and Sarah to God's similar promise in Genesis 17:17–18; 18:10–15. Zechariah's skepticism stands in contrast with Mary's acceptance of Gabriel's word (1:38), and it is severely punished. God expects his people to take him at his word. But as well as punishment, Zechariah's loss of speech serves as the "sign" of God's miraculous power that he has requested (1:18). From a literary point of view, Zechariah's loss of speech provides the basis for the striking scenes of the people's recognition of his "vision" (1:21–22), of his dramatic intervention in the naming of his son (1:59–63), and of the fluent outpouring of praise as soon as his speech is restored (1:67–79).

1:25 *The Lord has done this for me.* Elizabeth's reaction reminds us of Hannah's great prayer of thanksgiving in 1 Samuel 2:1–10, which also expresses the relief of one who has been rescued from the social stigma of barrenness. A much fuller echo of that prayer will be heard in 1:46–55. Compare Sarah (Gen. 21:1–7), Rebekah (Gen. 25:21), and Rachel (Gen. 30:22–23). God overturns situations of human helplessness and despair.

Theological Insights

The main theme is the dawning of the age of fulfillment. Echoes of the Old Testament throughout this passage combine with the angelic pronouncement to inform us that when Elizabeth's child has grown up and begins his mission of spiritual restoration, the long-promised "day of the Lord" will have arrived. Christians naturally think of John the Baptist as the forerunner of *Jesus*, but nothing has been said so far about a human messiah. Malachi's prophecy was that Elijah would come before *God himself* came to visit his people; the same implication will be found in Isaiah 40:3–5, quoted by Luke in 3:4–6. From this prophetic perspective, the coming of Jesus will be in effect the coming of God himself.

John will be filled with the Holy Spirit while still in his mother's womb (1:15). This is remarkable in view of the fact that Jesus's endowment with the Spirit will be mentioned only from the time of his baptism (3:22; 4:1). This is the first instance of a major emphasis in Luke's Gospel: the role of the Holy Spirit in effecting the work of salvation. In these opening chapters note 1:35, 41, 67; 2:25–27.

Teaching the Text

John the Baptist is often undervalued in Christian thinking. It is true that in the Gospel accounts he consistently points away from himself to Jesus, but Jesus himself declares that "among those born of women there is no one greater than John" (7:28); he is "more than a prophet" (7:26). In chapters 1–2 Luke invites us to consider the promise and birth of John and of Jesus side by side, and so to recognize John as an essential part of the fulfillment of God's plan of salvation. A message on this passage should focus *both* on John's subordinate position with reference to Jesus and on his critically important role in God's plan of salvation. Like John, every believer is uniquely gifted and has a unique role. Yet, ultimately, the role of *every* believer is to point to *Jesus,* and, like John, to say,

Luke 1:5–25

"He must become greater; I must become less" (John 3:30).

In this opening scene Luke's concern is to get us to recognize that John brings the end of the period of preparation and the dawn of the age of salvation. In doing this, John fulfills several strands of Old Testament prophecy, and in particular the prophecy of Malachi that Elijah would return to prepare people for the "day of the Lord." The promise of his birth by God's special power conforms to the pattern of other great figures in the story of salvation, especially Isaac, Samson, and Samuel.

The critical moment for which John is to prepare people is the "day of the Lord," the long-standing promise that God himself would come among his people to judge and to deliver. Many such prophecies in the Old Testament speak of God's coming and acting without mentioning a separate messiah figure, and the teacher should draw attention to the fact that no mention has been made so far of a human messiah and invite the hearer to consider the implications of this for our understanding of Jesus as "God with us."

A subsidiary message may also be derived from the experiences of Elizabeth and Zechariah. Elizabeth, in the "disgrace" of her inability to bear children, represents human helplessness, which is to be joyfully overcome by the power of God; despair gives way to praise. Zechariah, whose big day is suddenly turned upside down by the appearance of the angel, represents human slowness to accept God's power to change things (even though he apparently had been praying for precisely this outcome [1:13]) and contrasts with Mary's ready acceptance of a similar challenge to faith in 1:38. Compare Abraham and Sarah in Genesis 17:17–18; 18:10–15.

Illustrating the Text

God is able to overcome human helplessness and turn despair to joy.

Film: *The Nativity Story*, directed by Catherine Hardwicke. This somewhat overlooked movie (2006) includes strong acting and cinematography, a beautiful and subtle musical score, and many of the other sophisticated nuances that contribute to an exceptional film. It also uses a great deal of biblical text, providing a natural resource to illustrate many of the passages leading up to and including the birth of Christ. The film chronicles compellingly the actual events reported

The angel Gabriel appeared to Zechariah as he was offering incense before the Lord in the holy place. Incense shovels similar to the one shown here were used to transport hot coals on which the incense would be burnt. This bronze incense shovel is probably of Roman origin from the second century AD.

while filling in believably the human dynamics that make us see the story more fully. A very early scene shows Zechariah's unbelief in the face of the declaration that Elizabeth would become pregnant and Elizabeth's response, which, as Scripture notes implicitly, stands in contrast to her husband's.

God's intervention changes routine to drama.

Quote: *Telling the Truth: The Gospel as Tragedy, Comedy, and Fairy Tale*, **by Frederick Buechner.** In these words Buechner (b. 1926) underlines the drama of the Gospel—God's intervention through Christ in human affairs:

> It is a world of magic and mystery, of deep darkness and flickering starlight. It is a world where terrible things happen and wonderful things too. It is a world where goodness is pitted against evil, love against hate, order against chaos. . . . That is the fairy tale of the Gospel with, of course, the one crucial difference from all other fairy tales, which is that the claim made for it is that it is true, that it not only happened once upon a time but has kept on happening ever since and is happening still.[1]

Social Commentary: *Christ and the Media*, **by Malcolm Muggeridge.** Muggeridge expresses beautifully the drama Jesus's intervention in history would bring, "the great drama of the Incarnation, the Passion and the Resurrection." He adds,

> All the greatest artists, poets and musicians dedicated their genius to celebrating it, and . . . majestic cathedrals were built to enshrine it, and religious orders were founded to serve it. . . . Mystics spent their lives exploring it, and . . . for centuries it was the driving force behind all of the greatest human endeavour, the source of the brightest and most far-reaching hopes ever to be understood by the human will.[2]

Even a very pious person may experience incredulity in the face of mind-blowing data.

Poetry: "Zacharias in Advent," **by Francisco R. Albano.** This poem, which speaks of Zacharias (Zechariah) being "dumbfounded" by the prospect of "life flowing from impossibility," explores his dilemma upon the announcement of John the Baptist's impending birth to him and his wife as a conflict between his rational thought and his faith.[3]

The Birth of God's Son Announced

Big Idea *Jesus will be miraculously born from a virgin mother and will be the Son of God and the promised Messiah.*

Understanding the Text

The Text in Context

The mention of "the sixth month" in 1:26, 36 ties this episode in closely with the preceding one (note "five months" in 1:24), and the angel's news about Elizabeth (1:36) keeps the two angelic announcements closely linked, thus preparing for the meeting of the two pregnant mothers in 1:39–56. The similar announcements to Zechariah and to Mary by the same angelic messenger prepare the reader for the parallel accounts of the births of John and Jesus in 1:57–66 and 2:1–20. But there is also a significant escalation between the two announcements, both in the status of the one to be born (prophetic forerunner as compared with Son of God) and in the scale of the miracle involved (a woman beyond normal childbearing years compared with a virgin without sexual intercourse).

The direct and authoritative statement of Jesus's supernatural origin and of his status as Son of God provides the reader of this Gospel at the outset with essential, privileged information with which to make sense of the story that will follow.

Historical and Cultural Background

A Jewish girl would normally be pledged to be married at about twelve years old, and married about one year after that. Mary would therefore be in her early teens at this time, in striking contrast with the age of her relative Elizabeth, "well advanced in years" (1:7). Nazareth was a small, obscure hill village (cf. John 1:46) in the northern province of Galilee, far from the capital city of Jerusalem in Judea. In contrast with Gabriel's visit to Zechariah in the Jerusalem temple, therefore, he is now visiting a person of no social significance, even though her fiancé was of Davidic descent. The names "Mary" and "Joseph," like most of the names of characters in the Gospels, were both extremely common in first-century Palestine; nearly half of all Jewish women whose names are recorded at this period were called either "Mary" or "Salome."[1]

Interpretive Insights

1:26 *Nazareth, a town in Galilee.* Matthew 2:21–23 suggests that the family moved from Bethlehem to Nazareth after Jesus's birth only in search of political asylum. Luke, however, tells us that Nazareth was already the family's home, and that the visit to Bethlehem was only a temporary relocation.

1:27 *a virgin, pledged to be married.* The repetition of the word "virgin" and the explicit statement in 1:34 of Mary's lack of sexual experience leave no doubt about Luke's meaning. The point is underlined when Gabriel compares Mary's situation with Elizabeth's pregnancy despite her known sterility (1:36): this is to be a supernatural birth. Matthew 1:18–25 makes the same point no less explicitly though quite independently. Whatever the problems raised for modern genetics, these two Gospels insist that Jesus did not have a human father.

Joseph, a descendant of David. Joseph plays a minor role in Luke's birth narrative (he will be mentioned by name again only in 2:4, 16; note also "his parents" in 2:41–51 and "they" in 2:22, 39 [which the NIV translates "Joseph and Mary"])

Key Themes of Luke 1:26–38

- Jesus is to be born from a virgin mother by the power of the Holy Spirit.
- The child will be both Son of David and Son of God.
- Despite her initial incredulity, Mary willingly accepts her calling to be mother of the Son of God; she is "highly favored" by God.

compared with his centrality in Matthew 1–2, but neither evangelist mentions him in the period of Jesus's adulthood, hence the common supposition that he had died by then. The Davidic descent mentioned by Luke is the dominant theme of Matthew 1:16–25: it is because he is adopted and named by "Joseph, son of David" that Jesus becomes officially a member of the royal line. Luke will underline this Davidic theme in 1:32–33, 69 and in the location of Jesus's birth in "the town of David" (2:4).

1:31 *you are to call him Jesus.* The angel prescribes the names for both John (1:13) and Jesus. Neither name is explicitly interpreted in Luke, but the meaning explained in Matthew 1:21 would be a natural deduction from the name "Yehoshua" ("Joshua"), which means "Yahweh saves." "Jesus" (the Greek form of "Joshua") was one of the

Nazareth was only a small agricultural village in the mountains of Lower Galilee. This view of modern Nazareth from Mount Tabor shows how it nestles within a bowl formation in the Nazareth Range.

commonest male names in first-century Palestine,[2] so that its owner needed a further distinguishing epithet, in this case Jesus "of Nazareth."

1:32 *will be called the Son of the Most High*. (Cf. 1:35: "will be called the Son of God.") Jesus's status as Son of God is not dependent on his supernatural conception: Mark and John lay great stress on the title without ever mentioning Jesus's virginal conception. But the linking of the title here with the power of the Holy Spirit (1:35) makes it clear that "Son of God" is not being used merely honorifically, as it was in some cultures for kings or even specially holy people, but rather denotes a unique relationship with God. It is a pointer to Jesus's own divinity.

the throne of his father David. The prediction echoes the language of Nathan's prophecy in 2 Samuel 7:8–16, which was widely recognized as looking beyond Solomon to the ultimate messianic "son of David."

1:34 *How will this be?* This question makes sense only if Mary understands that the promise is of an immediate pregnancy rather than one to follow in the normal way after the marriage is consummated. In that case Mary, like Zechariah, understandably finds the angel's message hard to credit. But unlike Zechariah, she does not ask for a sign, and when the angel has explained the divine purpose, she shows

no reluctance in accepting it (1:38). The village teenager is more responsive to the promise of God's supernatural power than is the Jerusalem priest.

1:35 *The Holy Spirit will come on you.* Luke often speaks of people being "filled with the Holy Spirit" (cf. already 1:15), but this rather different expression speaks not of Mary's spiritual condition but of the means by which her pregnancy will be achieved. Compare the creative action of the Spirit of God in Genesis 1:2. The delicacy of expression here avoids the crude pagan idea of a god coupling with a human woman; this is a divine mystery. A child so conceived will be a "holy one," outside the normal pattern of purely human generation.

1:37 *no word from God will ever fail.* Literally, "will ever be impossible." It is a frequent biblical theme that what is humanly impossible is possible for God. Jesus states this explicitly in 18:27, and the same idea specifically in relation to an "impossible" childbirth appears in Genesis 18:14. As in the previous section,

Mary accepts the angel's message with a simple willingness to trust God. The traditional site of Mary's encounter with Gabriel is marked by the Basilica of the Annunciation, a modern Catholic Church in Nazareth. Archaeological excavations beneath the church have uncovered caves that may have been used as homes. These were later incorporated into buildings erected at this site: first a synagogue, later a Byzantine church, and now the Basilica of the Annunciation, which is shown here.

the experience of Abraham and Sarah remains in the background of Mary's story as well.

1:38 *I am the Lord's servant.* Mary's simple acceptance embraces not only the "impossibility" of what the angel has promised but also the personal cost of the special role that she has been called to undertake. Matthew 1:18–19 gives us a glimpse of that cost in relation to her immediate situation with Joseph. In Luke, Simeon's words in 2:34–35 will show that the cost will not be less when her child has grown up. As yet, Mary presumably knew little of this, but already her simple willingness to trust God makes her a shining example of faith (see 1:45).

Theological Insights

The virginal conception of Jesus is not a frequent theme in the New Testament. Indeed, this passage and the "parallel" in Matthew 1:18–25 are the only places where it is explicitly asserted. All the other New Testament writers are content to declare that Jesus is the Son of God without feeling the need to "prove" it by this means. Even Luke and Matthew do not refer back to this theme as they develop their portraits of Jesus as the Son of God. It is recorded as a fact rather than as a theological argument per se, though of course it fits appropriately with the theology of a Jesus who is both human and divine. The presence of this miraculous event at the beginning of the Gospel matches the equally "impossible" event of the resurrection of a brutally executed man at the end. A theology that cannot accommodate God's supernatural reordering of the "laws of nature" is never

going to find it easy to make sense of a Jesus whose life begins and ends in such a way.

Teaching the Text

The two main themes of this section are (1) Jesus as the promised Messiah from the line of David, the fulfillment of the messianic prophecies, and (2) his supernatural conception through the power of the Holy Spirit. For Luke, this extraordinary birth points forward to his role as the long-promised deliverer of God's people, who himself is "God with us." A message on this passage should not only trace the theme of the promise for the Messiah through its development in the OT (passages like 2 Sam. 7:11–16; Isa. 9:1–7; 11:1–9, etc.), but should also stress that God is doing something new and surprising here. The virginal conception is a unique and unprecedented creative act of God, accomplished through the Holy Spirit. Though the story of Jesus is grounded in the (traditional) Old Testament promises of the coming Messiah, those promises will be fulfilled in new and surprising ways.

There are other themes that might form the basis for teaching that emerge in this incident.

The paradox of a formidable heavenly messenger visiting (and greeting with respect) a simple village teenager illustrates dramatically God's habit of choosing the most improbable people through whom to fulfill his purpose. He delights to honor those whom the world would hardly notice. This theme will be developed in the Magnificat (1:46–55).

Mary will be held up in 1:45 as an example of faith (contrast the "unbelief" of Zechariah in 1:20). The passage demonstrates her willingness both to believe the impossible and to make herself available to God despite the upheaval that this would cause in her life. In this she is an example for all disciples. Note the initial address to her as "highly favored" (1:28) by God.

The angel's words in 1:37 draw out a persistent theme of these opening chapters: God's promises may be relied on even when they blow holes in natural human expectations.

How much a message should focus on the virginal conception must be determined by the purpose of the lesson and the nature of your audience. The supernatural conception of Jesus has also been the focus of much theological and philosophical debate, and in some contexts the teacher might encourage people to think about it from a number of angles:

- the prominence of miraculous events in the Gospel stories as a whole
- the extent to which this particular miracle is in a class of its own
- the possibility of a man born without a human father being truly human
- the relationship between the belief in Jesus's virginal conception and the belief that he is the Son of God
- the paradoxical combination of the divine and the human as a persistent feature of the Gospel stories and as the basis for the Christian doctrine of incarnation

All these issues are important, both for Christians' own doctrinal equipment and for their ability to deal with questions raised by others. They should be faced squarely and honestly. But at the same time, we must remember that Luke's emphasis is not primarily on apologetic concerns but on the grandeur of the angel's message.

Illustrating the Text

Art: *Ecce Ancilla Domini,* by Dante Gabriel Rossetti. Among the dozens of splendid annunciation scenes in Western art, this one ("Behold the Handmaid of the Lord") by the English poet and illustrator Rossetti (1828–82) is considered especially beautiful. It pictures Gabriel standing and Mary seated. Gabriel is holding out lilies, presumably emphasizing Mary's purity. The face of Mary has a look of fear and bewilderment that is particularly evocative. A haloed dove, representing the Holy Spirit, sits on the windowsill.

God chooses unlikely instruments to fulfill his purpose.

Film: *The Nativity Story,* directed by Catherine Hardwicke. In an early scene we see the annunciation and Mary's wonderment about it. She asks herself, "How is anyone to believe me? How is anyone to understand?" She indicates her awareness of the unlikeliness of the choice. Her interactions with Elizabeth, from the time they meet, are movingly portrayed.

Quote: Martin Luther.

Quite possibly Mary was doing the housework when the Angel Gabriel came to her. Angels prefer to come to people as they are fulfilling their calling and discharging their office. The angel appeared to the shepherds as they were watching their flocks, to Gideon as he was threshing the

Dante Gabriel Rossetti's (1828–82) *Ecce Ancilla Domini,* "Behold the Handmaid of the Lord"

grain, to Samson's mother as she sat in the field.[3]

Film/Biography: *The Inn of the Sixth Happiness*, based on the book *The Small Woman*, by Alan Burgess. In this marvelous, enduring older film, Ingrid Bergman (1915–82) plays the role of Gladys Aylward (1902–70), a woman who got herself to China after having been turned down by a missionary society. Born in London to a working-class family, Aylward worked as a maid, studying on her own to prepare for overseas missionary service. Seeing her education as inadequate, the mission that she applied to rejected her, contending that she could not learn to speak Chinese. Undeterred, Aylward spent her life savings to get to China, a journey filled with dangers, including a trip across Siberia. Aylward in time became a larger-than-life figure among the Chinese, advocating for prison reform, caring for and adopting orphans, and fighting against the terrible practice of foot-binding, not to mention spreading the good news of the gospel. This movie tells the story of her leading almost one hundred orphans across the mountains to safety when the Japanese invaded the region. Film clips would be effective illustrations.

God's promises can be relied on even when they violate natural human expectation.

Poetry: Antiphons for the Virgin, by Hildegard of Bingen. Hildegard (1098–1179) was a German abbess and poet, and her poems were intended to be chanted. These short poems have been translated by Barbara Newman and can be found online.

Mary's Song—the Magnificat

Big Idea *God has chosen the insignificant Mary for great honor. This is an example of how he overturns human values and conventions.*

Understanding the Text

The Text in Context

In our first two sections of Luke's text the angel Gabriel has announced two births to mothers who should not have been expecting a baby (one too old, the other not yet married). Before the births of John and Jesus are narrated, the two families are brought together, and we have in this domestic scene an opportunity to reflect on the significance of these two special people. The unborn John and his mother recognize the superior status of Mary's son, and Mary speaks with delight and wonder of the incredible honor of being the mother of God's Son.

The paradoxical values expressed in Mary's song prepare the reader for the repeated challenges to the status quo that will mark Jesus's ministry as this Gospel will describe it.

Outline/Structure

Mary's song in 1:46–55, the "Magnificat,"[1] is the first of three poetic declarations that are a striking feature of Luke's birth narratives; the others are the songs of Zechariah (the "Benedictus" [1:68–79]) and of Simeon (the "Nunc Dimittis" [2:29–32]). Their familiar Latin names derive from their use as canticles in church worship since the early Christian centuries. They have been valued as expressions of joy in God's saving work that can be applied far beyond their original context, even though each is clearly designed to reflect the specific circumstances in which they are uttered in Luke's narrative.[2] Their language and structure reflect those of the Old Testament psalms, with their poetic parallelism, so that their Semitic style stands out within Luke's generally more Hellenistic writing. The Magnificat in particular breathes the atmosphere of traditional Jewish piety and contains no specifically Christian language.

Historical and Cultural Background

Mary's visit to her relative Elizabeth involved a long walk of some seventy miles from Nazareth to somewhere probably in the Jerusalem area; the traditional site of the home of Zechariah and Elizabeth is Ain Karim, five miles west of Jerusalem. In 2:4 Mary will have to undertake almost the same journey in a much more advanced state of pregnancy.

Mary's song echoes, both in its opening words and in its general theme, the song of Hannah in 1 Samuel 2:1–10, though Hannah's song follows rather than precedes the birth of her child, Samuel. That too had been a birth against natural expectation (Hannah was believed to be unable to have children), and the child was recognized from birth as having a special role in God's saving purpose. Hannah, like Mary, celebrated God's choice of the despised and downtrodden rather than the world's natural leaders. But most of Mary's song does not repeat the actual words of Hannah's; rather, it is a collage of echoes of psalms and other poetic sections of the Old Testament.[3]

Interpretive Insights

1:41 *the baby leaped in her womb.* John is to have an important role in God's saving

purpose, but it will be a subordinate one, and already the unborn John, filled with the Holy Spirit (1:15), recognizes the presence of the Messiah, for whom he will prepare the way.

Luke's emphasis on the Holy Spirit is well known, and this is especially true of these opening chapters. The Spirit already

Luke does not specify the exact location of the home of Zechariah and Elizabeth, saying only that it was a "town in the hill country of Judea." Tradition identifies the town of Ain Karim as the meeting place of Mary and Elizabeth. Shown here is the Church of Saint John the Baptist and the surrounding neighborhood of Ain Karim.

fills John in the womb (1:15) and has been the means of Mary's pregnancy (1:35). He now inspires the prophetic utterance of Elizabeth, as he will also those of Zechariah (1:67) and Simeon (2:25, 27). So these words of Elizabeth are not simply an enthusiastic family greeting; they are a prophecy about Mary's role and status in the drama of salvation, as "the mother of my Lord."

1:45 *Blessed is she who has believed.* The customary English rendering "blessed" obscures the fact that two different Greek words are used here and in 1:42. *Eulogeō*, used twice in 1:42, speaks of God's blessing on Mary and on her unborn child. *Makarios* (a less directly religious word), used here and echoed by the verb *makarizō* in 1:48, speaks rather of how other people regard her: they recognize what God has done for her and congratulate her on the blessing that she has received. We will see in 6:20–22 how *makarios* is used to speak of the good life, to commend and to congratulate those who are in an enviable position. But Mary is to be congratulated not on good fortune, but on her own faith, which has been willing to take God at his word even when what is promised seems incredible.

1:47 *God my Savior.* This is a familiar Old Testament phrase (e.g., Hab. 3:18). In view of the exaggerated place that has been given to Mary in some Christian traditions, even describing her as "co-redeemer" with her son, it is salutary to notice that in this song she appears only as the grateful recipient of God's saving work. She is a model of faith (1:45) rather than the object of it, and it is as such that she is to be congratulated for all generations (1:48).

1:48 *the humble state of his servant.* This is the only part of the song that focuses

directly on Mary's situation. God has chosen a person of no social importance as the means of his saving work. As Paul later put it, God's "power is made perfect in weakness" (2 Cor. 12:9). See Paul's observations in 1 Corinthians 1:26–29 on the social insignificance and helplessness of those whom God has chosen as his people.

1:50 *those who fear him.* This phrase, together with "the humble" in 1:52 and "the hungry" in 1:53, recalls the frequent depiction in the psalms of the God-fearing "meek" or "poor," who are contrasted with the powerful and arrogant. The psalms depict them as downtrodden and exploited by the ungodly, who seem to have all the odds on their side, but as putting their trust in God to vindicate them over their callous oppressors. God's "bias toward the poor" and his saving action on their behalf mean that the world's power structures are overturned, so that "the meek shall inherit the earth" (Ps. 37:11 KJV). It is this subversive ideology that will underlie Jesus's own ministry, which will, as Luke notes, be "good news to the poor" (4:18).

1:51–53 *brought down rulers . . . lifted up the humble.* The direct reversal of earthly status and privilege in 1:51–53 is the most striking echo in the Magnificat of Hannah's song (1 Sam. 2:4–8). The past tenses indicate that this is no new pattern, but that God has always worked like this, even though in this song the focus is on what is still to come through the ministry of the as yet unborn Messiah. It is not so much that God's people will be given actual political power and material prosperity, but rather that under God's new regime there will be a new scale of values, and the old social divisions will cease to matter. The first will be last, and the last first.

1:54 *He has helped his servant Israel.* The spirituality of the Magnificat and of the Benedictus remains firmly within the tradition of Old Testament religion. It is only with the Nunc Dimittis that Luke's canticles will begin explicitly to look beyond the Messiah's primary role to envisage also "revelation to the Gentiles." Subsequent Christian history, with its increasingly universal scope, has made it inevitable that we think today of Jesus as primarily the Savior of the whole world, but these early chapters of Luke remind us that while he may be much more than the redeemer of Israel, he is never less. His coming is the fulfillment of God's promises to his chosen people throughout the Old Testament, beginning with Abraham.

1:56 *about three months.* Since Mary's conception was announced when Elizabeth was already in her sixth month of pregnancy (1:26, 36), Mary's stay with her relative lasts until close to the time when John is due to be born; if she stayed for the birth, Luke does not tell us so.

Theological Insights

Mary's song reveals two complementary aspects of the character of God well known from the Old Testament. He is the mighty warrior who overthrows those who oppose him, but he is also the God of the covenant whose love and faithfulness ensure the ultimate blessing of his chosen people.

So the theme of God's fulfillment of his Old Testament promises remains central to this passage. Mary's joyful exultation celebrates the entire scope of his saving work. But it is focused on his choice of an obscure and socially insignificant girl to be his servant and so to be advanced to the highest honor. This is how God works, defying human conventions of honor and importance. He is the God of the underdog. Luke will go on to narrate how the ministry of Mary's son will embody the radical values of the Magnificat.

Teaching the Text

It is possible to treat the Magnificat in isolation from its context as both a memorable celebration of the character of the God of Israel and a challenge to the world's values. As such, it has much to teach us in a society that unthinkingly assumes that might is right, and whose celebrity culture promotes the prosperous and successful as those to be envied and emulated.

God's role as powerful warrior is praised in Mary's song when she says in 1:51, "He has performed mighty deeds with his arm." This image is seen clearly on Egyptian reliefs like this one from Medinet Habu, in Karnak, Egypt. Here, Rameses III holds a weapon in his upraised hand ready to smite the prisoners he holds with the other (Twentieth Dynasty, twelfth century BC).

But the Magnificat comes to us as the inspired utterance of a particular person in a unique situation, and its message is best understood when Mary's own situation is taken into account. The teacher or preacher may helpfully encourage listeners to place themselves in Mary's shoes and to imagine her reaction to Elizabeth's striking greeting. The general truths of the Magnificat gain extra force when they are read as the amazed response of an insignificant girl whom God has chosen for an unimaginably important role in his plan of salvation.[4]

When Mary visits Elizabeth, even though both women have cause to praise God for what he has done for them, this is not a scene of *mutual* congratulation. All the focus is on Mary's pregnancy and on the future ministry of her child. It is this that both Elizabeth and her unborn baby recognize, and it is this that Mary sings about.

Mary's words challenge the modern reader to think how far our social and political life (and even our church life) can militate against God's scale of values. Recent movements such as liberation theology have reminded us of God's "bias toward the poor" and of the question marks that the biblical tradition places against privilege and power. The Magnificat assures us that this is not solely an Old Testament theme, and Luke's account of Jesus's ministry will constantly bring it back to our attention.

Many Protestants, reacting against the excessive devotion to Mary in some church circles, have tended to undervalue her importance. This passage provides a valuable opportunity to "rehabilitate" her both as a central figure in God's redemptive purpose and as a model for Christian faith, obedience, and vision. She is to be congratulated.

Illustrating the Text

Being undeservedly set apart for special service brings overwhelming awe and gratitude.

Television: Reference any current reality television series that is based on the idea of a talent search or progressive elimination (think *American Idol*, Miss America, etc.). Go as in-depth as you feel is appropriate, and use clips if you want. Point out how everyone likes to root for a regular person who begins as just a face in the crowd and who ends up set apart as one in a million. Focus on the moment in which the winner's name is announced and the confetti falls and the tears flow. Talk about the emotions the person feels at that moment: overwhelmed, overjoyed, honored, appreciated, grateful, and even deeply humbled. Explain that this phenomenon of being called out and set apart is what it means to be part of the church ("the called ones"), to be made holy ("set apart for special purposes"), and to be called a saint ("holy one"). Point out that, while contests are often about superficial qualities or skills that mark a person as comparatively unique, the specialness a saint feels is simply based on God's undeserved and gracious call.

Quote: John Lennon is quoted as saying, "Jesus was alright, but his disciples were thick and ordinary. It's them twisting it that ruins it for me." Point out that Mr. Lennon is fundamentally misunderstanding the fact that God intentionally chooses thick, ordinary disciples like Zechariah, Mary, Elizabeth, Peter, and all of us to reveal his amazing grace and power. Far from twisting the intent of Jesus's gospel, this undeserved sanctifying and deploying of regular, unremarkable people into amazing ministry proves the power of God and ensures a grateful, humble people of God.

God is the rescuer of the poor and afflicted, and responds generously to those who acknowledge their powerlessness.

Bible: This concept can be well illustrated with a brief look into a number of Scriptures, such as the Beatitudes (Matt. 5); Psalm 34:18; or the widow's oil (2 Kings 4).

Object Lesson: Use three clear glasses. The first should be filled with red wine or grape juice. The second should be empty. The third should be empty and broken or punctured so that it will leak. Tell your listeners that the three glasses represent three hearts. The first (wine/juice) is already filled to overflowing with rich things. The second is empty, but still rigid and proud. The last is both empty and broken by the trials and sorrows of this life. Show your listeners a bottle of olive oil and say it represents gifts and power as conveyed by the Holy Spirit. (1) Pour a little olive oil into the wine-filled glass, comment on how little room there is for God's gifts, and point out how they won't mingle with the rich things already there. The gift of God becomes a superficial layer that never penetrates to the depths of that heart. (2) Pour oil into the empty glass and point out that there is room to receive the oil but that heart is a dead-end for those

Mary is joyously welcomed by Elizabeth in this painting known as *The Visitation*, by Carl Bloch (1834–90).

blessings. The empty but proud heart is willing to receive and hoard, but the blessings will spoil over time. (3) Pour oil into the empty and broken glass (make sure to have something underneath to catch the leaks). Explain that an empty, broken heart pleases God since it must receive more of him daily, and always leaks his blessings out to others. Just as Mary proclaims, God delights to fill the poor, broken, and hungry with good things as a way of enriching the world and revealing his glory.

Mary is a role model and example who is worthy of our respect and honor.

Church History: Take some time to talk about your tradition's take on Mary. If you come from a tradition that venerates her, explain what that does and does not mean, and show how the honor paid her relates to her humility and modesty in the face of God's call. If you come from a tradition that shies away from special doctrines about her, take a moment to acknowledge the ways in which it *is* appropriate to respect and honor her as a sister in faith and as a role model for ordinary people who would be used by God.

The Birth of John

Big Idea *Both the extraordinary circumstances of his birth and his father's inspired utterance testify to John's pivotal role in the plan of salvation.*

Understanding the Text

The Text in Context

The two angelic announcements in 1:11–17 and 1:26–37 are now followed by accounts of their fulfillment in the birth of John and (in the next section) the birth of Jesus. Linking this passage closely with the opening scene of the Gospel are the return of Zechariah's power of speech, lost at the time of Gabriel's announcement (1:20–22) and recovered at the very moment of its fulfillment (cf. 1:20); the countercultural choice of the name "John," given by Gabriel (1:13); and the rejoicing at John's birth (cf. 1:14).

The fact that the second of Luke's Spirit-inspired canticles (cf. the Magnificat [1:46–55] and the Nunc Dimittis [2:29–32]) is uttered in relation to the birth of John rather than that of Jesus underlines the close connection between the two men and their future ministries and locates John firmly in the center of God's fulfillment of his Old Testament promises.

Outline/Structure

As in the previous section, a short narrative sets the scene for a lengthy prophetic utterance. Zechariah's song thus dominates this section. It celebrates the birth of John, suggesting an answer to the people's question "What then is this child going to be?" but it does not relate closely to the actual circumstances of his birth and naming narrated in 1:57–66.

See the previous section for the character of the three canticles. Zechariah's song, the Benedictus, falls into two parts, the first (1:68–75) speaking in more general terms of God's fulfillment of his promise of salvation for his people, the second (1:76–79) focusing more specifically on John's role in this process.

Historical and Cultural Background

The naming of a boy on the occasion of his circumcision is not otherwise attested at this period, but Luke will repeat the pattern for Jesus in 2:21. "John" was a common Jewish name, especially in priestly families, though apparently not in Zechariah's family. But names were sometimes chosen for their apparent meaning, in relation to the circumstances of the child's birth. "John" (Greek *Iōannēs*, representing the Hebrew *Yohanan*) was understood to mean "God is/has been gracious," and Zechariah's song takes up that theme. The announcement of this symbolic name by Gabriel superseded family tradition.

The language of the Benedictus is as full of Old Testament echoes as the Magnificat, though it does not have so clear a single model.[1] It is a typical Jewish hymn of praise, which in its first part recalls God's blessings to his people in connection with the key figures of David and Abraham.

Interpretive Insights

1:60 *He is to be called John.* Zechariah, despite his inability to speak, apparently has been able to share with Elizabeth what the angel had said, including the choice of the child's name (1:13). His dramatic confirmation in 1:63 of his wife's unexpected intervention reinforces the sense of specialness: this is not just a family matter.

1:62 *they made signs.* This suggests that Zechariah had become deaf as well as dumb; in that case, the visitors would be the more surprised at his agreement with his wife, whose words he would not have heard.

1:64 *he began to speak.* There is little point in speculating as to the medical cause of the nine months of dumbness (and deafness?) followed by

Key Themes of Luke 1:57–80

- Zechariah and Elizabeth's insistence on the name "John," given by the angel, shows that this child is not an ordinary member of the family.
- The restoration of Zechariah's speech marks a new beginning.
- Zechariah's song (the Benedictus) continues Mary's theme of God's fulfillment of his saving purpose.
- John's own role is again described as the forerunner of God's salvation; he prepares people for the true dawn that is coming.

sudden restoration of speech. Luke invites us to see this as God's direct intervention, which both adds to the astonishment of the neighbors and sets the scene for the prophetic utterance that follows, an appropriate first use of his restored voice.

1:65 *people were talking about all these things.* In chapter 3 Luke will describe a large, popular movement inspired by John's preaching. The widespread gossip at this point, some thirty years earlier, helps to explain that popular enthusiasm: John was already established in the folk memory as a man with a special mission.

1:68 *he has come to his people.* The Greek word translated here as "come" (*episkeptomai*) echoes the frequent accounts in the Old Testament of how God

Zechariah answers the question of his son's name by communicating with a writing tablet. This was a wooden board with a depressed area into which wax was poured. A sharp object like these styluses would then be used to scratch a message or drawing into the wax on its surface. The writing boards shown here are bound together as a book and still show Greek school exercises. The boards date from the fourth to fifth century AD, and the styluses are dated to the first and second centuries AD.

Luke 1:57–80

"visited" his people in order to save and bless them (cf. 7:16). It is a term full of the sense of divine grace. It occurs again in 1:78 in reference to how the rising sun will "come" from heaven. It is in the coming of Jesus the Messiah that God will come to his people. But the past tense here indicates that already in the birth of John God's saving program has begun.

1:69 *a horn of salvation.* The phrase, drawn from Psalm 18:2, denotes God's saving power, as an ox's horns symbolize its physical strength.

in the house of his servant David. Zechariah and Elizabeth belonged to the priestly tribe of Levi, but God's salvation is to come not through their son John, but through Jesus, whose Davidic descent is repeatedly emphasized in these opening chapters (1:27, 32; 2:4, 11), since Old Testament prophecy had declared that the messianic king was to be a "son of David."

1:73 *the oath he swore to our father Abraham.* God's covenant with Abraham (and the oath by which it was confirmed) was the essential basis of Israel's self-understanding as the special people of God. The oath focused on Abraham's descendants and on the possession of the land of Canaan (Gen. 22:16–18; Ps. 105:8–11), but the latter involved protection from their enemies. Zechariah here understands the covenant blessings in more spiritual terms. The covenant with Abraham included the blessing of all nations through Israel (Gen. 12:3; 22:18); that theme is not reflected in this canticle, but it will be central to the Nunc Dimittis (2:31–32).

1:76 *a prophet of the Most High.* John's role as the last and greatest of the prophets will be declared in 7:26–28. Here, as there, the emphasis falls on his role in preparing the way—but for whom? For Jesus, we naturally reply, but we noticed in 1:17 that the identification of John's role with that of Elijah means that he is to prepare the way for *God's* coming, and that is now made more explicit: he is to prepare the way *of the Lord.* Later Christians came to speak of Jesus as "the Lord," but for Zechariah, the title could refer only to God himself. Thus the impression grows stronger that when Jesus comes, God himself is visiting his people.

1:78 *the rising sun.* The KJV rendering "the dayspring from on high hath visited us" leads some to think that "dayspring" is a title for the coming Messiah, and indeed the Greek word *anatolē* was used in the LXX to translate the messianic title "Branch" in Zechariah 3:8; 6:12; Jeremiah 23:5. But *anatolē* itself simply means "the rising," usually with reference to sunrise. The expression speaks of the coming of light into the world, a light that derives from heaven and dispels earth's darkness. Zechariah does not link this light specifically with Jesus, but Luke's reader is by now well prepared to recognize that God's visitation (see on 1:68) for which John prepares will take place through the birth of his Son.

1:79 *those living in darkness and in the shadow of death.* This is an echo of Isaiah 9:2, the opening of the oracle that speaks of the child to be born to reign on David's throne, whose titles will include "Mighty God" (Isa. 9:6–7). Matthew too drew attention to this passage as a prophecy of the ministry of Jesus in Galilee (Matt. 4:12–16).

1:80 *he lived in the wilderness.* John's wilderness location will be further described in 3:2–6. The uninhabited area down near the Jordan was favored by those who wished to escape from normal society for a period of asceticism and spiritual retreat. The "wilderness" also featured in Israel's hopes of a new beginning, just as they had first got to know God in the wilderness (e.g., Isa. 40:3; Jer. 2:2–3; Hosea 2:14–15).

Theological Insights

The word "covenant" (1:72) occurs elsewhere in the Gospels only in Jesus's words at the Last Supper about a "new covenant" (22:20; cf. Matt. 26:28; Mark 14:24) through his death. But Zechariah's song here links the coming work of salvation with God's promises of blessing to his people throughout their history, and by going back to Abraham (rather than to the renewal of the covenant at Sinai) it makes clear the consistency of God's purpose from the beginning. Here, as in the Magnificat, the emphasis is on Jesus as the Messiah of Israel; his ministry to the whole world will come into focus later.

Whereas the covenant blessings promised in the Old Testament were primarily this-worldly (descendants, land, victory), Zechariah's song, like the rest of the New Testament, offers a less material and more spiritual perspective. His people will be enabled to serve him in "holiness and righteousness," they will have the "knowledge (experience) of salvation" through the "forgiveness of sins," they will see light in the darkness and know the blessings of "peace." Such a vision of God's purpose opens the way for the blessings of Israel to be made available to the whole world.

Teaching the Text

The account of the birth of John (1:57–66) focuses on the themes of the faithfulness and obedience of his parents in naming the

The wilderness in which John lived was most likely the area west of the Dead Sea near the mouth of the Jordan River. It was a desolate, barren region, as this photograph illustrates.

child and the recognition by all that God is uniquely at work in this child. A sermon or lesson on this material could touch on Zechariah's obedient response and "recovery" after his initial skepticism and the ensuing discipline by God (1:18–20). We all have times of doubt and skepticism that can

When Zechariah praises God because "he has raised up a horn of salvation" (1:69), he is referencing Psalm 18:2, which describes God's power. Because horns on an animal such as a bull or ox made these large animals even more formidable and dangerous, reliefs and statues throughout the ancient Near East often depicted gods and even kings wearing horned helmets to emphasize their might. In this plaque from Mesopotamia, a storm god wears a horned helmet and stands on top of a horned bull.

give way to faith and obedience. The greater theme, however, is the special role that John will play in God's plan and the recognition by the townspeople that God is at work. The awe and praise that accompany the restoration of Zechariah's speech is a recognition that the child is unique and will be a key player in God's plan of salvation. At the climax of the narrative, everyone asks, "What then is this child going to be?" and the narrator adds, "For the Lord's hand was with him" (1:66). In the broader context of Luke's Gospel, John's coming confirms that the prophetic voice—silent for all these years—has now been renewed in Israel and announces that God is about to visit and redeem his people through the coming of Jesus the Messiah (1:68, 76; cf. 3:4–6).

The Benedictus (1:67–80), in turn, develops this theme by inviting us to reflect on the relationship between the old and new covenants, and on John's position as the transitional figure between the two eras. This hymn of praise is steeped in Old Testament language, describing Jesus as the promised Messiah from David's line, the "horn of salvation . . . in the house of his servant David" (1:69). This is the fulfillment of the covenants made with Abraham and with David. A sermon or lesson here should remind hearers that God is always faithful to his covenant promises and that, no matter what difficulties or challenges we face in life or how dark the night, the "rising sun" has come "to shine on those living in darkness and in the shadow of death, to guide our feet into the path of peace" (1:78–79). The dawn of God's end-time salvation gives us hope for the future and peace in the present.

Illustrating the Text

God can use ordinary family events (in this case, a circumcision and naming) to demonstrate his presence and power.

Film: *The Nativity Story.* As noted earlier, this film is a natural resource for showing the dynamics of the account of Christ's birth and following events in a fresh way. The quiet dramatization is compelling; the listener really hears and sees what is happening.

Music: It would be good to let the audience hear a rendition of the "Benedictus," a term that may be unfamiliar to the average churchgoer. A variety of styles are available online, ranging from a Vineyard song to Gregorian chant.

God remains faithful to his covenant and raises up messengers to point to spiritual redemption, the path through the darkness into light.

Quote: Michael Milton. Milton, a professor and pastor, says that the song of Zechariah is "the song of a mind made clear" (1:69–73) and "the song of a soul revived" (1:74–75).[2]

Literature: *Cry, the Beloved Country*, **by Alan Paton.** This beautiful and moving novel (1948), by South African writer Alan Paton (1903–88), takes place in Johannesburg and the poor, rural South African countryside. It explores spiritual redemption as a path to healing, not only in the terrible racial tensions that afflicted South Africa during apartheid and that are still far from over but also in the conflict between a father and a son, and between families, white and black. What is clear throughout is that in the midst of loss, prejudice, family tensions, racial injustice, and even violent crime, God raises up person after person to enter into another's emotional, physical, and spiritual pain and bring healing, to become a part of reenergizing the disenfranchised community. In scene after scene God's work is displayed through both the prominent and invisible members of a community, in small moments and large, as they come to the stunning recognition, sometimes in unpredictable ways, that perhaps there will be a new dawn for those living in darkness. These individuals are led from a darkened understanding to light, from resentment to forgiveness, from inaction to action.

At the end, the main character, Stephen Kumalo, a pastor, falls asleep understanding that his life is almost over, and that he will probably not see his country restored. He later awakes and waits till the sun rises, at which time the narrator says, "But when that dawn will come, of our emancipation, from the fear of bondage and the bondage of fear, why, that is a secret."[3] This book, not a long read, renders many potential illustrations.

The Birth of Jesus

Big Idea *The Messiah is born in humble circumstances, but a blaze of heavenly glory shows his true significance.*

Understanding the Text

The Text in Context

With this scene, the fulfillment of the angel Gabriel's announcements (1:11–20, 26–37) is complete. Both John and Jesus have been unexpectedly conceived, celebrated in prophetic songs, and born in remarkable circumstances. Each is already revealed as having a central role in God's plan of salvation, but the angel's words now emphasize that the good news is centered on the Messiah rather than on his forerunner.

Historical and Cultural Background

Luke's account of an empire-wide census does not fit comfortably into the period when Herod was still king of Judea (1:5; cf. Matt. 2:1). The first recorded Roman census in Judea (not in the empire as a whole) was in AD 6, ten years after Herod's death, when Judea had been newly incorporated into the Roman province of Syria, under Quirinius. There is evidence from Egypt of a later census that required people to return to their ancestral homes, but no such provision is known in the rest of the empire. Perhaps Luke is referring here to a local census that was part of Caesar Augustus's empire-wide reorganization of the provinces.[1]

Luke's mention of a "manger" has led most Western readers to assume that Jesus was born in a stable, and that idea has become fixed in our Christmas traditions, even though Luke does not speak of a "stable." Rather, an ordinary Palestinian village home was a one-room house in which the

Although there is much speculation about the conditions under which Mary gave birth to Jesus, there is no need to conclude that it was in a lonely stable far from help. Jesus was placed in a manger because a typical home in Palestine would have included space for animals. The family living space, often a single room, was either adjacent to or above an area where the animals were housed in order to secure them for the night and provide warmth in winter. This drawing illustrates a home where the animal area is adjacent to the family's living space.

animals were kept on a lower level (not in a stable), with the mangers set along the side of the family's living area. The manger was therefore part of an ordinary living room, and there is no basis in Luke's account for the sentimental idea that Jesus was born excluded from human society. Since Bethlehem was Joseph's ancestral home, we may assume that they were staying with relatives.[2] See also the comments on the "inn" in 2:7 below.

Interpretive Insights

2:1 *Caesar Augustus.* Augustus was effectively emperor from 31 BC to AD 14. Luke mentions him here not only to provide a basis for the census that took Joseph to Bethlehem (see above) but also to set up an ironical contrast between the great commander and statesman who was celebrated as the political "savior" of the Roman world and the child born in an ordinary village home whose "salvation" was to be on a far higher level.

2:4 *from the town of Nazareth . . . to Bethlehem the town of David.* Even if Joseph and Mary had a donkey (Luke does not say so), this was a long and hazardous journey for a heavily pregnant young woman. Since the two were not yet married, it is surprising that Mary came too rather than giving birth among her family in Nazareth.

But it was symbolically important for the child to be born in the place where the Messiah was expected to be born (Matt. 2:4–6; John 7:42).

2:6 *her firstborn.* This implies that Mary subsequently had other children, Jesus's "brothers" (8:19; cf. Mark 6:3). It prepares us for the ceremony of the dedication of the firstborn in 2:22–24.

2:7 *there was no guest room available for them.* The Greek word traditionally translated "inn" (*katalyma*) normally denotes a guest room in a private house (as in 22:11); Luke uses a different word for a commercial inn in 10:34, and it is questionable whether Bethlehem was a large enough settlement to have an "inn" as such. A slightly more affluent village home might have an additional room for guests either alongside the main living room or built on the roof (cf. 2 Kings 4:10). Perhaps it was already

According to Luke 2:1, Caesar Augustus issued the decree for a census that required Mary and Joseph to travel to Bethlehem. Augustus was the Emperor of the Roman Empire from 31 BC to AD 14, and this statue was carved sometime during his early reign.

occupied by other relatives who were in town for the census. So Jesus was born among the family in the living room (see above for the "manger"). The circumstances were humble and perhaps inconvenient in contrast to an emperor's palace, but the scene is one of warmth and acceptance in a family home, not of rejection and squalor.

2:8 *there were shepherds.* Jews did not share the Egyptian disdain for shepherds (Gen. 46:34); after all, King David had been a shepherd. But these are ordinary workers, of no social standing, who are chosen to be the first witnesses of the Messiah's birth. Contrast the foreign dignitaries who fill a similar role in Matthew 2:1–12.

2:9–10 *an angel of the Lord.* The angel is not named this time (cf. 1:19, 26), nor is he alone. In the rest of Luke's Gospel angels appear only at the empty tomb (24:23). The striking concentration of angelic testimony in these first two chapters underlines the supernatural significance of these events that take place in such down-to-earth circumstances.

Whereas Matthew and Mark use the noun *euangelion*, Luke uses the verb *euangelizomai*, to "bring good news." It occurs frequently in this Gospel and Acts not only for the message proclaimed by Jesus (e.g., 4:18, 43; 8:1) but also for any communication that comes to people from God, whether through angels or humans (1:19; 3:18; 9:6). This Christian "good news" is thus on a different level from the "good news" of the

achievements and honors of the emperor, for which similar terminology was used.

for all the people. "The people" is a term specially used for Israel, God's chosen people. The focus remains firmly on Jesus's mission as the Jewish Messiah (note "born to you" in 2:11), even though the angels' song in 2:14 hints at a wider relevance when it refers to "the earth" and to "people on whom his favor rests" (see below).

2:11 *a Savior . . . the Messiah, the Lord.* This remarkable collection of titles spells out much of Luke's teaching about Jesus. He is the bringer of "salvation" (a key term for Luke), and he is the fulfillment of God's Old Testament promises to his people. Luke is the only Gospel writer to use "the Lord" editorially as a title for Jesus, and perhaps it is such later Christian usage that is anticipated here. But we have noted in 1:76 that at the time of Jesus's birth the title could be understood only as referring to God himself, so that there may be a further hint

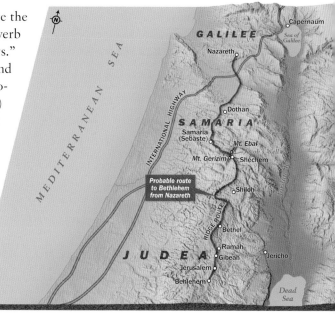

The distance from Nazareth to Bethlehem was seventy-five miles and would have been a three- to four-day journey. This map shows the route from Nazareth to Bethlehem.

here that when Jesus comes, God comes to visit his people.

2:14 *on earth peace to those on whom his favor rests.* The last phrase in Greek is literally "people of good will" (the traditional "good will to men" derives from a probably later reading of the Greek text). This might mean those who are well disposed, but it is better attested as a Jewish phrase describing those who enjoy *God's* favor. So this is not about peace for those whose "good will" deserves it, but about the unmerited grace of God, which brings salvation to those who enjoy *his* "good will."

2:18 *all who heard it were amazed.* Just as the events at John's birth led to popular speculation as to his future greatness (1:65–66), so now too for the birth of Jesus. But whereas in John's case the observers had to draw their inferences from uninterpreted events, now we have a direct divine communication through the angels, mediated through the shepherds who heard their song.

2:19 *Mary treasured up all these things.* Mary will do likewise in 2:51. Unless this is mere speculation on Luke's part, these comments suggest that he had personal access to Mary, and the fact that his first two chapters focus so consistently on Mary's experiences (whereas Matt. 1–2 is mainly about Joseph's) has suggested to many that she was the main source of Luke's information about the births of John and Jesus.

Theological Insights

Luke's account of the birth of Jesus is much more than a memorable story for children or the script for nativity plays. The words of the angel in 2:10–11 provide its theological focus. The "good news" is focused not so much on Jesus's birth as such, but on the role he has come to fulfill, as the promised Messiah and the source of salvation. This salvation is in the first instance for "all the people" (Israel), and Luke's account, unlike Matthew's, introduces no non-Israelites into the nativity scenes. But the song of the angels also offers a hint of blessing for the whole earth, and Simeon will make this theme explicit in 2:31–32.

This is a story of contrasts. The imperial pomp and political dominance of Caesar Augustus contrast with the humble village home in which the new world ruler is born. He is born in the royal "city of David," but he is there only as a visitor, without even a proper guest room. Although the news of his birth comes in an astonishing manifestation of heaven's glory, it comes to the most ordinary of mortals, agrarian workers, probably dirty and smelly. All this speaks of the God of the Magnificat, who brings down rulers from their thrones but lifts up the humble. The first are last, and the last first.

Teaching the Text

One good approach for teaching this passage is to focus on the strong contrast noted above between the glorious predictions for the coming of the Messiah and the lowly circumstances of Jesus's birth. The angel's words in 2:11 offer the teacher a strong christological framework: Jesus is born in the town of king David; he is the Savior, Messiah, Lord. An angelic choir announces his birth! Yet the audience is lowly shepherds and the birth is to poor peasant parents in a humble place where animals are kept. This is the paradox of the gospel. The great and glorious God has stooped down to become one of us, to meet us in our lowly fallen humanity.

The angels' song in 2:14 invites us to reflect on the true significance of the Messiah's coming. The balancing themes of heavenly glory and earthly peace point to a restoration of the pre-fall harmony between God and his creation, and *eudokia* ("good will") places the emphasis where it should be—on the unmerited grace of God, on which our salvation depends. "Peace" here, as usually in the Bible, is a more holistic concept than mere absence of conflict: it is *shalom*, the state where all is as it should be.

Luke's continuing focus on Mary also offers the teacher an opportunity to invite the congregation to enter into the story through her experiences. When she "pondered these things in her heart" (2:19), what did she make of it all? Remember that she was a very young village woman from a conventional Jewish home. This was quite an adventure, despite the physical discomfort and inconvenience. What would she have made of the shepherds' account of what they had seen and heard? At least she had been forewarned by Gabriel. What about the friends and neighbors, to whom it came without preparation? No wonder they were "amazed" (2:18).

A similar approach might be to compare the reactions of the three groups mentioned in 2:18–20: the onlookers "amazed," Mary "treasuring and pondering," and the shepherds "glorifying and praising God."

Most Western readers still take it for granted that Jesus was born in a stable. In my experience, a discussion of the likely domestic setting as noted above, though perhaps initially unsettling to some, usually leads to a welcome new perspective on the familiar story. It is easier to envisage Jesus as truly "one of us" if his entry into the world was in such an ordinary domestic scene rather than in the abnormal setting of a stable or cave (the latter was a persistent tradition in the early church).

Illustrating the Text

God's miraculous work and self-revelation bring different responses in different people, but all of them bring him glory.

Personal Stories: Tell about a time when you and a close circle of companions or family members all experienced the same miraculous moment, but each processed it differently. Perhaps you might reflect on the birth of a child, and how older siblings, mother, father, and doctors all responded differently. Some hearts need to process quietly and reflect, others need to talk about it, some give gifts, and still others feel led to do something celebratory or explicitly worshipful. All of these responses, though, have the potential to bring glory to God and to make us focus on his mighty acts.

Personal Testimony: Ask a variety of individuals to tell, in ten words or less, the first reaction they had when they comprehended the good news of the gospel. Some will say they cried, some will say they danced, some will say they called a friend, and so on. Compile these mini-testimonials into a short video, or have a panel share them in person. Explain that all of these different responses give great glory to God for his mighty works of salvation. (This would also be a great time to end by sharing the gospel concisely and offering listeners a

The Adoration of the Shepherds (AD 1500–1510), by Giorgione

chance to accept the gift of salvation and add their own response to those they have witnessed.)

Biblical "peace on earth" is more than the absence of conflict—it is reconciliation and restoration established by Jesus on the cross and conveyed to humanity by sheer grace.

Everyday Life: Talk about the difference between a home filled with the stillness that arises from cold disinterest and disconnection and a home filled with the real, chaotic, messy joy that comes from satisfying connection, true safety, hard-fought honesty, and unvarnished intimacy. Both families may claim they are experiencing a "happy, peaceful home," but one is defining peace and happiness as the mere absence of chaos and struggle, the situation that settles in when people stop caring and live *in spite of* each other. The other is defining these gifts as the hard-won fruit that blossoms when people live *for* God and each other. This fruit is messy and costly, but precious. Explain that peace on earth is not a matter of God and others merely leaving us alone and free to do as we please. Rather, it is the full reversal of the alienation brought on by sin; it is the restoration of all things begun by Jesus on the cross as he reconciled all things to himself. It will culminate in God and his church dwelling together forever, face-to-face.

Drama: Select two young people ahead of time and supply them with fencing foils, toy lightsabers, squirt guns, or foam dart launchers. Have them come onto the platform unexpectedly in the midst of a fierce battle. Stop them, and insist that they make peace with one another. They can reluctantly agree, then act out an uneasy ceasefire in which they keep circling, eyes locked, and weapons still pointed and ready as they twitch and posture. Try to resume the message, as they jockey for position around you and the pulpit, use you for a shield, and so on. Ask your listeners whether they have really made peace yet. Explain to your actors that the peace you want for them is not just a momentary ceasefire. Rather, you want them to fully release enmity and be restored to one another. Disarm them, place their hands in a handshake, and ask them to sit down side by side and enjoy the rest of the message together in the front row. Explain to your listeners that this is the kind of peace Jesus establishes. Our sin has put enmity and wrath between us and God, and a mere ceasefire will never suffice—we are not meant to live under the cloud of an uneasy standoff with God based on self-righteousness or cheap grace. Instead, Jesus became incarnate, died, and rose so that believers might be adopted into God's own family and eat at table with him in unbroken fellowship forever!

Luke 2:1–20

The Baby Messiah Recognized

Big Idea *The baby Jesus is recognized as the Messiah, and two holy people speak of his role in God's plan of salvation.*

Understanding the Text

The Text in Context

This scene completes the account of Jesus's infancy. His circumcision and naming echo those of John in 1:59–63, but, as with the account of his birth, the subsequent incidents are unique, and they lift the reader's expectations and theological understanding to a higher level. This scene provides the setting for the third of Luke's canticles in chapters 1–2, Simeon's song of praise, the Nunc Dimittis. This song, with its explicit recognition that Jesus is to be the Savior of the world, not just of the Jews, brings into the open a theme that so far has been only hinted at.

Historical and Cultural Background

Two different Jewish ceremonies are recorded in this section. The first, circumcision when the child was a week old (Gen. 17:12; Lev. 12:3), is linked here, as in 1:59, with the naming of the child, a link that is otherwise unattested for this period. The circumcision took place at home, but the second ceremony, when the child was forty days old, took place in the temple in Jerusalem (only about five miles from Bethlehem). Here Luke's wording does not closely correspond to contemporary records, but he apparently combines two elements—the purification of the mother after the "uncleanness" of childbirth (Lev. 12:1–8) and the "redeeming" of a firstborn son (Num. 18:15–16)—since after the exodus every firstborn male belonged to God (Exod. 13:2).

The purification offering of "a pair of doves" is permitted in Leviticus 12:8 in a case where the family cannot afford a lamb, and this

> According to Jewish law, forty days after giving birth a woman was required to offer a sacrifice for purification at the temple in Jerusalem. Mary brought two doves. This fragment from some type of stone vessel dated to the first century AD has simple line drawings of two dead doves and the Hebrew word for "offering" on its surface.

provides an interesting insight into the economic circumstances of Jesus's birth.

In this section, as in the Magnificat, Luke's account has several echoes of the story of the presentation of Samuel in the sanctuary at Shiloh (1 Sam. 1–2).

The Nunc Dimittis, like the earlier canticles, is full of Old Testament echoes, principally from the oracles of hope in Isaiah 40–55.

Interpretive Insights

2:21 *he was named Jesus.* For the commonness and the possible significance of the name, see above on 1:31. The words "Savior" (2:11) and "salvation" (2:30) show that Luke was aware of this meaning. But Luke's concern here is primarily to inform us that, as in the case of John (1:59–63), the angel's instructions were faithfully carried out.

2:22 *to present him to the Lord.* Luke does not mention the redemptive payment required in Numbers 18:16, and it has been suggested that he intends us to think that Jesus, like Samuel (1 Sam. 1:28), was actually dedicated to God's service rather than "redeemed" for normal life. But although Jesus was welcomed into the temple by Simeon, he, unlike Samuel (e.g., 1 Sam. 2:11, 18), did not remain in service there; so probably Luke simply leaves the regular payment to be assumed.

2:25 *Simeon.* Luke tells us little about him, though the fact that he "blessed" the family may suggest that he was a priest, and most readers assume from the opening of his song that he was an old man. His status is not what matters, but rather his spirituality and his God-given insight.

waiting for the consolation of Israel. On "consolation" as a term for Israel's hope, compare Isaiah 40:1, and note also Luke's comment about people "looking forward to the redemption of Jerusalem" (2:38). Simeon and Anna are portrayed as loyal, patriotic Jews who know from the Scriptures that God has promised a better future for his people. In view of this further evidence of the firmly Jewish setting of these infancy stories, it is the more remarkable that this same Simeon will also celebrate the Messiah's international mission (2:31–32).

the Holy Spirit was on him. By mentioning the Spirit three times in 2:25–27, Luke makes it clear that Simeon's words derive from more than natural insight. The personal revelation that he had received concerning the coming of the Messiah in his lifetime suggests that he, like Anna (2:36), should be understood as a prophet.

2:27 *he went into the temple courts.* Luke indicates that Simeon encountered Jesus not by happenstance of being on duty at the time Jesus's family arrived, but by special divine arrangement to ensure that he would "see the Lord's Messiah." This is what prompts his outburst of praise at God's fulfillment of his promise. The meeting must have been in either the court of the Gentiles or the court of women, since

Mary would not have been allowed into the inner courts.

2:30 *my eyes have seen your salvation.* Simeon echoes the Old Testament hope of "seeing" God's salvation (Isa. 52:10; cf. Ps. 98:2), but now it is not in the future but rather in the present. The fact that God's salvation is "seen" in a six-week-old baby born to parents who cannot even afford the regular sacrifice underlines the note of glorious paradox that runs through these first two chapters.

2:31–32 *in the sight of all nations . . . revelation to the Gentiles.* The inclusion of all nations in God's purpose of blessing for Israel was declared as early as the call of Abraham (Gen. 12:3). Here there is a clear echo especially of the role of God's "servant" in Isaiah 49:6 (cf. 42:6), who, in addition to restoring Israel, will be "a light for the Gentiles, that my salvation may reach to the ends of the earth." Luke's two-volume work will show how this prophetic vision began to be realized, in fulfillment of the apostolic commission in Acts 1:8.

2:34 *a sign that will be spoken against.* Simeon's additional words addressed to Mary provide a sobering counterpoint to the exultation of the Nunc Dimittis. Jesus's ministry will be uncomfortable and divisive. As he provokes opposition, people will be obliged to take sides ("the thoughts of many hearts will be revealed" [2:35]), and there will be those who fall as well as those who rise. This dark side of the coming of salvation will be underlined by Jesus's own words in 12:49–53.

2:35 *a sword will pierce your own soul.* Luke will not specifically mention Mary's presence at the cross (for this, see John 19:25–27), but in Acts 1:14 she is with the apostles after Jesus's resurrection, so that we may properly take Simeon's words as looking forward especially to her experience of bereavement. Less serious instances of the pain of being the mother of the Messiah will appear in 2:48; 8:19–21.

2:36 *Anna.* Luke likes to place a male character and a female character side by side. Here the presence of Anna ensures the validity of the testimony of two witnesses (see Deut. 19:15) to the coming of the Messiah. Although Luke will record no actual words of this woman, he accords her a surprisingly full and formal personal description compared with Simeon. If, as the Greek more naturally says, she had been a widow for eighty-four years (cf. NIV footnote), she must be over a hundred years old, though it is also possible to read "eighty-four" as her total age. Clearly, she was a familiar and respected figure to those who visited the temple, and her words would carry weight. Simeon's words may have been in private, but Anna spoke publicly.

2:40 *the child grew.* See on 2:52; these two rather broad summaries bridge over the "forgotten years" between Jesus's birth and his public ministry. But this first summary also serves to prepare us for our one canonical glimpse into those childhood years, in 2:41–51.

Theological Insights

This scene in the temple plunges us into the world of traditional Jewish piety and also into an atmosphere of prophecy. It is often said that the Jews believed that prophecy had ceased with Malachi, until John the Baptist revived it. But Luke here tells a different story, and modern scholarship agrees that there were strands of prophetic activity that were widely recognized among ordinary Jews in this "intertestamental" period.[1] Whereas Matthew's first two chapters concentrate on demonstrating Jesus's messianic role from Old Testament prophecy, Luke claims also the testimony of contemporary prophecy.

After the strongly Jewish focus of the salvation celebrated in the earlier canticles, the Nunc Dimittis provides a manifesto also for the Gentile mission that will be so central to Luke's developing account of the beginnings of Christianity.

Simeon's words, with their strikingly contrasted themes of joy (2:29–32) and foreboding (2:34–35), offer a microcosm of the paradox of the gospel, which brings both joy and pain, and in which the triumphant fulfillment of God's loving purpose is achieved through the rejection and death of his Son.

When Simeon sees Jesus he offers both praise to God and a prophecy concerning Mary and her baby. This scene of Simeon and Anna with Jesus in the temple courts has been the subject of many beautiful works of art. Shown here is a fresco from the Dominican convent of San Marco in Florence depicting the presentation in the temple painted by Fra Angelico (ca. 1437–46).

Teaching the Text

In some churches the events narrated in 2:22–38 are celebrated at the beginning of February in the festival traditionally known as Candlemas (the candles symbolize the "light to the nations"). Coming midway between Christmas and Easter, it is a bittersweet festival, looking back to the joy and hope of the coming of the Messiah, but also looking forward to the pain of Good Friday.

Simeon's words offer an opportunity to explore this paradox, as he both celebrates the dawning of the light of God's salvation and warns Mary of the pain that she must expect and of the division that her Son will provoke among God's people. A gospel of Christmas alone is not a whole gospel.

The Nunc Dimittis, with its echo of Isaiah 49:6, reminds us of a recurrent theme of

Luke 2:21–40

the Old Testament (though one probably little noticed by most Jews of the time): God's purpose of blessing extends beyond his chosen people, Israel, to include all the nations, which will be blessed through God's blessing of Abraham. This theme became increasingly prominent in Jesus's attitude toward non-Jews, and it would become a defining feature of the Jesus movement over against continuing Israel, leading eventually to the universal scope of the Christian church. Since most of our congregations consist of Gentiles, here is an opportunity to reflect on God's grace, which has brought the light of the gospel to us as well, and on the church's continuing task to bring that light to people outside our own "comfort zone."

Illustrating the Text

Anna and Simeon are models of the elderly whose hope in God has remained alive.

Anecdote: John R. W. Stott. John Yates, pastor of The Falls Church Anglican in Falls Church, Virginia, wrote the following after the death of John Stott (1921–2011): "I have had few heroes, but John Stott has indeed been not only a hero, but a teacher and friend to me, and so many of us. The last few weeks have been very difficult for him, and he was ready for this. Three old friends were at his bedside reading from 2 Timothy to him and listening to Handel's *Messiah*. When the chorus began to sing, 'I Know

> The meeting between Mary and Joseph and Simeon and Anna most likely occurred in the court of women or the court of the Gentiles in the temple complex. This model of Herod's temple from the first century AD shows the relationship of those courts to the temple itself.

court of the women

court of the Gentiles

That My Redeemer Liveth,' 'Uncle John' slipped away."[2]

Spiritual Autobiography: *Nearing Home,* **by Billy Graham.** This biography could be referred to for any number of quotes from Graham, whose attitude toward aging, by all reports, is full of grace and who notes in this biography that he has "liked growing older." He writes, "I invite you to explore with me not only the realities of life as we grow older but also the hope and fulfillment—and even joy—that can be ours once we learn to look at these years from God's point of view and discover His strength to sustain us every day."[3]

Music: There are many beautiful musical settings for the Nunc Dimittis (Canticle/Song of Simeon), which has been sung in the church for over fifteen hundred years and is part of Evensong in the Anglican liturgical tradition. Some of these would be Gustav Holst's wonderful setting as performed by, for example, the choir of Exeter Cathedral. One can sample these online. During the Reformation John Calvin's church sang the piece during Communion. In nonliturgical churches it would be very good to introduce this canticle to the audience in music and perhaps a carefully performed recitation.

Poetry: **"A Song for Simeon," by T. S. Eliot.** This poem, which can be found online, is written from Simeon's perspective and is full of images and personal reflections on the event.

The paradox of the gospel: Christ's salvation will bring joy as well as division and suffering.

Literature: *Shane,* **by Jack Schaefer.** In this classic Western (1949), considered among the best in the genre, Shane is a startling Christ-type. Coming out of the east, bearing no last name, he immediately inspires respect, even awe, and changes everything before he leaves. In this novel, based on historical realities and set in nineteenth-century Wyoming, Shane comes to bring hope to the homesteaders who are being threatened by the cattle barons.

Initially, he takes up residence with a homesteading family, exchanges his gunslinger clothing for a farmer's garb, lays down his gun, and helps out. But before long, he must pick up that gun again and take action against those threatening to bully and kill. While he leaves the homesteaders stable and joyful, he forces the situation to a painful crisis and incurs suffering for himself.

The Boy Jesus in the Temple

Big Idea *Already in his childhood Jesus is aware both of a special relation with God as his Father and of a special calling.*

Understanding the Text

The Text in Context

With this unique glimpse into the period of Jesus's adolescence, Luke bridges the thirty-year interval between Jesus's infancy and the beginning of his public ministry. His special relationship with God that is revealed in this story begins to fill out the promises associated with his birth. Mary and Joseph remain central to the story, as Jesus is still in their care; Mary in particular continues in her role as a thoughtful observer of her son's development (cf. 2:19, 34–35). But the setting in the temple among the religious teachers also foreshadows the confrontation that will take place in the same location when Jesus has grown up (chaps. 19–21).

Historical and Cultural Background

The annual Passover visit to Jerusalem was required in the law (Exod. 23:17; Deut. 16:16), and many Galilean Jews fulfilled this obligation (John 4:45). Jerusalem thus became seriously overcrowded for this period (perhaps up to six times its normal population), with many sleeping in camps around the city, so that the confusion as the Nazareth contingent set off for home is understandable.

The temple courts were the focal point of the festival and of the touristic interest of visitors to Jerusalem. The vast court of the Gentiles offered ample shaded space for teachers to gather listeners around them, which, as Luke notes, Jesus later did (19:47; 21:37–38). Because Luke mentions that Jesus was twelve years old, it is sometimes supposed that he was in the temple for his bar mitzvah, but there is no evidence until several centuries later for this Jewish coming-of-age ceremony (eventually fixed on the thirteenth birthday, when a boy was reckoned to become a full member of the religious community). In view of Luke's careful reference to the routine ceremonies after birth (2:21–24), it would be surprising if he failed to mention such a specific focus for this story. He presents it simply as a regular annual visit.

Interpretive Insights

2:44 *Thinking he was in their company.* The failure of Joseph and Mary to be aware that Jesus had stayed behind shows how relatively normal their family life must have been. It was natural for Jesus to be with his friends from the village, and his parents would not consider it odd for him to be elsewhere in the traveling group rather than staying close to them. Even though this story will reveal the special character of the boy, Luke knows nothing of the docetic tendency that in later Christian legends made Jesus more like an alien than a normal, sociable village boy.

2:46 *in the temple courts, sitting among the teachers*. Jesus would not have been the only person listening to teachers in the court of the Gentiles. The teachers may have been officially recognized scribes, though Jesus's own later practice shows that others could set themselves up as teachers without being formally licensed. The subject of teaching is likely to have been the interpretation of the law and its implications for both theology and ethics.

2:47 *amazed at his understanding and his answers*. Jesus seems to have attracted

attention, partly no doubt because of his age, but also because he knew what he was talking about. Luke's words do not necessarily suggest supernatural knowledge, but rather an ability to contribute to debate in a way that belied his years. He is not portrayed as offering his own teaching, as he would do some twenty years later, but as

Mary and Joseph found Jesus "in the temple courts, sitting among the teachers" (2:46). The porticos at the perimeter of the court of the Gentiles were shaded locations where Jewish teachers could conduct their classes. Education involved dialogue between teachers and students where both parties asked questions and offered answers. This photo from the Second Temple model focuses on the royal stoa, the portico area adjacent to the court of the Gentiles.

court of the Gentiles

royal stoa

asking questions and joining in discussion. Perhaps he was already trying out some of the radical ideas that later would lead to his rejection by the religious establishment.

2:48 *Son, why have you treated us like this?* This very natural protest contrasts with Luke's portrayal of Jesus elsewhere as the dutiful son. Objectively, his behavior appears at least thoughtless, but here, as later in 8:19–21, Jesus sets the natural expectations of family loyalty in contrast with a prior commitment to the service of God. In 14:26 he will demand the same sense of priorities from those who follow him, using the uncomfortably exaggerated language of "hating" parents.

2:49 *I had to be in my Father's house.* "House" is not in the Greek, which literally says "in the things of my Father," hence the traditional rendering "about my Father's business." Either rendering would fit the context, but since this is offered as a reason for not needing to search for him, it is perhaps more likely that he refers to a specific location. Jesus's reference to God as "my Father" is in striking contrast to Mary's phrase "your father and I" in 2:48. The adolescent Jesus is already aware, as surely his parents should have been, that he is God's Son rather than only theirs.

2:50 *They did not understand.* Given the clear indications that Mary and Joseph had received from Gabriel, from the angels, and from Simeon, this seems incongruous, especially in the light of the fact that Mary had "treasured up all these things and pondered them in her heart" (2:19). But perhaps we are to assume that twelve years of normal family life had blunted their awareness of the special character and destiny of their son.

2:51 *and was obedient to them.* Luke maintains the tension between the ordinary and the extraordinary. For all the unique self-awareness that we have just witnessed (and the apparently inconsiderate behavior that it had led to), Jesus continued to fit appropriately into the conventions of normal family life.

his mother treasured all these things in her heart. Luke has used very similar words in 2:19; see comment there. These "asides" given by Luke invite the reader to join Mary in thinking out what these stories reveal about the real Jesus.

2:52 *Jesus grew in wisdom and stature, and in favor with God and man.* This is Luke's second summary of Jesus's childhood development (cf. 2:40). It is interesting to compare these two summaries with that concerning the growth of John in 1:80: Jesus's childhood appears to have been more normal, and it did not involve separation from society as John's did. The two summaries in 2:40, 52, which remind us of the accounts of the child Samuel in 1 Samuel 2:21, 26, use the same Greek terms to speak of Jesus's "wisdom" and of the "grace (favor) of God," themes that have been illustrated in the story of 2:41–50. But this time we hear also of Jesus's good reputation in the village ("favor with . . . man"). His supernatural origin did not make him into the *enfant terrible* that some later Christian legends made him. We will discover in 4:16–30, however, that there was a limit to his fellow villagers' approval once the true nature of his mission became clear.

Theological Insights

Through this story runs the tension between Jesus being both Son of God and also son of Mary and Joseph. In view of Luke's clear affirmation in 1:34–38 that Jesus was not the biological son of Joseph, it is remarkable that he is prepared to include references to Joseph as Jesus's "father" in 2:33, 48 and to Mary and Joseph

as Jesus's "parents" (a term that normally implies biological parenthood) in 2:27, 41, 43. But this is not necessarily inconsistent, since by naming Jesus, Joseph has officially accepted him as his son (this point is more clearly explained in Matt. 1:18–25); so he is Jesus's "father" (and "parent") socially, even if not biologically. That term then allows Luke to play on the different levels of "fatherhood" in 2:48–49 ("your father and I" . . . "my Father's house").

Jesus's first recorded words thus emphasize his special relationship with God and his sense of a unique calling ("I *must* . . .").

Nevertheless, Luke portrays a normal home life. His Jesus is not the superhuman cuckoo in the nest suggested by later legends that reflect the docetic heresy (that Jesus was not truly human but a divine being masquerading as a human). The Jesus of the summaries in 2:40, 52 is special, and yet truly one of us. The fifth commandment ("Honor your father and your mother") applies to him as well as to us, though his special calling as Son of God puts it under strain in this episode. This same tension will run throughout Luke's Gospel.

Teaching the Text

This passage is primarily christological, emphasizing Jesus's growing awareness of his unique relationship with God. The prophecy of 1:32 is coming to fulfillment as the Messiah and Son of God prepares to fulfill his God-ordained mission. Yet equally important is the contrast between human and divine allegiances. Though Jesus remains faithful and obedient to his earthly parents, his greater (and ultimate) allegiance is to his heavenly Father. Invite your audience to consider this application for their own lives, as well as the lives of their children and grandchildren. Although we owe it to our families and neighbors to love and care for them (the second greatest commandment), our ultimate allegiance is to love God (the greatest commandment) and advance his kingdom purposes. The temptation for parents is to see our children as fulfilling our goals and our ambitions. Yet,

The Infancy Gospel of Thomas

This collection of legends from the mid-second century (not to be confused with the *Gospel of Thomas,* which is an early noncanonical sayings collection) includes the following stories:

- Jesus breaks the Sabbath by making model birds out of mud, but he gets out of trouble by making them fly away.
- Jesus curses the son of Annas because he has spoiled Jesus's game, and the boy withers up.
- A boy bumps into Jesus, who curses him, and he dies.
- Jesus is sent to school, and he humiliates his teacher by baffling him with allegorical imagery.
- One of Jesus's playmates is killed falling from a building, and Jesus is blamed; but he raises the child to life and is exonerated.
- A pitcher is broken, so Jesus carries the water in his garment instead.
- Joseph cuts a piece of timber the wrong size, but Jesus stretches it to fit.
- Another teacher slaps Jesus for answering back, and he is cursed by Jesus and collapses; but a third teacher praises Jesus's wisdom, and so Jesus is pacified and heals the other.
- People comment, "This child is not earth-born."
- The book finishes with a slightly expanded version of Luke 2:41–52.

Midwich Cuckoos will recognize the genre. The resultant portrait is impressive rather than attractive: *Infancy Gospel of Thomas* has been irreverently described as the "Gospel of the Superbrat."

By contrast, Luke's one brief glimpse into Jesus's childhood is reassuringly "normal," despite the theological tension outlined above. Consider why Luke, alone among the evangelists, decided to lift this corner of the curtain, and what his inclusion of this story has contributed to our understanding of who Jesus really was.

Illustrating the Text

Jesus's full humanity required that he live out an ordinary childhood, submitting fully to the guidance and care of his earthly parents under the fifth commandment.

Human Experience: Invite your listeners to think about a time when they saw a son or daughter of a business owner get involved in the family company. Point out the different ways this sometimes plays out: In some scenarios, the person is inserted into a high level of the organization based on status or relationship, and the other employees have a hard time respecting or receiving that person's leadership. In other cases, the relative starts at the bottom of the ladder like everyone else, and fully submits to the process of learning, slow promotion, and development that everyone else does. In these cases, everyone in the organization is more likely to admit the person is "one of us" who "knows the organization from the ground up." In the same way, Jesus's normal childhood and submission to a process of growth and maturation reveal how the Bible

ultimately, these precious ones are merely on loan to us and our role is to equip and prepare them for God's service—to give them back to him.

Another approach to this unique story about Jesus's childhood is to get people to imagine what it would be like to have an omnipotent, omniscient child growing up in a village home. The teacher might then introduce them to the legends about the child Jesus collected in the *Infancy Gospel of Thomas,*[1] an imaginative writing from the second century that testifies to the irresistible desire to fill in the gap in Jesus's biography left by the silence of the canonical accounts. See the sidebar for some of its contents. Those who have read John Wyndham's science-fiction novel *The* can declare that he is able to sympathize with us in our weakness.

Church Government: This is a great opportunity to give listeners a view into your congregation's leadership culture. You can point out how you believe leadership is an act of service done in submission to the will of God. If Jesus, though he was God in the flesh, still submitted to his earthly parents, then his church ought to be led by people who also know how to follow and submit in accountability and community. Explain that this is how leadership is defined within biblical organizations—everyone who would wield authority must also be willing to be under authority. If you have any printed staff covenants or accountability flow charts, point them out and invite listeners to learn more about how you live out loving submission as a board, staff, and congregation.

Jesus's full divinity required that he live out an extraordinary life, submitting fully to the will and mission of his heavenly Father under a complementarity and unity that existed before time.

Human Experience: Revisit your example about the owner's child working in a family business. Point out that, while that child

The reunion of Jesus with Mary and Joseph when they find him in the temple courts has been the subject of many painters over the centuries. This oil painting, *The Finding of the Savior in the Temple* (1854–60), is by William Holman Hunt (1827–1910).

may work up from the bottom of the ladder, he or she will always be an heir and future owner. Therefore, his or her parents will have a higher set of expectations for behavior, and the stakes of investment and risk will be higher than for other employees. In the same way, while Jesus lived out a normal childhood, he was also responsible and aware in a way that his peers never were. He lived in our midst, aware that the little sins he saw around him would fall on his own shoulders one day. He worked in humanity's "mailroom," aware that he had also built every brick in the building itself. He came to that which was his own knowing that he would be rejected, crushed, buried, and then resurrected before ever receiving his inheritance.

John the Baptist

Big Idea *John calls the people to a new beginning, and so prepares the way for the Messiah.*

Understanding the Text

The Text in Context

We now move into the story proper, and it begins, as chapter 1 led us to expect, not with Jesus but rather with John, the forerunner. At 3:21 the focus will turn to Jesus, but John's call to repentance, and the considerable impact that it had on public opinion, will remain in the background of Jesus's own ministry. In many ways Jesus will be, as he was popularly perceived to be, the successor to John (7:33–34; 9:7–9, 19; 11:1; 20:1–8), and Jesus himself will emphasize the pivotal importance of John's ministry (7:24–28). Here the scene is set for that later linkage.

Historical and Cultural Background

In 3:1–2 Luke is keen to set the story of Jesus in its wider historical context within Roman and Jewish history. The date that he describes is probably AD 28/29 (depending on how the beginning of Tiberius's reign is calculated). The "Herod" who is now tetrarch of Galilee (and Perea) is Herod Antipas, the son of the "King Herod" of 1:5; all subsequent references to "Herod" in the Gospel (3:19–20; 8:3; 9:7–9; 13:31; 23:7–12) are to Antipas.

The historical significance of John the Baptist is shown by the fact that the Jewish historian Josephus devotes more space to him than to Jesus. His account is similar to Luke's, but he attributes Antipas's action to the political threat that he perceived in John, as a popular leader with a volatile following.

Ritual purification was important in Judaism, but normally on a continuing basis before each act of worship, not as a one-time rite of initiation. John's innovative practice may have been modeled on the baptism that non-Jews were required to undergo in order to become Jewish proselytes (though some argue that this practice originated later); see below on 3:8 for the implications of this background.

Interpretive Insights

3:2 *the high-priesthood of Annas and Caiaphas.* There was only one high priest at a time, but Annas, whom the Roman governor deposed in AD 15, continued to be influential, and he was probably still regarded by many as the true high priest, during the period of office of his son-in-law

Caiaphas (ca. AD 18–36); see John 18:19; Acts 4:6, where Annas is still described as "the high priest" at the time of Jesus's execution and resurrection.

the word of God came to. This is a familiar scriptural formula (e.g., Jer. 1:1–2; Hosea 1:1) that marks John out as a prophet in succession to the Old Testament prophets.

wilderness. The Jordan Valley north of the Dead Sea was a wild area remote from the nearest town, Jericho. For "wilderness" as a theologically pregnant term, see above on 1:80.

3:3 *a baptism of repentance for the forgiveness of sins.* This "dipping" in the Jordan, in an area far from recognized places of worship, was different from the routine washings before worship in the temple and in synagogues. It was not about ritual cleanness, but about moral and spiritual renewal. The Gospel reports indicate that it was a once-for-all experience, indicating

Key Themes of Luke 3:1–20

- John's baptism is a symbol of repentance and a new beginning.
- He fulfills Isaiah's prophecy of one who would prepare for God's coming.
- His baptism challenges Jews not to rely on their Jewishness for salvation.
- True repentance leads to a practical change of life.
- John's revival movement is highly significant, but he himself is not the Messiah.
- His fearless confrontation of Herod Antipas leads to his imprisonment.

a complete change in a person's relation to God, and in this it prepared the way for Christian baptism.

3:4 *A voice of one calling in the wilderness.* Luke's full quotation of Isaiah 40:3–5 (cf. the shorter quotations in Matt. 3:3; Mark 1:3; John 1:23) emphasizes John's role as the one who prepares for God's coming to save his people. We have noted in the earlier references to John's role as Elijah

John preached a "baptism of repentance for the forgiveness of sins" (3:3). His ministry was concentrated in the region around the Jordan River (shown in the photo) north and west of the Dead Sea.

and in the Benedictus that the Old Testament texts refer to a forerunner of *God*, not specifically of the Messiah, and the same implication is even clearer in Isaiah 40:3–5: the "Lord" who is coming is Yahweh himself. By extending the quotation to Isaiah 40:5—which in the LXX speaks of "God's salvation" made known to "all people," not just to the Jews—Luke ensures that this key theme of his Gospel is heard already in John's ministry.

3:7 *You brood of vipers!* Not very diplomatic language! Matthew 3:7 says that these words were addressed to Pharisees and Sadducees visiting the scene, but Luke is content to leave it as applied to the whole crowd, presumably to emphasize the sinfulness from which they are to be cleansed.

3:8 *Produce fruit.* This is a regular metaphor for the ethical and spiritual response God seeks (cf. 6:43–44; 13:6–9; 20:10). The baptism itself is not enough; it must lead to changed lives. In 3:10–14 we will be provided with three concrete examples of what this means.

We have Abraham as our father. Jewish expectation was that God's salvation was for his own people, the descendants of Abraham (cf. John 8:39, 53). John challenges that belief. His pun on the two very similar Aramaic words for "stones" and "children" pokes fun at this narrow nationalism. If his baptism was recognized as a development from the baptism of proselytes (see "Historical and Cultural Background" above), it was in effect saying to his Jewish hearers, "You are no better than pagans; without repentance you do not even belong to God's people."

3:9 *thrown into the fire.* The focus of John's preaching is on the judgment that will be the prelude to God's work of salvation. It will be for Jesus to bring the fullness of that salvation, though judgment will remain a key element in his mission as well (cf. 3:16–17).

3:10–14 *What should we do then?* The "fruit" that John specifies is ethical. The tax collectors and soldiers are simply told to play by the rules and not to exploit their position of power over ordinary people. That in itself would be proof enough of a serious change of life in a society where corruption and exploitation were normal. But the message to the people in general in 3:11 goes much further. For the haves to share with the have-nots, even to the extent of bringing them up to a position of equality, is a radical social ethic worthy of the most idealistic reformers. No wonder people listened to John!

3:16 *one who is more powerful than I.* Nothing has previously been said about a messiah figure, and John's hearers might still have assumed that he was talking, in the light of passages such as Isaiah 40:3, about God himself soon coming to judge. But by mentioning people's speculation whether John himself was the Messiah, Luke prepares us for the natural Christian assumption that the "one who is more powerful" refers to Jesus, whom the reader already knows to be the Messiah. The contrast between baptism with water (outward and symbolic) and baptism with the Holy Spirit (a real inward change) sums up the difference between John's preparatory ministry and the true role of the Messiah.

the straps of whose sandals. A rabbi's pupil was expected to undertake all sorts of mundane service for his teacher, but the removal of the sandals was too low even for the pupil; it was the slave's job.

Holy Spirit and fire. In the light of 3:9, 17, it is more likely that "fire" here refers to judgment on the unrepentant as the flip side of Jesus's mission of salvation than that it denotes the purification of those who are saved. Luke might also be thinking, however, of the fire that would accompany the coming of the Spirit at Pentecost (Acts 2:3).

3:19 *John rebuked Herod.* Antipas's recent marriage (in AD 26) to Herodias, who had divorced her previous husband (Antipas's brother) contrary to Jewish law, was a scandal to his Jewish subjects. A popular preacher who dared to challenge it was a threat to public order as well as a personal embarrassment. John was clearly not one to compromise, and he paid the price. Luke mentions his imprisonment here, and in 9:9 he will refer to his subsequent execution, which is graphically related in Mark 6:17–29.

Theological Insights

Luke describes John's mission as "preaching good news" (3:18). Its focus, as Luke records it, is mainly on coming judgment and the call to repent. Even when he speaks of the future ministry of Jesus, he says more of judgment than of salvation (3:16–17). This "bad news" is part of the good news. There is a great deal wrong with God's people that must be put right before salvation becomes a reality.

Baptism with water (3:16) is not itself salvation. It is a symbol of the repentance (change of direction) that is the prerequisite of salvation. True salvation

John, the son of Zechariah and Elizabeth, began his ministry sometime during the reign of Herod Antipas, the tetrarch of Galilee. Herod Antipas ordered the minting of these coins. The one on the left records the mint location, "Tiberius," and the one on the right shows a palm tree and the words "Herod the Tetrarch."

depends also on the work of the Holy Spirit, which makes a person new inside. The reference here, of course, is to John's baptism, but the same principle applies once Christian water baptism has taken its place. "Baptism with the Holy Spirit" here and elsewhere in the Gospels and Acts speaks not of a separate ritual, or even of a separate spiritual experience, but of the inward reality that the outward act of water baptism signifies. These are not two stages of initiation in Christian discipleship; they are the outward and inward aspects of the one life-changing experience that we call "conversion."

Teaching the Text

Luke's intense interest in the historical foundations of the Christian faith is on display in verses 1–2 and would be good to bring out in a sermon or lesson. Verse 3 echoes the language of the Old Testament prophets and shows John the Baptist's role as a link and bridge between the old age of promise and the new age of fulfillment.

As with various passages in the birth narrative (1:4–25; 2:57–80), a message here should deal with the relationship between Jesus and John. What is John's role in relation to that of Jesus? It would be good to challenge listeners to think out from this passage *why* Jesus rated John's importance so highly (7:24–28). What new notes did John's ministry introduce that had not been heard before in Judaism? How fair is the common Christian view of John as simply a "warm-up act" before the real hero comes on the scene? John is in important ways a model for the Christian teacher/preacher. Note, for example,

- his unwillingness to curry favor ("You brood of vipers"),
- his challenge to entrenched assumptions about who are really God's people,
- his consistent pointing away from himself (just "a voice") to the one he prepares for,
- his insistence that repentance must be more than just words,
- his radical social ethics, and
- his refusal to be silent about the moral scandal of the most powerful man in the land.

Can you add other ways in which John is an example to follow?

This may also be a good opportunity to think through the meaning of baptism in relation to Christian salvation, especially in the light of your particular church's baptismal practices. There is, of course, some awkwardness in arguing from John's baptism to the meaning of later Christian baptism, but John himself gives a pointer forward in 3:16. And if "baptism with the Holy Spirit" is contrasted to John's water baptism, how does it relate to Christian water baptism?

Illustrating the Text

In his courage and refusal to be silent about moral scandals, John the Baptist is an outstanding example of a religious leader standing up to a political leader.

Biography: **Thomas Becket.** Thomas Becket, or Saint Thomas of Canterbury (1118–70), was made archbishop of Canterbury under the reign of King Henry II. He was murdered in Canterbury Cathedral, and is recognized as a martyr in both the Anglican and the Catholic Churches. Initially having grown close to the king, he was made chancellor, and he enforced the king's will. However, upon being made archbishop of Canterbury, he refused to indulge the king's wishes above the authority of the church. He stood his ground, and it is thought that the king had him murdered. The story became the inspiration for a number of works of film and literature, among them *Murder in the Cathedral* (1935) by T. S. Eliot (1888–1965), and the film *Becket* (1964), starring Richard Burton and Peter O'Toole.

Literature: *Murder in the Cathedral,* by T. S. Eliot. In one portion of this play (first performed in 1935) Becket articulates his loyalty to God over political powers when he says,

> Temporal power, to build a good
>   world,
> To keep order, as the world knows
>   order.
> Those who put their faith in worldly
>   order

Not controlled by the order of God,
In confident ignorance, but arrest
    disorder,
Make it fast, breed fatal disease,
Degrade what they exalt. Power with
    the King—
I *was* the King, his arm, his better
    reason.
But what was once exaltation
Would now be only mean descent.[1]

Speech: In the tradition of John the Baptist's principled moral stance, a speech such as "I Have a Dream," by Martin Luther King Jr., certainly could be shown as a modern-day example of this kind of courage.

Biography: George MacDonald. MacDonald (1824–1905), who greatly influenced C. S. Lewis, was a Scottish minister and the author of varied works, including novels, mysteries, children's works, and poetry. He never considered himself important or allowed others to elevate him. In fact, he was reported to sometimes sit on his works if someone tried to read them aloud. In one of his novels, *Donal Grant*, the following dialogue ensues:

"But almost no community recognizes its great men till they are gone. The strongest influences are from their very nature of the most hidden working. They are deep out of sight."

"Where is the use then of being great?" suggested Miss Graeme.

"That depends on what the use of greatness is. The desire to be known of men is destructive to all true greatness; nor is there any honor worth calling honor but what comes from an unseen source."[2]

Thomas Becket, Archbishop of Canterbury (AD 1162–70), was martyred for upholding the authority of the church during the reign of King Henry II of England. This panel from a twelfth-century AD reliquary portrays his murder.

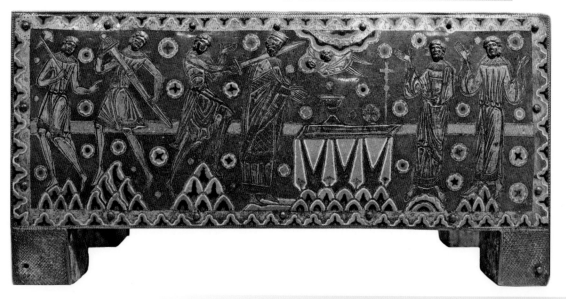

The Baptism of Jesus

Big Idea *Jesus is anointed as the Messiah at his baptism, and God publicly declares that Jesus is his Son.*

Understanding the Text

The Text in Context

This is the first appearance of the adult Jesus in Luke's narrative. This and the following passage record his preparation for public ministry, which will begin in 4:14. The sequence from 3:20 is not strictly consecutive, in that John is here apparently still at liberty to baptize Jesus. Luke has rounded off John's story, and now he goes back to locate the beginning of Jesus's story within it.

The declaration that Jesus is God's Son is a pivotal moment, picking up Gabriel's announcement in 1:32, 35 and initiating a christological theme that will be developed in the recognition of Jesus by supernatural beings (4:3, 9, 41; 8:28), in a further divine announcement in 9:35, and in some pregnant sayings by Jesus himself (10:22; 20:13) before it finally comes into the open at Jesus's trial in 22:70.

Outline/Structure

Most of this section is taken up by a lengthy family tree. Whereas Matthew put this at the very beginning of his Gospel, Luke has fitted it in here at the beginning of Jesus's adult story, perhaps because his non-Jewish readers might have found the genealogy to be an unappealing way to open the book, or possibly in order to bring together God's declaration that Jesus is his Son with a genealogy that traces Jesus back to "Adam, the son of God."

Historical and Cultural Background

The many genealogies in the Old Testament illustrate how important ancestry was to the Jews. Josephus, writing at the end of the first century AD, lists his own ancestors for six generations and claims the support of publicly available genealogical records (Josephus, *Life* 1–6; *Ag. Ap.* 1.30–36). It is not unlikely that such lists were kept, either orally or in writing, especially for the (royal) family of David.[1]

But Luke's list differs substantially from that in Matthew 1:1–17, not only in that it goes in the reverse direction and extends back from Abraham to Adam but also in that between Jesus's father, Joseph, and David there are only two names in common, Luke's list being significantly longer. The popular suggestion that Matthew gives Joseph's genealogy and Luke gives Mary's is unlikely because Jewish genealogies at that time were not traced through the mother (in contrast to modern Jewish practice), and in any case Luke begins his list explicitly with Joseph (who has already been introduced as a descendant of David in 1:27; 2:4). No explanation is generally agreed upon, but one helpful observation is that Matthew's focus is on the royal throne succession (he follows the Old Testament list of the kings of Judah down to the exile), whereas Luke traces Joseph's ancestry not through Solomon the king but through another son of David who did not become king. Is Luke's then more a biological genealogy, as against an official throne list presented by Matthew, the two lists coming together briefly in Shealtiel and Zerubbabel and then again with Joseph?[2]

Interpretive Insights

3:21 *Jesus was baptized.* Later Christians, who taught that Jesus was sinless, were embarrassed that he had submitted to a "baptism of repentance for the forgiveness of sins." Luke shows no such embarrassment, perhaps because he regarded this as

Key Themes of Luke 3:21–38

- Jesus is baptized along with other people.
- A special revelation marks him out as different.
- The Holy Spirit comes upon him in preparation for his mission.
- He is declared to be God's Son.
- Luke provides a family tree that links Jesus back to David, to Abraham, to Adam, and so to God.

Luke 3:23–37 is a genealogical record for Jesus. The "Jesse tree" shown in this photograph is one example of an artistic way to represent the ancestry of Jesus. A typical Jesse tree has a reclining figure of Jesse at its base with a branch coming out of his side. Side branches, foliage, or tendrils embrace figures that represent the ancestors of Jesus, and the number of ancestors shown depends on the genealogy used and the space available for the tree. Mary is usually included just beneath the topmost figure, which is Jesus. This ivory carving from Bavaria (AD 1200) shows a Jesse tree with two prophets on either side of Mary and Jesus.

an act of solidarity with John's religious revival movement rather than as a matter of personal consciousness of sin. By speaking of Jesus as being baptized along with "all the people," he allows the reader to reflect on Jesus's identification with those whom he had come to save from sin.

Luke will mention Jesus at prayer more frequently than do the other Gospel writers. Here, at his first adult appearance, Jesus is already a man of prayer.

heaven was opened. Mark's account of this event can be read as a private experience of Jesus, who "saw" heaven opened and to whom alone the heavenly voice was addressed. Matthew's version makes it more objective: heaven "was opened," and the voice spoke about Jesus in the third person (as at the transfiguration). Luke maintains the second-person address, but his description of the Spirit coming "in bodily form" suggests something that other people could see (as indeed John did "see," according to John 1:32–34). The opening of heaven is an Old Testament way of alerting the reader to a divine communication (Ezek. 1:1).

3:22 *The Holy Spirit descended on him.* In the Old Testament the Spirit "came upon" people to empower them for God's service, and Luke will speak in Acts about the apostles being "filled with the Holy Spirit" on specific occasions. But this visible "descent" of the Spirit sounds more like an initial endowment that sets the tone for the whole of Jesus's ministry to be in the power of the Spirit (cf. the visible coming of the Spirit on the apostles at Pentecost [Acts 2:3]). Endowment with God's Spirit was to be a mark of the Messiah (Isa. 11:2; 42:1; 61:1). For the sequel in Jesus's ministry in Luke, see 4:1, 14, 18.

in bodily form like a dove. The dove was one of the commonest and most familiar birds in Palestine, and there is no need to search for any more specific symbolism in the "bodily form" in which the Spirit appeared. As the dove (or any other bird) can be seen coming down to alight on a perch, so the Spirit was seen coming down on Jesus.

A similar divine declaration in 9:35 will authenticate Jesus to his closest disciples as God's true messenger. In the New Testament God's voice is normally heard either internally or through a prophet. A directly audible communication like this (cf. John 12:28–29; Acts 9:4–7; 10:13, 15) marks out a very special act of revelation.

Commentators sometimes devote so much attention to the possible Old Testament background to the words from heaven

that they fail to focus on what the voice actually says. Jesus, the hitherto unknown man from Nazareth, is the Son of God. The reader should not be surprised, in the light of 1:32, 35, but this is a declaration addressed to Jesus himself, confirming what he has no doubt already been told by his parents, and what he was already aware of at the age of twelve (2:49). Most interpreters find in these words an echo of the first introduction of God's servant in Isaiah 42:1, upon whom God puts his Spirit, and possibly also of Psalm 2:7, which was understood as looking forward to a messianic king of the line of David. Such echoes would indicate Jesus's messianic role as well as his special relationship with God. A further possible echo of Genesis 22:2 would suggest the thought that God himself, like Abraham, was prepared to sacrifice his own son.

3:23 *about thirty years old.* If Jesus was born just before Herod's death in 4 BC, he would have been about thirty-three at the time that Luke specifies in 3:1. Thirty was probably the age at which a priest began his official service (cf. Ezek. 1:1). It was also the age at which David became king (2 Sam. 5:4).

Luke uses careful language here because he has made clear in 1:34–38 that Jesus is not biologically Joseph's son. So what is the point of the following genealogy? Socially speaking, Jesus would be known as Joseph's son (see above on 2:41–52). This genealogy therefore establishes his official place in society. But it does more. It links Jesus with David, the king and prototype of the Messiah, and with Abraham, the revered ancestor of the Jewish people. So much is in common with Matthew, though the names listed are different (see the "Historical and

Cultural Background" section above). But Luke then follows the Old Testament story right back to creation, thus showing Jesus's solidarity with the whole of humanity, not just the Jews.

3:38 *The son of Adam, the son of God.* No other known Jewish genealogy includes the name of God. Clearly, by adding "the son of God" Luke is wishing to make a point (see the "Theological Insights" section below).

Theological Insights

Luke's interest is not in Jesus's baptism as such (which he simply takes for granted, mentioning it only in a participle) but rather in the revelation that followed it. It combines elements that emphasize Jesus's messianic mission (endowment with the Spirit, and the echoes of Isa. 42:1; Ps. 2:7) with the assertion that he is in a special sense the Son of God. Other cultures might speak of important men, especially kings, as sons of the gods, but in the Old Testament, apart from a few references to Israel corporately as God's "son" (Exod. 4:22–23; Hosea 11:1), the term is used only of the future ideal "son of David," the Messiah (2 Sam. 7:14; Ps. 2:7). Here in Luke, coming after 1:34–38 and pronounced by the very voice of God himself, it is clearly more than simply an honorific term for a human leader.

In 3:22, then, Jesus is declared to be God's Son in a unique and theologically significant sense. But then in 3:38 the genealogy concludes that he is "the son of Adam, the son of God." This is a different kind of "divine sonship," one that Jesus shares with all created humanity. By placing

Luke's genealogy of Jesus traces back to Adam, perhaps to show the solidarity of Jesus with all humanity. Adam is included in the genealogy depicted in this beautiful fourteenth-century AD mosaic dome in the Chora Monastery, now Museum, in Istanbul, Turkey. Christ Pantocrator (Almighty) is at the center. Surrounding him are Old Testament figures, ancestors from Adam to Jacob. The lower ring includes the twelve sons of Jacob.

the two so close together, Luke perhaps intends to alert us to the paradox of a divine/human Jesus, who fully shares the nature of God (his "real" Father) and at the same time is fully one of us. By tracing Jesus's ancestry back to Adam, Luke may also be alluding to the Pauline idea of Christ as the "second Adam," the representative man by whose obedience humanity is rescued from the consequences of Adam's disobedience (Rom. 5:12–19; 1 Cor. 15:21–22, 45–49).

Teaching the Text

A sermon or lesson on this passage will want to bring out the significance of Jesus's baptism. Why would Jesus, the sinless Son of God, experience a baptism of repentance? Especially important for Luke is the role of the baptism as Jesus's messianic anointing for ministry (3:21–22; 4:1, 14, 18). Important, too, are the three Old Testament allusions made in the voice from heaven. These provide a good summary of Jesus's identity and mission: he is the Davidic Messiah (Ps. 2:7), the Suffering Servant (Isa. 42:1), and the beloved Son, whom God will offer as a sacrifice for sins (Gen. 22:2).

The different senses of "son of God" in 3:22 and 38 provide an opportunity to work through the significance of the term, as suggested in the "Theological Insights" above.

Preaching through the genealogy can be challenging, but also very rewarding. Genealogies are not favorite teaching aids, and Luke's unadorned list lacks the clearly royal focus of Matthew's. So why did Luke include it? Are we missing something in our Western culture, where many people consider genealogies to be "boring"? In many cultures genealogies are of enormous importance, establishing a person's identity, social position, and even destiny. Melba Maggay, a Filipino theologian, writes, "Our notions of the core of the gospel may not be the same for other cultures where these genealogies are important. It's certainly important in my culture, where we want to know exactly where you have come from: Who are your ancestors? . . . I think the Chinese know this, the Filipinos know this, the Africans know this. The genealogies are important."[3] As Joel Green asserts, this is because, "as a literary form, genealogies are concerned as much with theological and apologetic issues as with historical; *in them resides remarkable social power*."[4]

To teach the genealogy, identify key figures and bring out their role in God's plan of salvation. Seek to show the importance of a genealogy for your audience through a contemporary example, such as where a legitimate heir might inherit a vast estate, or where someone might gain access to a famous person's papers and memoirs because of ancestral claims.

Illustrating the Text

God the Father personally bore witness about the divine lineage of Jesus, his Son.

Popular Saying: There is an old saying that "the apple doesn't fall too far from the tree." When the Father spoke words of blessing and acceptance over his only Son at his baptism in the Jordan, he gave onlookers the expectation that Jesus would bear an accurate family resemblance in his ministry. Jesus was endorsed as a chip off the old rock of ages.

Human Metaphor: Talk about the importance to a young person of being initiated into adulthood by parents. Ask your listeners to reflect on a time when a parent affirmed them and let them know they had reached maturity. Some will not be able to recall such a moment; invite them to reflect on the pain and loss that lack can bring. Then, speak about the blessing that Jesus must have experienced in hearing his Father speak words of approval of who he had become. Jesus had taken the long and humble road to maturity in a carpenter's shop, and was finally hearing his Father's assessment of his journey: "This is my beloved Son in whom I am well-pleased." In other words, "I approve of the person you have become, and I love you—you are exactly who and where you were meant to be." Invite your listeners to reflect on how this approval must have sustained Jesus in times when others accused him of blasphemy, demonic possession, and even immorality.

Luke's genealogy allows the chosen people, Israel, to bear witness about the human lineage of Jesus, the new Adam and royal heir of David.

History: The Daughters of the American Revolution is an organization dedicated to preserving and celebrating the history of the men and women who fought to establish American independence and freedom in the American Revolutionary War. Not surprisingly, one of the organization's most important functions is the keeping of genealogies, cemetery records, and artifacts that establish

When Jesus was baptized, the Holy Spirit descended on him in the form of a dove. This scene from an ivory panel shows John baptizing Jesus and the dove descending (fifth century AD).

and trace lineages of present-day members to significant people in the early United States. The link between the past and the present is essential to the DAR in establishing a sense of continuity with the great men and women of America's past. How much more must the early Jewish Christians have treasured the genealogies that connected their Savior to the great men and women of faith who had come before them? How significant must it have been to know that Jesus was the descendant and heir of King David and was the very seed promised to Adam, Eve, and Abraham?

Testing in the Wilderness

Big Idea *The Son of God is tested in preparation for his mission, and he defeats the devil's attempts to drive a wedge between him and his Father.*

Understanding the Text

The Text in Context

The devil's proposals echo and depend on the declaration that Jesus is God's Son, which has just been made in 3:22. This scene, still set in the wilderness where John has been baptizing, now completes Jesus's preparation before his public ministry begins in 4:14. That ministry will take him back up north to his home province, among the ordinary population of Galilee.

> Jesus was led into the wilderness, where he was tempted by the devil. The traditional location of the temptation of Jesus is a mountain known as Jebel Quarantal near Jericho.

But first, in an area away from human population, he must face a crucial spiritual test as he confronts the "leader of the opposition." This scene thus provides the unseen background to the struggles ahead; behind human opposition stands a more threatening supernatural force.

Historical and Cultural Background

This private experience can only have been related by Jesus himself to his disciples. It is told in terms of physical relocation to a "high place" and to Jerusalem, but no actual high place commands a view of all the kingdoms of the world, and we should think rather in terms of visionary

experiences while Jesus was still in the wilderness (cf. Ezekiel's "visit" to Jerusalem while still in Babylon [Ezek. 8–11]), from which he will return to Galilee in 4:14.

We have noted at 1:80 how significant the wilderness was in Jewish thought as a place of meeting with God and of new beginnings. This ideology derived from Israel's forty years in the wilderness, where they were formed into a nation under God. In Deuteronomy 6–8 Moses reminded Israel of the lessons that they had learned during that period, and it is from those chapters that all three of Jesus's responses in 4:4, 8, 12 are drawn. Deuteronomy 8:2–5, the source of the first of those responses, describes Israel as God's "son," "tested" and learning to depend on his Father through the discipline of deprivation in the wilderness. This is the background for Jesus's own testing as the Son of God.

Interpretive Insights

4:1 *full of the Holy Spirit . . . led by the Spirit*. This double mention of the Spirit leaves no doubt that this was a divinely planned and necessary experience, from which Jesus will then return "in the power of the Spirit" (4:14). Like Israel's testing in the wilderness (Deut. 8:2), it is designed by God to prepare his Son for what lies ahead.

4:2 *for forty days he was tempted by the devil*. Forty is a round number, which may be intended to echo Israel's forty years in the wilderness. The three recorded tests come at the end of the forty days, but Luke tells us that the devil had been tempting Jesus throughout that time.

The verb *peirazō* can mean both to "test," in a good sense, and to "tempt" to do wrong. Both senses apply here,

> ## Key Themes of Luke 4:1–13
>
> - Jesus's wilderness experience is initiated by the Spirit, and so it serves the positive purpose of "testing" as well as the devil's aim of "tempting."
> - The devil's proposals focus on the title "Son of God" and aim to disrupt the relationship between the Father and the Son.
> - Jesus's replies from Deuteronomy 6–8 reveal a close parallel with the testing of God's "son" Israel in the wilderness.
> - Jesus comes through with his loyalty to God uncompromised.
> - The devil's retreat is only "until an opportune time."

corresponding respectively to the intentions of God and of the devil. In biblical thinking the devil operates only within the overall sovereignty of God, and God can even sometimes use the devil's hostile actions for his own good ends. This story is traditionally referred to as Jesus's "temptation," but that is perhaps to give too much weight to the devil's aim over against God's design: hence the term "testing" in the title for this section.

4:3 *If you are the Son of God*. The "if" here and in 4:9 need not imply doubt. Following the unambiguous declaration in 3:22, it is instead an inference from what Jesus now knows for certain. The devil therefore assumes that Jesus already has the miraculous power that belongs to the Son of God. His strategy is rather to probe the dynamics of that relationship and to suggest that Jesus exploit it for his own benefit.

God fed his people with manna in the wilderness (Exod. 16). So surely God's Son need not be hungry. The temptation is for him to use his undoubted authority as God's Son simply to satisfy his personal need.

4:4 *Man shall not live on bread alone.* Israel's hunger had been part of God's scheme of testing (Deut. 8:2–3). Jesus too must keep his priorities clear and accept God's plan for him rather than use his miraculous power to escape that plan and thus assert his independence.

4:6 *It has been given to me.* Compare the description of the devil as "ruler of this world" in John 12:31; 14:30; 16:11. His authority is limited but real, and he can reward those who serve him. Jesus's mission to the whole world (see Luke 2:31–32), as the "son of man" set over all the nations (see Dan. 7:13–14; cf. the messianic destiny set out in Ps. 2:8), must lead to conflict with the devil, who already "rules" it. But instead the devil offers a gentlemen's agreement. It is not a very subtle temptation, but it goes to the heart of Jesus's mission as Son of God. Note too that the devil offers the "splendor" of the kingdoms along with the authority; is this an appeal to the self-importance that might be expected of the Son of God?

4:8 *Worship the Lord your God and serve him only.* Israel's status as the people of God depended on their refusing the attractions of other gods when they came into the promised land (Deut. 6:13–15). Jesus too must be uncompromisingly loyal to his Father, even if it means mortal conflict with the devil.

4:9 *the highest point of the temple.* Perhaps we should think of the corner of the temple portico that overhung the Kidron Valley. Even now, with the superstructure destroyed, it is a dizzying drop; at that time, according to Josephus, the portico rose a further thirty meters.

4:10 *it is written.* The devil too can quote Scripture. Psalm 91:11–12 is a promise of God's protection for all who trust him; how much more, then, should the Son of God be able to take it literally?

4:12 *Do not put the Lord your God to the test.* Jesus's reply, from Deuteronomy 6:16, recalls the experience at Massah narrated in Exodus 17:1–7. There, Israel refused to trust God's promise of provision in the wilderness, and they forced God's hand by demanding that Moses produce

The devil led Jesus to the highest point of the temple. Although the exact location is unknown, it has been suggested to be the roof of the royal portico on the southeast corner of the Temple Mount complex, which drops down to the Kidron Valley. This view looks upward at the more recent Ottoman walls at the southeast corner.

water from the rock. God gave them what they wanted, but the relationship of trust had been irreparably damaged. Similarly, if Jesus had jumped, presumably God would have saved him, but the filial relationship would be broken. True trust in God does not demand tangible proof. To put oneself in unnecessary danger is to force God's hand.

4:13 *until an opportune time*. This phrase warns us that Jesus's victory over the devil, though complete, does not mean that the danger has gone away permanently. The devil will not again appear in person in Luke's Gospel (though see 10:18; 22:3, 31), but Jesus will be confronted by demonic forces, as well as by people and situations that will place his loyalty to his Father under strain, most notably in the mental conflict of Gethsemane (22:39–46). The whole process of Jesus's arrest, trial, and execution is to be understood as the devil's renewed assault (22:3).

Theological Insights

Luke shares the general Jewish belief in a personal devil, whom he elsewhere generally calls "Satan," as the leader of opposition to God's purposes for his world. Under Satan's control are the demonic forces most frequently met in the Gospel as evil spirits possessing people (11:17–18). There is an ambivalence in the biblical view of Satan, who is regarded not only as a real and powerful force determined to destroy God's work but also as operating under the overall sovereignty of God. This tension, never fully resolved in Scripture, comes out clearly in this passage, where the devil's (evil) temptation is the means of God's (good) testing of his Son.

Jesus's thrice-repeated formula "It is written/said" expresses his constant appeal to the Old Testament as the word of God and the ultimate arbiter of truth and right action. He will question accepted interpretations of Scripture, but never the authority of Scripture itself.

His repeated references here to Deuteronomy 6–8 develop the important typological theme of Jesus as the new Israel. Israel was tested in the wilderness as God's "son," and Jesus now takes up that role. Israel was a disobedient son, but Jesus's perfect submission to his Father's will enables him to fulfill Israel's mission to be a light to the nations.

This story therefore focuses on the testing of that filial relationship, as the repeated challenge "If you are the Son of God" reveals. Some interpreters have suggested that the spotlight falls on Jesus's messianic agenda, with the devil suggesting shortcuts to achieving public acclamation. But nothing is said of feeding anyone but himself (and only a single loaf is mentioned), nor is there any indication of the presence of spectators for the jump from the temple. This is a personal transaction between the devil and Jesus in relation to his Father.

Teaching the Text

Three quite different approaches may be suggested for teaching the temptation of Jesus.

First, a sermon or lesson could focus on the nature of temptation/testing. Point out to your audience the dual sense of the verb *peirazō*; discuss what temptation involves and whether/how it may be used for good as well as for evil. Important issues that could be discussed here include the relation between good and evil, the relation between God and Satan, and the whole big issue of divine providence. Provide examples of how God uses trials to strengthen our faith, to bring us closer to him, and to enable us to face even greater challenges.

A second approach is to explore the theme of Jesus as the new Israel, and also the nature of typological thinking in relation to the Old Testament as it is illustrated here by the use of Moses's speech in Deuteronomy 6–8. Consider other ways in which this Israel/Jesus typology is developed in Luke's Gospel (e.g., Luke 9:30–31) and the New Testament generally (e.g., Matt. 2:15, where "son" in Hosea refers to Israel). What are its implications for thinking about the theological significance of Israel in the period of messianic fulfillment?

Third, look individually at the three temptations and discuss whether there are parallel ways in which our own relationship with God is put under strain—and if so, how the Old Testament precepts quoted by Jesus can apply to us as well. Some interpreters have compared Jesus's three temptations to those named in 1 John 2:16: the lust of the flesh, the lust of the eyes, and the pride of life. We need to be careful here, since the present passage is primarily christological and Luke's *primary* purpose is not to teach us how to resist temptation but rather to demonstrate that Jesus is indeed the Messiah and the Son of God,

well equipped to accomplish the messianic task. Jesus's filial relationship with God is on a different level from ours. But are there basic principles of trust and loyalty here that should also govern our relationship with our Father in heaven?

Illustrating the Text

Christ's temptation in the wilderness provides a nuanced demonstration of the subtlety of Satan's attacks and of the way God may allow temptation to be used for good as well as for evil.

Literature: The temptation in the wilderness has been the inspiration for great writing. Two particular works, one written in the nineteenth century and one in the twentieth century, warrant further mention. A thorough reading of both will render gripping illustrative material that will put flesh on the nuances of these temptations in different settings.

Jesus was tempted by the devil for forty days in the wilderness. This artistic interpretation by Ivan Nikolaevich Kramskoy (1837–87) called *Christ in the Wilderness* captures Christ's deep anguish (oil on canvas, 1873).

The first is "The Grand Inquisitor" section of *The Brothers Karamazov*, by Fyodor Dostoevsky (1821–81). In this powerful section of Dostoevsky's final novel (1880) the agnostic Karamazov brother Ivan engages his believing brother Alyosha in a story about Christ's return to earth during the Spanish Inquisition, and the inquisitor's anger at Christ for how he handles people. Christ will not manipulate people with bread, power, or authority as the inquisitor has done with those he has enslaved in the name of the church. Ivan's story, ironically, turns on itself, and he becomes a great defender of Christ. It is important to read the chapter just prior to this section to more fully understand the nature of Ivan's grief, which is about the terrible plight of children he has seen abused, even murdered, something for which he has trouble forgiving God.

The second work is *Christ and the Media*, by Malcolm Muggeridge. In a thought-provoking passage Muggeridge (1903–90), a renowned English journalist, talks about media as the "fourth temptation in the wilderness" and proceeds to speculate how Christ would have responded to the temptation to appear on television, a move that would make him world-famous. He paints a scene in which the media moguls approach Jesus, sure Christ would not be that "crazy." Muggeridge writes, "Jesus *was* crazy," and "did turn it down . . . as he did the other three temptations. He was concerned with truth and reality," the media with "fantasy and images." Jesus was "involved in another scenario altogether . . . the great drama of the Incarnation, the Passion and the Resurrection."[1] This work contemporizes the way Christ's temptations might manifest themselves in modern society.

Jesus's Manifesto

Big Idea *Back in Nazareth, Jesus sets out on his mission of deliverance, but his own townspeople in Nazareth reject him because of his vision for the salvation of all people everywhere, which includes the Gentiles.*

Understanding the Text

The Text in Context

Jesus's return from the wilderness area marks the beginning of his public ministry, which will be focused in his home province of Galilee until he sets off for Jerusalem in 9:51.

Mark and Matthew record a single visit to Nazareth, which they place later in their narratives. Luke not only tells the story in much more detail, and with his typical focus on Jesus's mission of deliverance, but also has inserted it at the very beginning of his account of Jesus's public preaching to act as a sort of frontispiece (a decorative illustration facing a book's title page) for Jesus's ministry as a whole. The themes of deliverance, of good news for the poor, and of the universal scope of Jesus's mission set the tone for all that is to follow. The hostility of Jesus's own fellow villagers serves as a warning of the opposition that his ministry will provoke from conservative Jewish interests.

Historical and Cultural Background

Nazareth was a small Jewish village in the hill country of Galilee.[1] Matthew 4:13–16 records that Jesus deliberately relocated to Capernaum, a more prominent lakeside center, when he began his public ministry, and that move is presupposed here in 4:23. So the sermon in Nazareth is not Jesus's first public appearance; he already has a reputation as a healer in Capernaum.

Jesus read the words of the prophet Isaiah in the synagogue at Nazareth. Here is a portion of the Isaiah Scroll, one of the Dead Sea Scrolls found at Qumran. This is the kind of scroll Jesus would have been given to read.

That is why he is invited, as a distinguished visitor, to preach in his home synagogue when he returns.

Synagogue worship was based on the readings from the Torah and from the prophets. Our information does not make it clear whether there was at this period a set system of prophetic readings following a lectionary. If Isaiah 61 was the set reading, it was a remarkably appropriate one for the occasion, but we should probably think rather of Jesus being free to select his own passage and deliberately choosing this well-known portrayal of the anointed deliverer. This is not normally regarded as one of the "servant passages" of Isaiah, but it picks up and develops the theme of the first such passage, Isaiah 42:1–4 (which has already been echoed in God's declaration in 3:22). Here the prophet speaks in the first person, but the passage was probably already widely regarded as a blueprint for the mission of the expected messiah (it is used in that sense in Qumran texts).

Luke's quotation follows the LXX version of Isaiah 61:1–2a, except that one clause is omitted ("to heal the brokenhearted," after proclaiming good news to the poor) and one added ("to set the oppressed free"), the latter being drawn from Isaiah 58:6, a passage that similarly lists acts of deliverance. This substitution makes little difference to the overall thrust of the oracle, though it results in an emphatic repetition of the term "setting free." More important is that the LXX that Luke quotes matches more closely the actual ministry of Jesus, in that it makes explicit reference to restoring sight to the blind. This corresponds to a Hebrew phrase that is usually translated "release to the

prisoners," though the word for "release" is used elsewhere only of opening eyes or ears.

Interpretive Insights

4:15 *He was teaching in their synagogues.* It is questionable whether at this time most local communities, especially one as small as Nazareth, would have a synagogue *building* as such (though Capernaum certainly did [7:5]). The term meant originally a "gathering," which may have been in a suitable large building or in the open. Such gatherings on the Sabbath were the natural place for a man with a religious message to find an audience.

4:16 *He stood up to read.* Worship was under the direction of the local synagogue leader (see 8:41; 13:14), but other competent men might be invited to read and to comment on the readings (cf. Acts 13:15). They stood to read and then sat (4:20) to teach.

4:17 *the scroll of the prophet Isaiah was handed to him.* Each prophetic book was contained in its own scroll (the twelve "minor prophets" from Hosea to Malachi together making up the "Book of the Twelve"). We do not know whether Jesus asked for Isaiah, or whether it simply came up by rota. But Luke's words suggest that Jesus deliberately turned to (what we now call) chapter 61.

4:18 *The Spirit of the Lord is on me.* The opening of the Isaiah text echoes Jesus's experience at 3:22, which has already been reiterated in Luke's comment that Jesus began his ministry "in the power of the Spirit" (4:14). The following clauses make it clear that this endowment is specifically for the unique mission of preaching and deliverance that Jesus has come to fulfill, as he will declare in 4:21.

There is no record that Jesus literally freed prisoners (though such events will occur in Acts 5:19; 12:6–11), and Luke is probably thinking here of Jesus's exorcisms (of people "held captive" by a demon) and healings (note the language of "setting free" in 13:16). But the later history of Jesus's followers contains fine examples of the literal application of this principle, notably in relation to the abolition of slavery.

4:19 *to proclaim the year of the Lord's favor.* Some interpreters think that Jesus was calling for the literal observance of the Old Testament principle of Jubilee (Lev. 25) as a social reform, but neither the words of Isaiah nor the Gospel accounts of Jesus's ministry support this. The reference seems rather to be to the Lord's chosen time to bring salvation and judgment (the following words in Isaiah are "the day of vengeance of our God," which does not sound like Jubilee). That time has now come, with the ministry of Jesus.

4:21 *Today this scripture is fulfilled in your hearing.* The fulfillment is not completed in a day, but as Jesus begins his public proclamation the fulfillment has begun. By this claim, Jesus identifies himself as the one who brings God's eschatological salvation. The term "messiah" (the anointed one) is not used, but the reference to "anointing" in Isaiah's prophecy makes this in effect an open messianic claim.

4:22 *All spoke well of him.* Literally, "bore witness to him." The initial impression is apparently favorable (though some have suggested that they "bore witness" *against* him—i.e., they were hostile from the start). How has a local boy ("Joseph's son") turned out to be such an impressive speaker? The Greek phrase translated "gracious words" could be understood either of the quality of Jesus's speaking or of its content: he has been speaking about the grace of God, which it is his mission to promote.

After standing to read the Scriptures, Jesus sits before starting to teach. This was common protocol at the synagogue, and this practice may be supported by the discovery of special seats or chairs as part of synagogue architecture. Shown here to the left of the doorway of the second-century AD synagogue at Chorazim is an elaborately carved seat. It is thought to have been meant for someone of importance such as an elder or synagogue official. It has been suggested that it was the "seat of Moses," which is where the teachers of the law would provide instruction.

4:23 *Physician, heal yourself.* Jesus quotes a proverb that picks up the comment about "Joseph's son." If he belongs to the village, surely the village has a right to benefit from his ministry at least as much as Capernaum, his new home. His reputation as a healer has gone ahead of him and has created a natural expectation of healings in Nazareth too.

4:24 *no prophet is accepted in his hometown.* Similar sayings are recorded about Greek philosophers. We have the proverb "Familiarity breeds contempt." The better you think you know a person, the more difficult it is to accept that person as being out of the ordinary.

4:25–27 *there were many widows in Israel.* Jesus defends his concern for people away from home by taking as a precedent stories about two of the most famous miracle workers of the Old Testament, Elijah and Elisha (1 Kings 17:7–24; 2 Kings 5). Both Sidon and Syria were traditional enemies of Israel, yet the Israelite prophets had used their miraculous power to benefit, in the one case, an obscure widow and her son and, in the other case, the commander of the enemy army.

4:29 *to throw him off the cliff.* The admiring congregation has become a lynch mob. Luke does not explain the crowd dynamics that resulted in this excessive reaction to Jesus's supposedly unpatriotic comments, but it is an ominous foretaste of what is to follow when the Nazareth preacher eventually provokes the anger of vested interests in Jerusalem.

4:30 *he walked right through the crowd.* Was this natural charisma or supernatural protection? Luke does not say.

Theological Insights

The phrase "good news to the poor" neatly summarizes Luke's characteristic emphasis on Jesus's concern for the marginalized and oppressed. See above on 1:50–53, and below on 6:20. Isaiah 61:1–3 is also echoed in the opening beatitudes in Matthew 5:3–4. In choosing Isaiah 61:1–2 for his opening manifesto, Jesus places himself firmly on the side of the underdog. The words of the prophecy could be understood either in a sense of sociopolitical liberation or in a sense of spiritual deliverance; note that the repeated term for "setting free" (*aphesis*) in 4:18 is the same word that means "forgiveness" in 1:77; 3:3; 24:47. The best guide to how Luke understood them is his following record of Jesus's actual ministry, where the focus falls on physical and spiritual deliverance of the sick and possessed, and on giving hope to the hopeless and a voice to the voiceless, rather than on a concrete attempt to reform the social or political system. But the values here expressed have provided an important incentive to radical Christian sociopolitical involvement in subsequent generations.

We have had hints already (notably in 2:31–32) of the universal scope of God's concern and therefore of Jesus's mission. Here in 4:25–27 that universality is underlined in a most provocative way. Luke's Gospel is the enemy of parochialism.

Teaching the Text

One good approach to teaching this episode is to invite listeners to consider why Luke placed it in this prominent position as the opening salvo of Jesus's public ministry. The

Nazareth sermon plays out in miniature the whole ministry of Jesus, including his proclamation of the gospel in the power of the Spirit and his ultimate rejection by his own people. It would be illuminating to go through the Isaiah text clause by clause and point out how each of these statements finds expression in Jesus's later ministry as Luke records it. This might lead on to a discussion of how literally the clauses should be understood, and thus of how far this text provides a blueprint for Christian social and political action. For example, are the "poor" the literal poor or the spiritual poor? (This important theme will be revisited throughout Luke's Gospel—compare, for example, Luke's beatitudes [6:20–23] with Matthew's [5:3–12]). Is the "freedom for prisoners" (4:18) noted by Isaiah pointing ahead to Jesus's exorcisms, where he is setting people free from the power of Satan?

The rapid swing of the crowd from approval to murderous rejection invites us to consider what factors determine our response to the word of God. Are there lessons here for all of us in our listening and responding, and also for teachers and pastors in how they present the message? In what circumstances is it right, and even necessary, to provoke hostility by challenging entrenched prejudices? How far is the "rejected prophet syndrome" a model that we should expect to follow?

Illustrating the Text

Christ's public teaching in this passage is a powerful opening manifesto setting the tone for his life's work.

Church History: Martin Luther. Martin Luther (1483–1546) posted the Ninety-Five Theses in 1517 in response to the abuse of indulgences in the Catholic Church.[2] His bold declarations set off a furor that instituted broad and historic changes and introduced the German Reformation, which became the hallmark of his career. Luther wrote the theses in Latin for an academic audience and pinned them to the church door in Wittenberg, as was the practice. But someone took them, translated them into German, and published them for the general public, reaching many who had been abused by the practice.

History: Mohandas K. Gandhi. Gandhi (1869–1948) mobilized millions of followers into joining a cause that is like very few the world has seen, a nonviolent protest method and lifestyle that set the tone for his life's work. "'Those who are in my company,' he warned his followers, 'must be ready to sleep upon the bare floor, wear coarse clothes, get up at unearthly hours, subsist on uninviting, simple food, even clean their own toilets.'" "They fought," comments Philip Yancey, "with the weapons of prayer, fasting, prison terms, and

In 4:29 the residents of Nazareth are most likely intending to stone Jesus as they take him outside of town to a cliff. There is no modern consensus on a location. The traditional site for this event is known as Mount Precipice and is shown here.

bodies bruised from beatings, and in the end their unorthodox methods helped liberate half a million people."[3]

In his teaching, Jesus's emphasis on "good news to the poor" places him decisively on the side of the underdogs, to give them a voice and a sense of hope.

Anecdote: Leighton Ford tells of visiting Mother Teresa and her Sisters of Mercy, who ministered to the poor of Calcutta, India. They sought to give the underdog, in this case the dying poor, voice and hope. They found her in "a modest building marked by a simple sign on a brown wood door." When Mother Teresa finally came to meet them, she apologized for keeping them waiting. Ford and his wife then engaged her in conversation about these "dying poor" in their final days whom she and the sisters reached out to. "How do you keep going" Ford asked, "with so much poverty and death and pain all around?"

Mother Teresa answered, "We do our work for Jesus and with Jesus and to Jesus, . . . and that's what keeps it simple."[4]

Jesus was not afraid to challenge entrenched prejudices.

Anecdote: Pastor John Killinger recounts a story he heard from D. T. Niles at Princeton University. After World War II, wanting to account for money given to parts of the Balkan peninsula, the World Council of Churches sent John Mackie, president of the Church of Scotland, and two others from a more "severe" denomination to visit the villages where the money had been sent.

When they visited an Orthodox priest who was "overjoyed to see them," the priest gave the men "a box of Havana cigars," one of which Dr. Mackie took, "bit off the end, lit it, puffed a few puffs, and said how good it was." The other two men looked "horrified" and commented that they didn't smoke.

The priest, suspecting he had offended them, tried to make up for the offense by bringing out a bottle of his best wine. Dr. Mackie drank some and "praised its quality." The men with him were visibly more offended by this gift and declined firmly.

Later, when the two men were alone with Dr. Mackie, they asked him how someone in his position could "smoke and drink." As the story goes, Mackie's "Scottish temper got the best of him," and he said, "I don't, but *somebody* had to be a Christian."[5] Mackie seems to have understood that there are times to break the "rules."

Christian Living: *Extreme Righteousness: Seeing Ourselves in the Pharisees,* **by Tom Hovestol.** In this insightful book, Hovestol writes,

> Jesus' way of dealing with the self-righteous and religious people was instructive. First, *Jesus seemed to specialize in using shock therapy with the religious.* He was fearless in putting His divine finger on the faults of the faithful. He did not sugarcoat his message or attempt to burrow His way into religious hearts by tiptoeing around sin and cultivating a "positive mental attitude.". . . He loved them enough to break through, often in shocking ways.[6]

Sabbath in Capernaum

Big Idea *A typical day in Jesus's ministry in Capernaum reveals his power over both spiritual and physical oppression.*

Understanding the Text

The Text in Context

Luke has characterized Jesus's Galilean ministry as one of teaching (4:14–15), though his words in Nazareth presuppose that he has also been healing (4:23). Now, by setting out the events of a typical day in Capernaum, Luke fills out the picture. The resultant portrait of an authoritative exorcist and healer as well as an impressive teacher will provide the backdrop for the whole of the following account of Jesus's ministry in Galilee. This section thus continues the general account of the Galilean ministry that began in 4:14–15 but has been interrupted by the striking episode at Nazareth that Luke has inserted. The location in Capernaum now takes us back to Jesus's regular base during this period, though 4:43–44 also emphasizes that his scope was to be much wider than just the one town. The (overly) enthusiastic response of the people of Capernaum to Jesus in 4:42 contrasts strikingly with his expulsion from Nazareth in 4:28–30.

Historical and Cultural Background

Capernaum was a more significant place than Nazareth. It was a lakeside town, with a flourishing fishing industry. Its location as the last town in Galilee on the road

Jesus returned to Capernaum after his rejection at Nazareth. Capernaum was located on the northwestern shore of the Sea of Galilee. Archaeological evidence from the second and third centuries AD indicates it was a thriving town supported by fishing, agriculture, and trade. This aerial view of the area of Capernaum shows the Sea of Galilee and some of the excavations, including the fourth-to-fifth-century AD synagogue, the octagonal roof covering Peter's house, and walls outlining many insulae and individual dwellings.

around the north side of the lake made it a border post where taxes were collected (5:27) from traders en route between the tetrarchies of Antipas and Philip (see 3:1), as well as from boats coming across the lake. The presence there of a detachment of Roman troops (7:1–2) testifies to its importance, as does the fact that it already had a purpose-built synagogue at this period (7:5). The synagogue shown to visitors in Capernaum today is, however, a later structure, probably built on the same site.

The Synoptic Gospels make it clear that Jesus not only healed physical illness and disability but also carried out exorcisms, and the two are normally clearly distinguished, even when, as here, they are mentioned together. Luke records three specific exorcisms in addition to this one (8:26–39; 9:37–43; 11:14), but his summary statements (6:18; 7:21; 8:2; 11:15–20) show that this was a central element in Jesus's ministry, and one that he shared also with his disciples (9:1; 10:17) and even with one outsider (9:49–50). Modern Western society is generally uncomfortable with the idea of demonic possession and sometimes tries to dismiss it as a primitive explanation for mental illness, but in the society in which Jesus lived, as in most of the non-Western world today, the reality of malign spirits and their ability to take possession of people was not doubted, and exorcism was a valued ministry of deliverance, practiced also by Jews outside the Christian movement (Matt. 12:27; Acts 19:13–16) and by some pagans. Among all the surviving records, however, there is no individual figure credited with an exorcistic ministry on the scale of the one conducted by Jesus.

Key Themes of Luke 4:31–44

- Demonic spirits recognize and submit to Jesus's authority as the Son of God.
- He is able to heal all sorts of spiritual and physical ailments.
- He has a strong and growing reputation as a healer.
- He also has a ministry of proclaiming the good news, which he is unwilling to have sidelined by the popular demand for more healing.
- His teaching, like his exorcism and healing, is marked by a unique authority.

Interpretive Insights

4:31 *on the Sabbath he taught the people.* On the nature of synagogue worship on the Sabbath, see "Understanding the Text" on 4:14–30. The invitation to teach after the readings from the Scriptures would indicate that Jesus must already have gained some reputation in his adopted home.

4:33 *a demon, an impure spirit. He cried out.* As usual in an exorcism account, the words are attributed not to the "host" whose voice is used but rather to the possessing demon, and Jesus's response will be specifically to the demon.

4:34 *Have you come to destroy us?* The plural "us" is not likely to indicate that this is a case of multiple possession (as in 8:2, 30; 11:26), since the demon will go on to use the singular "I." More likely, this demon speaks on behalf of his whole class; with the coming of Jesus they are all under threat.

the Holy One of God. In 1:35 the promised "Son of God" has already been described as "the holy one," and in 4:41 demons will recognize Jesus as the "Son of God" (cf. 8:28) and as the Messiah. As supernatural beings, they have an insight into Jesus's real nature that is not yet open to human observers, and they recognize him as their natural antagonist. The title "Holy One of God" suitably contrasts him with the "unclean" demon. In John 6:69 it denotes Jesus's role as the Messiah.

4:35 *came out without injuring him.* Contrast 9:42 and the more graphic description in Mark 9:26. Demon possession was understood to have physical as well as mental effects, and the lack of any physical damage in this exorcism no doubt added to the favorable reaction from the synagogue congregation.

4:38 *the home of Simon.* Simon Peter will be introduced in 5:1–11 and 6:13–14 as Jesus's leading disciple, and it was probably in his house that Jesus lived when in Capernaum. The sequence of Luke's account here suggests that there was already a connection between Jesus and Simon before his dramatic "call" while fishing (as John 1:40–42 also indicates). The low-key domestic nature of this miracle, which contrasts with the spectacular and very public exorcism in the synagogue, is underlined by the delightfully down-to-earth observation that the immediate concern of Simon's

mother-in-law upon being healed was to fulfill her duties as host.

4:40 *At sunset.* The Sabbath finished at sunset. The legitimacy of healing on the Sabbath will be a matter of dispute in 6:6–11; 13:9–17; 14:1–6, but in this case the issue does not arise, for the people dutifully waited until the Sabbath was over before carrying others to Jesus for healing, thus avoiding a breach of current Sabbath restrictions.

4:41 *he rebuked them and would not allow them to speak.* Jesus's demand for silence after his miracles is not so prominent a theme in Luke as it is in Mark. Here (as in 4:35) it is addressed to the demons rather than to human observers, and it is explicitly linked to their supernatural recognition of him as the Messiah. Compare the similar command to the disciples when Peter reached the same conclusion (9:20–21). This surprising caution is probably best explained by the likelihood that popular

Jesus performs a miracle of healing in Simon Peter's house when he cures Peter's mother-in-law of a fever. Shown here are the archaeological remains of a fifth-century church that many scholars believe was built over Peter's house in Capernaum.

ideas of the messianic agenda would be at odds with Jesus's own understanding of his mission. He prefers to spell out his messianic role in his own terms, as we have seen in 4:16–30, and the adverse reaction on that occasion shows that his caution was justified. A further factor here is that *demons* are not the sort of witnesses Jesus would welcome, even if their perception was true.

4:43 *I must proclaim the good news of the kingdom of God to the other towns also.* Proclaiming good news is at the heart of Jesus's mission, as we have seen in 4:18 (and see on 2:10), but this is the first time its content has been spelled out as "the kingdom of God." It is a central theme of Jesus's teaching in the Synoptic Gospels that God's reign is being established through his own ministry. It was Israel's national hope that in the last days God would establish his kingship over all people, and that hope is now being fulfilled (cf. 4:21). Such a message cannot be confined to Capernaum and must not be subordinated to the admittedly messianic work of healing and exorcism, which the local people clearly wanted to keep "in-house" for their own benefit.

that is why I was sent. Many people are "sent" (*apostellō*) to do God's work, and the use of that Greek verb here need mean no more than that Jesus has a God-given mission (cf. "He has sent me" [4:18]). Some interpreters suggest, however, that Gospel references to Jesus's "being sent" or "coming" for a given purpose may also express a belief in Jesus's preexistence before his "coming into the world."[1]

4:44 *in the synagogues of Judea.* In Luke's narrative Jesus will not reach Judea proper (the southern province focused on Jerusalem) until chapter 19, but here he uses the term in the wider sense (familiar to his Gentile readers) of the whole area occupied by Jews (cf. 6:17; 7:17), thereby emphasizing the wide scope of Jesus's ministry.

Theological Insights

The careful selection of traditions that make up this typical "day in the life" of the Messiah produces a wholesome balance of three elements: the supernatural (exorcism), the physical (healing), and the mental (teaching/proclamation). This range of concern embodies well the manifesto declared at Nazareth in 4:18–19. But the concluding cameo in 4:42–44 tells us that within this integrated program the proclamation of good news takes precedence. Jesus is more than just a healer.

The encounter with Satan in 4:1–13 has signaled that there is to be a supernatural dimension to Jesus's mission. His work of exorcism belongs to that dimension, and Luke makes clear from the beginning that Jesus, who has already "defeated" Satan in the wilderness, has authority also over all demonic forces. The people notice his parallel *authority* both in teaching and in exorcism. The christological implications of this, which are already clear to the demons, will take longer to become clear to human observers, but already the raw material for that Christology is being set out.

Note the contrast with 4:1–13. There, Satan tried unsuccessfully to get Jesus, as the "Son of God," to misuse his power. Here, that power is deployed to good effect against spiritual evil, and the demons recognize his authority as the "Son of God" (4:41).

Teaching the Text

Demon possession and exorcism are matters of puzzlement and even embarrassment to some modern readers of the Gospels, and of unhealthy fascination to others. This passage gives the teacher the opportunity to engage with the issue and to attempt to foster a more balanced biblical approach. Notice Luke's emphasis on the simple authority of Jesus, which contrasts with the more elaborate exorcistic techniques and magical formulae used by some of his contemporaries. Because of *who Jesus is*, a word of command is enough.

The integration of teaching, healing, and exorcism in Jesus's ministry may profitably be explored in relation to the agendas of our churches today. Is due attention given to the needs for spiritual deliverance and for physical well-being, along with the more "cerebral" aspects of gospel and pastoral ministry? On the other hand, is there a danger of the more "caring" aspects of ministry taking undue precedence over the teaching and proclamation?

And do we, like the people of Capernaum in 4:42, sometimes try to tie Jesus down to our own limited agenda, so that he needs to break loose and move on? Jesus's ministry of healing in Capernaum was good, but the good (and popular) can sometimes be the enemy of the best.

In the synagogue at Capernaum, Jesus exorcises the demon with the authoritative command, "Come out of him!" Remains of the first-century AD synagogue have been exposed and can be seen as the black basalt stones below the white limestone of the fourth- or fifth-century building.

Illustrating the Text

The Christ who defeated Satan in the wilderness also has authority over all demonic forces.

Quote: *Jesus, a New Vision*, by Marcus Borg.

> More so than extraordinary cures, exorcism is especially alien to us in the modern world. In part, this is because we do not normally see the phenomenon (though are there cases of "possession" which we call by another name?). Even more, it is because the notion of "possession" by a spirit from another level of reality does not fit into our worldview. Rather, possession and exorcism presuppose the reality of a world of spirits which can interact with the visible world; that is, they presuppose the truth of "primordial tradition."[2]

Anecdote: *Fresh Wind, Fresh Fire*, by Jim Cymbala. While careful to assert that "the Bible speaks more about *resisting* the devil than it does about *binding* him," Cymbala has been part of necessary exorcisms in the process of leading a church with a very complex and troubled population in the middle of Brooklyn. He tells one story of a Hispanic girl who came forward to the front of the church in a "daze." Cymbala and those coming with him to pray felt instantly alerted. As soon as the name of Christ was mentioned, the small girl lunged for the pastor's throat and "body-slammed Cymbala against the front edge of the platform." At the same time, a "hideous voice from deep inside her began to scream, 'You'll never have her! She's ours! Get away from her!'" Obscenities followed. In the name of Jesus, those praying with her addressed the spirits, and in a few minutes the girl was set free and now serves the Brooklyn Tabernacle. Her testimony has been a great encouragement to those coming to the church.[3]

Jesus's ministry included teaching, healing, and exorcism; he said and he did.

Biography: D. L. Moody. Moody (1837–99) was famous for frequently saying, "I would rather save one soul from death than have a monument of solid gold reaching from my grave to the heavens." He spent his entire postconversion life both emphasizing the absolute importance of learning and teaching Scripture (he was involved in the creation and perpetuation of institutions of learning) and caring for and encouraging the disadvantaged. His range of influence is immeasurable. In the introduction to his biography of Moody, Lyle Dorsett writes, "The testimonies . . . are legion from people who chose to enter Christian service after sitting under the preaching and teaching of Moody. . . . American home missionaries to Native Americans, recently freed slaves, the urban and rural poor, and prison inmates claimed Moody nudged them toward lives of full-time service." He believed in the "healing and nurture of souls as well as the rescue of souls, or evangelism."[4]

The First Disciples

Big Idea *Being a disciple of Jesus means recognizing our own unworthiness before a sovereign God, having a willingness to leave all to follow him, and recruiting others for the task of discipleship ("fishing for people").*

Understanding the Text

The Text in Context

Luke's account has hitherto depicted Jesus acting alone, though the unexplained mention of Simon in 4:38 has hinted that others are already associated with him. Now Luke fills in the background to that mention by telling of the recruitment of the first and closest of the disciples who will accompany Jesus in his ministry. They are the first of a growing number of people publicly associated with Jesus (5:33; 6:17), of whom the Twelve will be only a select few chosen to be his closest associates (6:13). From here on this will be the story not of Jesus alone but of Jesus and his disciples, and he will very seldom be seen apart from their company until he is taken from them in Gethsemane. Even where they are not specifically mentioned, their presence is assumed. At the end of the book it will be to

this group that the continuation of Jesus's mission is entrusted (24:44–49).

The present story takes the place in Luke of the much shorter account in Matthew 4:18–22 and Mark 1:16–20. The location is the same, and the same fishermen are involved (except that Luke does not mention Andrew specifically); the same metaphor of "fishing for people" (though using a different Greek word to refer to fishing) is the basis of their call. But Luke's story is independent in that it locates the call in the context of a fishing miracle parallel to that in John 21:1–14.

Historical and Cultural Background

There was a flourishing fishing industry especially along the northwest shore of the Lake of Galilee. The setting of this

This boat, known as "the Jesus boat," is a first-century fishing boat. Its buried remains were found in 1986 along the shore of the Sea of Galilee. This kind of boat is thought to be similar to those used by Jesus and his disciples in the Gospels.

incident is presumably at Capernaum, one of the principal fishing centers, where Simon lived (4:38). A surprisingly well-preserved boat from this period has been discovered at nearby Ginosar (probably the "Gennesaret" mentioned in 5:1). It measures 8.27 meters long by 2.35 meters wide, and it may well be similar to those used by Simon and Andrew and the sons of Zebedee.

Jewish rabbis typically had disciples who traveled around with them, looking after their material needs and absorbing their teaching, with a view to later becoming rabbis themselves. But rabbinic disciples normally chose their own teacher. Jesus, for all his growing reputation as a teacher, was not an officially recognized rabbi. His initiative and authority in calling his own disciples mark him out as distinctive.

Interpretive Insights

5:1 *the Lake of Gennesaret.* Matthew and Mark call it the "Sea of Galilee," John the "Sea of Tiberias." Luke's term is that normally used by Josephus. Gennesaret was just along the shore southwest of Capernaum. The designation "lake," which Luke uses consistently, better fits our modern usage, since this is a stretch of water measuring only some thirteen by eight miles that, even though well below sea level, has fresh water.

5:3 *the one belonging to Simon.* Luke makes no mention of Andrew at this point, though he will include him in the list of the Twelve as Simon's brother (6:14). Matthew and Mark depict two pairs of brothers fishing in partnership, and the plural verbs that Luke uses in 5:6–7 show that Simon was not alone (cf. "all his companions" [5:9]). Indeed, even two men would hardly

Key Themes of Luke 5:1–11

- Jesus's ministry will not be exercised alone but with colleagues.
- Jesus's first disciples are ordinary workers.
- Their occupation as fishermen provides a model for a key element in discipleship: the recruitment of other disciples.
- Jesus's miraculous power evokes a sense of unworthiness in us, but also of his unique authority.
- To follow Jesus means to leave all else behind.

be enough to manage a boat of the type mentioned above. But all the emphasis falls on Simon, not only as the leading apostle but also as the one whose experience and response on this occasion are a model for discipleship.

he sat down and taught the people from the boat. For sitting as the accepted posture for teaching, see 4:20. The use of a boat as a "mobile pulpit" facing the crowd gathered on the shore is mentioned by Matthew and Mark as the setting for their collection of Jesus's parables (Matt. 13:2; Mark 4:1). By teaching the crowd from the boat, Jesus begins to model the metaphor of "fishing for people," which he will develop in 5:10.

5:5 *because you say so, I will let down the nets.* It is unlikely that Jesus, a landsman, had a better natural awareness of the habits of fish than an experienced fisherman. The best fishing is at night and close to the shore, not in deep water in daylight. Simon is nevertheless willing to go against his professional judgment because he recognizes in Jesus a special authority. This may be the result of a longer acquaintance with Jesus than simply this one sermon (see on 4:38). His reaction to the subsequent catch shows that he did not attribute it to natural causes.

5:8 *Simon Peter.* Luke will mention that Jesus gave Simon his nickname (6:14), but he does not record when it was given (cf. Matt. 16:18; John 1:42), and so he is free to add the better-known name "Peter" at this early stage.

Go away from me, Lord; I am a sinful man! Like the demon in the synagogue (4:34), Simon instinctively recognizes Jesus as holy. The demon felt threatened, and so did Simon. But whereas for the demon Jesus represented a dangerous enemy, what Simon displays is the natural discomfort of an ordinary laborer in the presence of supernatural power.

5:10 *James and John, the sons of Zebedee.* Their names will follow Simon and Andrew in the list of the Twelve (6:14), and on two occasions (8:51; 9:28; cf. Mark 13:3; 14:33) they with Simon will form an "inner circle" of Jesus's closest disciples. Matthew tells us that their mother was also closely associated with Jesus (Matt. 20:20; 27:56), and some have argued for a family connection, possibly even that James and John were first cousins of Jesus.[1]

from now on you will fish for people. Jesus's declaration is addressed specifically to Simon, but it is clear from the following verse that James and John saw it as applying to them too. In Jeremiah 16:16 the same metaphor is used with a clearly hostile sense: the "fishermen" are to catch people for judgment. And that is a more natural sense: it is no blessing for a fish to be caught in order to be killed and eaten. But the Greek verb used here for "to fish" (*zōgreō*) more literally means "to capture alive." Jesus's choice of this metaphor is suggested by Simon's actual occupation, but the sense is presumably that just as Jesus is now summoning Simon to follow him, so Simon in turn will bring others to share in the blessings of salvation. Catching fish is a skill requiring training, experience, and patience, and so is evangelism.

5:11 *they . . . left everything and followed him.* The same will be said of Levi,

Peter, James, and John left their boats and nets behind to follow Jesus. Here is a modern fisherman with his nets on the Sea of Galilee.

the only other disciple whose calling Luke specifically records (5:28). In this they are model disciples. In 14:33 we are told that an essential requisite for discipleship is to "give up everything you have," and in 18:29–30 disciples are those who have left home and family for the sake of the kingdom of God. On the other hand, the continued availability of a boat for the journeys of Jesus and the Twelve (8:22, 37), along with the likelihood that Jesus was based in Simon's home in Capernaum, cautions against too absolute an understanding of the phrase "left everything."

Theological Insights

Following the account of Jesus's exorcisms and healing, this is the first of three so-called nature miracles (those that do not have a human being as the subject) that are recorded by Luke; for the others, see 8:22–25; 9:10–17. This miracle has the same motif (an incredible catch of fish following Jesus's directions) as the postresurrection story in John 21:1–14. As with all the nature miracles in the Gospels, there is no attempt to explain how it was done; we are simply left to assume that Jesus commanded power and/or insight beyond normal human experience. It is that supernatural authority that evokes Simon's sense of unworthiness.

The miracle itself is not, however, the main point of this story. It is about discipleship. While the authority of Jesus displayed in the miracle underlies the prompt response of those he first calls to be disciples, the focus is on these first disciples as models for all other disciples, who may not be called in such spectacular circumstances. Two aspects of discipleship stand out. First, the immediate and unconditional response

to Jesus's call ("they left everything and followed him") is a paradigm for the life of discipleship, in which loyalty to Jesus takes priority over all other claims and concerns. Second, to be a disciple is to be commissioned to win other disciples. "Fishing for people" is a vivid metaphor that aptly encapsulates the essentially missionary nature of the Christian faith. We do not merely wait for recruits to volunteer; we go looking for them.

Teaching the Text

A good way to teach this passage is to show the contrast between Peter's (and our) total unworthiness to be Jesus's disciple and his perfect suitability to be used by God. Jesus takes imperfect instruments and uses them to accomplish his purpose. Peter is not ready or able to follow Jesus wholly until he experiences Jesus's power and majesty and recognizes his own sinfulness. Then Jesus can take him, transform him, and teach him to fish for people. Encourage your listeners to reflect on their own calling to discipleship. In what ways are we both unworthy and perfectly suited to fulfill God's call in our lives? Related to their calling, what does it mean to "leave everything and follow him"? What might be the appropriate outworking of that principle in our very different cultural setting? Will it be the same for all disciples? If not, why not?

Another teaching or discussion point might focus on the "fishing for people" metaphor and its implications for evangelism. What does this metaphor mean? Were your listeners conscious of being deliberately "fished for" when they came to faith? What are the appropriate means of "fishing" in our setting? And again, is this going to be the same for all disciples, or should there be different types of "fishing" to suit different personalities and situations?

A third topic for teaching or discussion might be the nature and implications of Jesus's miracles, especially those that do not involve a human subject. In this case, the miracle does not directly override the "laws of nature." An unusually large catch of fish is not in itself impossible—the habits of fish are not totally predictable. But what is remarkable about it is the timing of the catch after a night of failure in the same area—the presence of the fish in the "wrong" place at the "wrong" time. And even if, as some have speculated, Jesus was aware of a shoal likely to hold fish, how did he know of one that experienced fishermen had not detected? What is meant by calling this "miraculous," and what does it tell us about Jesus?

After their miraculous catch of fish, Peter, Andrew, James, and John recognize the authority of Jesus and respond to his call to "fish for people." This sixth-century AD mosaic in the main nave at San Apollinare Nuovo in Ravenna, Italy, is called *St. Andrew and St. Peter Responding to the Call of Jesus.* One lucky fish is escaping, a detail that brings humanity to the scene and a touch of humor that serves to make one pay more attention to the familiar.

Illustrating the Text

There have been stories throughout history of people leaving everything and following Christ as the disciples were called to do.

Biography: William Booth. Booth (1829–1912), an English Methodist preacher, was the founder and the first general of the Salvation Army. The story of his leaving his comfortable pulpit to work with street people, the poor and unloved, is stirring; the legacy and ongoing work of the Salvation Army everywhere is proof of the obedience of its founder.

Missions History: The Student Volunteer Movement. This movement started in 1886, on the campus of the Mount Hermon School in Northfield, Massachusetts, though earlier than that it is reported that seven Cambridge University students forsook their career goals to go to foreign missions. Missiologist Herbert Kane reports that the movement was very active for fifty years, during which it was "instrumental in sending 20,500 students to the foreign mission field, most of them from North America." Some estimates say that student volunteers composed half of the total Protestant foreign missionary force. They were "driven by intensity of purpose that has been rarely equaled." Among these individuals who gave up their early ambitions were C. T. Studd, John B. Mott, Joseph H. Oldham, and Stanley E. Jones.[2]

Literature: *The Hobbit*, by J. R. R. Tolkien. In this fantasy tale, which comes before Tolkien's epic *Lord of the Rings*, Gandalf prods Bilbo to leave all he has ever known and loved (safety, quiet, good friends, good food, and a cozy hobbit home) to help Thorin and a band of dwarfs reclaim the Lonely Mountain and its treasures from a dragon named Smaug. This creates a significant personal struggle for Bilbo between his mother's "Tookish" adventurous side and the much-more-sedentary "Baggins" genes by which he has been living. Although he is initially very resistant to leaving, he submits his will to something he can sense is right and agrees to go. He leaves quickly, taking his walking stick. Several clips from the movie version (*The Hobbit: An Unexpected Journey*, 2012) could be used.

Fishing for people, the dominant metaphor of this passage, encapsulates the missionary nature of Christian faith, which can take many forms.

Christian Ministry: Rebecca Manley Pippert. Pippert, who trains evangelists, is the head of Salt Shaker Ministries. She tells about people who have "fished" for others in remarkably different ways and in different places. In one article, Pippert tells the story of the late Ruth Siemens, who pioneered student campus ministries, starting with individuals and small groups in Peru, Brazil, and Spain. Pippert lived with Siemens for a time in Spain. During Pippert's time there, Siemens was very persistent in encouraging her to start a Bible study for friends who were "seekers." Even though she wanted to have some type of ministry, she was a bit doubtful that anyone would be interested. Pippert finally went ahead, coached by Siemens on actual topics to introduce, such as a study "on the biographies of Jesus Christ." However, when the moment came to invite people to the study, Pippert, overcome by fear, said to those gathered, "You don't want to come to a Bible discussion, do you?" To Pippert's "amazement and alarm, they all said they would." What she discovered was that unlikely people were open to being "fished"; she had limited the categories.[3]

Two Memorable Healings

Big Idea *Jesus brings not only physical healing and social restoration but also spiritual liberation by the forgiveness of sins.*

Understanding the Text

The Text in Context

These two episodes develop Luke's portrait of Jesus the healer, a theme that was alluded to in 4:23 and spelled out in 4:40, and that will remain a prominent feature of his ministry throughout the time in Galilee and on the road to Jerusalem. In 4:40 we learned of Jesus's ability to heal "various kinds of sickness," and here that bald statement is filled out by a focus on two specific physical complaints. The first is particularly striking because of the deep-seated fear of "leprosy" and the belief that it was humanly incurable.

In this section we are told of Jesus's strong popular following but at the same time of the beginning of official opposition, focused in the scribes' accusation of blasphemy. These twin themes of popular support and official opposition will run side by side through Luke's narrative, until the issue comes to its final resolution in

Jerusalem. The controversy motif, with the Pharisees as chief opponents, will continue in our next two sections, up to 6:11.

Historical and Cultural Background

The term "leprosy" was used for a variety of skin complaints, not necessarily

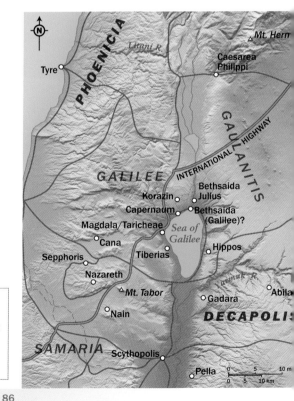

In 5:17 the Pharisees and teachers of the law are described as coming to hear Jesus teach from "every village of Galilee and from Judea and Jerusalem." Jesus's main focus during this period of his ministry is in the area of Galilee. This map shows the cities, towns, and major roads in the region of the Sea of Galilee.

leprosy proper as we know it today (Hansen's disease). Those affected were regarded as unclean and were forced to live outside normal society for fear of contagion (see Lev. 13:45–46). "Leprosy" was regarded as incurable (2 Kings 5:7). Yet Leviticus 14 made provision for someone whose "leprosy" had been "cleansed" (the term regularly used for this disease, rather than "healed"), presumably by direct divine intervention, to be examined by the priest and so restored to society.

In ancient society a connection between physical illness or disability and sin was often assumed, with some directly attributing disease to sin as its cause. Paul seems to suggest such an idea in 1 Corinthians 11:29–30, but in John 9:1–3 Jesus refutes that simple equation, and much of the book of Job is devoted to questioning it. Jesus's comments on the forgiveness of the paralyzed man must be read in the light of that popular view.

Interpretive Insights

5:12 *covered with leprosy.* This indicates an advanced state of the disease, so it is all the more remarkable that the man simply assumes that Jesus *could* heal him if he wished, given the general view that the disease was incurable.

5:13 *Jesus reached out his hand and touched the man.* To touch someone with "leprosy" was automatically to contract ritual defilement. It is an interesting question whether Jesus simply ignored the taboo, or whether the healing touch itself nullified the defilement.

5:14 *Don't tell anyone.* For Jesus's demand for silence after miracles, see on 4:41. In this case there is no demonic dimension,

and the most obvious reason is Jesus's desire to avoid being mobbed by other potential patients. If so, 5:15 tells us that it was unsuccessful. In any case, it would be hard to conceal the restoration of a man who had "leprosy," given the ostracism shown to those with that condition.

show yourself. For this man to show himself to the priest would require a long journey to Jerusalem, where the necessary sacrifice must be offered.

as a testimony to them. Probably all that this means is that the prescribed sacrifice (see Lev. 14) would attest to the man's cure, so that he could be received back into society. The plural pronoun suggests that it is not a testimony to a skeptical "priest" (singular) about Jesus's supernatural power. There has not yet been any suggestion of hostility to Jesus on the part of priests; his opponents in 5:17–26 will be Pharisees and scribes, not priests.

5:16 *Jesus often withdrew to lonely places and prayed.* Luke tells us more about the priority of prayer in Jesus's ministry than do the other evangelists (see 3:21; 6:12; 9:18, 28; 11:1). Because of popular pressure he often needed to retreat to a "solitary

Scribes and Pharisees

"Teachers of the law" (*nomodidaskaloi*) in 5:17 is another term for the "scribes" (*grammateis*) in 5:21 (the NIV regularly uses "teachers of the law" to translate *grammateis*, whereas many other versions use "scribes"). They were the professional interpreters and teachers of the Mosaic law, also called "rabbis," from whose labors the massive legal corpus of the Mishnah and the Talmud was eventually compiled. Their concern was to make the Mosaic laws applicable as regulations for every aspect of life, a concern that inevitably led them into conflict with Jesus's more flexible and creative attitude toward the law.

The Pharisees were a relatively small but highly respected group of Jewish laymen who devoted themselves to the careful observance of the law, both in its Mosaic form and in its later scribal elaboration, and to persuading others to do likewise. Because of this convergence of interests, many scribes were also Pharisees (see 5:30). The Pharisees became the dominant force in the rabbinic establishment that developed in the latter part of the first century AD.

place," as in 4:42, and this general statement is deliberately placed alongside the mention of persistent crowds in 5:15.

5:17 *Pharisees and teachers of the law.* See the sidebar "Scribes and Pharisees." That these teachers, some of whom came from Jerusalem, had come to hear Jesus teaching may already indicate that they had suspicions about his orthodoxy.

5:18 *A paralyzed man.* Paralysis may result from a number of causes, such as polio, a stroke, or an injury, but the Gospels never spell out the underlying cause. The cure of a paralyzed person, with the sudden restoration of movement, is a particularly striking public proof of supernatural healing power.

5:19 *lowered him on his mat through the tiles.* Mark 2:1–2 tells us that on this occasion Jesus was teaching inside a house. Ordinary Palestinian homes had a flat roof accessible by an outside staircase. The roof normally was made of thatch and clay over wooden beams, but sometimes also of tiles. This dramatic plan to get access to Jesus must have caused a lot of noise and debris, but we are spared the details of how it affected Jesus's teaching in the room below.

5:20 *Your sins are forgiven.* See "Historical and Cultural Background" above. It is possible that either the man or his friends (or both) thought that the paralysis was the result of sin, but it is equally possible that they were looking only for physical healing, whereas Jesus was aware of a further spiritual dimension to the man's need, or indeed of a psychosomatic element in his disability of which they may have been unaware. In that case, Jesus's opening declaration would have taken them by surprise as much as it does the modern reader. The forgiveness of sin is presented not as the means of healing, but rather as itself the fundamental need, with the healing serving, almost as an afterthought, to demonstrate the authority of Jesus the forgiver.

A paralyzed man was brought to Jesus by lowering him down through the roof. Homes during this time period had flat roofs with an outer staircase leading to the top similar to those shown in these photos from the modern village of Der Samet near Hebron in the Palestinian territory.

5:21 *Who is this fellow who speaks blasphemy?* A later rabbinic ruling defined "blasphemy" as the uttering of the name of God, but here it carries the broader sense of a human infringing on the divine prerogatives. Anyone might declare that God forgives, but here they understood Jesus to be forgiving on his own personal authority. This is something that belongs to "God alone."

5:23 *Which is easier: to say . . . ?* It is easier to *say* that sin is forgiven because there is no visible result by which the outcome may be tested, whereas a claim to heal paralysis is clearly spurious if no visible change results. So Jesus uses the more falsifiable claim to reinforce the less tangible.

5:24 *The Son of Man has authority on earth to forgive sins.* See the sidebar "The Son of Man." Here the title reflects the earthly authority given to the "one like a son of man" in Daniel 7:13–14.

Theological Insights

Luke has already told of Jesus's authority in healing and exorcism and in a nature miracle. Now a new dimension is added: his authority to forgive sins. This is one of a number of ways in which the Gospels depict him as quietly assuming the authority of God himself. Normally such assumptions go without challenge, but here the reaction of the scribes, accusing Jesus of blasphemy, brings the underlying boldness of the claim into the open. It is therefore significant that Jesus does not back off from the claim, but rather reaffirms it and offers as proof an undeniably visible healing. His power over physical illness is thus paired with his spiritual authority, and the reader (and the crowd whose awed reaction is noted in 5:26)

The Son of Man

This term occurs twenty-five times in Luke's Gospel, always as a title of Jesus, and always in his own words. In Hebrew and Aramaic a "son of man" simply means a "human being," but Jesus coined "*the* Son of Man" (which is not a natural idiom in Greek) as a title specifically for himself. Indeed, it is his only regular public title in the Gospels.

He probably derived the idea from Daniel's vision of a human figure ("one like a son of man") who was to receive the ultimate sovereignty over all peoples (Dan. 7:13–14), but he then used the title for different aspects of his mission, including his earthly authority (as in Dan. 7:14) but also more frequently his destined suffering and death and his subsequent vindication and glory. Because it was not already a recognized messianic title, it deliberately challenged people to think out in a new way what Jesus had come to do.

is left with a sense that Jesus really is "God with us."

Teaching the Text

These two healings may be taught separately, since they represent two episodes, or together, since both illustrate Jesus's extraordinary power to heal. Below are teaching points for each.

1. In teaching about the man healed from leprosy, it is essential to bring out the nature and significance of defilement, or "uncleanness." The man's disease made him a social and religious outcast, isolating him from family, friends, and community. Jesus's willingness to touch him, despite this uncleanness, reveals Jesus's power to bring healing and restoration to brokenness and isolation. The following are some teaching points to consider:

- The man's isolation and hopelessness before meeting Jesus. Try to identify some areas where you or your audience might experience similar feelings.

- The poignant blend of faith ("you can make me clean") and doubt ("if you are willing"). Are there times when we simultaneously experience both faith and doubt?
- The effect of Jesus's *touch* on a man whom others have shunned for years as unclean. In what ways do we have opportunities to "touch" those who are outcasts?
- The ordeal of the priestly examination. You might discuss the reason for Jesus to have made this command. Why was priestly verification important? Consider how this impacted the man's place in his community.
- The impossibility of keeping quiet about the good news (despite Jesus's prohibition). How should we respond to the good news of Jesus's healing and saving power?

2. The healing of the paralyzed man has several important themes that ought to be brought out in a teaching session:

- The remarkable faith of the friends. Be sure to explain the nature of first-century Palestinian roofs and what these friends went through to get the man to Jesus. They must have had significant faith in Jesus's healing power to risk the ire of the homeowner. It can be fun and interesting to your congregation to describe in humorous detail the process of opening the roof and the likely response of those present.
- Jesus's surprising response, "your sins are forgiven." How was this response different from the expectations of the friends and others present? What were

A leper came to Jesus and asked to be made clean, and Jesus healed him. Although a section is missing, this portion of a large fourteenth-century Byzantine ceiling mosaic shows the leper making his request to Jesus.

they expecting? Does Jesus sometimes give us something different than what we ask or hope for?

- The christological implications of Jesus's statement. How did the religious leaders respond to Jesus's statement? What does this tell us about Jesus? What does it tell us about his authority as the divine Son of Man and Son of God?
- The relationship between physical and spiritual healing. Jesus does not just heal the man to prove that he could forgive sins. Like his other healings and exorcisms, this is an object lesson, illustrating the reality that the kingdom of God is breaking into human history, bringing healing and wholeness. There is an intimate relationship between the spiritual salvation of individuals and

the restoration of creation from its fallen state.

Illustrating the Text

Jesus's power to heal covers all diseases, including the horror of leprosy.

Autobiography: *Pain: The Gift Nobody Wants*, **by Paul Brand and Philip Yancey.** Although biblical "leprosy" does not always refer to the dreaded disease known today as "leprosy" (Hansen's disease [see "Historical and Cultural Background" above]), the man in Luke 5:12–14 might well have had Hansen's disease, in which case the terrible and dreaded nature of the disease could be an important part of the sermon or lesson. Paul Brand (1914–2003) worked for fifty years as a physician, particularly as a hand surgeon specializing in leprosy. He spent a number of years among lepers in India, where he had been born to missionary parents, his work leading to amazing breakthroughs in the treatment of leprosy. This book describes one experience when he had what he calls "the darkest night of my entire life."

> Feeling very unwell and feverish, he realized that he could feel no "sensation of touch whatsoever in the area around his heel," one of the disease's first symptoms. He had always checked himself carefully for skin patches as leprosy workers were instructed to do. What followed for him was a night full of despair, plagued by questions and anxieties. "What would this do to my life . . . my work? I had gone to India in the belief that I would serve God by helping to relieve suffering. Should I now . . . go underground so as not to create a stir? I would need to separate myself from my family, of course, since children were unusually susceptible to infection. I knew all too well what to expect. My office files were filled with diagrams charting the body's gradual march toward numbness. Ordinary pleasures in life would slip away. Petting a dog, running a hand across fine silk, holding a child—soon all sensations would feel alike: dead."[1]

Bible: The story of Naaman (2 Kings 5).

Quote: The first-century AD Jewish historian Josephus describes a leper as "no different from a corpse" (*Ant.* 3.264).

Jesus discerned spiritual need as well as seeing physical disability.

Anecdote: *The Gospel of Ruth: Loving God Enough to Break the Rules*, **by Carolyn Custis James.** James tells the story of her husband, Frank, whose brother died while climbing Mt. Hood. At the rescue site and in deep grief, Frank, who had come quickly from Florida without enough warm clothing, was giving press interviews. A CNN producer noticed his cold hands and offered his gloves to Frank. The producer refused to take them back later, a detail which, writes James, "seems hardly worth mentioning. But," she continues, "he [Frank] often refers to that simple act of kindness . . . as a moment that touched him deeply." She concludes with a reflection on Christ's concern for Frank's physical well-being as well as his grief: "When you're sitting in the darkness with a heart that aches for [God], the slightest sign of his presence is monumental."[2]

Feasting and Fasting

Big Idea *The joyful inclusiveness of Jesus's ministry contrasts with the joyless ritual of formal religion.*

Understanding the Text

The Text in Context

The note of controversy that came into Luke's story with the accusation of blasphemy by scribes and Pharisees against Jesus in 5:21 is now further developed in two scenes in which he is criticized first for mixing with people regarded as irreligious and second for not imposing a proper disciplinary regime on his disciples. The impression thus grows stronger that Jesus's whole approach to religion is fundamentally different from that of the scribes and Pharisees, and the Sabbath controversies in 6:1–11 will underline this difference. This theme will lead up to his eventual confrontation with the authorities in Jerusalem.

But alongside the controversy, and indeed largely responsible for it, is a growing sense of the sheer joy and exuberance of Jesus's message and ministry, which bring the hope of liberation for those who are oppressed, as was first set out in the Nazareth manifesto (4:18–19). Luke's characteristic theme of *salvation* is being progressively filled out as the story develops.

Historical and Cultural Background

Mark locates the call of Levi in Capernaum, which was the border post between Galilee and the tetrarchy of Philip across the Jordan. Levi's "tax booth" there would probably be concerned with the customs duties levied on

Levi was sitting at his tax booth when Jesus came and said, "Follow me." This relief from a funeral stele shows a tax collection scene (second to third century AD, Germany, Neumagen-Dhron).

goods in transit between the tetrarchies of Philip and Antipas as well as across the lake. But the presence in the town of "a large crowd" of other tax collectors suggests that in this thriving town there were also those responsible for the taxation of the general population.

Jews disliked tax collectors not only because they were known to get rich by charging arbitrary amounts above the official dues (see 19:8) but also because they represented and were answerable to an oppressive and (despite Antipas's part-Jewish pedigree) pagan regime. This made them unclean in the eyes of the religious purists, and no respectable teacher would be seen in their company. Luke makes a great deal of Jesus's controversial openness to tax collectors; see 7:29, 34; 15:1, and note especially the parable in which a tax collector is the unexpected "hero" (18:9–14) and the story of the "chief tax collector" Zacchaeus (19:1–10).

Interpretive Insights

5:27 *by the name of Levi.* The story is clearly the same as that of "Matthew" in Matthew 9:9–13. The fact that Mark and Luke tell this story like that of the calling of the other apostles (Mark 1:16–20) and yet do not mention Levi in their lists of the Twelve suggests that "Matthew" (whom they do list among the Twelve) and "Levi" were two names for the same man.

5:28 *left everything and followed him.* The same was said of Simon, James, and John in 5:11. See comments there for the implications of this statement as a model for discipleship. As a member of the itinerant group, Matthew/Levi would have little

chance to return to his profession after hosting the "great banquet" of 5:29.

5:29 *held a great banquet for Jesus.* Luke uses the same term in 14:13 for what appears to be a special meal with formal invitations. Levi's profession had made him wealthy enough to be a generous host. Not only were his professional and social associates invited, but also Jesus's disciples along with Jesus himself (5:30 is Luke's first use of the term "disciple"; he will introduce the disciples more formally in 6:13–16). This looks like a deliberate attempt by Levi to introduce Jesus and his circle to a particular sector of society, with Jesus as the guest of honor. This is the first of several scenes in Luke's Gospel set at meals.

5:30 *Why do you eat and drink with tax collectors and sinners?* Maintaining ritual purity was a central concern of the Pharisees. To enter a tax collector's house was perhaps a formal breach of purity, and certainly no respectable religious teacher would mix socially with such people (note the addition of "and sinners" to underline the point). Sharing a meal was an important mark of social identification.[1]

5:31 *It is not the healthy who need a doctor, but the sick.* Similar proverbs are attributed to some ancient philosophers. A healer must expect to get his hands dirty.

5:32 *I have not come to call the righteous, but sinners to repentance.* The contrast between the self-satisfied righteous and the repentant sinner is typical of Luke; see the parables of the two sons (15:11–32) and of the Pharisee and the tax collector (18:9–14). Only Luke includes the phrase "to repentance," an important caveat: Jesus offers spiritual salvation, not mere acceptance for those who have failed morally.

5:33 *They said to him.* The questioners are left unidentified. The third-person reference to "disciples of the Pharisees" makes it unlikely that these are the same objectors as in 5:30. It is perhaps a topic raised at the dinner table.

John's disciples. Given the initial impact of John's revival movement (3:7–18), it is not surprising that we hear of groups of his followers continuing long after his death. See 7:18–19; 11:1; John 4:1–2; Acts 18:25; 19:3.

often fast and pray. Our knowledge of the ascetic discipline of the "Baptist" movement comes only from this text, though 7:33 attests the popular view of John as an ascetic. Pharisaic groups fasted for two days each week (18:12; *Did.* 8:1). A religious movement that did not impose such a discipline was easily dismissed as frivolous (compare the popular estimate of Jesus in 7:34).

5:35 *the bridegroom will be taken from them.* The wedding imagery depicts the new life of the kingdom of God as one of joy and celebration. But the "taking

away" of the bridegroom follows on from Simeon's imagery of the sword (2:34–35) as a pointer toward Jesus's eventual violent death, for which the growing note of official disapproval is increasingly preparing us.

in those days they will fast. There is no suggestion that fasting per se is wrong, but rather that it is simply inappropriate to the present time of celebration. For Christian fasting, see Matthew 6:16–18.

5:36 *the patch from the new will not match the old.* In Mark and Matthew this saying focuses on *damage* to the old cloth, but Luke's version stresses incompatibility. New and old in religion do not mix.

5:37 *the new wine will burst the skins.* Here the theme of damage is added. The (powerful, effervescent) new wine represents the gospel message and those who embrace it; they cannot be confined within the worn-out structures of formal religion. The parable is left uninterpreted, leaving readers to think out for themselves what sort of religious structures may be required for the new wine of the kingdom of God.

5:39 *The old is better.* This unexpected

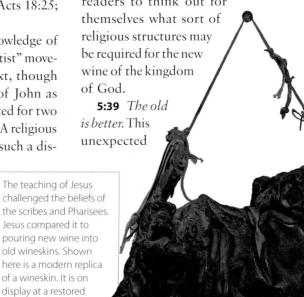

The teaching of Jesus challenged the beliefs of the scribes and Pharisees. Jesus compared it to pouring new wine into old wineskins. Shown here is a modern replica of a wineskin. It is on display at a restored third-century AD home at Qatzrin on the Golan Heights.

addition seems to turn the preceding imagery on its head. But perhaps that is the point: while Jesus offers new wine, most people prefer to stay with the old—a wry comment on the deadening effect of the religious conservatism represented here by the Pharisees.[2]

Theological Insights

The proverbial saying of 5:31 and Jesus's programmatic declaration in 5:32 together set out the theology of salvation that underlies Luke's whole Gospel, and that comes to its climax in the manifesto of 19:10: "The Son of Man came to seek and to save what was lost." Sin and repentance are therefore at the heart of this message. But the ironical reference to "the righteous" in 5:32 warns us that repentance does not come easily to those who see themselves as already sufficiently religious. In this context, Jesus's welcome to tax collectors and sinners is socially and religiously radical in itself, and his expectation that it will be among such outsiders that his message finds a welcome mounts an uncomfortable challenge against all more formal religion.

The same perspective runs through the parables of 5:34–38. It is easy for us to recognize in the old cloth and the old wineskins the rule-bound approach of Pharisaic Judaism, against which so much of Jesus's teaching will be directed in this Gospel. But it is not only in Judaism that overly formal religion can occur, and large areas of Christian church history and of church structures today also show more resemblance to old wineskins than to the new wine of the kingdom of God. There are still "righteous" people in Christian churches who show little appetite for a gospel of salvation for the "sick."

Teaching the Text

The pronouncement in 5:31–32 is the climax of the call of Levi and should be the central point of a message on 5:27–32. Jesus did not come to call those who consider themselves righteous (that is, the self-righteous), but rather those who recognize their need of him. Invite your listeners first of all to recognize that all of us should fit into the latter category. We all must come to God as sinners, desperately in need of the Divine Physician's healing touch. We are saved by his grace alone, apart from anything we have done to earn that salvation (Eph. 2:8–9).

Listeners could then be invited to think about how Jesus's involvement with people outside respectable religious circles might appropriately be followed in our own social and religious setting. What are some contemporary examples of ministries that similarly go outside the church's comfort zone to reach those in most need? What could we do to expand our ministry in this direction? Are there dangers in such outreach? Why is it not more prominent in modern Christian ministry?

Luke 6:33–39 is one of the few passages about fasting in the New Testament and so may profitably be used to teach the nature and benefits of fasting. Was Jesus's sidelining of fasting in this passage appropriate only to the time of his earthly ministry (while the bridegroom was still present)? What place, if any, should be found for fasting in modern Christian discipleship? You may even consider using this passage as preparation for a period of prayer and fasting for your congregation or Bible study group.

Yet while fasting is an important secondary point of this passage, Jesus's primary point should not be missed. The coming of Jesus, the bridegroom, has brought in a whole new era in salvation history. The new wine of the gospel is incompatible with the old. Invite your hearers to consider what Jesus means by this. What aspects of the new wine of Christianity are incompatible with the old wine of Judaism? What are critical points of continuity that must be maintained between the two? Is Jesus contrasting purely ritualistic religion with a living and dynamic relationship with God? Or is something else at work here? Consider how the imagery of the patch and the wineskin might apply to the present situation in your church circles.

Illustrating the Text

Jesus calls and is welcomed by people from all walks of life.

Christian Ministry: *Teen Challenge.* This Christian recovery ministry, which later came to be called "Teen Challenge," was started in New York by the late Dave Wilkerson (1931–2011). It is a well-known example of providing welcome. Wilkerson spent time in small pastorates in Pennsylvania. Late one night, he saw a picture in *Life* magazine of a group of teenagers in New York City charged with murder. He felt strongly called to go to minister to the gangs and addicts of this great city. His book *The Cross and the Switchblade* (1963), written with John and Elizabeth Sherrill, is the story of gang leader Nicky

Jesus did not avoid the social outcasts of the day. He ate with them. Father Damien followed Christ's example when he was sent to minister to the quarantined lepers on the island of Molokai. He served them compassionately until his death. This photo of Father Damien was taken just before he died in 1889.

Cruz's conversion. It became a best seller, has been translated into many languages, and was one of the most influential books of its time. It was later made into a film of the same name. Anecdotes from the book would be very helpful to illustrate this principle.

Biography: Jackie Pullinger. Not well known to American audiences is the story of Pullinger (b. 1944), founder of St. Stephen's Society (a rehabilitation facility), who felt called to go to Hong Kong to reach out to drug addicts. Hundreds of those addicts have been brought to Christ as a result of her ministry, which is described in her book *Chasing the Dragon* (1980). Information about and interviews with her can be found online.

Film: *Molokai: The Story of Father Damien*, directed by Paul Cox. This beautiful film (1999) chronicles the story of Father Damien (1840–89), a Catholic priest from Belgium who went to work among the lepers on the island of Molokai and died from leprosy at the age of forty-nine. His courage and his outreach to the people are unforgettable.

Christ will not be held back in his outreach by the false expectations of Pharisaical religion.

Christian Nonfiction: *Extreme Righteousness: Seeing Ourselves in the Pharisees*, by Tom Hovestol. In this unusually insightful book (1997) Hovestol points out the commonality that the average evangelical Christian maintains with the Pharisees, who, as he notes, were not at all completely bad. He writes,

> The Pharisees were well-meaning religious people. However, it was their essential goodness and godliness that was part of the problem they had with Jesus, and He with them. The Pharisees received such "harsh" treatment from Jesus not because they were so far from the truth but because they were so close. Yet, as is often the case, those who are furthest from the kingdom of God are those closest to it, who cannot see the forest for the trees.[3]

Anecdote: The Pharisaic reaction is well exemplified by the response of the Church of England to John Wesley and George Whitefield in their open-air preaching to miners, which violated regulations regarding preaching and parish boundaries. The formation of the Methodist Church (despite Wesley's own reluctance) is an example of new wine needing new wineskins.

Lord of the Sabbath and Appointing the Twelve

Big Idea *Jesus, the Son of Man, declares that he has the authority to determine how the Sabbath should be observed.*

Understanding the Text

The Text in Context

The two Sabbath incidents in 6:1–11 complete the series of confrontation stories that began in 5:17–26, and the concluding discussion of "what they might do to Jesus" sets an ominous note for the further development of the story.

But alongside the official opposition, we are now more fully introduced to the contrasting group of Jesus's committed followers. We have read of the call of some of them in 5:1–11, 27–28, but now the inner circle of the Twelve is formalized. It is they who will form the primary audience for Jesus's teaching on discipleship in 6:17–49, and who will be a constant presence during the story of Jesus's itinerant ministry right up to the final week in Jerusalem.

Historical and Cultural Background

Observance of the Sabbath was (along with circumcision and the food laws) one of the main distinguishing marks of Jewish religion, culture, and national identity, and so it was a matter of primary importance in scribal teaching and discussion.

The Old Testament commanded God's people to keep the Sabbath holy by doing no work on it. But what constituted "work"? A major concern for the scribes was so to define "work" that no one was left in any doubt as to what was and was not permitted on the Sabbath. Their Sabbath rules eventually filled two whole tractates of the Mishnah. Thirty-nine primary categories of "work" were established (see the sidebar "Rules for the Sabbath") and then subdivided and elaborated so that every aspect of daily life was covered. Strict observance of the Sabbath was thus a major element in the Pharisees' agenda of scrupulous obedience to the law, written and oral.

Healing is not listed among the forbidden categories, but scribes seem to have assumed that it qualified as work. So they discussed when medical help might exceptionally be given on the Sabbath, and they allowed this when there was imminent danger of death or when childbirth took place (*m. Yoma* 8:6; *m. Shabb.* 18:3). The principle seems to have been to allow only what could not be postponed until after the Sabbath (see on 4:40). A paralyzed arm clearly did not fall into this category.

Interpretive Insights

6:2 *Why are you doing what is unlawful on the Sabbath?* The act itself of plucking and eating grain in someone else's field was not against the law (see Deut. 23:25), but to pluck grain and rub it could be classed as "reaping" and "threshing," both of which were forbidden under Pharisaic Sabbath rules (see the sidebar "Rules for the Sabbath").

6:3 *Jesus answered them.* As in 5:30, the accusation was addressed to the disciples, and only they are said to have plucked the grain. But a teacher was held to be responsible for his disciples' behavior, and Jesus's reply assumes that he has sanctioned what they are doing.

6:4 *Have you never read what David did?* An argument drawn from outside the books of Moses (1 Sam. 21:1–6) does not formally solve the legal question, but Jesus's argument is not at that level. What David did is not a straightforward precedent because it concerned a different law. (It was on the Sabbath that the sacred bread was changed and so became available for eating [Lev. 24:8], so this incident may have occurred on a Sabbath day; but the text does

Key Themes of Luke 6:1–16

- Jesus claims the authority to defy current conventions for Sabbath observance.
- He puts the meeting of human need before strict Sabbath rules.
- A serious breach is thus opened between Jesus and the traditional religious leaders.
- Jesus sets up his own alternative leadership group by selecting his twelve closest associates as "apostles."
- The Twelve are an unconventional and, in some ways, surprising group.

not say so.) Jesus cites David's action not simply as a case where Scripture recorded a law being set aside, without condemnation. It is rather a matter of *why* it was set aside, and especially of *who* did it. David used the holy bread, with the priest's permission, because he and his men were hungry; so strict observance of the rules gave way to human need. But is that alone a sufficient reason for breaking the law? Jesus's following words in 6:5 suggest that this is more about *authority* to override the law. David could do it because he was David, the Lord's anointed. Jesus is the Son of David, indeed David's Lord (20:41–44).

6:5 *The Son of Man is Lord of the Sabbath.* If David could set aside a legal ruling, how much more can the Son of Man (for this as Jesus's self-designation, see the sidebar "The Son of Man" at 5:12–26). Here, as in 5:24, the reference is to his authority during his earthly ministry, but

When the Pharisees criticized the actions of the disciples on the Sabbath, Jesus pointed to the example of David taking and eating the consecrated bread from the tabernacle. Human need outweighed strictly following the regulations of the law. This model of the table of showbread holding the consecrated bread is part of the tabernacle replica at Timna, Israel.

underlying it is Daniel's vision of the universal sovereignty of the "one like a son of man" (Dan. 7:13–14). Jesus might have disputed the scribes' definition of "work"; this was, after all, only a scribal ruling, not a matter of explicit Mosaic law. But he prefers to set the whole question of legal observance under the weightier heading of his own personal authority, leaving all the scribal debate, and the authority of the scribes, on one side.

Jesus chose twelve of his followers to be apostles. This illustration is known as the *Ordaining of the Twelve Apostles* and is from a series called The Life of Our Lord Jesus Christ, by James Jacques Joseph Tissot (1836–1902).

6:6 *whose right hand was shriveled.* The Greek term for "hand" (*cheir*) may indicate the arm, not just the hand. "Shriveled" is literally "dry" (*xēra*), and this may denote a deformed growth, but probably more likely paralysis. A nonfunctional right arm is a great inconvenience but not an immediate threat to life (see above under "Historical and Cultural Background").

6:7 *they watched him closely.* This looks like a deliberately planted test case rather than a spontaneous healing, with the same objectors (Pharisees and scribes) now clearly intent on discrediting Jesus as a lawbreaker.

6:9 *I ask you, which is lawful on the Sabbath?* Jesus deliberately challenges the scribes. He is shifting the ground away from definitions of "work" to first principles. Of course no one would say that you should "do evil" or "destroy" on the Sabbath or on any other day. So Jesus, by his own authority, subjects Sabbath rules to human need. By framing the issue in these terms, Jesus undercuts the whole scribal enterprise. No wonder they "were furious"!

6:12 *spent the night praying to God.* The priority of prayer in Jesus's ministry is a

regular theme in Luke; see on 5:16. But we should probably also understand this note as underlining the significance of the choice to be made.

6:13 *chose twelve of them.* The number would inevitably recall the twelve tribes of Israel derived from the twelve patriarchs. Jesus will later speak of these twelve disciples as sitting on thrones judging the twelve tribes of Israel (22:30). Here Jesus is setting up the leadership structure for the true Israel of the kingdom of God.

whom he also designated apostles. The Twelve are drawn from a wider circle of "disciples," committed followers of Jesus (see 6:17); seventy-two of them will be mentioned in 10:1. The Twelve are singled out to be Jesus's regular traveling companions, and in 9:1–2 they will be given a special mission as "apostles" (those sent out, envoys), a term that Luke frequently uses for them both in the Gospel and especially in Acts, where they feature corporately as the central leadership group of the growing church in Jerusalem. It is thus the more remarkable that most of those listed remain merely names to us; only Simon (Peter), James and John, and, though of course for a different reason, Judas Iscariot are individually mentioned elsewhere in the Gospel or Acts.

Theological Insights

Jesus nowhere questions the Decalogue principle of Sabbath observance as such, but he had no time for the meticulous scribal definitions that had the effect of elevating the prohibitive element of the Sabbath ("You shall not do any work") to a primary level of significance. For Jesus, it was overshadowed by the general principle of "doing good," which for the scribes was infuriatingly vague and open-ended. Mark 2:27 sums up his approach: "The Sabbath was made for man, not man for the Sabbath."

Jesus's claim to be "Lord of the Sabbath," following after his claim to forgive sins (both under the title "the Son of Man"), adds to the sense that he claims to be on a level above merely human authorities. He will not openly claim to be divine, but the reader who remembers the angel's message in 1:30–35 will have no difficulty in reading between the lines.

But alongside this exalted understanding of Jesus, it is salutary to note that those whom he chooses as his helpers and representatives come not from the top layer of society but rather from ordinary life: the ones whose professions we know are four fishermen and (if Levi = Matthew) a tax collector. Luke will later describe Peter and John as "unschooled, ordinary men" (Acts 4:13). Nor were the Twelve an altogether

Rules for the Sabbath

"The main classes of work are forty save one: sowing, plowing, reaping, binding sheaves, threshing, winnowing, cleansing crops, grinding, sifting, kneading, baking, shearing wool, washing or beating or dyeing it, spinning, weaving, making two loops, weaving two threads, separating two threads, tying, loosening, sewing two stitches, tearing in order to sew two stitches, hunting a gazelle, slaughtering or flaying or salting it or curing its skin, scraping it or cutting it up, writing two letters, erasing in order to write two letters, building, pulling down, putting out a fire, lighting a fire, striking with a hammer and taking anything from one domain into another" (*m. Shabb.* 7:2).

compatible group: Simon "the Zealot" was not necessarily a committed freedom fighter (the later meaning of "zealot"), but he was at least a keen nationalist and upholder of the law (the meaning of "zealot" in Acts 21:20; 22:3; Gal. 1:14), which would have made him an uncomfortable colleague for Levi/Matthew the tax collector.

Teaching the Text

This passage introduces two important themes that could be profitably developed in a lesson or sermon. The first is the nature and significance of Sabbath observance. While these Pharisees were interested in legalistically enforcing their Sabbath rules, Jesus emphasized the true purpose of the Sabbath, which was to benefit mankind. Listeners might be invited to consider their experiences of traditional restrictions on Sunday activity, and to think how far these were justified. What is the fundamental purpose of the Sabbath law, and how far is it literally applicable in modern Christian practice? What were the dangers inherent in the scribal approach to the Sabbath, and why did Jesus think it necessary to challenge them? Did Jesus fulfill the whole law, including Sabbath observance? What does this mean for the continuing authority of the Old Testament law?[1] In addition to God's blessing of the seventh day of creation (Gen. 2:2) and the Old Testament Sabbath laws (Exod. 20:8–11; Deut. 5:12–15), consider Paul's words about our freedom in Christ in Romans 14:5–6 and Colossians 1:16.

Try also to get hearers to see the situation from the scribal point of view. Why did they regard Jesus's attitude to legal rules as dangerous? What risks are inherent in his more positive and flexible approach to the issue? Do we need such rules and regulations now, and if so, what is their purpose?

The second key issue in this passage is the authority of Jesus as Messiah and Son of Man. The authority of the scribes to interpret the law and impose their decisions on others came from their recognized position in society, and more particularly from their formal training and the respected tradition to which they belonged. Jesus's

authority was personal, because of who he was. It was the authority of a charismatic teacher to whom people responded instinctively and also the unique authority of the Son of Man. Consider the extraordinary authority implicit in Jesus's words. God alone established the Sabbath command. Yet Jesus identifies himself as "Lord of the Sabbath" (6:5). This same remarkable authority continues in the next passage, as Jesus chooses and appoints the Twelve (6:13–16). Remember that it was God himself who chose the twelve tribes of Israel to be his special people. Since the Twelve in some sense represent a reconstituted or restored Israel, Jesus is again claiming the authority of God to call out a new people for himself.

Illustrating the Text

Sometimes it is highly instructive when the authority of an established power group is challenged by a newcomer's reaction.

Literature: "The War Prayer," by Mark Twain. This bitterly ironic, short prose indictment of war is told in the form of a very short story. It was published in 1916, several years after Twain (1835–1910) died.

The discussion of what types of work should not be done on the Sabbath resulted in complex rules and regulations transmitted and enforced by the religious leaders of Jesus's day. Two examples of classes of work that were forbidden were plowing and threshing. A farmer of the first century would have used a plow and a threshing sledge (wooden sled with stones or sharp metal pieces embedded in the underside to loosen the grain) similar to the tools shown here.

Twain attacks more than people's mere attitudes about war; he asks them to examine their prayers. In the piece, an older stranger, claiming to be a "messenger" from God, comes into a church service where the people have been sincerely, but probably smugly, asking God to preserve their boys in war, to grant them victory and bring them back safely. The old stranger asks the minister to step aside, which the "startled" minister does. Then, in a "deep voice" he begins to speak, picturing vividly what their prayers may invoke upon the enemy. "If you would beseech a blessing upon yourself, beware! Lest without intent you invoke a curse upon a neighbor at the same time. If you pray for the blessing of rain upon your crop . . . by that act you are possibly praying for a curse upon some neighbor's crop which may not need rain and can be injured by it." Continuing, he parodies, "Help us to tear their soldiers to bloody shreds with our shells. Help us to cover their smiling fields with the pale forms of their patriot dead. . . . Help us to lay waste their humble homes with a hurricane of fire." The story ends with the narrator commenting on the church's reaction, "It was believed afterward that the man was a lunatic, because there was no sense in what he said."[2]

One person can become a significant force for change.

Documentary Film: *The Singing Revolution*, directed by James Tusty and Maureen

Castle Tusty. This documentary (2006) about a populist, nonviolent revolution in Estonia between 1986 and 1991 chronicles the people's successful attempt to push back on the Soviet occupation and oppression of their country. Hundreds of thousands of people gathered publicly to sing revolutionary songs.

Not widely known in the West, the account is inspiring and amazing.

Sometimes Christians create restrictions that inhibit the gospel's outreach.

Quote: *Extreme Righteousness: Seeing Ourselves in the Pharisees*, by Tom Hovestol.

> Sometimes our traditions compromise our theology; they even encourage us to look toward wrong solutions to the sin problem. We Christians at times produce lists of rules that protect us from defilement. Though it may not be packaged as such, defilement is viewed as "out there in the world." Certain people are designated as defiling. . . . Certain places are inherently compromising: wherever alcohol is served or pot smoked, wherever rock music is played . . . —wherever secular activities occur. . . . While there is wisdom in many of these rules, they subtly communicate the antithesis of bedrock biblical theology, namely, that defilement is internal and not external.[3]

The Good Life

Big Idea *Jesus contrasts the blessings of life in the kingdom of God, with all its hardships, with most people's idea of the good life.*

Understanding the Text

The Text in Context

Following after the selection of the Twelve, this is the beginning of a programmatic sermon on the blessings and demands of discipleship, which continues to the end of the chapter. The parameters are thus established for the role that the disciples will play in the developing story.

Outline/Structure

Luke 6:20–49 is a much shorter "equivalent" to the Sermon on the Mount in Matthew 5–7. Both sermons begin with beatitudes and end with the parable of the two houses. Most of what Luke includes in between is paralleled in Matthew's longer discourse (though not always in the same order, and often in quite different words), but Matthew has also integrated a lot of Jesus's other teaching on discipleship (some of which occurs elsewhere in Luke) into this sermon outline. Both discourses are explicitly addressed to Jesus's "disciples" in the presence of a larger crowd, and both concentrate on how those addressed must be distinct from the wider society in their lifestyle and values; they are to be an "alternative society."

The beatitudes here in Luke 6:20–22 differ from those in Matthew not only in that there are four (with four balancing woes) rather than eight (with no woes), but also in that they are addressed to the disciples in the second person; they are specifically about what it means to be a disciple, not about people in general. And whereas Matthew's beatitudes have a more obvious spiritual dimension ("poor *in spirit*," "hunger and thirst *for righteousness*"), Luke's are more down to earth ("you who are poor," "you who hunger now"), focusing on the deprivations entailed in being a disciple. Each set of beatitudes should be interpreted on its own terms, not by reference to the other.

Historical and Cultural Background

"Beatitudes" (statements of the form "Blessed is/are . . .") occur often in the Old Testament, especially in Psalms (see Pss. 1; 32; 119; 128), and, usually singly, in the Gospels of Matthew and Luke. See above on 1:45 for the meaning of *makarios*, traditionally translated as "blessed," but perhaps better as "happy," "enviable," or "to be congratulated." Such statements are not so much theological assertions about how or whom God blesses, but rather commendations (found also in secular literature, with the connotation "fortunate") of a good way of life. Here the formulae "Blessed are" and "Woe to" set out respectively the way to be embraced and the way to be avoided, and the following "for" clauses spell out what is to be the outcome of those choices. These are the reasons why it is worthwhile to be a disciple, despite the hardships that this brings. Luke is unusual in spelling out the negative alongside the positive by including four balancing woes.

Interpretive Insights

6:17 *stood on a level place.* Luke uses in 6:12 the same phrase that Matthew 5:1 uses for the location of the sermon ("to the mountain," or "into the hills"). Jesus has first taken the Twelve higher up the hill, but now he returns with them to rejoin the larger group of "disciples" and other hangers-on at a level place on the hillside, which would provide a natural amphitheater.

a large crowd of disciples . . . and a great number of people. In 6:13 we learned that there was a wider circle of "disciples" from whom the Twelve were chosen. Now we find that they are "a large crowd." But even that is not the full extent of Jesus's following. Despite official disapproval, he is now well known over a wide area far beyond Galilee.

In 6:20–49, Jesus preaches a sermon to his disciples as well as to a large crowd that has gathered. This view from the Sea of Galilee looks toward the north shore and the hilly region around the Church of the Beatitudes, which marks the traditional location of Jesus's sermon.

Key Themes of Luke 6:17–26

- Jesus teaches his disciples in the presence of a larger crowd of less committed followers.
- He uses a balancing set of "blessings" and "woes" to portray two contrasting philosophies of life.
- The disciple's life is one of earthly deprivation and hardship, but of ultimate satisfaction.
- Those who enjoy worldly success have no more to look forward to, but for true disciples there is a reward in heaven.
- True disciples must expect to be misunderstood and persecuted.

The motivation for following him up the mountainside is mixed (6:18), and probably the expectation of more healing miracles accounts for much of the crowd.

6:19 *power was coming from him and healing them all.* This sounds almost magical, but a specific case of such a healing by touch will be recorded in 8:43–48, and there we will find that the secret was "faith," not magic. Other such healings by a mere touch are mentioned in Matthew 14:36; Mark 3:10; Acts 19:12 (cf. Acts 5:15).

6:20 *Looking at his disciples, he said.* As in Matthew 5:1–2, the specific target audience is not the wider crowd but rather the disciples, and the teaching that follows focuses on their distinctive situation and

calling. But the fringe audience will not be forgotten, as in 6:46 Jesus questions the reality of the discipleship of some of those he addresses. The woes of 6:24–26 are perhaps directed more to that wider part of his audience.

Blessed are you who are poor. Here is the "good news to the poor" that was promised in 4:18. Luke's wording gives no indication that the poverty here is anything but literal. The "poor" disciples will be contrasted in 6:24 with the "rich" who are comfortably off in this world. It is thus assumed that

The target audience of Jesus's sermon was his disciples, as he preached about the costs and benefits of discipleship. This sixth-century mosaic is one of a series that illustrates scenes from the life of Christ. This is the depiction of the Sermon on the Mount (Byzantine School, San Apollinare Nuovo, Ravenna, Italy).

to be a disciple entails the loss of earthly possessions and security. Such concerns have been subordinated to "the kingdom of God" (see on 4:43). When Jesus says that "yours is the kingdom of God," the implication is that those who are not disciples fall outside the sphere of God's rule and therefore also of his blessing. If to enter such a state entails poverty, then *that* poverty is a blessing. Jesus is not saying that being poor is a commendable state *in itself*.

6:21 *Blessed are you who hunger now . . . who weep now.* Again the language (and its converse in 6:25) is literal, but as in 6:20, the implication is not that literal hunger and sorrow are good in themselves, but rather

that to accept a life of hunger and sorrow "now" as a disciple is good because of the satisfaction and joy that will come later. Again it is assumed that to be a disciple is to be outside the number of those who *in this world* are well fed and laughing (6:25). The future tenses "will be satisfied" and "will laugh" (and their counterparts in 6:25, "will go hungry," "will mourn and weep") probably envisage the final state of disciples and of nondisciples (contrasted with the "now" repeated here and in 6:25) rather than a reversal of fortunes within this life.

6:22 *Blessed are you when people hate you.* Here it is even more explicit that the condition described is specifically that of disciples: they will meet with rejection and abuse "because of the Son of Man"; that is, this is the direct result of their loyalty to Jesus. Jesus is already aware that his ministry is rousing violent opposition, and he expects those who are identified with him to experience the same hostility. "Exclude you" denotes at least social ostracism, but possibly also that they are not welcome in the worshiping community (cf. the references to disciples being "put out of the synagogue" at a later date in John 9:22; 12:42; 16:2). "Your name" perhaps looks forward to the later name "Christian," which began as a term of dissociation, if not of abuse (1 Pet. 4:14–16).

6:23 *Rejoice in that day.* The paradox of rejection being a cause for congratulation is explained by two clauses, one looking forward, the other looking back. They may look forward to a heavenly reward; compare the future satisfaction and laughter in 6:20–21. But they may also look back and see that this has been the consistent experience of those who have stood for God in a rebellious world, "the prophets." The Old Testament is full of examples, of whom Jeremiah is perhaps the most memorable: his was not a happy life from the worldly point of view, but he fulfilled his divine commission and, we may assume, has received his ultimate reward.

6:24–26 *But woe to you.* The four woes in 6:24–26 set out the obverse of the four beatitudes. In all these respects, what appears on the surface to be a happy and successful life turns out in the end to be empty. As Jesus memorably puts it in Matthew 6:2, 5, 16, "they *have received* their reward in full" (using the same word for receiving [*apechō*] payment in full as used here in 6:24).

Theological Insights

In these opening verses, and throughout this sermon, a clear distinction is drawn between the disciples ("you") and other people. The presence on the hillside of a large crowd of less committed followers (some of whose discipleship will be questioned in 6:46) indicates that the distinction is not always easy to discern, but in principle there are only two responses to Jesus's message, either wholehearted commitment to the kingdom of God, with all the hardships that may bring, or continued pursuit of the way of the world, putting present satisfaction before the will of God and its ultimate rewards. In 13:24 Jesus will characterize the way of discipleship as the "narrow door," through which only a few will enter (and see more fully Matt. 7:13–14).

What makes this a wise choice is not the promise of a better life in this world, but instead the prospect of "reward in heaven." Jesus had no hesitation in promising rewards for faithful service (especially in Matthew [see Matt. 6:1–6, 16–18; 10:40–42; 20:1–16]). Luke notes that sometimes there is "payback" already in this life (18:29–30), but the main focus of the disciple's reward is beyond death (12:32–34). Some modern Christian teaching has been slow to recognize this essentially otherworldly aspect of discipleship.

This section echoes the theme of the reversal of fortunes that was so prominent in the Magnificat (1:49–53); note especially the "humble" being "blessed" (1:48), the "hungry" filled and the "rich" dismissed (1:53). For the same theme, compare 13:30; 14:7–11; 16:19–31; 18:9–14. Jesus's gospel in Luke turns conventional values on their heads; those whom the world congratulates Jesus pities, and those whom the world regards as losers Jesus declares to have gotten it right.

Teaching the Text

As noted above, Luke's beatitudes have a stronger focus on physical poverty and need (e.g., "Blessed are the poor," 6:20) than Matthew's, which have a greater spiritual emphasis (e.g., "Blessed are the poor *in spirit*," etc.; Matt 5:3–10). This theme, which runs throughout Luke's Gospel, can produce challenges as well as opportunities for the pastor and teacher. In a society where wealth, privilege, and power are so cherished and sought after, how can poverty, hunger, weeping, and persecution be avenues of blessing? Think of experiences in your life or the lives of others where need and want have actually been opportunities for God's blessing. Consider also the implications of Jesus's teaching for the so-called prosperity gospel, the claim that God promises to bless his people in material as well as spiritual ways.

You should also consider the meaning and significance of the great reversal that Jesus seems to be predicting (note the future tenses). Is this a future prediction or a present reality or both? You might cross-reference here to important Lukan parables like the rich fool (12:13–21) and the rich man and Lazarus (16:19–31). Get people to think about the meaning of "blessed" and "woe" in this passage. What, if anything, would be lost if we substituted "congratulations" and "commiserations"?

Encourage listeners to consider or discuss from experiences (their own or those of others) whether modern Christian life agrees with Jesus's assumption that to be a disciple entails poverty, hunger, sorrow, and rejection. Have we gone wrong somewhere, or was it never meant to be as simple as that? They might usefully consider also how Jesus's own life exemplifies what he says here. Did it leave him any room for enjoyment and satisfaction?

Illustrating the Text

The word "beatitude" needs to be carefully understood.

Definition: The beatitude form, using *makarios* ("lucky," "fortunate"), may be illustrated from various classical Greek texts that have no religious dimension. One example is from Aristophanes, *Wasps* (lines 1292–93), who recounts that Xanthias, while undergoing a beating, reflects on how lucky (*makarios*) the tortoise is to have a hard protective shell. A famous saying of Ben Sira is likewise instructive: "Call no one blessed [*makarios*] before they die" (Sir. 11:28). His point here is that blessedness denotes the person's overall life experience and reputation rather than a specific experience of "blessing." Defining *makarios*

Jesus says in 6:22 that the disciples are blessed when people "exclude you." This social ostracism may even extend to the synagogues, where they would no longer be welcome to attend. Only a few first-century AD synagogues have been excavated. The one shown here is located at Gamla on the Golan Heights.

carefully will avoid the oversimplification that sometimes is connected to the concept of blessing.

Being a disciple may entail deprivation and hardship.

Biography: Jim Elliot. Elliot (1927–56), a famous missionary to Ecuador who was killed by the Auca people, said, "He is no fool who gives up what he cannot keep to gain what he cannot lose." Certainly, the experience of Elliot, whose story is well recorded in books and articles, as well as in film, would bear out the truth of what appears on the surface as unrewarding discipleship.

Biography: Erle Frederick Rounds. The highest goal of Rounds (1901–43) was to take the love of Christ to unreached areas of the world. Multitalented and able to fill a variety of roles, Rounds and his family ended up in the Philippines. What interrupted their successful work, including his forays into rugged mountains of the Philippines, was the bombing of Pearl Harbor in 1941, after which the Japanese invaded Manila and surrounding areas. Unable to leave the country, the Rounds family continued with their work and then took refuge in the mountains. The people kept them hidden among them, and Erle, a strong and athletic man, continued his outreach, this time to American guerrillas resisting the Japanese. Another camp where many missionaries were staying during this time was eventually attacked by the Japanese, and all of the missionaries were executed.

In one of Erle's last letters before escaping to the mountains, he wrote, "I believe the missionaries are going to see real persecution before the thing is over. . . . But it is one of the greatest privileges I can think of to be here as a missionary. . . . We hope to see you all again, but, if we should be denied that blessed joy, we can meet again in a land that is fairer than day."[1] The Roundses' camp, Hopevale, was captured by Japanese troops late in 1943, and Erle and the other missionaries were executed.

Hymn: "So Send I You," by Margaret Clarkson. Seen by many as one of the greatest missionary hymns of the twentieth century, this beautiful and moving piece was written out of the tremendous loneliness and isolation endured by Clarkson (b. 1915) while living at a logging camp in Ontario. The words of this hymn are commanding and powerful.

The first two verses are as follows:

So send I you to labour unrewarded,
To serve unpaid, unloved, unsought,
  unknown,
To bear rebuke, to suffer scorn and
  scoffing,
So send I you to toil for Me alone.

So send I you to bind the bruised and
  broken,
O'er wand'ring souls to work, to weep,
  to wake,
To bear the burdens of a world
  a-weary,
So send I you to suffer for My sake.

"Love Your Enemies"

Big Idea *We should treat other people as God treats us, looking not to our own advantage or satisfaction, but to what is good for them.*

Understanding the Text

The Text in Context

This is the middle section of the sermon that began at 6:20. Its first section set out the choice between two ways of life and commended that of discipleship. This section now explores some of the ethical implications of discipleship, with special reference to how we should treat other people and to the effect that this may have on our own relationship with God. The sermon will then conclude in 6:39–49 with a series of parables about the demands and the outcome of discipleship. This whole complex of teaching adds to our growing awareness of the unique authority of Jesus, who can make such radical demands on the allegiance of those whom he has called to follow him.

Historical and Cultural Background

The attitudes and lifestyle that Jesus here demands strike us, as they would have struck those who first heard them, as profoundly "unnatural" in that they challenge the essentially self-centered way human society operates. A man who taught like this would easily be dismissed as hopelessly otherworldly and out of touch with real life. In the Greco-Roman world of that time this might have placed Jesus in a similar light to the Cynic philosophers, who were famous for their countercultural challenges to social convention, though there is little evidence for the direct influence of Cynics in Palestine at the time of Jesus, nor for any close Cynic parallels to these particular sayings of Jesus.

The call to love one's "enemies" seems to relate in context more to personal enemies than to the politics of Jewish resistance to Rome. But Palestinian life was lived in the constant consciousness of political subjection and oppression, made worse by the ideological shame of the people of God being under the control of a pagan power. To talk of loving enemies in that context might seem to many at least starry-eyed if not downright unpatriotic. New Testament scholar Gerd Theissen, in his narrative theology on Jesus, draws a telling contrast between the "unrealistic" call of Jesus of Nazareth to love one's enemies and the hard-nosed political pragmatism of Jesus Barabbas, the freedom fighter.[1]

Interpretive Insights

6:27 *Love your enemies.* Jesus's famously radical instruction goes well beyond the Mosaic imperative "Love your neighbor as yourself" (Lev. 19:18), where "neighbor" stands parallel to "your own people." There is a closer Old Testament parallel in the remarkable instruction to help "someone who hates you" if their donkey is in trouble (Exod. 23:5), but Jesus goes beyond calling for limited practical help to demand a totally positive attitude of loving, doing good, blessing, and praying for them (the four verbs of 6:27–28 provide a wholesome contrast to the four verbs of hatred and rejection in 6:22). The fact that the "enemy" is depicted as actively cursing and mistreating the disciple makes this the more remarkable. Compare Jesus's own prayer for his executioners in 23:34 and also his example as Peter remembered it: "When they hurled insults at him he did not retaliate; when he suffered he made no threats" (1 Pet. 2:23).

6:29 *If someone slaps you on one cheek . . . If someone takes your coat.* The focus of these two scenes is not just on violence and theft but also on legal rights. A slap on the cheek was a calculated insult, for which damages could be claimed. And if the coat is being taken by litigation (so clearly Matt. 5:40), this more valuable outer garment was legally protected from confiscation (Exod. 22:26–27).

Key Themes of Luke 6:27–38

- Disciples should love and do good to those who do not love them.
- We should be prepared to help others, even to our own disadvantage.
- Such an attitude reflects the way God treats people.
- Our treatment of others should be generous and forgiving, not critical and condemning.
- Those who put others first will themselves be treated generously by God.

Yet, not only are disciples to forgo their rights to claim compensation; they are even to offer voluntarily more than their opponent demands.

6:30 *Give to everyone who asks you.* If the previous verse appears to be hopelessly idealistic, this one seems even more so. In a society where beggars, thieves, and con men abound, this is not a sustainable lifestyle. The suspicion grows that Jesus is not so much prescribing a practical rule of life as making his point by exaggeration. And that point is that our motive should be the other person's interests and "rights" before our own.

6:31 *Do to others as you would have them do to you.* Similar principles to this "golden rule" are attributed

The coat that Jesus refers to in 6:29 was most likely the outer Greek garment known as a *himation* (usually translated "garment" or "cloak"). This was a rectangular piece of soft wool cloth that could be draped across the body any number of ways. This first-century BC statue shows a young man wearing a *himation*.

to other ancient teachers, but seldom in so comprehensive and positive a form as this. More commonly the injunction was to avoid doing to others what you would not like done to you, which is arguably less demanding. The spirit of this rule is close to that of Leviticus 19:18, "Love your neighbor as yourself," though without the restriction to the "neighbor" that will be examined in 10:25–37.

6:32 *Even sinners love those who love them*. This and the two parallel statements in 6:33–34 express the natural human principle of mutuality. What is being demanded of disciples is the much less natural principle of extending love and help to those who are unlikely or unable to return it, so that the motive is altruistic, not self-interested. The self-interested approach is that of "sinners," a term that in 5:30 denoted the undesirable members of society but here is used more broadly of ordinary people who do not share the radical ideology of discipleship. This sermon regularly divides people into only two classes; on that principle, all who are not disciples are "sinners."

6:35 *Then your reward will be great*. As in 6:23, the "reward" promised to disciples is not at the level of worldly advantage. It is precisely because their generosity extends beyond the quid pro quo of normal human commerce that they can expect a reward instead from God, whose character they have reflected in their own unselfishness.

he is kind to the ungrateful and wicked. In Matthew 5:45 this "kindness" is spelled out as God's gifts of sun and rain, which are given to all regardless of their character. This principle of "common grace" does not entail, however, that God condones wickedness. The creator is also the judge.

6:36 *Be merciful, just as your Father is merciful*. This exhortation goes beyond generalized philanthropy and so prepares for 6:37–38, where the focus is on a non-judgmental, forgiving attitude to others. Disciples themselves are fallible and in need of forgiveness, and they must recognize this need in others. Ultimate forgiveness is for God alone to grant, but disciples are called to reflect his compassionate recognition of human weakness. There is no place for arrogant superiority.

6:37 *Do not judge . . . Do not condemn . . . Forgive*. The reference is to personal relationships, not to the judicial function of a court of law. What Jesus prohibits is taking a hard, critical, dismissive view of other people's failures rather than offering understanding and compassion. This does not mean that we are never called to take a stand against wrong, or to warn others of ethical and spiritual danger; it is the attitude that is at issue, a desire for the good of others instead of simply pointing out their flaws and failures.

and you will not be judged . . . condemned . . . and you will be forgiven. The passive verbs allow some ambiguity. This might simply mean that other people will treat you in the spirit you treat them, that people who live in glass houses should not throw stones. But often in New Testament Greek a passive verb denotes how God will act, and most interpreters take these passives in that way; in that case, this is a warning that the unforgiving cannot credibly ask God to forgive them (11:4; cf. Matt. 6:14–15).

6:38 *Give, and it will be given to you*. This principle of reciprocity may be understood literally, picking up the theme of generous giving in 6:30, or metaphorically of the generous spirit of mercy and forgiveness spelled out in 6:36–37. The "measure for measure" saying is used also in a different context in Mark 4:24 with reference to how we hear God's message. In these various uses, the principle is that what you receive depends on what you contribute, an extension of the principle of 6:37: "Forgive, and you will be forgiven."

Theological Insights

Two apparently opposite principles are brought together in these verses. On the one hand, there is the uncalculating generosity that looks for no returns but rather is modeled on the free grace of God to the undeserving. But on the other hand, there is the promise that those who give will also receive; indeed, 6:38 ("good measure, pressed down, shaken together and running over") indicates that in the end the giver will be richly compensated far beyond mere reimbursement.

The difference is that while we should not be looking for recompense at the human level (that is the point especially of 6:32–34), 6:37–38 speaks not of human response but of God's blessing on those who give and forgive. Humans may not repay or even appreciate the disciple's love and generosity, but God will not be in debt to anyone.

Underlying specific ethical instructions is the fundamental principle expressed in 6:35–36: disciples should reflect the character of the God they serve. Discipleship is a process of growing into the family likeness. However, this is to be achieved not merely by adopting a new set of behavioral rules but also by absorbing God's own values and attitudes. This means, above all, an outgoing, uncalculating love that puts the needs and interests of others before our own. A community that lives by such principles will stand out against natural human self-centeredness as an alternative society, incomprehensible perhaps, but undeniably attractive.

Teaching the Text

This passage bristles with ethical challenges, and in my experience it often provokes incredulity. Could Jesus really have meant us to follow literally such guidelines as these?

loving *enemies* (6:27–28, 35)

not standing up to abuse and exploitation, but rather forgoing our rights (6:29)

Jesus exhorted his listeners to give generously to others and so receive God's immeasurable goodness, which Jesus compared to a container packed down and running over with grain. This farmer's measuring bucket is full to overflowing with grain from the harvest.

Luke 6:27–38

never refusing a request (6:30)

not trying to get back what is due to us (6:30, 35)

not judging others (even when they are clearly wrong?) (6:37)

forgiving everyone (6:37)

It is important when teaching this passage to distinguish between personal revenge and societal justice. Though Christians are not to lash back at others, neither are they to look the other way in the face of evil or injustice. As God's children, we are to be agents of justice, actively opposing evil in the world. Yet in a world of sin, where violence produces violence and evil begets evil, believers are called to a radically different standard. Teaching this passage can take your audience to the heart of the gospel, because loving enemies and doing good to those who hate reflects exactly what God did for us. While we were sinners and enemies of God, Christ died for us (Rom. 5:6, 8). To love our enemies means to reflect the nature of God, who loved the world despite its rebellion (John 3:16). Just as Christ's remarkable act of self-sacrificial love produced reconciliation between God and human beings, so our self-sacrificial love and service to others, in the power of the Spirit, can break the cycle of hate and violence and produce authentic reconciliation.

Share with your audience examples from your life or the life of others where authentic self-giving resulted in reconciliation. Suggest some practical ways that this might be achieved in their own lives. It might also be instructive to suggest some examples where turning the other cheek (6:29) or allowing someone to take what belongs to you (6:30) would be wrong or unjust. What are the key principles enshrined in these commands and when might following them literally be inappropriate? A good cross-reference here is Romans 12:9–21, and especially verse 21, where Paul says, "Do not be overcome by evil, but overcome evil with good." The goal is not to be passively exploited by others, but to actively overcome evil with good. That is what God did for us in Christ.

Illustrating the Text

We are to love our enemies and those who mistreat us in word and practice, an uncompromising ethical challenge that can seem almost impossible.

Literature: *Crime and Punishment*, by Fyodor Dostoevsky. This is a dark novel (1866) about a terrible human being, Raskolnikov, who calculatingly murders two people and arrogantly insists on the reasonableness of his deed. Despite his horrific deeds, Raskolnikov is shown grace and love by a converted prostitute, Sonya. She not only enjoins him with passion and wisdom "to accept suffering and achieve atonement," but also lovingly stays by his side, even going with him to Siberia when he serves his sentence there. She refuses to compromise her belief that all must accept the consequences of sin and submit to the mercy of God. In a final scene Dostoevsky writes, "Love had raised them from the dead and the heart of each held endless springs of life for the heart of the other. . . . He was restored to life and he knew it and felt to the full all his renewed being."

Raskolnikov's relationship with other prisoners in his barracks changes, and "other convicts, formerly so hostile, were already looking at him differently. He had even spoken to them and been answered pleasantly."[2] This classic work illustrates powerfully the redemptive effect of love.

Biography: Fyodor Dostoevsky. Philip Yancey, in his book *Soul Survivor: How My Faith Survived the Church*, discusses Russian author Fyodor Dostoevsky (1821–81). Yancey writes,

> In a world ruled by law, grace stands as a sign of contradiction. We want fairness; the gospel gives us an innocent man nailed to a cross who cries out, "Father, forgive them.". . . Having embraced Christ in the hellhole of a Siberian prison, among cell mates who mocked his infirmities and despised his advantages, Dostoevsky understood grace at its most contradictory. In his novels, it enters stealthily, without warning, silencing the skeptics and disarming the cynics. They think they have life figured out until suddenly an encounter with pure grace leaves them breathless.[3]

Portrait of Fyodor Mikhaylovich Dostoevsky (1821–81) by Constantin Chapiro (nineteenth century)

Biography: There are many fine examples, especially from WWII prison camps, of persons loving their enemies and of the effect that this could have on the guards. Examples include Bishop Leonard Wilson in Changi Prison in Singapore, and Laurens van der Post in POW camps at Sukabumi and Bandung.

Anecdote: A story about the renowned Rabbi Hillel is told in the Babylonian Talmud (*b. Shabb.* 31a). When challenged by a Gentile, "Teach me the whole Torah while I am standing on one leg," Hillel replied, "Do not do to your neighbor what is hateful to you. This is the whole Torah; the rest is commentary."

Literature: *The Water-Babies: A Fairy Tale for a Land-Baby,* **by Charles Kingsley.** This children's novel, by English writer and clergyman Charles Kingsley (1819–75), was first published as a magazine serial in 1862–63. In it, the good fairy is Mrs. Do-as-you-would-be-done-by, and the wicked fairy is Mrs. Be-done-by-as-you-did.

True and False Discipleship

Big Idea *It is not enough to hear and approve Jesus's teaching; it must also be lived out.*

Understanding the Text

The Text in Context

The sermon that began at 6:20 concludes with a series of parables and pithy sayings that together challenge those who heard the sermon to model their lives on what they have heard. The following chapters will contain several shorter sections of Jesus's teaching as well as many examples of his dealings with other people, and so a fuller picture will be built up of what it means to be a disciple and to adopt the radical values of the kingdom of God. An increasingly sharp distinction will thus be drawn between God's true people and others, between the saved and the lost. The parable of the two houses that concludes this sermon gives a memorably stark portrayal of those alternatives.

Historical and Cultural Background

Rabbis often followed the example of Old Testament prophets in teaching by means of parables. The word "parable" was used more broadly than in our common usage, and it included all sorts of challenging and memorable sayings, proverbs, epigrams, similes, and so on, as well as the more extended story parables that we are familiar with. Parable, in this broader sense, was at the heart of Jesus's teaching style. We have already noted striking sayings such as "Physician, heal yourself" and "fishing for people," and in 5:31–39 we saw a series of parables of the doctor, the wedding, and the patch and the wineskins. Now Luke draws attention again to Jesus's use of a parable (6:39), and the rest of this chapter will consist of little else.

Parables are more than explanatory asides. They come with a message of their own that often is left unexplained, so that the hearer has the responsibility of working out what Jesus is getting at. Sometimes the meaning seems obvious, or is determined by the context, but often the imagery used allows a variety of applications, so that different hearers may hear different messages and challenges. Some may respond in one way, some in another, and others may simply choose to be left undisturbed. Because parables do not just illustrate, their pithy form and often surprising imagery aim to get around the hearer's defenses and to subvert unquestioned assumptions. If you have understood a parable, you will not be the same again.

Throughout this commentary the notes inevitably contain *my* reading of Jesus's parables. But that is not necessarily the only way of responding to them, and yours may well be different, and no less valid for that.

Interpretive Insights

6:39 *Can the blind lead the blind?* The verse following this one is about teachers and pupils, and that suggests one way of understanding this "parable." One who shows the way must first be able to see the way. It is useless trying to teach others if you yourself have not been taught. The same parable is used specifically of the Pharisees in Matthew 5:14, and after the confrontations of Luke 5:17–6:11 they might be thought to be the target here too. But the immediate context within the sermon does not suggest such a specific application of what is a quite general principle: teaching without understanding is a recipe for disaster.

6:40 *The student is not above the teacher.* As an observation on social status, this is true only as long as the relationship between teacher and pupil is in force; the pupil may subsequently not only equal but also surpass the teacher's standing and achievement. Jesus, however, is not just a human rabbi, one link in a chain of tradition. His authority is unique because of who he is. So is it not presumptuous to speak of *his* pupils ever being "like their teacher"? But Jesus will in fact both delegate his authority to his disciples during his ministry and expect them to continue it after he is gone, so that "Whoever listens to you listens to me" (10:16).

6:41 *the speck of sawdust . . . the plank.* This playfully exaggerated scenario from the workshop

Key Themes of Luke 6:39–49

- You cannot teach before you have learned.
- You cannot correct others when you yourself need correcting.
- The way you live and speak reveals the sort of person you are.
- It is futile to claim to follow Jesus if you do not live by his teaching.
- There is no salvation in hearing without obeying.

makes essentially the same point as 6:37 (see comments there): do not criticize others when you yourself deserve criticism far more. Those who are aware of their own failings will be less critical of the failings of others. But since the previous two verses were about teaching, this saying may also apply particularly to those who set themselves up as teachers of others when it is they themselves who need to be taught—the blind leading the blind.

6:42 *You hypocrite.* It is not a long step from the classical Greek sense of "hypocrite" as an "actor" to our use of the word to indicate deliberate deceit, pretending to be what you are not. But the term is used frequently in Matthew for religious leaders whose distorted understanding

In 6:40 Jesus says, "The student is not above the teacher, but everyone who is fully trained will be like their teacher." This relief from a column base shows a teacher with a pupil (second century AD).

In Jesus's parable of the trees and their fruit he reminds his listeners that trees are recognized by their fruit. Grapes (shown here) are produced by grape vines, not briers.

leads them to miss the point of God's laws—not so much deliberate deceit as self-deception. Here it carries a similar sense: the sheer moral inconsistency of seeing others' faults but being unaware of your own.

6:43 *No good tree bears bad fruit.* Both literally and metaphorically this is not strictly true: there may be rotten or malformed apples among a good crop, and good people sometimes do bad things. But the focus is on the crop as a whole, and thus on a person's whole lifestyle. The way one lives testifies to what sort of a person one is. Disciples should stand out as different by the way they live. Christian profession must be validated by Christian living. For the metaphor of "fruit," see John the Baptist's message in 3:8–9 and its practical elaboration in 3:10–14.

6:45 *A good man brings good things out of the good stored up in his heart.* A different image—treasure brought out from a storehouse—develops the same idea. What is true of behavior (6:43–44) is equally true of speech. What one says reveals the real person inside. Again the whole of a person's

"speech style" is in view. Anyone, perhaps having a bad day, can speak out of character. It is also sadly possible to deliberately conceal one's true character by the way one speaks, so that the test of "fruit" (6:44) may be needed to unmask a deliberately false profession. But it is not easy to keep up such an act consistently, and truth will come out.

6:46 *Lord, Lord.* The word *kyrios* may be used simply as a polite form of address: "sir." But addressed to a Galilean villager, it is a notable mark of respect, and its repetition suggests a serious recognition of Jesus's special authority. But authority demands obedience. Note the quiet assumption of authority in the phrase "do what *I* say" (not "do what God says"). Discipleship is a matter of following *Jesus*, and he claims authority equal to that of God.

6:47 *hears my words and puts them into practice.* Note that both men in the parable represent people who *heard* Jesus's words.

This parable is not left unexplained: it divides even those who are listening to Jesus (not the people who have never bothered to come and listen) into two groups. There are people in the audience whose supposed discipleship may yet end in ruin if they do not follow up on what they hear. It has always been so; not everyone in church belongs to the kingdom of God.

6:48 *laid the foundation on rock.* This fundamental rule of safe building is well illustrated by Kenneth Bailey from Middle Eastern practice. Bailey points out the temptation of avoiding a very laborious excavation by building on hardened clay, which in the summer may seem as solid as rock but will "turn into the consistency of chocolate pudding" when the winter rains come.[1] Jesus's imagery of good and bad foundations echoes that of Isaiah 28:14–18. Ezekiel 13:10–16 uses similar imagery of a flimsy wall that cannot withstand bad weather.

6:49 *its destruction was complete.* A sobering end to the sermon! Discipleship is not about an optional lifestyle decision; it is about life and death, in the ultimate sense.

Theological Insights

The different parables and epigrams in this section focus mainly on the distinction between true and false, between profession and performance, between outward appearance and inward reality. Disciples must be on their guard against those who claim to be true teachers but will only lead others into their own errors. Both deeds and words may be used to test the reality of personal profession: one's true character is made evident in the fruit that one bears.

Illustrating Parables

When illustrating parables, it is suggested that the speaker study the already-built-in images in the parables, picturing them vividly and creatively before your Christian audience has time to subconsciously dismiss them because of years of familiarity.

Gordon Fee and Douglas Stuart, in their book *How to Read the Bible for All Its Worth* (pp. 160–62), provide helpful advice for applying and illustrating the parables. First discern the central point of the parable for the original audience, then find an analogous situation for today. Fee and Stuart retell the parable of the good Samaritan, where the wounded man is represented by a poor, disheveled family broken down on the side of the road. They are passed by first by a local bishop and then by the president of the Kiwanis club, only to be picked up and aided by a local, outspoken atheist.

Find a way to retell the parable in such a way that your audience will experience the same shock and surprise that Jesus's audience did. The speaker might also ask the audience or congregation ahead of time for personal examples that illustrate these stories. With permission, these could be used in your presentation, giving a personal and local feel to the message.

But these verses also bring the challenge nearer to home. There are those who appear to others (and even to themselves?) to be true disciples but who do not come up to the mark. They call Jesus "Lord, Lord" but do not follow his teaching; they listen to his words but do not obey them. A key word of this section is "do," which occurs five times in 6:43–49 ("bears [fruit]" twice in 6:43 is the same word in Greek). There is scope here not only for examining others but also for disciples to test their own performance. Those who discern a speck of dust in someone else's eye may be quite unaware that they have a plank in their own.

Jesus's teaching in this sermon, then, is probing and discomforting. It keeps before us the two possibilities of being saved and being lost, and it invites those who hear it to apply that distinction not only to other people but also to themselves.

Teaching the Text

The parables and sayings in this section focus primarily on authentic Christian living and the need for a firm and genuine foundation that will carry us through in difficult times. Jesus's engaging teaching style here provides a variety of word pictures for the teacher or preacher. Invite your listeners to think through one or more of the six parabolic images in these verses and discuss how they may apply to our own situation as disciples today:

- the blind leading the blind (6:39)
- the teacher and the pupil (6:40)
- the speck of dust and the plank (6:41–42)
- the tree and its fruit (6:43–44)
- the treasure from the storehouse (6:45)
- the two house builders (6:47–49)

These images provide fertile ground for both illustration and application. What are some examples of "the blind leading the blind" in society or in the church today? In what ways do we see teachers replicating themselves (for good or for bad) in their students? Consider some current trends of teaching in the church that might need to be tested against the imagery of fruit and treasure (deeds and words) in 6:43–45. What exactly is involved in digging adequate foundations for our discipleship? Are there tempting shortcuts that we need to be alert to?

Illustrating the Text

You must follow up the hearing of the word by putting what you hear into practice.

True Story: Kenneth Bailey, in his helpful book *Jesus through Middle Eastern Eyes*, gives a relevant example of a building in Jerusalem that collapsed in 1991 because it was built on loose soil rather than bedrock.[2] Sadly, natural disasters seem to provide constant examples and pictures of similar collapses of shoddily built houses, such as those vulnerable to mudslides following heavy rain.

We have no right to criticize others unless we ourselves are free of faults.

Quote: G. K. Chesterton. Chesterton once wrote wryly about critics, giving words of caution that certainly apply to any person who criticizes others: "Now the mistake of critics is not that they criticize the world; it is that they never criticize themselves. They compare the alien with the ideal; but they do not at the same time compare themselves with the ideal; rather they identify themselves with the ideal."[3]

The way you live and speak reveal the sort of person you are.

Personal Story: When I (R. T. France) lived in West Africa, I wanted to grow bananas, but banana trees and plantain trees seemed to be indistinguishable. I asked a botanist friend how to tell the difference. He said that the two different types cannot be identified until the fruit develops. "Each tree is recognized by its own fruit."

Story: *The Arabian Nights.* In this collection of classic Middle Eastern stories the traditional Arabic response to a command from a superior, found throughout, is, "I hear and I obey." This is a declaration of a firm intent to actively receive and respond to admonishment.

Anecdote: It is possible almost immediately to know what the ethos of a church service will be like when one enters the sanctuary. Everything communicates it: the look of the sanctuary, the way the clergyperson is dressed, the kind of instruments that are absent or present, and the program for the service. A Catholic or a Lutheran church, which observes a formal liturgy, is profoundly different from a Pentecostal or a Quaker church. The former will have a liturgical book that guides the service, the priest or pastor will usually be robed, and the look of the sanctuary will likely be more formal. The latter will probably have a printed bulletin or none at all, the pastor (if there is one) probably will wear a suit, and the atmosphere will be far less formal. The start of the service will confirm the differences. The way a church looks and practices worship often confirms its philosophy and sometimes its identity.

Obeying the words of Jesus is like building a house on a rock foundation. It provides a firm foundation when adversity comes. In 1927, an earthquake occurred in the Jordan River Valley near the Dead Sea. Houses built on unstable foundations such as clay and soft bedrock, like the one shown here along the Jordan, could not withstand the movement of the earth. Houses built on solid rock remained standing, protecting their inhabitants.

Luke 6:39–49

Power over Illness and Death

Big Idea *Jesus has unique authority to heal, which extends even to raising the dead.*

Understanding the Text

The Text in Context

After the controversies of 5:17–6:11 and the collection of teaching on discipleship in 6:12–49, Luke now resumes his account of Jesus's public activity in and around Capernaum with two instances of Jesus's spectacular healing power. These two healings are of men, one of whom is already dead; in 8:40–56 Luke will tell of the healing of two women, one of whom is already dead. Luke often likes to balance male and female in the stories he tells. This section also brings together two stories in which Jesus responds to the needs of first a man and then a woman, each facing the loss of a loved one.

Matthew's account of the healing of the centurion's servant (8:5–13) emphasizes the centurion's status as a Gentile and develops that theme with a powerful saying about the universal scope of the kingdom of heaven (8:11–12), which Luke has elsewhere (13:28–29).

The story of the widow's son, which Luke alone includes, is one of three cases recorded in the Gospels (the others are in Luke 8:40–56; John 11:1–44) of restoring to life those who have recently died. Luke's two accounts of resuscitation are told with surprisingly little fanfare, as two healings among others, this one in public and the other in private.

Historical and Cultural Background

A centurion in Galilee would be in charge of a detachment of auxiliary troops in the service of Herod Antipas (the Roman legions were not deployed in Palestine at this time). Such troops were drawn from the non-Jewish population of surrounding regions such as Phoenicia and Syria. The centurion thus represented the Roman-supported government of an unpopular Hellenistic ruler. His good relations with the local Jewish community (7:3–5) are an important counterbalance to the general impression of an oppressive Roman occupation of Palestine. In Acts 10 Luke will tell of another centurion with strong Jewish sympathies.

Nain is located some twenty-five miles from Capernaum, in the plain of Jezreel south of Mount Tabor and about six miles from Nazareth. Jesus's ministry is not confined to the area around the lake.

Both Elijah and Elisha are credited with restoring to life someone who had recently

A centurion was part of the Roman military and supervised about one hundred soldiers. During this time period in Galilee, the centurion whose servant Jesus healed was probably in the service of the tetrarch of Galilee, Herod Antipas. This portrait of a centurion is from a second-century AD grave monument.

- Jesus can heal by the power of a word alone.
- He heals in response to faith.
- The faith of a Gentile officer is greater than any within Israel.
- One of the two "patients" in these stories is close to death, the other has just died; even death is subject to Jesus's authority.
- Jesus is motivated by compassion.
- People recognize a divine dimension to his healing power.

died (1 Kings 17:17–24; 2 Kings 4:18–37; see also 2 Kings 13:21). Luke shows that Jesus has already quoted Elijah and Elisha as precedents for his own activity (4:25–27), and readers with knowledge of the Old Testament stories would easily make the connection here. Hence the cry "A great prophet has appeared among us" (7:16). Luke tells the story of the widow's son in a way that deliberately echoes that of Elijah in Zarephath.

Interpretive Insights

7:2 *sick and about to die.* Luke does not tell us the nature of the servant's illness. Matthew says that he was "paralyzed."

7:3 *sent some elders of the Jews to him.* The centurion's explanation in 7:6–7 reveals the delicacy of the situation: a Jewish teacher ought not to contract ritual impurity by entering a Gentile house. A personal approach to Jesus would not in itself be improper, but the centurion is sensitive to the social dynamics of such a cross-cultural appeal and decides to "play it safe" by using Jewish intermediaries. Matthew, by ignoring the Jewish envoys, emphasizes the cultural confrontation.

7:4 *This man deserves to have you do this.* Jesus does not elsewhere deploy his healing power on the basis of merit, and in 7:9 it will be the centurion's faith, not his worthiness, that Jesus comments on. But the elders assume that Jesus will need persuasion to extend his ministry outside his own people. The centurion himself sees the matter differently (7:6–7).

7:5 *built our synagogue.* Probably only the more important centers of population had a specific synagogue building at this period (see on 4:15). The imposing remains of the synagogue that visitors to Capernaum admire today date probably from the fourth century, but there is evidence of an earlier building underlying them. It would be remarkable for a relatively junior officer to have the resources to finance a public building even if he wanted to; did he perhaps deploy his troops as laborers?

7:6 *I do not deserve to have you come under my roof.* See on 7:3. There is no record that Jesus ever entered a Gentile house (except under compulsion at his eventual trial). Compare Peter's reluctance to do so in Acts 10:28–29 and the reaction in Acts 11:3. The centurion, with remarkable ethnic sensitivity, wants to spare Jesus that dilemma.

7:7 *But say the word, and my servant will be healed.* Another such healing at a distance is recorded in Mark 7:24–30, again involving a Gentile "patient."[1] The centurion has no doubt of Jesus's ability to heal, only of his willingness to enter his house. But the latter is no barrier to effective healing.

7:8 *a man under authority, with soldiers under me.* A soldier is used to unquestioned authority, whether imposed on him or exercised by himself. He recognizes Jesus's power over illness as in the same category: a word is enough.

7:9 *I have not found such great faith even in Israel.* Israel is where the Messiah should expect to find faith, but this non-Jew puts Israelite faith to shame. Luke is gradually building up the theme of Jesus as a "light to the Gentiles" (2:32), and here

is a foretaste of a church in which racial origin will cease to be the defining factor.

7:12 *a dead person was being carried out.* Cemeteries were located outside the towns. Burial normally took place within twenty-four hours of death, and it was an event for the whole community.

7:13 *his heart went out to her.* "To have compassion," the traditional rendering of the term *splanchnizomai*, is sometimes associated in the Gospels with Jesus's healings and other miracles. They are not displays of power but rather responses to perceived need. A widow would have been dependent on her only son for her livelihood. Normally, Jesus healed in response to a request, but here he seems to take the initiative. Luke's spare narrative does not satisfy our curiosity as to why this particular case moved Jesus to action.

7:15 *The dead man sat up.* This and the other Gospel "raisings of the dead" should not be described as "resurrections" on par with Jesus's own. They are resuscitations to normal earthly life, and in due course the person will die again; these are physical restorations rather than spiritual transformations.

Jesus gave him back to his mother. This is a clear echo of 1 Kings 17:23; the whole story has been told in a way that recalls Elijah's miracle of restoring a widow's only son.

As Jesus approached the gate into the town of Nain, he encountered a funeral procession heading toward the burial place outside the village. The town of Nain was on the north side of Mount Moreh, twenty-five miles from Capernaum and about six miles across the Jezreel Valley from Nazareth. The modern village is shown in this photograph. No excavations have been done to locate the biblical site.

7:16 *They were all filled with awe and praised God.* Such comments follow many Gospel accounts of miracles, but here the two reported exclamations underline the astonishing character of what has just happened. "A great prophet" puts Jesus in the company of the two special prophets Elijah and Elisha, who also raised the dead. "God has come to help his people" at least recognizes a supernatural power working through Jesus. We need not suppose that in the narrative context people now encountering Jesus for the first time saw him as God incarnate, but Luke would expect his readers to read this acclamation in a more literal sense than the crowds perhaps realized.

Theological Insights

Healing by a word from a distance and bringing a dead man back to life both extend the reader's growing awareness of Jesus's special powers, which go far beyond a gift for psychosomatic healing. The Gentile centurion recognizes Jesus's unique "authority," while the Jewish crowds at Nain speak of him as a "great prophet" and exclaim that in Jesus God is visiting his people. The implicit Christology revealed in 5:20–26 in Jesus's claim to forgive sins, which only God can do, is steadily being strengthened by what we see of Jesus in action.

In the first of these stories the basis of Jesus's healing is the *faith* of the centurion. Notice that, as in 5:20, it is not the faith of the patient that is mentioned, but rather that of the one who appeals to Jesus on the patient's behalf. Faith is commonly mentioned in the Gospels as the basis of healing, but not always. Where it is not

mentioned, should we assume that it is implied? Perhaps, but the Nain story gives us pause, in that Jesus comes apparently as a stranger into the scene, no one appeals to him for help, and neither the mother nor, of course, the son is said to have faith. What is mentioned in this case is simply Jesus's compassion.

Teaching the Text

While these two passages share the common theme of Jesus's extraordinary authority to heal, they also have important differences in emphasis, the first focusing on the faith of a non-Israelite and the second on Jesus's remarkable ability to raise the dead. They may profitably be taught either together or separately.

1. *The centurion's servant.* A sermon or lesson on this passage should focus both on Jesus's authority to heal and (especially) the surprising faith of a non-Jew, which foreshadows the gospel going to the Gentiles in the book of Acts. A central theme of Luke-Acts is God's love for *all* the lost, whether sinner, tax-collector, Samaritan, or Gentile. In your message you might focus on the social and religious dynamics of this encounter between a junior officer of the occupying forces (a pagan) and a respected Jewish rabbi. Why did the centurion think it necessary (or at least diplomatically desirable) to send his Jewish friends rather than meet Jesus himself? Notice the description of the centurion in 7:4–5 and the respect for him in the Jewish community. What implications does this have for those Gentiles who are most responsive to the gospel?

In 7:6 Jesus appears willing to go to the house. So why did he accept the centurion's proposal of healing from a distance rather than breaking the social taboo by going into the house? What would be the effect of this mode of healing on the Jewish friends? Consider the implications of 7:9. How far is this a foretaste of a radical change in the economy of salvation, with faith taking precedence over race? Are there lessons that we still can learn from this about the irrelevance of our traditional boundary markers?

2. *The widow's son.* A sermon or lesson on this passage should emphasize Jesus's remarkable authority to raise the dead. He is indeed the resurrection and the life (John 11:25). This passage can be dramatically taught: encourage listeners to picture a big funeral, with the whole community involved, and then to put themselves in the place of those who witnessed this stranger's dramatic intervention.

Be sure to discuss the response of the crowds in 7:16. How much theological depth should be found in these acclamations? Did the people see Jesus as a prophet on a par with Elijah and Elisha? As much more than a prophet? Did they think that Jesus was actually God? Notice that in one sense the crowd gets it right (acknowledging God has visited his people), yet in another sense they fall short (claiming Jesus

In 7:14 Jesus "touched the bier they were carrying him on, and the bearers stood still. He said, 'Young man, I say to you, get up!'" This ivory panel from the Magdeburg Cathedral, Germany, illustrates the scene (AD 962–68).

is merely a prophet). You might discuss this as part of Luke's narrative strategy. Notice that in the resurrection account of the disciples on the road to Emmaus (24:13–35), these two followers have an inadequate view of Jesus as merely a great prophet (24:19). Jesus corrects them to show that *the Messiah* (not merely a prophet) had to suffer in order to accomplish our salvation.

3. *Life and death.* This passage also provides a good opportunity to discuss with your audience the difference between resuscitation and true resurrection. When Jesus raised people from the dead in the Gospels, they returned to normal human existence (resuscitations). Jesus's resurrection, by contrast, as well as our future resurrection, will be to an immortal, eternal existence. These resuscitations, like Jesus's healings and exorcisms, are merely snapshots that foreshadow the full restoration of creation that will one day be completed through Jesus's life, death, resurrection, and ascension.

Illustrating the Text

The centurion's faith was extraordinary.

True Story: *In Light of Eternity: Perspectives on Heaven,* by Randy Alcorn. In this book (1999) Alcorn tells about praying for twenty-two years for his father, who, as Alcorn puts it, "dug in his heels" when it came to "religious stuff." Then, at the age of eighty-four, Alcorn's father was stricken with cancer and given six months to live. One day Alcorn had to rush him to the hospital. While there, he directly asked him if he had confessed his sins and asked Christ for forgiveness. Hesitatingly, his father said, "No," and after a long pause he added, "But I think it's about time I did." Alcorn, shocked, led his father in a prayer of confession, read Scripture to him, and told him how long he had prayed for him. "The prayers of so many—beginning with my mother and me twenty-two years earlier—had finally come to fruition. To have prayed so long for a miracle and now to see it actually happen was truly amazing." Alcorn then prayed that his father would be miraculously preserved. His father lived five more years.[2]

Human Experience: In 7:7–8 Luke gives us a soldier's down-to-earth approach to the issue of authority. The testimony of active or retired military personnel in the congregation may help to show how their understanding of relationship to Jesus relates to their military experience.

Theological Reflection: William Barclay (1907–78) argues that the centurion was "no ordinary man," not only because he was a "sergeant major"—a backbone of the Roman army—but also because he had such a remarkable spirit toward his slave. Furthermore, he had "an extremely unusual attitude toward the Jews." Gentiles were known for despising the Jews; yet, for someone accustomed to giving orders, he was a humble man. Finally, he was a man of faith, coming "with that perfect confidence which looks up and says, 'Lord, I *know* you can do this.'"[3]

Jesus's compassion had multiple dimensions.

Sermon Notes: Charles Haddon Spurgeon. Some of well-known preacher Charles Spurgeon's (1834–92) notes on Christ read as follows:

> Our Lord Jesus is nearest and dearest
> to us as Man.
> His Manhood reminds us of;—
> His incarnation, in which He assumed our nature.
> His life on earth, in which He honored our nature.
> His death, by which He redeemed our nature.
> His resurrection, by which He upraised our nature.[4]

These verbs, "assumed, honored, redeemed, and upraised" cover the numerous ways in which men and women need to be approached and cared for.

The reaction of the crowd is extraordinary.

Bible: The reaction of the crowd in Luke 7:16 may be illustrated from within the New Testament by the Lycaonians, in Acts 14:11, who responded to a miracle by saying, "The gods have come down to us in human form!"

Jesus and John the Baptist

Big Idea *Jesus affirms the exceptional importance of John as the prophetic herald of the kingdom of God.*

Understanding the Text

The Text in Context

John's public activity had ended with his imprisonment (3:20), though we have heard since of his continuing influence (5:33). Now Luke invites us to consider how the ministries of John and Jesus relate to one another, and he ensures that his readers will not devalue John. This is important in the developing story, as Jesus will be perceived by others as John's successor (9:7–9, 19) and will himself affirm that connection (20:1–8). This section is linked with the immediately preceding narrative (7:1–17) in that those incidents provide important evidence of Jesus's messianic role, as he will claim in 7:22.

Outline/Structure

Three separate units make up this complex of material concerning the relationship between John and Jesus. First comes John's question and Jesus's answer (7:18–23), then Jesus's comments about the significance of John's ministry (7:24–28), and finally a parable about how people have responded to the contrasting ministries of John and Jesus (7:31–35). All this material is parallel to Matthew 11:2–19, where the three sections occur in the same order. Luke has inserted his own editorial comment in 7:29–30.

Historical and Cultural Background

Josephus tells us that John, accused of sedition, was imprisoned and then executed in Antipas's fortress-palace of Machaerus, east of the Dead Sea and some one hundred miles from Capernaum. Mark 6:17–29 fills out the story. This episode is set during that imprisonment.

Messianic expectation was widespread among Jews in the first

John the Baptist was imprisoned at Machaerus, the palace fortress of Herod Antipas located on this mountaintop to the east of the Dead Sea.

century, but it took various forms. Some looked primarily for the political restoration of Israel through liberation from Roman occupation, some for a more apocalyptic vengeance on God's enemies, some for a more spiritual restoration of God's people. Jesus's teaching and activity did not fit everyone's expectation of what the Messiah should do, and John apparently shared this uncertainty.

There was a strand in Jewish thinking that believed that prophecy had come to an end with Malachi. Not everyone held that view (see on 2:21–40), but to speak of John as a "prophet" would strike many as a far-reaching claim, putting John on a level above other human teachers and suggesting a radical new beginning in God's dealing with his people. Jesus's comments build on that perception.

Interpretive Insights

7:18 *told him about all these things.* If John recognized the Nain incident as a parallel to Elijah's miracle, the expectation of a returning Elijah (see on 1:17) may have helped to prompt his question.

7:19 *the one who is to come.* "The coming one" was not, as far as we know, a familiar messianic title as such. Here it relates more directly to John's specific prediction of someone "more powerful" who is "coming" after him to execute wrath and judgment (3:7, 9, 16–17). Was John then disappointed that Jesus's ministry of deliverance and good news to the poor fell short of that expectation? The contrast between Jesus's and John's disciples in 5:33 may also suggest that John found Jesus's attitude toward religious observance too

> ### Key Themes of Luke 7:18–35
> - John the Baptist needs to be reassured that Jesus really is the Messiah.
> - Jesus's ministry of deliverance and good news proves that he is the Messiah, here to restore God's creation.
> - Jesus affirms that John is not just any prophet, but the final prophet before the coming of the kingdom of God.
> - John, like Jesus, has met with a divided response among Jewish people.
> - The ministries of John and Jesus are very different, but both have their vital place in the purpose of God.

free and easy, perhaps especially his table fellowship with sinners.

7:21 *At that very time Jesus cured many.* This need not mean a deliberate display of healing for the sake of the messengers, but rather that they came when Jesus was busy healing people.

7:22 *Go back and report to John what you have seen and heard.* The messianic works listed here are partly drawn from prophetic predictions of eschatological blessings that are typical of Jesus's healing and preaching ministry as a whole (especially Isa. 35:5–6; 61:1) but also recall more specifically two miracles that Luke has already recorded ("leprosy" [5:12–15]; raising the dead [7:11–17]). Specific cases of healing the blind (18:35–43) and the deaf (11:14) will be narrated later.

7:23 *Blessed is anyone who does not stumble on account of me.* The immediate reference is to John, whose concept of messiahship seems to differ from that of Jesus. "Stumbling" is often used in the Gospels to indicate spiritual disaster, but here it need mean no more than a failure to appreciate Jesus's mission where it does not conform to John's preconceived ideas. What Jesus will go on to say about John does not suggest any more-ultimate "stumbling."

7:24 *A reed swayed by the wind?* Perhaps this is to be taken literally: you did not go all that way just to admire the scenery. But in view of the following verse, it is probably also an implied characterization of John, who was not a man easily swayed by opposition.

7:25 *A man dressed in fine clothes?* Luke has not mentioned John's rough garb (cf. Mark 1:6), but this would have been part of the traditional memory of his ministry. John was a rough and rugged individualist, not a smooth courtier. "In palaces" is ironic in that John was in fact now located in Antipas's palace of Machaerus, but in prison not in luxury.

7:26 *more than a prophet*. John's preeminence derives from his unique place in salvation history. The quotation from Malachi 3:1 in 7:27, like that of Isaiah 40:3–5 in 3:4–6 (see comments there), speaks of one who is privileged to announce the coming of Yahweh himself in judgment and salvation, the last prophet before the age of fulfillment finally dawns, the returning Elijah (Mal. 4:5–6; see on 1:17). But the wording of Malachi 3:1 has been modified (drawing on the wording of Exod. 23:20) so that it now introduces the forerunner of *Jesus* ("you") rather than of God himself.

7:28 *no one greater than John; yet the . . . least . . . is greater than he.* This paradox underlines the pivotal place of John in the development of God's purpose: there has as yet been no one greater (a remarkable accolade: greater than Abraham, Moses, and David?), but now that the kingdom of God has become a reality, everyone who belongs to it, even the "least," is on a new

In 7:27 Jesus says of John the Baptist, "This is the one about whom it is written: 'I will send my messenger ahead of you, who will prepare your way before you.'" This mosaic from the Hagia Sophia in Istanbul, Turkey, depicts John the Baptist. The words on the mosaic can be translated to read, "Saint John, the forerunner."

footing before God. Those who live in the age of fulfillment are privileged beyond even the greatest of those who lived in the age of preparation.

7:29 *acknowledged that God's way was right, because they had been baptized by John.* Translated literally, the Greek reads "they justified God." Matthew 21:31–32 makes the same point: the social and religious outsiders responded to John's mission, while the religious authorities refused. By including this editorial comment here Luke draws attention to a clear line of development between John's ministry and that of Jesus, to which tax collectors and sinners responded but which authorities criticized (5:27–32). Both are part of a "subversive" movement outside the channels of official

Judaism, and it is there that God's purpose is being fulfilled.

7:32 *They are like children sitting in the marketplace.* This little parable envisages some children complaining that others refuse to join in with their game of weddings and funerals. Its application could be either that John and Jesus called on the people, respectively, to repent and to rejoice in God's salvation, but there was no response to either, or that the people wanted John to dance but he remained dour, while they wanted Jesus to fast but he insisted on feasting. I think that the former better suits the following verses, but either way there is a general sense of incompatible attitudes toward life and to God.

7:33–34 *John the Baptist came . . . The Son of Man came.* We have seen in 7:29–30 the sense of continuity between the ministries of John and Jesus, but there was a difference between their lifestyles and so between their public images. Compare 5:33–35, where the fasting of John's disciples is contrasted with the feasting of Jesus and his disciples. For John's abstention from wine, see on 1:15; Jesus was not a Nazirite, and so he could participate freely in social life and entertainment. But even so, people dismissed them respectively as mad and frivolous. There was no pleasing those people.

7:35 *But wisdom is proved right by all her children.* "Wisdom" often appears in Jewish literature as a personified way of speaking of God's governance of his world. "Children of wisdom" therefore refers to people who share God's perspective. In this context it probably means that both John and Jesus, for all their differences, represent wisdom, and so they will meet with the approval of all who are guided by wisdom, even though the thoughtless majority are not persuaded. Thus, wisdom will be vindicated. This conclusion picks up the thought of 7:29–30: the ordinary people and the tax collectors prove, shockingly, to be wisdom's children in place of the Pharisees and lawyers (scribes).

Theological Insights

This passage illustrates the ambivalence that runs through all the Gospel accounts of John the Baptist. On the one hand, he is a great prophet, the one privileged to prepare the way for the kingdom of God, and in that sense there is a direct continuity between his ministry and that of Jesus. On the other hand, he is never more than the forerunner; he stands at the point of transition, and 7:28 places him outside the blessings of the kingdom of God. He prepared for the coming of one "more powerful" (3:16) than he, and once that one has come, as John himself says, "He must become greater; I must become less" (John 3:30).

We have here two indications of how Jesus's ministry was perceived by some of those around him. John perhaps found Jesus's approach too open and gentle, compared with the fierce judgment that he himself had predicted. Some of the people wrote him off as a *bon viveur* (lover of fine things in life), lacking the seriousness of the ascetic and formidable John. Both estimates failed to grasp the totally new perspective of the kingdom of God, which broke through conventional expectations of what true religion was about, and so put Jesus on a collision course with the religious establishment.

John may have been expecting Jesus to accomplish a physical deliverance from the Romans and so began to doubt that Jesus was "the one to come." Jesus, however, directs him to Old Testament passages that indicate he is here to accomplish something much greater than physical conquest. He is here to restore a fallen creation (Isa. 35:5–6; 61:1–2). This is the radical new thing that Jesus is doing—the inauguration of the kingdom of God. Although John is the greatest of all the prophets, he is part of the old age, so that even "the least" in the kingdom of God is greater than he.

Teaching the Text

In teaching or preaching this passage it is important to bring out the ambivalence related to John described above. The first key point is that John is a distant second to Jesus. John is merely the forerunner, a prophet who prepares the way for the Lord (1:76). Jesus *is* the Lord, the Messiah, and Son of God (1:32–35), who will accomplish God's salvation. John's understanding of Jesus's ministry is also inadequate. He is evidently expecting a powerful, conquering Messiah who will destroy the Romans. When Jesus is not fulfilling this role, he sends his disciples to question whether he is the One. Jesus responds by defining his ministry as even greater than John can imagine. When teaching this passage, be sure to bring out the profound significance of Jesus's allusions to Isaiah 35:5–6 and 61:1–2 in 7:21–22. Jesus links his healings and exorcisms to the end-time restoration of creation predicted in Isaiah. Jesus's role is much greater than physical victory over Israel's enemies. It is to reverse the results of a fallen creation and to restore it to a right relationship with God. It is to accomplish the ultimate defeat of humanity's greatest enemies—sin, Satan, and death.

The second key point to bring out in a sermon or lesson on this passage is that while John is a distant second to Jesus, he plays a profoundly important role. Although he is "merely" the herald of salvation and precursor to the Messiah, Jesus surprisingly affirms that he is the greatest person ever born (to that time). This is because he has the unique privilege of announcing the arrival of God's final salvation. Just how important this role is can be seen in the view of salvation history Jesus expresses in 7:26–28. Though John is the greatest human being ever born up to that point, he is still the least in the kingdom of God. This is because everything is now changing. The age of promise is giving way to the age of fulfillment; the old covenant is about to be superseded by the new, when God's people will receive complete forgiveness of sins and will truly know God through the abiding presence of his Spirit (Jer. 31:31–34). This is why John—who represents the old age—is the "least" in the kingdom of God.

Illustrating the Text

In his humanity, John the Baptist brooded about Jesus as he lay in jail.

Anecdote: **William Barclay.**

Think what was happening to John. John, the child of the desert and of the wide-open spaces, was confined in a dungeon cell in the castle of Machaerus. Once, one of the MacDonalds, a highland chieftain, was confined in a little cell in Carlisle Castle. In his cell was one little window.

To this day you may see in the sandstone the marks of the feet and hands of the highlander as he lifted himself up and clung to the window ledge day by day to gaze with infinite longing upon the border hills and valleys he would never walk again. Shut in his cell, choked by the narrow walls, John asked his question because his cruel captivity had put tremors in his heart.[1]

Biography: Simone Weil. Weil (1909–43), a brilliant French Jew, was a scholar, author, and political activist who, though born into an agnostic family, after a number of mystical encounters converted to Christianity. Always devoted to the poor and helpless, she joined the French Resistance and starved herself to death in protest of what was happening to the Jews. Her writings are widely known and read. Her description of affliction could certainly describe what John the Baptist must have felt: "Affliction causes God to be absent for a time, more absent than a dead man, more absent than light in the utter darkness of a cell. A kind of horror submerges the whole soul."[2]

As a forerunner to Christ, John the Baptist's position was difficult.

Christian Living: *Prophetic Untimeliness,* by Os Guinness. In this articulate book, Os Guinness compares John the Baptist to other "unheeded messengers." The first of these is Alexander Solzhenitsyn, who issued a warning to the West in his 1978 Harvard commencement speech, "A World Split Apart," and was savaged in some circles for it. Guinness also points to Winston Churchill "during his 'wilderness years' in the 1930s, when his insistent warnings about the mounting menace of Hitler left him out of the government and out of favor with much public opinion." These men suffered for their messenger's perspective, for the burden of their prophecy. These men had "seasoned wisdom born of a sense of history and their nation's place in it . . . a note of authority in their message born of its transcendent source."[3]

The coming of Jesus marks the radical transition from the age of promise to the age of fulfillment.

Film/Story: Superhero movies and stories often deal with the release of a captive, evil world by the superhero. Any one of many of these could illustrate the paradigm shift spoken of here, ranging from *Beowulf,* the Old English heroic poem (made into a movie in 2007) in which Beowulf delivers the people of Scandinavia from the terrible monster Grendel, to the Batman and Superman movies, among others.

Although John the Baptist was in prison at the fortress palace of Herod Antipas at Machaerus, he was able to send messengers to Jesus asking him, "Are you the one who is to come?" (7:19). These ruins at Machaerus are the remains of Herod's palace. The pillars in the background are part of a reconstruction and surround one of the courtyards.

Jesus and Women

Big Idea *Jesus's work of salvation extends to people shunned or ignored by Jewish society; women play an unusually large part in his mission.*

Understanding the Text

The Text in Context

After the characterization of Jesus as a *bon viveur* and a friend of the disreputable (7:34), we now find him at a dinner party and befriending a disreputable woman. Two themes from earlier in the Gospel reemerge in this story: Jesus's openness to and welcome by unrespectable members of society (5:27–32) and his claim to forgive sins (5:17–26). It develops further Luke's characteristic theme of Jesus's concern for those who lived outside the circles of privilege and respectability. In particular, this story (7:36–50) together with the following verses (8:1–3) shows that Jesus valued women as much as men, and that women were coming to play a more significant role in his movement than the reader might have thought from the choice of twelve male disciples in 6:13–16.

Outline/Structure

The other three Gospels (Matt. 26:6–13; Mark 14:3–9; John 12:1–8) tell of a woman who anointed Jesus at Bethany on his final visit to Jerusalem; John identifies her as Mary of Bethany. But beyond the fact of a woman anointing Jesus with perfume in the house of someone called "Simon" (a very common name), this episode has little in common with that one: the setting here is quite different (in Galilee, in a Pharisee's house, and relatively early in the story), and the theme of the woman's sinfulness, forgiveness, and love is quite distinctive, as is also the dialogue with Jesus's host. The problem here is not the waste of valuable ointment, but the moral character of the anointer. The two stories are better treated separately.

The traditional chapter division obscures the significant link between this story and the following account of other women associated with Jesus's ministry. On the other hand, however, too much was made of the juxtaposition of the two stories when later tradition supposed that Mary Magdalene (8:2) was formerly a prostitute. There is no biblical warrant for that idea. Luke makes no suggestion that Mary was the woman of 7:36–50, and he describes her deliverance in quite different terms.

Historical and Cultural Background

Women had a subordinate place in Jewish society. All of the guests at a dinner such as this likely were males. Rabbis typically took care to avoid being in female company (cf. John 4:27), let alone the company of a woman known to be "a sinner." Jesus's contrasting attitude was bound to raise eyebrows. To include female followers not only in his wider circle of supporters but even in the traveling group together with the twelve male disciples (8:1–3) was potentially scandalous. Here, as always, Jesus seems unconcerned by what conventional society might think.

Interpretive Insights

7:36 *he went to the Pharisee's house and reclined at the table.* Jesus was as much at home in "polite" society as in Levi's house; he did not "belong" to one side of the social divide. For other such invitations by Pharisees, see 11:37; 14:1. At a more formal dinner guests reclined in the Roman style on couches around a central table, so that their feet would stick out away from the table; that is the scenario envisaged in 7:38.

7:37 *A woman in that town who lived a sinful life.* This is probably a euphemistic way of referring to a town prostitute; hence the host's scandalized reaction in 7:39. Given the Pharisaic concern for ritual purity, she "comes into

this scene like an alien, communicable disease."[1]

an alabaster jar of perfume. Luke does not mention the value of the perfume, which is the central motif of the other anointing story. This is simply a woman's more lavish substitute for the plain olive oil that a guest might have expected as a courtesy (7:46).

7:38 *she stood behind him at his feet weeping.* Clearly she wants to make contact with Jesus, but can get no closer than his feet (see on 7:36). Luke records no words spoken by her; she speaks by her actions, which here are spelled out so as to form the basis for Jesus's comparison in 7:44–46. In order to wipe Jesus's feet with her hair, she would have to uncover it and let it down, which no respectable woman would do in company.[2]

When Jesus was invited to have dinner at the home of a Pharisee, he reclined at the table. This was the typical posture for men at a banquet. The dining area in the homes of the wealthy contained couches rather than chairs, and the centrally located table was low. Banquet participants would lay on their left side, so they could eat with their right hand, with their feet extended away from the table, as illustrated in this drawing.

Putting perfumed ointment on the feet is extraordinary; normally, it was the head that was anointed. Her actions taken as a whole could easily be seen as erotic as well as "over the top."

7:39 *If this man were a prophet.* The Pharisee repeats the popular estimate of Jesus that presumably he has heard from local gossip. He will address Jesus by the more conventional title "teacher" in 7:40. The impression given is that he has invited Jesus to dinner in order to make up his own mind about the man's credentials. He is not impressed by Jesus's failure to rebuke such a suggestive act by an obviously disreputable woman.

7:40 *Jesus answered him.* Simon's thought was unspoken. By discerning it nonetheless, Jesus shows something of the prophetic insight that Simon was questioning.

7:41–43 *Two people owed money.* Like Nathan's famous parable to David (2 Sam. 12:1–7), this little parable invites Simon to pronounce the verdict that will be turned against him. Its message, that love results from forgiveness, will be important for the interpretation of the potentially ambiguous saying in 7:47. For another parable that uses the cancellation of debt as a symbol for God's forgiveness of sin, see Matthew 18:23–35.

7:44–46 *You did not give me any water.* Simon's welcome to Jesus fell short of the normal social courtesies of footwashing, kissing, and anointing. All these would be expected, and their omission looks like a deliberate social snub. Simon was not a fan of Jesus, but the woman's actions had more than made up for his discourtesy, and they revealed her, by contrast, as the one who truly valued him.

Jesus taught about love and forgiveness by telling a parable about two debtors who owed large amounts of money; one owed five hundred denarii and the other fifty denarii. The denarius was a Roman coin equivalent to a day's wage. This particular denarius was minted to show the achievements of Emperor Augustus.

7:47 *her many sins have been forgiven— as her great love has shown.* A literal translation is "Her many sins have been forgiven because she loved much." Taken alone, these words could mean that her love was the *basis* of her forgiveness, but that would be to turn on its head the message of the preceding parable in 7:41–43 and of the following clause, in which little love is the *result* of little forgiveness. Thus, most versions, like the NIV, find ways of indicating that her love is the evidence of her (antecedent) forgiveness rather than the basis for it.

7:48 *Your sins are forgiven.* Jesus speaks directly to the woman for the first time. As in 5:20, his declaration provokes theological questions (7:49), but this time the issue is not pursued. Following the logic of the parable in 7:41–43, we must suppose that the woman's loving actions show that she is already aware of being forgiven, and that Jesus here simply makes it explicit. (The verb is in the perfect tense, lit., "have been forgiven.") Perhaps we should assume that she has met Jesus, or at least listened to his preaching, before coming to make this gesture of appreciation.

7:50 *Your faith has saved you.* This formula is used elsewhere of physical healing (8:48; 17:19; 18:42), but the forgiveness of sin is no less "salvation." This conclusion further underlines that she was forgiven not because she loved (see on 7:47), but because she believed.

8:2 *Also some women.* The allegiance of these women derived from their experience of healing and exorcism through Jesus's ministry. Three are mentioned by name, but there were also "many others." In Matthew and Mark it is not until the end of the story that we are informed that women had been among Jesus's traveling companions (Matt. 27:55; Mark 15:41), but Luke makes it clear at this early stage. The women are not included in the Twelve, but even so, their presence was a potential cause for scandal in Jewish society at that time.

Mary (called Magdalene) from whom seven demons had come out. Subsequent tradition has built much onto this brief description, notably (since the sixth century) by associating this Mary with the unnamed woman of 7:37. Luke gives no support to this speculation. Mary's prominence in the resurrection stories indicates that she had a leading role among the disciples, but that is as far as biblical evidence takes us. For Luke, Mary is simply someone who had been the object of a very remarkable exorcism. On possession by multiple demons, see also 8:30; 11:26.

8:3 *These women were helping to support them out of their own means.* For the dependence of the Jesus movement on the material support of well-wishers, see 9:3–4; 10:4–7. By mentioning the influential social position of Joanna's husband, Luke indicates that Jesus's followers included some from the more affluent strata of society. We do not know whether Chuza himself supported Jesus. The sharing of resources mentioned here will be developed more fully in Acts 4:32–37.

Theological Insights

Jesus's dealings with women and their involvement in his ministry are an important element in Luke's presentation of the universal scope of the gospel of salvation and of its tendency to overturn the conventional barriers of society. Jesus's open attitude contrasts with the patriarchal norms of most ancient societies, including Judaism. The book of Acts and the letters of Paul will go on to reveal the significant role that some women played in the mission and ministry of the early church. All this needs to be set against the reluctance in some modern churches to accept the full involvement of women in mission and leadership, and it suggests that a simplistic view of women as essentially subordinate to men (on the basis of Paul's so-called submission texts) does not represent all the biblical data on the subject.

Teaching the Text

A sermon or lesson on this passage should bring out its central theme, one that appears again and again in Luke's Gospel: *the recipients of God's salvation are those who come to him humbly, recognizing their unworthiness and need of him.* Simon, the self-righteous Pharisee, looks down on the woman as a lowly sinner and shows no reverence for Jesus, failing to provide even basic hospitality for his guest. As Jesus's parable makes evident (7:41–42), this is because Simon thinks he is good enough for God and needs no forgiveness. The woman, by contrast, shows her profound gratitude because of the forgiveness she has received. The key to the passage is Jesus's authoritative pronouncement in 7:47: "her many sins have been forgiven—as her great love has shown. But whoever has been forgiven little loves little."

When teaching the passage, encourage listeners to put themselves in the shoes of the sinful woman. What had she heard about Jesus (or had she actually listened to his preaching?), and how did she already know that she was forgiven? What was her aim in making this unorthodox approach to Jesus in such a public setting? What emboldened her to break social taboo in this way? Would she have been surprised by the outcome?

Other themes may also be important to bring out here. Jesus's authority to forgive sins is again on display (cf. 5:18–26). This is also a good opportunity to think through Jesus's attitude toward women more generally than just in this passage. Do listeners have experience of societies (whether Christian or not) in which women are still treated as subordinate to men? Thinking of such situations, encourage them to envisage the feelings likely to have been aroused by Jesus's dealings with women. What sort of community would Jesus himself have promoted? How far did the early church follow his lead? In view of the prominent and distorted portrayal of Mary Magdalene in some recent popular literature (e.g., *The Da Vinci Code*), it would be good to take this opportunity to point out how later speculation differs from the New Testament evidence.[3]

Illustrating the Text

Jesus welcomes those marginalized by society.

Spiritual Song: "The Welcome Table"/ "Some of These Days"/"Members Don't Get Weary." Called by various names, this nineteenth-century civil-rights song would be worth playing for a congregation or group, as it expresses the longing of the hearts of those who have been neglected and sidelined. Some of the words are as follows:

> I'm going to sit at the Welcome table
> Shout my troubles over
> Walk and talk with Jesus
> Tell God how you treat me
> One of these days!

How full this anointer's heart must have been to be accepted by Jesus so beautifully in the house of a hostile Pharisee.

Literature: "The Welcome Table," by Alice Walker. Walker (b. 1944) tells the tale of an old black woman "nearly blind with age" who has "staggered" her way to a white church on a cold day. Focused on being in church, the woman "brushes" past the pastor, who has said, "Auntie, you know this is not your church?" Everyone is unsettled by her presence, and the women finally ask their "burly indecisive husbands" to throw her out. Bewildered, the old woman stands on the church steps looking down the highway and sees "something interesting and delightful." It is Jesus coming "at a firm though leisurely pace. . . . There was a sad but joyful look to his face, . . . and he walked with sure even steps in her direction." The only thing Jesus says to the woman as he approaches her is "Follow me," and "she bounded down to his side with all the bob and speed of one so old." She then proceeds to tell him what has happened to her, and that she is "so happy to be out walking along the highway with Jesus," disturbing the silence only to tell him how "glad she was that he had come" and how "she had often looked at his picture hanging on her wall."[4]

Women, some with complex and sinful backgrounds, were part of the group who traveled with Jesus, helping to support him.

Christian Ministry: She Is Safe. This is only one of many ministries around the world designed to come alongside women who have been abused and exploited. They recognize that these are women whom Christ wants to be brought into the kingdom and restored for ministry in the body of Christ. Based in Atlanta, this particular ministry seeks to "mobilize Christians against poverty, oppression, exploitation and spiritual darkness in the world's hardest places through practical grassroots projects." Ministry founder Michelle Rickett has coauthored two books, *Forgotten Girls* and *Daughters of Hope*.[5]

In 7:46 Jesus says to Simon, "You did not put oil on my head, but she has poured perfume on my feet." These small ointment bottles would have been used for oil or perfume (first century AD).

Hearing and Responding

Big Idea *When God's word is proclaimed, there are different levels of response, ranging from those who take no notice to those whose lives are transformed.*

Understanding the Text

The Text in Context

At the heart of Jesus's mission as announced in 4:14–21 is teaching and the proclamation of good news. We have had an important section of his teaching in 6:20–49, which concluded with trenchant comments on the importance of putting into practice what is heard—a theme that runs through this whole section. Since then, Jesus has continued to proclaim the good news all over Galilee (8:1). So it is time now to think about how that proclamation has been received. In particular, we have already seen that while some embrace the message with enthusiasm, others are skeptical or downright hostile. How can it be that the same good news meets with such varying results? That is the issue explained here in the parable of the sower and associated sayings. Before long Jesus will be sending his disciples out with the same message (9:1–6; 10:1–16); they too will meet with a mixed response. This section of the Gospel prepares them for that experience.

Outline/Structure

As in Mark 4 and Matthew 13, the parable of the sower is accompanied by an explicit interpretation, and between the parable and interpretation is a brief statement (fuller in Matt. 13:10–17) about revelation and response. This statement focuses on the way parables work, so that in effect the parable of the sower becomes a parable not just about teaching in general but about teaching in parables. The appended sayings in 8:16–18 (which follow the same parable in Mark 4:21–25 but all also occur separately later in Luke) take up the same theme of revelation and response. The brief story about Jesus and his family in 8:19–21, though a freestanding unit, is appropriately

In the parable recorded in Luke 8:5–15, the farmer goes out to sow seeds using the broadcasting technique where handfuls of seed are carefully tossed in the air so most of them settle on the cultivated ground. This Palestinian farmer is sowing seeds using this method.

included here because it too focuses on hearing and responding.

Historical and Cultural Background

See the comments on teaching in parables introducing 6:39–49. The enigmatic and challenging nature of parables is indicated by the disciples' request for an explanation in 8:9. The detailed interpretation that follows (8:11–15) is unusual, and it may reflect the special importance of this parable, as a "parable about parables."

Several of Jesus's parables draw on imagery from farming, a familiar scenario for his Galilean audience. This parable reflects the agricultural practice of a Palestinian peasant farmer, whose ground is not of uniform quality, and whose broadcast sowing inevitably results in some of the seed falling into unsuitable places.

The sobering experience of Isaiah's mission to an unresponsive people (Isa. 6:9–10) was taken by the early church as a precedent for widespread Jewish rejection of the Christian gospel. In addition to the Synoptic parallels here, see John's editorial comment in John 12:37–43 and Paul's verdict on the Jews in Rome in Acts 28:24–28.

Interpretive Insights

8:5 *some fell along the path*. The traditional title "parable of the sower" (taken from Matt. 13:18) misses the focus of the parable, which is not on the sower but rather on the seed and on the different soils into which it fell. Literally, "*one* fell": Luke speaks of four individual seeds (Mark has six individual seeds, three in bad places and three in good soil; in Matthew they are all plural).

8:6 *Some fell on rocky ground*. To fall directly onto rock (as Luke's text literally says) would be no better than along the path, and the seed could not "come up" at all. The NIV therefore assumes that Luke, like Mark, refers to "rocky ground," where there was a thin covering of soil over the bedrock.

8:8 *It came up and yielded a crop, a hundred times more than was sown*. Because Luke mentions only a single seed in the good soil, he cannot reproduce Mark's more nuanced version, with different seeds producing different levels of yield. A hundredfold yield is a very good crop (cf. Gen. 26:12) but not in the realm of fantasy; one ancient Jewish writer (*b. Ketub.* 111b–112a) imagined, as a sign of God's ultimate blessing, a miraculous 1,500,000–fold yield!

8:10 *The knowledge of the secrets of the kingdom of God has been given to you*. The theme of God's "secrets" (*mystērion*, from which we get "mystery") is prominent in the book of Daniel, where God's truths, hidden from other people, are revealed to his faithful servant (Dan. 2:17–30, 47; 4:7–9). Jesus's disciples are in the same privileged position of understanding what is hidden from others, not because they are cleverer but because they, like Daniel, have been "given" special insight by God himself. His way of salvation ("the kingdom of God") is a matter not of natural insight, but of special revelation.

to others I speak in parables. Because parables demand considered response, they suit the situation where some have the God-given insight to grasp their significance but others do not. The "so that" that introduces the quotation from Isaiah 6:9 does not necessarily mean that Jesus deliberately stops some people from understanding, but that the difference in people's receptivity is such that in fact not all will respond. In that situation parables are an appropriate method of teaching: to some they reveal truth, but others are left unmoved.

8:11 *This is the meaning of the parable.* Like all parables, this one could have various meanings and applications if left without interpretation. Jesus's interpretation focuses on the issue of divided response to his proclamation and explains why not all have responded positively. The first three scenes represent typical hindrances to effective response: total lack of interest, inadequate commitment, and competing priorities. The balance of the parable, with its four carefully delineated scenes, indicates that such a detailed analysis is intended, rather than simply an assurance that there will be a harvest in the end.

The seed is the word of God. The parable speaks to any situation where a message from God is conveyed. The allusion to Isaiah 6:9 reminds us that this has already been the experience of the Old Testament prophets. The immediate reference here is probably to Jesus's own preaching, but the parable will apply equally to the disciples' subsequent mission and to all evangelists and preachers who come after them.

8:16 *No one lights a lamp and hides it.* This little parable (used again in 11:33) counteracts any defeatism that the preceding parable might have engendered: the fact that not all will respond is no reason for withholding the message. The disciples have been "given" special knowledge (8:10) so that they may pass it on to others.

8:17 *For there is nothing hidden that will not be disclosed.* This is another repeated saying (cf. 12:2). Just as the disciples have been given access to the "secrets" of the kingdom of God, so others must also be shown the light. This is an important counterbalance to the "pessimism" of 8:10, and it rules out interpreting that verse as

In 8:16 the lamp that Jesus refers to may have been a small clay oil lamp like this one from the Roman period. Olive oil was poured into the central cavity, and a wick that was placed in the hole at the pointed end would be lit. The lamp would be set in an alcove or on a stand where it would give light throughout the room.

suggesting that Jesus's ultimate purpose was to conceal the truth from all but a few.

8:18 *Whoever has will be given more.* This proverbial saying (used again in 19:26, and cf. 6:38) is appropriate in this context because parables depend on the hearer's capacity to respond. What you get out of them depends on what you bring to them. *what they think they have will be taken from them.* Like the "righteous" who think that they have no need for Jesus's message (5:32), those who think that they already know it all will find in the end that their supposed knowledge was illusory. The seed finds nowhere to grow in such people.

8:19 *Jesus' mother and brothers.* Mark 6:3 tells us more about Jesus's family back in Nazareth. Luke does not hint at any sinister motive in their coming to see Jesus (contrast Mark 3:21), but Jesus's comments here probably indicate that they had not yet responded to his message (which they will do later [cf. Acts 1:14]).

8:21 *My mother and brothers are those who hear God's word and put it into practice.* This statement *could* be taken as commending Jesus's mother and brothers themselves as model disciples, but the fuller versions of this scene in Mark 3:31–35 and Matthew 12:46–50 suggest instead that they are *contrasted* with true disciples. In 14:26 Jesus will demand that discipleship take precedence over family loyalty. Obedient discipleship creates a new "family" bond that can supersede that of natural kinship. Stated so briefly, this seems an unnecessarily negative way for Jesus to speak of his own family, but the issue is one of priority. For the emphasis on hearing and doing, see 6:43–49, as well as the parable of the sower.

Theological Insights

This whole section is about how to "hear" God's word in the right way: all can hear it, but not all hear it profitably. So everyone is responsible for the way he or she responds to God's message with faith and by living it out. But 8:10 raises the difficult question of whether some are in fact *unable* to respond; not everyone "has ears to hear" (8:8). If the ability to grasp "the secrets of the kingdom of God" is *given* only to some, can the others be blamed for their failure to grasp it? Does Jesus's teaching in parables then merely confirm some in their unbelief, since they do not have the capacity to understand the parables and respond to them?

The parable of the sower, however, is not designed to answer these questions. It sets out the *fact* of unbelief and of inadequate response, but it neither explains its *origin* (except perhaps briefly in the reference to the devil in 8:12) nor prescribes its cure. It is clear that enlightenment is possible, since it has already been given to the disciples (8:10), and 8:16–17 insists that truth is meant to be made known. Truth is there for all who seek it, but this passage does not explain *why* some do not want to know or how they too may make the vital transition to the privileged place where the disciples already are.

The mysterious interaction of human responsibility and divine enabling confronts us at many points in the New Testament, and it is easier to recognize that both sides of the paradox are true than to provide a neat, logical reconciliation.

Teaching the Text

The primary theme that should be brought out in a lesson or sermon on this passage is the importance of not only hearing the message of the kingdom of God but also responding to it with faith and obedience, thereby producing fruit. It is important to interpret the parable first of all in light of its original context in Jesus's ministry. The religious leaders have rejected Jesus's preaching. They have ears but do not hear and eyes but do not see. Others, however, are responding positively to Jesus's message and so are bearing fruit.

Of course, the parable also relates to the present-day proclamation of the gospel, and the teacher will want to identify contemporary examples of the different kinds of soils. Consider, for example, what the choking "thorns" of worry, riches, and pleasures (8:14) look like in today's world.

Teachers and preachers sometimes get bogged down in the question of whether any of the first three soils are actually "saved." But this misses the point of the parable. In Jesus's ministry there are only two kinds of people, those who accept the message of the kingdom and those who fail to receive it. All three of the failed seeds represent the latter. Authentic faith produces spiritual fruit (James 2:14–26).

Some teachers will want to delve deeper into the apparently "predestinarian" language of 8:10 and tease out the sort of issues raised in the "Theological Insights" above. Consider cross-referencing Paul's discussion in Romans 9, where he shows how God uses even unbelief and rejection to accomplish his purpose.

> The parable of the sower might more accurately be called "the parable of the seeds" or "the parable of the soils." This area near Capernaum shows the rocky fields and hard paths common to the area, two of the environments onto which the seeds fell.

Illustrating the Text

Jesus illustrates the reasons why people do not respond to his word.

Personal Stories: Every pastor of a congregation or teacher in a classroom can tell personal stories illustrating the three negative responses in this passage: seeds that are dropped on the path, those that fall upon rocks, and those scattered among thorns. One could even call upon individuals for stories illustrating these nuances so that they understand them better.

Literature: *The Brothers Karamazov*, **by Fyodor Dostoevsky.** This demanding but worthwhile novel (1880) was Dostoevsky's (1821–81) last. The attitudes of the brothers and father in this novel parallel not only the negative responses of the hearers of the word in this parable but also the positive. The catalyst of this family is Alyosha, the believing youngest son, a winsome character who has communicated and lived the truth to his family. The father is a buffoon who pays little attention to his sons. The oldest son, Dimitri, is a sensualist much like his father but also is very close to his brother Alyosha. The second son, Ivan, is a profound thinker whose view of God's lack of intervention for suffering children has made him agnostic.

A great deal of material is available online and in libraries about this work, considered one of the greatest novels of all time.

In order to be part of Christ's true family, one must practice what one has heard.

Hymn: "Trust and Obey," by John H. Sammis. A businessman who became a Presbyterian minister, Sammis (1846–1919) wrote over one hundred hymns. This old hymn reflects obedience to Christ in the simplest terms. In 1887 a young man stood up to speak after a meeting in which D. L. Moody had preached. Showing plainly that he was not conversant with Bible teaching and doctrine, he nevertheless moved the audience when he said at the end of his testimony, "But I'm going to trust; I'm going to obey." Daniel B. Towner, a music composer in the audience, was struck by the young man's words and gave them to Sammis, who developed them into the hymn text. This hymn became a great favorite and is still beloved in many circles. The well-known refrain is "Trust and obey, for there's no other way / To be happy in Jesus, but to trust and obey." Some of the verses are as follows:

> When we walk with the Lord in the light of His Word,
> What a glory He sheds on our way!
> While we do His good will, He abides with us still,
> And with all who will trust and obey.
>
> But we never can prove the delights of His love
> Until all on the altar we lay;
> For the favor He shows, for the joy He bestows,
> Are for them who will trust and obey.
>
> Then in fellowship sweet we will sit at His feet,
> Or we'll walk by His side in the way.
> What He says we will do, where He sends we will go;
> Never fear, only trust and obey.[1]

An Encounter across the Lake

Big Idea *Jesus displays his unique power over both the natural elements and supernatural oppression.*

Understanding the Text

The Text in Context

Thus far, Jesus's mission has been confined to the Jewish areas of Galilee, though we have heard of crowds from a wider area coming to hear him (6:17–18). The decision now to cross the lake takes him into Gentile territory on the eastern shore. It is only a brief visit, but it symbolizes the wider extension of the Jewish Messiah's ministry to non-Jewish people, already signaled in 2:31–32; 4:24–27; 7:9.

This is the most spectacular and most fully narrated exorcism recorded by Luke. It thus brings to a climax a developing theme of the Gospel: Jesus's power over supernatural evil (see 4:31–37, 41; 6:18; 7:21; 8:2). This power will soon become a central issue and source of controversy in 11:14–26.

The disciples' question in 8:25, "Who is this?" introduces the christological theme that will dominate

the story of the remainder of the Galilean ministry. This question will come to the surface again in 9:9, 18–20, 32–35, but it is an underlying motif in all the incidents up to 9:51, when Jesus sets off for Jerusalem.

Historical and Cultural Background

On the likely size and type of the boat caught in the storm, see "Historical and Cultural Background" on 5:1–11. Jesus and twelve disciples would fill such a boat pretty well to capacity.

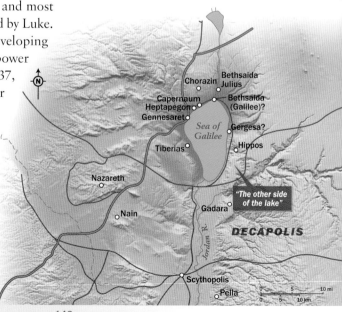

This map shows "the other side of the lake" (8:22), the region known as Decapolis.

Galilee was a mainly Jewish area, though with a significant Gentile minority. Most of the settlements on the western shore of the lake, where most of Jesus's ministry was focused, were Jewish (as was Nazareth, where he was brought up). But the eastern shore of the lake lay outside Galilee and was the territory of a group of Hellenistic towns (the Decapolis) with a largely non-Jewish population. The presence in this story of a large herd of pigs (unclean for Jews) indicates that Jesus and his disciples had landed in a Gentile area.

On the nature and significance of demon possession, see "Historical and Cultural Background" under 4:31–44. Here in a Gentile area it is as serious an issue as it had been in the Jewish town of Capernaum (4:33–36).

Interpretive Insights

8:23 *As they sailed, he fell asleep.* The reader may be reminded of Jonah, who likewise slept during a storm at sea and had to be awakened (Jon. 1:4–6), but if so, the relation is one of contrast rather than similarity: Jonah is the guilty fugitive and helpless victim, Jesus the one who controls the elements.

they were in great danger. The Lake of Galilee is large and deep enough to present real danger in a storm. Strong winds funneling through the valleys between the surrounding hills can produce waves that would easily overwhelm a shallow-drafted fishing boat.

8:24 *rebuked the wind and the raging waters.* The graphically personal term "rebuke" (*epitimaō*), which is used also of Jesus's commands to demons (4:35, 41; 9:42), has led some to suggest that the storm is

viewed as demonic. But the same verb is used of a fever (4:39). It is the narrator's vivid way of portraying Jesus's authority over inanimate forces.

8:25 *Where is your faith?* In Luke's Gospel "faith" is usually linked with miraculous power, especially in the formula "Your faith has saved you" (7:50; 8:48; 17:19; 18:42). It is not, of course, faith that actually saves, but rather Jesus (or God [see 17:5–6]), in whom that faith is placed. For Luke, faith is not an intellectual conviction so much as practical reliance on supernatural power.

Who is this? Luke may expect his readers to reflect on various passages in the psalms that celebrate God's mastery of the elements, and especially on Psalm 107:23–31, which speaks of God's rescuing those caught in a storm at sea and bringing them safely home: "He stilled the storm to a whisper; the waves of the sea were hushed" (Ps. 107:29). So what Jesus has just done has displayed divine power over the created order.

8:26 *the region of the Gerasenes.* Gerasa, one of the largest and best-known towns of the Decapolis, was some thirty-five miles from the lake. Matthew locates the incident in the territory of Gadara, only six miles from the southeast corner of the lake.

Several ancient texts substituted "Gergesa," which may have been closer to the shore. The exact location must remain uncertain, though the only part of the eastern shore where the ground rises steeply from the water (see 8:33) is toward the northern end (where Gergesa may have been located).

8:27 *had lived in the tombs.* Ancient tombs were often quite elaborate structures or artificial caves in the hillside, and they would have provided shelter for a man excluded from society. Tombs were ritually unclean to Jews and thus provided a fitting home for one possessed by an "unclean spirit" (8:29).

8:28 *Jesus, Son of the Most High God.* As in 4:34 (cf. 4:41), the demons not only know Jesus's name but also recognize his supernatural nature, though here the title "the Most High God" probably has a pagan flavor. And again, as in 4:34, they see God's Son as their natural enemy. The "torture" that the demons envisage might be merely the threat of expulsion from their "home" (on the discomfort of an expelled demon, see 11:24) but perhaps also expresses fear that Jesus, as the Son of God, is now about to initiate the final destruction of all evil spirits, which Jewish belief expected in the last days; this is probably what is meant by "go into the Abyss" in 8:31.

8:30 *"What is your name?" "Legion," he replied.* It was believed that to know the name of a demon gave the exorcist power over it. The demons already know who Jesus is (8:28), and he now reciprocates. A Roman legion consisted nominally of six thousand soldiers, but the imagery does not require literally six thousand demons. It simply means that the condition of this demoniac is unusually severe. The term also prepares us for the "large herd" of pigs to be occupied by these "many demons." For the idea of several demons possessing one person, see also 8:2; 11:26.

8:32 *he gave them permission.* Jesus has complete authority over the demons. The problems that modern readers see here in the destruction of many innocent

Although the exact location where Jesus encountered the demon-possessed man is unknown, one possibility is the area near Gergesa on the eastern side of the Sea of Galilee. The steep hillside (shown here) provides a logical setting for the pig stampede.

animals and the loss of livelihood for the owners of the pigs do not seem to have occurred to the Gospel writers. Indeed, Jewish readers might have rather enjoyed the idea of the destruction of "unclean" pigs through the agency of "unclean" demons. The point of this feature of the story is the visible confirmation that it provides that the demons had really gone out from their "host."

8:35 *and they were afraid*. The restoration of such an apparently incurable (and frightening) man was in itself a natural cause of awe. But the emphasis on the report of those tending the pigs in both 8:34 and 8:36 suggests another reason for fear: the miraculous power that had already destroyed a valuable herd of pigs might be expected to take other violent forms. Jesus was not safe to have around. Hence the statement in 8:37 that the local people "asked Jesus to leave them, because they were overcome with fear." This uninvited visitor from the Jewish side of the lake spelled trouble, and he was not welcome.

8:39 *Return home and tell how much God has done for you*. To add a Gentile member to Jesus's disciple group would perhaps have been a step too far as a challenge to the Jewish sense of propriety. In any case, the man's place is as a witness among his own people. We are not told what success he had, nor whether pagans from this area turned to the Jewish God or became followers of Jesus.

Theological Insights

These two stories record not merely the deliverance of people in danger or distress but also the nature of Jesus the deliverer. In the first incident we see Jesus deploying miraculous power over nature such as the Old Testament attributes to God himself (Ps. 107:23–31). In the second incident his authority over spiritual evil, even in its most exaggerated form, also reveals someone who is far more than just a human teacher and healer.

The response of those who witnessed this power is instructive: "fear" is repeatedly mentioned. The disciples' natural panic (8:24) gave way in the light of Jesus's supernatural authority to a different type of "fear" mixed with amazement (8:25). The Gerasenes who had been afraid of the violent demoniac (8:27, 29) were filled with a different type of "fear" of the man who had made the demoniac harmless (8:35, 37). Jesus's ministry was characterized by love, compassion, and gentleness, but at the same time there was an inescapable element of otherness about him that left people feeling uncomfortable. In the case of the Gerasenes, this discomfort prevented them from gaining any further benefit from the presence of the Jewish Messiah.

Teaching the Text

These two passages can be taught either separately or together. See the "Theological Insights" above for some of the common themes.

1. *The storm on the lake*. A sermon or lesson on this passage could be called "Lord of Life's Storms," a title that brings out its two main themes. The first is christological. As noted above, Jesus's authority over the wind and the waves recalls passages in the Old Testament about God's sovereign authority over all of creation. What does this tell us about Jesus's identity?

The second main theme is our response to this authority. If Jesus is sovereign over all of creation, he is surely sovereign over anything we face in life. Jesus's challenge to the disciples, "Where is your faith?" is a challenge to us as well. Are we willing to trust God through life's difficulties? Discuss some of the spiritual and physical "storms" that we face today and provide examples of how God's sovereign authority and divine protection can carry us through.

One dramatic way to teach this passage is to encourage listeners to imagine themselves in the situation of the disciples, with Jesus asleep in the boat, and to follow through their changing emotions and impressions. How would they have reacted to the challenge "Where is your faith?" What answer may already be implied in their

Jesus and his disciples probably sailed across the Sea of Galilee in a common fishing boat. Shown here is a first-century AD mosaic from the ancient town of Magdala featuring a fishing boat with sails, oars, and rudder.

rhetorical question, "Who is this?" especially if they were familiar with Psalm 107?

2. *The demon-possessed man.* The theme in this passage, like the previous one, is Jesus's extraordinary authority. While it was over the chaotic powers of the deep in the first passage, here it is over demonic forces. Perhaps invite listeners to put themselves in the place of the pig herders (who would already know, and be afraid of, the possessed man) and follow through the story as they would perceive it. What would they make of (a) the man's restoration, (b) Jesus's authority, (c) the fate of the pigs, (d) the public response when the story got around, and (e) the man's telling of his own story after Jesus had gone?

For more on demon possession, see "Teaching the Text" on 4:31–44. If you have tackled the issue of demon possession more generally there, what has this story added to your understanding? If you have not, here is another good opportunity to help your audience consider the issue in relation to modern thinking.

Illustrating the Text

Jesus has power over the created order, and he is able to intervene in a crisis.

Biography: **Alexander Solzhenitsyn.** In his book *Loving God*, Charles Colson tells about the experiences of Alexander Solzhenitsyn (1918–2008) in a Siberian work camp, experiences on which Solzhenitsyn also partially based his novel *One Day in the Life of Ivan Denisovich.* Colson describes Solzhenitsyn's plight: "a pattern of backbreaking labor and slow starvation" leading to a "hopelessness [that] became too much to bear."

He put down his shovel and sat down on a bench, knowing full well that such an action could cost him his life. Amid his dejection he suddenly felt a powerful presence. Beside him, hunched over, an old man was drawing a stick through the sand at his feet, making the sign of the cross. Colson recounts that

> as Solzhenitsyn stared at that rough outline, his entire perspective shifted. He knew he was merely one man against the all-powerful Soviet empire. Yet in that moment he also knew that the hope of all mankind was represented by that simple cross—and through its power, anything was possible. Solzhenitsyn slowly got up, picked up his shovel, and went back to work—not knowing that his writings on truth and freedom would one day enflame the whole world.

Colson concludes, "Such is the power God's truth affords one man willing to stand against seemingly hopeless odds."[1]

Jesus has authority over the devil and can deliver anyone from his power.

True Story: *The Rise of Fallen Angels*, **by Mark I. Bubeck.** Among many other stories of deliverance, Bubeck tells about the experience of a new believer, Ahmed, in the southern Philippines. Fellow villagers who were critical of his faith challenged him to cast the devil out of a disturbed woman, saying that if he did so, they would put their faith in Christ. After praying and waiting on the Lord, Ahmed "confronted the powers controlling the woman." What ensued is proof of Christ's power. "Words flowed from her lips, indicating the battle to come. 'You are nobody to me, I can eat you alive,' a voice from within the woman said. 'The only one I'm afraid of is the Holy One within you,' the voice continued." Ahmed then ordered the demon to depart in the name of Jesus Christ the Savior. The demon said that he would go away, and after some physical torment, the woman became sane and free from Satan.[2]

Literature: *Madman*, **by Tracy Groot.** Anyone preaching or teaching this passage would be well served to read this fine novel (2006), which received some acclaim when it came out. The author did a great deal of research into why the madman of Luke 8 was mad, then created a believable fictional setting for him that vividly shows the dimension of the uncontainable evil that the madman falls into, evil that no one around him can subdue or redeem. The darkness of sin's power is palpable, and the marvel of the madman's redemption is profound in ways possibly not imaginable even to those familiar with the account. Christ is never called by name in the novel and is referred to only as the "man across the sea," nor does he appear in the story until the end, in a scene that is breathtaking and moving without sentimentality. Reading this scene (chap. 19) aloud could prove effective in helping your audience to put themselves there, seeing with their own eyes Christ's powerful deliverance over the most wretched evil, an exorcism that finally delivers the madman into beauty, freedom, and relief as he looks upon the face of Jesus.[3]

A Sick Woman and a Dead Girl

Big Idea *Jesus's extraordinary power to heal extends even to someone who has just died.*

Understanding the Text

The Text in Context

Two further miracles of healing add yet more weight to the impression of unlimited power that characterizes the whole of the Galilean phase of Jesus's story and that form the basis for the key question of 9:18–20: Who is Jesus? After his authority has been asserted over the natural elements and the supernatural powers of evil (8:22–39), he now restores two women to life: one literally, from a recently fatal illness, the other metaphorically, in that she is rescued from a long period of ostracism and misery. In these incidents Jesus acts alone, but these further demonstrations of his power provide the background for his subsequently sending his disciples out to extend his ministry of proclamation and deliverance (9:1–6; 10:1–17).

Outline/Structure

The insertion of one story (that of the woman with the hemorrhage) within another (that of Jairus's daughter) is a well-known rhetorical technique, especially characteristic of Mark but quite commonly employed by storytellers both ancient and modern. Such "sandwiching" or "intercalation" not only retains the interest of the reader, who is impatient to discover how the first story will finish, but also often prompts the reader to note the common elements in the two stories—in this case, two women (one young, one older) with contrasting conditions, the danger of ritual defilement, Jesus's unique power, and the pivotal role of faith. All three Synoptic writers combine these two stories in the same way, perhaps simply because Matthew and Luke have adopted Mark's outline, but perhaps also because those who were present remembered the striking interruption of the journey to Jairus's house, so that the girl died before Jesus could get there.

Historical and Cultural Background

Two of the standard sources of ritual defilement in Old Testament law were through contact with someone with a bodily discharge and, more seriously, through touching a dead body. For defilement through touching a corpse, see Numbers 19:11–16; for the law regarding a woman with an abnormal flow of blood, see Leviticus 15:25–30. The latter condition led to social exclusion (a Qumran text prescribes segregated areas in a town for menstruating women as for lepers [11Q19 48.14–17]). Each of these two incidents raises at least the possibility of ritual defilement for Jesus. For a similar issue, see 5:13.

For Old Testament accounts of the restoration of those who had recently died, see "Historical and Cultural Background" on 7:1–17.

Interpretive Insights

8:41 *a man named Jairus, a synagogue leader.* The place is presumably again Capernaum, Jesus's base at this period, so that Jairus is an official of the newly built synagogue mentioned in 7:5. The preservation of his name (unusual in such Gospel stories) probably indicates that he was a leading figure in the community. That such a man should prostrate himself before Jesus shows the respect in which Jesus was now held among Jews (in contrast with his recent rejection in the Decapolis).

8:43 *subject to bleeding for twelve years.* This is normally assumed to be a menstrual disorder, but no details are given. The ritual defilement associated with such a problem (see above), both for herself and for all associated with her, not only would be an embarrassment and an inconvenience but also would likely put her in social isolation. Her surreptitious approach to Jesus reflects this delicate situation.

8:44 *touched the edge of his cloak.* For the belief that healing could be conveyed by a touch, see on 6:19. The *kraspedon*

A woman who had been bleeding for twelve years touched the edge of the cloak of Jesus and was instantly healed. This scene was one of several miracles of Jesus carved onto the front side of a sarcophagus (AD 375–400).

- Jesus's healing power operates even without his conscious intention.
- But he perceives that "power has gone out from me."
- Healing comes as a result of faith.
- Jesus is able to reverse the process of death.
- Death is described as only a "sleep."
- The danger of ritual impurity through contact with discharge and death does not deter Jesus from bringing restoration.

("edge") is probably the tassel required by the law (Num. 15:37–38) to be attached to the corners of men's outer garments. It is not clear whether her "uncleanness" was understood to be communicated to Jesus by such a touch; the issue is not raised in the narrative.

8:46 *I know that power has gone out from me.* The "mechanical" sound of this statement, suggesting an "automatic" transfer

of power, is modified by Luke's statement that many were "pressing against" Jesus; yet only one of them drew on his "power," and he was immediately aware of what had happened. It was not the physical contact in itself that conveyed healing, but rather the faith that prompted it and to which Jesus will attribute the healing in 8:48.

8:48 *Daughter, your faith has healed you.* This is the only time Jesus addresses someone as "daughter" (though cf. 13:16), a reassuringly intimate term for this distressed woman. "Healed" is literally "saved." The primary reference here (as when the same formula is used in 17:19; 18:42) is to physical healing, but in view of this woman's condition, there may also be a wider sense of "salvation" to include the restoration of the full normal life from which she had been excluded (cf. the same formula in a nonphysical sense in 7:50).

8:49 *Your daughter is dead.* The careful progression of tenses from 8:42 ("was dying") to this perfect tense (lit., "has died") leaves no doubt that Luke intends us to read this as a case of actual resuscitation after death, despite Jesus's puzzling words in 8:52 (see below).

8:50 *Don't be afraid; just believe, and she will be healed.* "Healed" is again literally "saved." The assumption of the messenger in 8:49 was that death made the appeal to Jesus no longer relevant, but Jesus begs to differ: even a dead person can be "saved." What matters, as in 8:48, is faith. Jairus has just witnessed Jesus's healing power, but now the challenge to faith has become even more extreme.

8:51 *Peter, John and James.* These three formed a sort of "inner circle" of disciples (cf. 9:28; Mark 13:3; 14:33).

8:52 *She is not dead but asleep.* The derision that greets this pronouncement suggests that the onlookers took it literally: Jesus was disputing the diagnosis and believed that the girl was only in a coma. But the way Luke has told the story (see on 8:49) does not allow that possibility; nor does the following statement that they "knew she was dead." In that case, Jesus must be speaking figuratively: her death is real but only temporary, so that she can "wake up" again. ("Sleep," using a different Greek word, was a common euphemism for death, but that cannot be all that is involved here, since "not dead but dead" would make no sense.)

8:54 *He took her by the hand.* Luke does not mention the ritual defilement that resulted from contact with a corpse. See on 5:13. Even if Jesus's words "not dead but asleep" are metaphorical, his touch overcame death and, with it, defilement.

8:55 *Her spirit returned.* The wording echoes Elijah's miracle of resuscitation in 1 Kings 17:21–22.

8:56 *he ordered them not to tell anyone what had happened.* Even though only five people were allowed to see the miracle (8:51), the reappearance of a girl previously known to be dead could hardly be kept quiet. As in 5:14, Luke records Jesus's demand for silence but does not pursue the theme. See on 4:41.

Theological Insights

These two intertwined miracles are very different, but in each a hopeless situation (an incurable and isolating illness, and death itself) is overcome by the life-restoring power of Jesus, exercised in response to "faith" (8:48, 50). Faith is frequently mentioned, and is probably always presupposed, in accounts of Jesus's physical healings. Any impression of "automatic" or "magical" healing, such as the story of the woman with the hemorrhage might otherwise suggest, is thus excluded.

Jairus's daughter, like the widow's son (7:11–17) and Lazarus (John 11), was resuscitated only to die again subsequently; this was not "resurrection." But Jesus's words about death as "sleep" can, with hindsight, have a relevance beyond these exceptional cases. His own resurrection (not just resuscitation to die again) opens up a new view of death, not as the end of everything but rather as a "sleep" followed by awakening into a new life.

Teaching the Text

Each of these two stories has its own message and gives a different insight into what it means to be healed by Jesus. But the weaving of the two together in the narrative perhaps suggests that we should notice especially the common themes:

- two women in extreme distress—typical of Luke's special interest in Jesus's concern for women
- two cases where normal human resources have failed to bring healing
- the issue of ritual defilement (Luke does not make this explicit, but it is likely to have been in the mind of a Jewish audience who knew the significance of ritual purity in the law.)
- the vital role of faith in healing
- Jesus's divine authority to heal the sick and to raise the dead

There are two main angles from which to approach these passages in a sermon or lesson, one focused on Jesus's healing power (Christology) and the other focused on the faith of those seeking help. When dealing with the first, be sure to emphasize both (a) Jesus's *ability* to heal and (b) his *willingness* to do so. Our God is both all-powerful and all-compassionate. If he were only the former, he would not care about our human needs. If he were only the latter, he would

Jairus was a leader in the synagogue. This is the restored fourth- to fifth-century synagogue at Capernaum. Remains of a first-century AD synagogue have been found beneath the white limestone.

not be able to deliver us. Since he is both, we can have absolute confidence that he will bring us through life's difficulties.

The other angle is the importance and nature of faith. To teach this, encourage your listeners to enter into the woman's situation (physical discomfort, despair over healing, social exclusion due to defilement, embarrassment in public, the shock of Jesus's discovery of her secret attempt, eventual relief). What does this teach about the nature of and the challenges to faith?

Similarly, the story of Jairus's daughter may be approached through Jairus's own experience: his approach to a known healer; his frustration at the delay caused by the other woman; his despair at the message from home; Jesus's unexpected response; the small group allowed in the room; Jesus's enigmatic words about death and sleep (what would he have thought Jesus meant?); the banal instruction to give her something to eat; his reaction to the demand for silence. Describe the challenges to faith that he faced and how we might face similar challenges.

See also the last paragraph in "Teaching the Text" on 7:1–17. This story allows similar reflections on life, death, and resurrection.

Illustrating the Text

Jesus's power is only unleashed by his grace and received by faith.

Nature: Lightning is an amazing natural phenomenon that almost everyone has seen or experienced. The static charges that build up in air masses store unimaginable potential energy that hovers over our heads every day. Only under the right conditions, however, can that energy be released and transmitted to objects below. The object that is struck by lightning has to be grounded; that is, it has to be able to receive a massive influx of electrons and conduct them into a medium that can absorb them. If an object is insulated from the ground, it cannot conduct the electrons and the lightning passes it by. In fact, there is a moment right before a lightning strike when viable targets develop a glowing tongue of flame (a "positive streamer") created as positive charges in the grounded object attempt to unite with the negative charges ("stepped leader") descending from the air mass above. (You can find incredible images and slow-motion videos of this phenomenon online via a search for "lightning in super slow motion" or "lightning strike positive streamer.") In the same way, if a heart is grounded in faith, it can receive power from Jesus; if it is insulated from the Lord by unbelief, however, the Lord's power passes by untapped.

Jesus can be fully attentive to every individual in every situation.

Human Experience: Describe a time when you missed something important because you were distracted or when you let someone down because you were inattentive to their needs. In this passage, Jesus is not only able to notice an individual touching his garment in the middle of a crowd, but he is also able to sense the faith and trust behind that touch. Nor does stopping to pay attention to this woman detract from his perfect timing and provision for Jairus's daughter. Invite your listeners to wonder at the miracle that Jesus's attention is never divided like ours is by a world full

of simultaneous needs—he is enough to satisfy all of us with personal care.

Death is never the final word when Jesus gets involved.

Film: Take a moment to retell or show a movie scene where a character seems to be defeated and then repeatedly comes out of trouble or even apparent death to fight again. (Think about epic movies and adventures, like the *Indiana Jones* films, *The Princess Bride*, etc. You may even want to show a scene from the *Princess Bride* where the protagonist, Wesley, explains "death can't stop true love—all it can do is delay it for a while.") Explain that, in the same way, when Jesus enters a person's story, death ceases to be the final word—whether it is through a miraculous healing in this life, or a complete healing in heaven, Jesus upends death and brings the victory.

"Who Is This?"

Big Idea *Jesus shares his mission with his disciples, but his unique authority is further recognized and is demonstrated in another astonishing nature miracle.*

Understanding the Text

The Text in Context

The Twelve disciples chosen by Jesus in 6:13–16 have hitherto been merely his companions and audience; now they become his agents as he extends the scope of his mission. In 10:1–12 that delegation of his mission will be further expanded. The reader is thus prepared for the eventual continuation of the movement after Jesus's death.

The immense popularity of Jesus and his mission is contrasted with the suspicion of Herod Antipas. This parenthetical note prepares the reader for the later death threat from Antipas (13:31) and for the scene in which Antipas eventually meets Jesus directly (23:7–12). Antipas's question "Who is this?" in 9:9 repeats that of the disciples in 8:25 (and cf. 5:21) and further escalates the christological question that will come into direct focus in 9:18–20. In the meantime, the further astonishing miracle in 9:10–17 makes that question the more pressing.

Historical and Cultural Background

The Greco-Roman world at this time was familiar with itinerant teachers in the form of the Cynics, who were famous for their simple lifestyle and their dependence on material support from the local population. It is not clear, however, how prominent Cynics might have been in Palestine. More typically Jewish was the itinerant exorcist (9:49; 11:19; Acts 19:13–16). Josephus (*J.W.* 2.124–25) also describes how Essenes traveled without provisions and were given hospitality by other Essenes. Hospitality for visiting strangers was, and still is, a deeply rooted tradition in Middle Eastern life.

On Herod Antipas, see "Historical and Cultural Background" on 3:1–20.

The feeding of a large crowd in an uninhabited area, in the absence of any regular food supply, strongly recalls for a Jewish audience the experience of Israel in the wilderness (Exod. 16), with the miraculously multiplied bread corresponding to the divinely provided manna. There is also a more directly parallel miracle story about Elisha (2 Kings 4:42–44), which is clearly echoed in this story.

Interpretive Insights

9:1 *he gave them power and authority.* The roles for which the Twelve are authorized—exorcism, healing, proclamation—mirror closely Luke's depiction of Jesus's own Galilean mission. He thus delegates his own authority to them, and the mission is extended.

9:3 *Take nothing for the journey.* The aim is not so much asceticism or "living simply" for its own sake (like the Cynics, as noted above) as the recognition that hospitality should be expected, and that the work of the kingdom of God deserves its own support (cf. 10:7).

9:5 *If people do not welcome you, . . . shake the dust off your feet.* Jews returning from pagan territory shook off its dust in order to leave behind any contamination. So this was a gesture of dissociation and judgment (see 10:10–12; Acts 13:50–51). To reject the messenger is to reject the message and the one who sent it (10:16). The message is for all, but where it is not received, they are not to waste time "flogging a dead horse."

9:7 *heard about all that was going on.* Antipas's main concern will be shown to be Jesus himself, but the sudden appearance of a dozen itinerant spokesmen for the new movement would naturally increase his alarm.

some were saying that John had been raised from the dead. Luke has recorded John's imprisonment (3:20)

but not his execution (Mark 6:17–29), which is, however, made clear in 9:9. We have seen in 7:18–35 that Jesus was popularly seen as the successor to John the Baptist, and he himself encouraged that understanding (20:1–8). That he might actually be John restored to life is a superstitious extension of that idea (though one that Antipas finds hard to credit because John no longer has a head [9:9]!). Note that all three reported popular assessments of Jesus, which will be repeated in 9:19, place Jesus in the category of a prophet and therefore a true messenger of God.

9:8 *Elijah had appeared.* For the expectation of Elijah's return, see on 1:17.

> When Jesus sent the disciples out to proclaim God's kingdom, they were to carry nothing with them, "no staff, no bag, no bread, no money, no extra shirt" (9:3). This statue shows a young man wearing a tunic, the garment that would have been worn next to the skin (nineteenth-century copy of a fourth-century BC original).

9:9 *he tried to see him.* Antipas's desire to see Jesus will be fulfilled in 23:8.

9:10 *they withdrew by themselves.* Mark 6:31–34 makes it clear that this was a deliberate attempt to find respite from the crowds, but that popular insistence thwarted the planned retreat. Bethsaida, which was outside Galilee proper, had recently been developed into a sizable fishing town (the original home of Peter and Andrew [John 1:44]), but the location of this incident in a "remote place" (9:12) suggests that they went to a rural area within its territory rather than to the town itself.

9:12 *Send the crowd away.* This does not show a lack of hospitality in principle, but rather the apparent impossibility of providing it when away from home and faced by a huge gathering.

9:13 *You give them something to eat.* The obvious impossibility of this

instruction sets the reader up for the amazing sequel: human resources are totally inadequate. Compare Elisha's similar instruction in 2 Kings 4:42–43. Note how in this story the disciples have now become active participants in Jesus's ministry, not just spectators.

five loaves of bread and two fish. The "loaves" would each be enough for a single meal for one person. Even Jesus and his disciples apparently did not have enough with them for their own needs on this retreat, and they would have been dependent on local hospitality.

9:14 *About five thousand men were there.* The Greek for "men" would normally denote only males; Luke says nothing of women and children (contrast Matt.

The exact location where Jesus multiplied the loaves and fishes is unknown. Two possibilities are the plain of Bethsaida, favored by most recent commentators, or the traditionally venerated site at Tabgha visited by pilgrims since the fourth century AD.

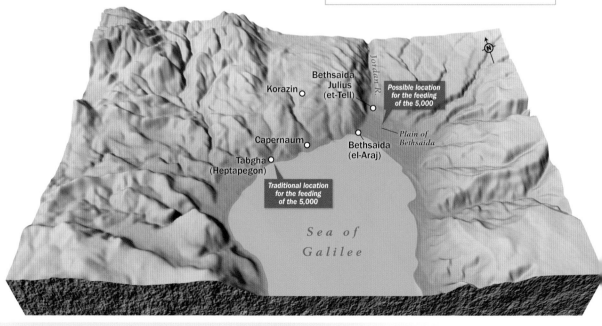

14:21). John's version of this story suggests a political and even military flavor to the gathering (John 6:15), so that the crowd may have been mainly or only men. A similar connotation has been suggested on the basis of the "groups of about fifty," like military platoons. But Luke does not suggest that Jesus encouraged, or even recognized, any such intention.

9:16 *Taking the five loaves and two fish . . . , he gave thanks and broke them. Then he gave them . . .* This sequence of verbs is virtually the same as used in 22:19 to describe Jesus's actions at the Last Supper (and in 24:30 for the meal at Emmaus). Although these are the actions that would be expected of the host (in a family, the father) at a Jewish meal, it is likely that Luke intended his Christian readers, familiar with eucharistic language, to find here a foreshadowing of the Christian fellowship meal.

9:17 *They all ate and were satisfied.* The wording rules out the suggestion that only a token amount of bread and fish was received by each person.

twelve basketfuls of broken pieces that were left over. There was far more left at the end than was available at the beginning. That seems to be the point of the note, rather than a concern for either tidiness or the avoidance of waste. There is also a clear echo of 2 Kings 4:44: "They ate and had some left over"; the reader familiar with the Elisha story will not fail to note the much greater scale of Jesus's feeding miracle. Note also the collection of leftover manna in Exodus 16:23. "Twelve" probably simply reflects the number of disciples assisting Jesus rather than being a symbolic number.

Theological Insights

When Jesus called his first disciples, he commissioned them to "fish for people" (5:10). When the Twelve were designated, we were told nothing of their "job description," except insofar as it was encapsulated in the term "apostle," referring to someone sent out (6:13–16; repeated here in 9:10). Now the nature of that "sending out" (9:2) becomes more explicit, and it will be further clarified as a second wave of emissaries is sent out in 10:1–12. In view of Luke's massive emphasis on the unique authority and supernatural power of Jesus, it comes as a surprise to find his mission shared in this way with fallible disciples. He remains the source of that authority, of course, and sometimes they will fail in their task. But the message of the kingdom of God is now clearly more than a one-man campaign, and the way is being prepared for the awesome responsibilities and authority of the church as Luke will later describe it in Acts.

Modern attempts to remove the miraculous element from the feeding story (e.g., everyone shared food that they had previously concealed, or only a token amount was received) find no basis in the wording of the Gospel accounts. Here, as in the amazing catch of fish, the calming of the storm, and the resuscitation of the dead, is another striking example of Jesus's ability to go beyond natural possibility in providing needed help. As the calming of the storm evoked echoes of the power of the creator God over the sea, so this incident recalls God's supernatural provision of food in the wilderness. Another significant brick is added to Luke's growing structure in answer to the christological question "Who is Jesus?" That question, already raised incidentally

in this section by Antipas in 9:9, will be tackled directly in the next paragraph.

The use of the same verbs for Jesus's actions here as in the accounts of the Last Supper probably indicates that the Gospel writers saw this supernaturally provided meal as a foretaste of the Christian Eucharist (despite its different menu and circumstances) and thus perhaps also of the eschatological messianic banquet (Isa. 25:6–8). The inclusion of a large and mixed group of people in such a meal, not just the disciples, speaks of the breadth of the coming kingdom of God.

> This bread-and-fish mosaic is from a fifth-century Byzantine church built at Tabgha over an earlier church for Christian pilgrims who venerated this site as the location where Jesus multiplied the loaves and the fishes.

Teaching the Text

The mission of the Twelve is probably best approached in conjunction with the mission of the seventy-two in 10:1–12, since the principles of the mission are very much the same but are more fully spelled out there. But here in 9:1–2 we have a more explicit listing of the tasks entrusted to them. There are three elements: (1) drive out demons, (2) cure diseases/heal the sick, and (3) proclaim the kingdom of God. Consider how this agenda compares to the current concerns of the church, both in its general manifestation and as it is expressed locally. In what ways is our commission the same? In what ways is it different? Have we lost our way?

The feeding miracle may be brought to life by encouraging listeners to put themselves in the place of one of the Twelve and to follow through the phases of the story. In particular, how would they have responded to Jesus's unexpected answer in 9:13 to a perfectly sensible request? How would they describe what had happened as they cleared up the leftovers? While modern hearers will readily recognize the miracle as the blessing of a free lunch, be sure to bring out the important biblical parallels, including the provision of manna in the wilderness and the future messianic banquet (Isa. 25:6–9). Jesus is not just performing a charitable act. He is also illustrating the nature and blessings of the kingdom of God.

Illustrating the Text

Be discerning about when to shake the dust off your feet.

Personal Stories: Many individuals have had experiences of persevering in relational and spiritual encounters in which the other person has either been hostile to or had no real interest in the counsel offered. It might be good to elicit stories of some of these situations that may still be present in the persevering person's mind.

Literature: *The Lion, the Witch and the Wardrobe*, by C. S. Lewis. This novel (1950) is the best known of the seven books in the Chronicles of Narnia series, written by Lewis (1898–1963). In it, the four children visit Narnia when it is still frozen over. They are traveling with the Beavers and have just had a wonderful meal when they discover that Edmund, the disgruntled brother who has eaten the witch's food and been infected by her, has disappeared. Wise Mr. Beaver instantly knows that he has gone to find the witch because she has tempted him with power. Peter and Lucy are terribly worried and want to go look for him. Mrs. Beaver responds, "Go to the Witch's House? Don't you see that the only chance of saving either him or yourselves is to keep away from her?" Lucy wails, "Oh, can *no* one help us?" "Only Aslan," says Mrs. Beaver, "we must go on and meet him. That's our only chance now."[1] Both Mr. and Mrs. Beaver insightfully teach the children that they cannot bring back someone who is not ready to join their righteous cause. Only God can take care of that.

Divine provision goes far beyond basic needs.

Commentary: Pastor and author Warren Wiersbe (b. 1929) writes,

> Our Lord was not the kind of person who could teach the Word and then say to hungry people, "Depart in peace, be ye warm and filled" (James 2:16). The disciples were only too eager to see the crowd leave. . . . They had not yet caught the compassion of Christ and the burden He had for the multitudes, but one day they would. . . . This miracle was more than an act of mercy for hungry people, though that was important. It was also a sign of our Lord's messiahship and an illustration of God's gracious provision for man's salvation.[2]

The Messiah and His Glory

Big Idea *Jesus, at last recognized as the Messiah, speaks of his own rejection and death but then is revealed in glory.*

Understanding the Text

The Text in Context

This is the climax to the christological theme that has been developing through the first part of the Gospel: the question "Who is this?" now receives two definitive answers, one from the human witness Peter ("God's Messiah"), the other from God himself ("my Son"). Here too is the answer to John the Baptist's question in 7:19. But Peter's acclamation leads, to the reader's surprise, to a declaration by Jesus that the Messiah's mission is to suffer and die, before being raised to life again. This will now become the central theme of the Gospel, as Jesus repeats the warning at intervals (9:43–45; 13:31–35; 14:25–27; 17:25; 18:31–34). His determined progress toward Jerusalem to meet his fate will provide the framework of the story from 9:51.

The revelation of Jesus's glory on the mountain stands out as a unique experience for the disciples. It provides the reader with a reassuring glimpse behind the scenes, a "moment of truth," to offset the dark events to come. God's repetition of his testimony to Jesus, first given at his baptism (3:22), gives the reader a theological background against which to interpret what follows.

Historical and Cultural Background

On the meaning of "messiah," see the sidebar "The Messiah."

The ascent of a mountain with three chosen companions recalls Moses at Sinai (Exod. 24). That same passage also speaks of God's glory seen in a cloud on the mountain, into which Moses entered; cloud and bright light are understood as signs of God's presence in the Old Testament.

Interpretive Insights

9:18 *Once when Jesus was praying in private.* This is a typical situation in Luke; compare 11:1, when again the disciples are present. Note that the revelations of 9:18–20, 28–36 both occur in the context of Jesus's prayer. Luke does not mention the location near Caesarea Philippi, north of Galilee (so Mark and Matthew).

9:19 *Some say John the Baptist.* The answer echoes the popular opinions mentioned in 9:7–8; see comments there.

9:20 *Peter answered, "God's Messiah."* To see Jesus as a prophet, as the people did, placed him on a level with many other prophets in the Old Testament and since. Peter's insight is that Jesus is unique. There was to be only one Messiah (see the sidebar "The Messiah"). The reader already knows that Jesus is the Messiah (2:11, 26; 4:41); now the disciples have caught up.

9:21 *not to tell this to anyone.* This surprising reticence is probably best explained by the likely connotations of the term "messiah" for the popular mind (and possibly also in Peter's intention; cf. Mark 8:30–33). The mission that Jesus goes on to outline is diametrically opposed to any notion of the triumphant expulsion of the Roman armies, and he does not want to stir up such misleading hopes (or give a political handle to his enemies) before his paradoxical mission has been accomplished. He is the Messiah, but not that sort of messiah.

9:22 *The Son of Man must.* On this term, see the sidebar "The Son of Man" at 5:12–26. Its use here, as a deliberate substitute for Peter's term "Messiah," is designed to avoid the potentially misleading connotations of that title and to allow Jesus to set his own, unexpected agenda.

the elders, the chief priests and the teachers of the law. These three groups together made up the Sanhedrin in Jerusalem, the official representa-

tives of the Jewish people. This is therefore a formal rejection of the Jewish Messiah by the Jewish leadership.

he must be killed and on the third day be raised to life. Here and in 18:33 Jesus links resurrection to his predicted death. In 24:6–8 the women will be expected to remember this prediction, but it is clear in 24:11–12 and in the Emmaus story that the disciples had not grasped it.

Key Themes of Luke 9:18–36

- Jesus is more than a prophet; he is the Messiah.
- As such, his mission is, paradoxically, to be rejected and killed by his own people.
- Those who follow him must expect the same treatment.
- But beyond the suffering there is glory in the kingdom of God.
- A chosen group of disciples is given a vision of Jesus's true glory.
- God again declares that Jesus is his Son.

The Messiah

"Messiah" means "anointed." In the Old Testament kings and priests were anointed for their special offices. "The Lord's anointed" became a familiar term for the Davidic king. After the fall of the monarchy there was a growing hope of a new king of the line of David, and while the term "messiah" was not used in this way within the Old Testament, it became more common in later Jewish literature. Different groups had different notions of what sort of deliverer God would send to his people, but the kingly ideal was fundamental for most and led many to see the Messiah's mission in essentially political terms, especially in the light of Israel's subjection to Rome.

Luke does not name the place where Jesus asks his disciples his pointed question, "Who do you say I am?" (9:20). Matthew and Mark locate this exchange in the region of Caesarea Philippi, the modern site of Banias. One of the sources of the Jordan River flows through this region and is shown here.

9:23 *take up their cross daily.* Jesus has not specified crucifixion as such, but Jews knew what form Roman execution was likely to take. So "take up the cross" meant to face the prospect of a shameful death. Luke's addition of "daily" suggests that he also took the phrase less literally, as a metaphor for public humiliation and self-denial.

9:24 *whoever wants to save their life will lose it.* This paradoxical statement depends on the fact that *psychē* is used to refer to both physical life and the spiritual self, or "soul."

9:25 *to gain the whole world.* The same principle is extended beyond life itself to the values that govern most people's lifestyle. "Gain" and "forfeit" are commercial metaphors.

9:26 *the Son of Man . . . when he comes.* The imagery is drawn from Daniel 7:13–14, where the "one like a son of man" comes before God to be enthroned in glory as sovereign and judge of all nations. That judgment is ultimately more important than human opposition, even if it leads to physical martyrdom.

9:27 *will not taste death before they see the kingdom of God.* In the light of the parallel in Mark 9:1, the reference is probably to Jesus's triumphant establishment of God's kingdom on earth, despite his own death. This would become "visible," before some of them had "tasted death" in martyrdom, as the gospel spread and the church grew after Jesus's resurrection. But it is also possible, especially since this is said of only "some" of those present, that it refers to the experience of witnessing the transfiguration, which follows immediately.

9:28 *went up onto a mountain to pray.* The location (traditionally Mount Tabor) is not important; it was a place apart from normal life, as often when Jesus prayed. For the "inner circle" of Peter, John, and James, see on 8:51.

9:29 *the appearance of his face changed.* In this unique event the "human incognito" of the Son of God is transcended, and his true glory is revealed (note the mention of "glory" in 9:31–32).

9:30 *Two men, Moses and Elijah.* The reappearance of men from the distant past (both of whom had left this earth in mysterious circumstances [Deut. 34:5–6; 2 Kings 2:11]) adds to the numinous atmosphere. Both were prophets, and both had met God

We can only speculate about the mountain where the transfiguration of Jesus occurred. Two locations have been proposed. One is Mount Hermon, which is near Caesarea Philippi; the other, shown here, is Mount Tabor, the traditional site.

on a mountain. Both were expected in Jewish belief to be part of the eschatological scenario. Their presence confirms Jesus's status as the Messiah.

9:31 *They spoke about his departure.* "Departure" (*exodos*) probably focuses on Jesus's death, but perhaps it also includes his resurrection as the completion of his triumphant "exodus" progress. Glory and death are thus inextricably linked. Jesus's death is not an accident; it is the center of his messianic mission, soon to be "brought to fulfillment."

9:33 *He did not know what he was saying.* Overwhelmed by the awesome spectacle, Peter blurts out his first thoughts. Such distinguished visitors need suitable shelter on the mountain, and it is a good thing that the disciples are there to provide it. Peter does not realize that this vision is not meant to last.

9:35 *This is my Son, whom I have chosen; listen to him.* What God declared in the second person to Jesus in 3:22 is now repeated (with "chosen" rather than "beloved") for the benefit of the disciples. The added instruction "Listen to him," uttered after the appearance of Moses with Jesus, echoes Moses's prophecy (which featured in some messianic expectations) of a future prophet like himself to whom "You must listen" (Deut. 18:15); Jesus the Messiah now takes the place of Moses. But the central element in this declaration is again the identification of Jesus as the Son of God.

Theological Insights

This passage is packed with christological significance. Jesus is, as people supposed, a prophet (perhaps *the* prophet like Moses), but he is also more than a prophet—the Messiah. The appearance of Moses and Elijah with him adds to the sense of eschatological fulfillment. But the supernatural glory of the vision on the mountain and the divine declaration from the cloud take us beyond a merely human messiah to the Son of God, who himself shares in the essential glory of God.

Yet mixed in with this positive Christology is the strong note of suffering and death, not as an unfortunate diversion from the messianic mission but rather as its heart. The Son of Man who will appear in glory (9:26) is the same one who must be rejected by his own people (9:22). So to follow him is to take the road not to popularity and influence but instead to self-denial and the real possibility of martyrdom. And yet beyond his death is his resurrection and, for his disciples, the prospect of sharing his glory in the kingdom of God.

What a rich yet paradoxical theological harvest from a mere nineteen verses!

Teaching the Text

These verses contain at least three sections, each of which could be taught on its own:

- the revelation of Jesus as the Messiah, and the paradoxical nature of that messiahship
- the teaching of Jesus on discipleship
- the revelation of his glory on the mountain

But to isolate any of these from the others is to lose the remarkable overall balance that makes this section as a whole such a satisfying, if surprising, complex of teaching. It is better if the whole section can be taken together.

A lesson or sermon on this material should focus on both its implications for Christology (the identity of Jesus) and for discipleship. Luke's Gospel reaches a key turning point here as Peter recognizes and confesses that Jesus is the Messiah. Yet Jesus surprisingly defines that messiahship not as physical conquest but as suffering and sacrifice. This theme—the Messiah must suffer—is an important one in Luke-Acts and will reach its climax in the Gospel in the account of the Emmaus disciples after the resurrection (24:25–27). Jesus's teaching about suffering here applies not only to himself but also to his disciples, who must take up their cross daily and follow him (9:23). The transfiguration that follows both confirms the glorious identity of Jesus as Messiah and also provides assurance for the disciples that after suffering will come vindication and glory.

The prominence of Peter in the final scene invites us to use him (as a typical disciple) as a lead-in to grasping the significance of these events, as we follow the rollercoaster of his perceptions and emotions:

- his pride in at last grasping Jesus's messiahship
- his dismay when Jesus not only forbids them to speak of this but also apparently undermines it immediately by talking about rejection and death at the hands of the very people whom the Messiah has come to deliver
- his perception of what was meant by being raised on the third day

- the sinking feeling when Jesus speaks of the need to take up the cross and not to be ashamed of him
- the exhilaration of the mountaintop experience, but also the scary sight of a transformed Jesus and two dead men returned
- the embarrassment of his inappropriate words
- his possible shift of perceptions about Jesus from 9:20 to 9:36

Illustrating the Text

Sometimes one must lose one's life in order to gain it.

Literature: *Till We Have Faces*, by C. S. Lewis. This novel (1956), based on the myth of Cupid and Psyche, is reputed by some sources to be one of Lewis's own favorite works. In it, the protagonist, Orual, has a lifelong battle with the gods (God).

She tries to meet the longings of her troubled soul through a series of people in her life, claiming to love them, but using them for the sake of her own needs. The gods pursue her relentlessly. Finally, having lost many of those around her and unable any longer to fill the God-shaped vacuum, she begins to submit. She says, "But when the craving went, nearly all that I called myself went with it. It is as if my whole soul had been one tooth and now that tooth was drawn. I was a gap." And at the end, when Orual is about to die, she writes in the second book of her recorded battle with the gods, "I ended my first book with the words *no answer*. I know now, Lord, why you utter no answer. You are yourself the answer. Before your face questions die away. What other answer could suffice?"[1]

Beyond the suffering, there is glory.

Literature/Film: *Henry V*, **by William Shakespeare.** In this famous St. Crispin's Day speech, Henry V inspires his troops during the Battle of Agincourt (1415). It emphasizes (especially in the last few lines) the glory that follows heroic suffering. Kenneth Branagh's rendition of the speech from the 1989 film version is particularly powerful.

> This day is called the feast of Crispian:
> He that outlives this day, and comes
>   safe home,
> Will stand a tip-toe when the day is
>   named,
> And rouse him at the name of
>   Crispian.
> He that shall live this day, and see old
>   age,
> Will yearly on the vigil feast his
>   neighbours,
> And say 'To-morrow is Saint Crispian:'
> Then will he strip his sleeve and show
>   his scars.
> And say 'These wounds I had on Crisp-
>   in's day.'
> Old men forget: yet all shall be forgot,
> But he'll remember with advantages
> What feats he did that day: then shall
>   our names,
> Familiar in his mouth as household
>   words
> Harry the king, Bedford and Exeter,
> Warwick and Talbot, Salisbury and
>   Gloucester,
> Be in their flowing cups freshly
>   remember'd.
> This story shall the good man teach
>   his son;
> And Crispin Crispian shall ne'er go by,
> From this day to the ending of the
>   world,
> But we in it shall be remember'd;
> We few, we happy few, we band of
>   brothers;
> For he to-day that sheds his blood with
>   me
> Shall be my brother; be he ne'er so vile,
> This day shall gentle his condition:
> And gentlemen in England now a-bed
> Shall think themselves accursed they
>   were not here,
> And hold their manhoods cheap whiles
>   any speaks
> That fought with us upon Saint Crisp-
>   in's day.[2]

Jesus's Fallible Followers

Big Idea *The disciples show that they have not yet absorbed the message and values of the kingdom of God.*

Understanding the Text

The Text in Context

Luke 9:51 marks the end of the Galilean ministry and the beginning of the long "journey section" of the Gospel, which lasts until Jesus reaches Jerusalem in chapter 19. This is not a tightly organized travel narrative (indeed, the occasional geographical indications do not fit into a coherent sequence), but rather a collection of varied incidents and (mainly) teaching, including many of Luke's parables, loosely set within the journey motif. Overshadowing it all is the declaration in 9:22, now echoed in 9:44, of the coming rejection and suffering of the Son of Man. Much of the material in this journey section is found only in Luke; parallels in Mark are very few.

The short paragraphs surrounding this turning point are remarkable as repeatedly showing Jesus's disciples in an unflattering light. Even though now commissioned to represent Jesus (9:1–6), they still have much to learn, and one significant element in the

chapters between now and the arrival in Jerusalem will be the process of their education in the revolutionary values of the kingdom of God.

Historical and Cultural Background

On demon possession and exorcism in the ancient world, see "Historical and Cultural Background" on 4:31–33. Two of the incidents in this section relate to exorcism.

The hostility between Jews and Samaritans was by this time proverbial (John 4:9; 8:48). Each side regarded the other as religiously deviant, even though both derived their religion from the books of Moses. The Samaritans rejected the temple and priesthood in Jerusalem, and they had had their own temple near Shechem, until it was destroyed by the Jewish king Hyrcanus in 128 BC. Galilean pilgrims en route to Jerusalem often crossed to the east side of the Jordan to avoid passing through Samaritan territory. Mark never mentions Samaritans, and Matthew does so only once, to exclude them from the disciples' mission. Jesus's involvement with Samaritans in John 4 is narrated as a daring breach of protocol. Luke, however, presents Samaritans as the objects of God's concern here and in 17:11–19, and he will go on to speak of a successful apostolic mission among them in Acts 8; and most famously, a Samaritan will be the unlikely hero in one of Jesus's best-known parables (10:25–37). The disciples'

Key Themes of Luke 9:37–56

- Jesus succeeds in exorcism where his disciples have failed.
- The disciples do not yet understand Jesus's messianic mission.
- They need to learn that human ideas of greatness do not belong in the kingdom of God.
- The boundaries of God's work and grace are wider than the disciples suppose.
- Jesus now leaves Galilee and takes the road to Jerusalem.
- He rebukes the disciples' desire to retaliate.

conventional Jewish attitude here is out of step with that of Jesus (and of Luke).

Interpretive Insights

9:39 *A spirit seizes him.* All three Synoptic Gospels describe the symptoms of this boy in a way that sounds similar to epilepsy, and some interpreters suggest that his supposed demon possession is simply an unscientific way of describing epilepsy. But epilepsy was well known in the ancient world, and none of the Gospel writers here use the normal Greek terms for "epilepsy"; all describe the cure explicitly as an exorcism.

9:40 *I begged your disciples to drive it out, but they could not.* The disciples involved would not include Peter, John, and James (9:28). But all the apostles, not just the leading three, had been given authority to exorcize in 9:1 (and compare the experience of the seventy-two in 10:17), so this failure is surprising. In Matthew 17:20 it is attributed to a lack of faith on the disciples' part, and in Mark 9:29 to a lack of prayer. Luke does not explain their failure, but this note warns against any automatic view of spiritual power. Even apostles can fail.

9:41 *You unbelieving and perverse generation*. Here we have an echo of Moses's complaint in Deuteronomy 32:5, 20. It is not clear whether this is addressed specifically to the disciples, who had lacked the faith to perform the exorcism, or more generally to Jesus's contemporaries, as in 11:29. Perhaps there is no need to decide.

how long shall I stay with you and put up with you? This is a passing reminder that the human Jesus is also a "visitor" from heaven, as the supernatural glory on the mountain has revealed.

9:44 *delivered into the hands of men*. The passive verb indicates that the initiative is with God rather than with Jesus's human opponents. This explains the paradox that the Son of Man, whose role it is to rule over all nations (see the sidebar "The Son of Man" at 5:12–26), is to be subject to human power. This prediction summarizes what is more fully spelled out in 9:22 and especially 18:31–32.

9:45 *They did not understand*. Luke emphasizes the point by repeating it in different words three times in this one verse, in striking contrast to Jesus's instruction to "listen carefully" (9:44). By further adding that they were afraid to ask Jesus, he suggests that they failed not so much in intellectual comprehension as in willingness to face an unwelcome new perspective. The following verses will illustrate their more self-centered attitudes.

9:46 *which of them would be the greatest*. This issue will resurface explicitly in 22:24–27, and Jesus will attack conventional notions of importance in 14:7–14. The disciples have not yet absorbed the principle of the kingdom of God that the last will be first and the first last (13:30).

9:47 *Jesus . . . took a little child*. The child represents the lowest social status, the bottom of the pecking order, and so serves as a visual aid for the reversal of conventional values: the least is the greatest. The "welcome" that Jesus demands for the child is thus not just a matter of being nice to children, but of taking seriously, and indeed giving priority to, those (of whatever age) whom one may be tempted to despise or ignore. In 18:15–17 the disciples will show that they have not yet learned this lesson. Such "welcome" will also be conspicuously lacking in the story that follows in 9:49–50.

9:49 *someone driving out demons in your name . . . not one of us*. Compare Acts 19:13. Jesus's reputation as an exorcist tempted other Jewish exorcists (see 11:19) to try to "get in on the act."[1] John's instinct was to protect the distinctiveness of the Jesus "brand," but this too was a worldly motivation, defending the group's own interests. Is John's attitude also perhaps motivated by jealousy over this man's success as compared with the disciples' failure (9:40)? Jesus, by contrast, welcomes all who are "on the right side," whether formally affiliated with him or not. Compare Moses's similarly generous reaction to "unauthorized" prophecy in Numbers 11:26–29.

9:51 *As the time approached for him to be taken up to heaven*. Luke looks forward, beyond the rejection and suffering that Jesus has predicted, to Jesus's ascension, with which this Gospel will close (24:51). It is almost as if the terrible events in Jerusalem are a mere parenthesis within Jesus's progress to glory. This was the "exodus in Jerusalem" of which Jesus had spoken with Moses and Elijah on the mountain (9:31). "Taken up to heaven" also reminds the reader of Elijah (2 Kings 2:1–11), but 9:54 will contain a different echo of Elijah.

Jesus resolutely set out for Jerusalem. Jesus knows full well what is to happen in Jerusalem (cf. 13:32–35; 18:31–33); hence Luke's comment on his resoluteness to go there. The journey that begins here will reach its goal in 19:41, in time for the final Passover.

9:52 *went into a Samaritan village to get things ready for him.* Galilean Jews on pilgrimage to Jerusalem frequently traveled down the east side of the Jordan to avoid passing through Samaritan territory. Jesus's more inclusive attitude is revealed again by this chosen itinerary.

9:53 *the people there did not welcome him, because he was heading for Jerusalem.* This is not hostility to Jesus himself so much as to any Jewish pilgrim group going through their territory to the "apostate" temple.

9:54 *James and John.* This incident perhaps explains why Jesus gave this pair of brothers the nickname "Sons of Thunder" (Mark 3:17). Their proposal to call down fire from heaven recalls the story of Elijah in 2 Kings 1:9–15. Their sense of special authority is greater than their human compassion, and again Jesus has to rebuke their self-centered interest.

9:56 *went to another village.* Jesus puts into practice the principle of 9:5 (cf. 10:10–11) by not staying where he is not welcome. But instead of threats of judgment, he seems to quietly accept their decision. For the change of route that Luke seems to indicate as a result, see on 17:11.

Jesus is journeying to Jerusalem, ultimately to his suffering and death followed by his victorious resurrection and ascension. The trip from Galilee to Jerusalem through Samaritan territory usually took three days. Jesus chose to stop in Samaria even though Jewish travelers usually timed their walk to make it through the territory quickly in one day. Sometimes this road was avoided completely and travelers followed the route down the east side of the Jordan, which added two to three days onto the journey. This map shows the main travel routes from Galilee to Jerusalem.

Theological Insights

Two themes seem to dominate this section.

1. *The fallibility of disciples.* Though called, chosen, and empowered by Jesus, these ordinary men fail repeatedly: they are unable to exorcize because of a lack of faith, they do not understand Jesus's prediction of his own death and do not want to have it explained to them, they squabble about their relative status, and they show an exclusive group mentality that would drive away a potential ally and bring violent destruction on those who do not welcome them. To be a follower of Jesus is no guarantee of spiritual maturity.

2. *The revolutionary values of the kingdom of God.* Conventional ideas of status and importance have no place in Jesus's program. The "least important" are the ones who matter most. The natural cliquishness of human society gives way to a warm inclusiveness. The self-interest that wants to retaliate violently to a perceived insult is rebuked.

And all of this is under the shadow of Jesus's knowledge that it will be his own fate to be rejected and killed in Jerusalem, a fate that he will not resist.

Teaching the Text

There are five distinct elements in this section (9:37–43a, 43b–45, 46–48, 49–50, 51–56), any of which could be taken as a basis for teaching on its own, depending on which the teacher perceives to have the most relevant message for the group.

But it is also possible to trace related themes through the different sections, as I have done in "Theological Insights" above, and so to teach about the following:

1. *The fallibility of disciples.* The disciples illustrate weakness in various ways in these texts, including lack of faith (9:40), lack of spiritual discernment (9:45), pride (9:46), and exclusivity (9:49). In what ways do believers today manifest these same failings? Notice how Jesus responds in each case. What does this teach us about the ideal qualities of Christian leaders? What contemporary Christian figures do listeners most admire? Is there a danger of unrealistic hero worship? Do you know of examples of Christian leaders with "feet of clay"? If so, what is the right response to this? Who is in a position to cast the first stone? How

does the grace of God operate in relation to human fallibility?

2. *The revolutionary values of the kingdom of God.* Jesus's teaching in these verses is strikingly countercultural to contemporary values. He calls for self-sacrifice instead of self-exaltation, humility and dependence on God as the key to greatness, and collaboration with others instead of competition. Consider situations today where these principles can be applied in order to challenge accepted conventional values. Are there other areas of current concern where similar subversive thinking and action are needed? In our society today, who are the first and who are the last? Have we got it right from the perspective of God's kingdom?

"Whoever is not against you is for you" is a particularly challenging principle to apply to modern church life, with its cliques and mutual exclusion. How does it relate to the apparent opposite in 11:23, "Whoever is not with me is against me"? You might point out that both principles are valid depending on the circumstances and discuss where each applies.

Illustrating the Text

Self-preoccupation prevented the disciples from understanding Jesus's message and messianic mission.

Human Experience: *Photography and the Art of Seeing,* **by Freeman Patterson.** In this book (1965) Patterson (b. 1937), a top-notch Canadian photographer, instructs on photography and visual design. He describes what it takes to have vision, the vision that has power and understanding. Patterson writes, "Letting go of self is an

Jesus ministered in a culture where illness or abnormal behavior was attributed to supernatural causes. Amulets were worn to ward off demonic activity, and healers and exorcists were valuable members of society. Freeborn Roman boys were given pendants (*bullae*) to wear to provide protection against evil spirits. The young boy standing between his parents in this funerary relief wears a Roman *bulla* (first century AD).

essential precondition to real seeing. When you let go of yourself, you abandon any preconceptions about the subject matter which might cramp you into photographing in a certain, predetermined way. . . . Preoccupation with self is the greatest barrier to seeing, and the hardest one to break."[2] Similarly, in their self-preoccupation, the disciples were not ready or able to comprehend Jesus's message.

In the face of the disciples' quarreling, Jesus attacks conventional notions of what is important.

Literature: "Revelation," by Flannery O'Connor. O'Connor (1925–64) was a renowned American writer and essayist whose Christian faith shone through her work. In this wry tale published posthumously in 1965, Ruby Turpin, the protagonist, is a very self-assured woman who is convinced that she has satisfied Jesus. She knows she is fat, but she also asserts that she has been given a good disposition, a good complexion, and a little bit of everything. She is completely self-satisfied and puts herself above almost everyone she meets, always commenting internally on their lesser position. She finally has an encounter with God when a seemingly deranged girl named, not accidentally, Mary Grace, throws a book at her that hits her in her head (affecting her understanding). In the end, after Ruby has argued with God, she is granted the vision of a procession of people on their way to heaven, with all those she has disparaged in front of the line, and she and those like her at the end of the procession. She can see "by their shocked and altered faces that even their virtues were being burned away."[3]

Christian Living: *The Jesus I Never Knew*, **by Philip Yancey.** In this well-known book (1995), Yancey addresses Jesus's unconventionality. He writes,

> Jesus did not mechanically follow a list of "Things I Gotta Do Today.". . . He let himself get distracted by any "nobody" he came across. . . .
>
> Jesus was "the man for others," in Bonhoeffer's fine phrase. He kept himself free—free for the other person. He would accept almost anyone's invitation to dinner, and as a result no public figure had a more diverse list of friends, ranging from rich people, Roman centurions, and Pharisees to tax collectors, prostitutes, and leprosy victims.[4]

Discipleship and Mission

Big Idea *To follow Jesus and share his mission demands full commitment.*

Understanding the Text

The Text in Context

Ever since 5:1–11 Jesus has been gathering disciples. In 6:13 he chose the Twelve from among a larger number. It is clear that the Twelve will be his principal companions on the journey to Jerusalem, but who else will go with them? We are not told whether the three potential recruits in 9:57–62 did in fact join the group, but they represent the difficult choice to be made. So it is surprising to find so large a group as seventy-two who are ready and suitable to be added to the mission team. They will not appear again after 10:17, but they, like the women mentioned in 8:1–3, remind us that there was more to the Jesus movement than just the tightly knit group of Jesus and the Twelve. The journey to Jerusalem is taking on the aspect of a substantial missionary enterprise.

Historical and Cultural Background

In Jewish culture family loyalty and family responsibilities took precedence over almost any other obligation. And one of the most significant roles of an eldest son was to arrange a suitable burial for his father. To fail to do so not only reflected badly on the character of the son but also brought shame on the whole family. Jesus's apparent overriding of this sacred responsibility would have been profoundly shocking.

On itinerant preachers in the Jewish world, see "Historical and Cultural Background" on 9:1–17.

When Jesus asks a man to follow him, he responds, "Let me go and bury my father" (9:59). Families who were wealthy buried their loved ones in rock-cut tombs. The bodies would be wrapped and placed in the long niches whose openings you can see in the remains of this tomb on the Mount of Olives from the Second Temple period. After a year, only the bones remained, and a second "burial" would occur as the bones were placed in a limestone box known as an ossuary.

In modern Western culture decisions, especially those relating to religious commitment, tend to be a matter for the individual. By contrast, Jesus's instructions to the seventy-two envisage not just a household but a whole town making a corporate decision to welcome or reject their mission. Compare the rejection of Jesus by the whole community in Nazareth (4:22–30). This is much more typical of Middle Eastern culture, then and now.

Interpretive Insights

9:58 *the Son of Man has no place to lay his head.* Jesus's title "the Son of Man" derived from the majestic figure in Daniel 7:13–14, but we have already seen the paradoxical notion of the Son of Man rejected and killed. Now the paradox is extended to his earthly lifestyle. What even the nonhuman creation can take for granted is denied him, and those who choose to follow him must expect no better.

9:59 *He said to another man, "Follow me."* The potential disciples in 9:57, 61 are volunteers, but this man, like Levi (5:27), is personally selected.

Lord, first let me go and bury my father. If the father had just died, it is unlikely that the son would have been free to be away from home listening to Jesus. More likely he means that he needs to stay at home to deal with the funeral arrangements when his father dies; in that case, he is effectively saying that he is not at present available to follow Jesus.[1]

9:60 *Let the dead bury their own dead.* This paradoxical epigram probably implies that those who do not follow Jesus are spiritually "dead." Jesus's rejection of the man's reason for not following him places

the demands of the kingdom of God (and therefore of discipleship) above even the most basic of family duties—a radical break with cultural norms.

9:61 *first let me go back and say goodbye to my family.* This seems an even more natural and innocuous request (cf. Elisha in 1 Kings 19:20–21), and Jesus's reply is deliberately extreme.[2] A plowman who looks back is likely to produce a crooked furrow; the job demands full concentration. So to be concerned with family ties is to jeopardize one's discipleship. For a similarly "hardline" statement of priorities, exaggerated to make the point, compare 14:26.

10:1 *The Lord appointed seventy-two others.* They are "others" compared with both the Twelve (9:1–6) and with the advance guard sent in 9:52. Textual evidence is divided between "seventy-two" and "seventy" as the original text, but the rounder number is more likely to have been a "correction" for the surprisingly precise "seventy-two." There is no obvious symbolic reason for this number. Genesis 10 probably lists seventy nations in the world (seventy-two in the Greek text), but since this is a mission specifically within Jewish territory, that seems an unlikely allusion. A slightly more plausible allusion is to the seventy associates appointed by Moses

(Num. 11:16–25; note that two more are added in 11:26–29). It is a surprise to find so many disciples sufficiently committed and available at this stage. After the report of their return in 10:17 they will not be referred to again.

two by two. Jesus probably sends them out in pairs for companionship and mutual support, but perhaps also because two witnesses were required for valid legal testimony (cf. Deut. 19:15).

10:2 *The harvest is plentiful, but the workers are few.* The following verses make it clear that the harvest is of people, to be won for the kingdom of God. Compare "fishing for people" in 5:10. The role of the seventy-two as "harvest workers" is more fundamental than merely as advance guards for Jesus's own visit (10:1; cf. 9:52). In 10:17 they will report back on their own independent mission.

10:3 *Go! I am sending you out like lambs among wolves.* The immediate answer to their prayer for more workers (10:2) is that they themselves will fulfill that role. They are "sent out" (apostles = "sent ones") just like the Twelve in 9:2 and, like them, will be exposed to danger and rejection.

10:4 *do not greet anyone on the road.* Their lack of normal traveling equipment (as in 9:3) expresses their vulnerability and dependence on hospitality. But now there is a new element of urgency: the harvest is ripe and must be gathered immediately. Even the customary greetings will take too much time and distract the disciples from their mission. This is probably hyperbole for extreme urgency, since it is not obvious why people whom they meet on the road should not also receive their message.

10:5 *Peace to this house.* The instructions in 10:5–12 spell out more fully the principle set out in 9:4–5. The greeting "Peace" (*shalom*) is not just a wish but rather a "performative utterance," which, like God's word in Isaiah 55:11, has its own dynamic. Only if it is rejected will it "return" like an uncashed check.

10:7 *the worker deserves his wages.* This principle, which Paul upheld but refused to invoke for his own benefit (1 Cor. 9:5–18), goes beyond mere conventional hospitality: the work of the gospel, and therefore those

Jesus told his followers, "The harvest is plentiful, but the workers are few" (10:2). Shown here is a field ready for harvest near the Palestinian village of Yanoun.

who are engaged in it, should be maintained by those who benefit from it. But all that is needed is basic support; they should not "shop around" for better accommodations.

10:9 *Heal the sick.* As usual, healing is linked with proclamation as an essential element in the mission of Jesus and of his disciples (as in 9:1, 6). Exorcism is not mentioned at this point, but in 10:17 we will see that this too is part of the mission of the seventy-two.

The kingdom of God has come near you. This slogan, repeated in 10:11, sums up their proclamation. It is more than an announcement of something future: in Mark 1:15 it is parallel to the statement "The time has been fulfilled." Compare here 11:20: "has come upon you." In the ministry of Jesus the kingdom of God has already come into being, even though it remains open to people to either accept it or reject it.

10:12 *it will be more bearable on that day for Sodom.* The destruction of Sodom in Genesis 19 was the paradigm of God's judgment on those who reject his sovereignty. But these Jewish towns have been offered a more explicit call to repentance than pagan Sodom received.

Theological Insights

No ordinary rabbi would have dreamed of making the demands on potential disciples that Jesus makes. But such was his authority that he could make such demands and expect to be obeyed. Even the most basic of family responsibilities must give way before the imperative to proclaim the kingdom of God. There is a similar radicalism about Jesus's instructions to those whom he sends out as his emissaries. There is no scope for conventional politeness; both the task of proclamation and the response that it demands have an "all-or-nothing" quality that sits uncomfortably alongside many people's experience of discipleship today.

The missions of the Twelve (9:1–6) and now of the seventy-two show that what began as Jesus's solo messianic mission is becoming a sizable movement with a potentially universal scope (though as yet confined to the Jewish community). The kingdom of God is not merely an option for a religious few; it is a manifesto presented to everyone and requires a clear response of acceptance or rejection.

Teaching the Text

The teacher could focus on two groups: potential disciples and those sent out to make disciples.

1. *Potential disciples (9:57–62).* Outline the situation. Jesus, having declared his intention to go to Jerusalem to his death, now sets off determinedly. Who will go with him, and what can they expect to face? Then encourage listeners to think through the principles involved in each of the three cameos of potential disciples and Jesus's response to them. In what ways might we face similar challenges in our discipleship today?

We are not told whether any of these three did actually join Jesus on the journey. What might have happened to them?

2. *The seventy-two (10:1–12).* This passage may be considered together with 9:1–6, where similar principles are more briefly expressed. It raises a number of issues:

- The need for workers and the sequence "Ask the Lord to send" followed by

"Go, I am sending you." Is there a pattern here for our involvement in mission?

- The practice of sending them two by two. Why, and what may this teach us?
- The lack of equipment/resources and the prohibition of greeting. How, if at all, might these be relevant to Christian ministry today?
- The principle of staying if welcomed but moving on if rejected. How might this principle apply to pioneer evangelism and to settled church ministry? Does this mean that an "unsuccessful" ministry is a reason to move elsewhere?
- The disciples' message "The kingdom of God has come near to you." What does this teach us about priorities in our ministry?

Illustrating the Text

Personal security and even family duties must give way to the demands of discipleship.

Hymn: "Take My Life and Let It Be," by Frances Ridley Havergal. In this beloved hymn (1874) Havergal (1836–79), a poet and hymnist who suffered greatly in her life, spells out the kind of dedication and commitment that this principle teaches.

Take my life, and let it be consecrated,
   Lord, to Thee.
Take my moments and my days; let
   them flow in endless praise.
Take my hands, and let them move at
   the impulse of Thy love.
Take my feet, and let them be swift and
   beautiful for Thee.

Take my voice, and let me sing always,
   only, for my King.
Take my lips, and let them be filled
   with messages from Thee.
Take my silver and my gold; not a mite
   would I withhold.
Take my intellect, and use every pow'r
   as Thou shalt choose.

Take my will, and make it Thine; it
   shall be no longer mine.
Take my heart, it is Thine own; it shall
   be Thy royal throne.
Take my love, my Lord, I pour at Thy
   feet its treasure store.
Take myself, and I will be ever, only, all
   for Thee.

The instruction to go without resources and to depend on hospitality was influential in the development of Christian "faith missions," a legacy and example that must be remembered and honored.

Missions History: *From Jerusalem to Irian Jaya*, **by Ruth Tucker.** This book (1983) by Tucker (b. 1945), a missions historian, is wide-ranging in its history of Christian missions. The term "faith missions" was connected with missions that did not have a set income for their missionaries. In fact, some of the missionaries would not solicit funds, relying exclusively for provision on God. But it went even further. Speaking of the Christian Missionary Alliance (1887), Central American Mission (1890), Sudan Interior Mission (1893), and Africa Inland Mission (1895), to name but a few, Tucker says, "These missions were born out of faith, often at great risks and resulting in a high mortality rate among the early faith missionary pioneers." They risked their lives to take the gospel to those who had never heard it. They were motivated "by a vivid picture of hell. For them the purpose of missions was to save lost souls from the eternal torment of hellfire and brimstone." Associated with conservative evangelicalism, many of the recruits had never been to college or were graduates of Christian colleges and Bible institutes, particularly Moody Bible Institute in Chicago. Faith missions spread Christianity; their founders had different methods and traveled to different places, but they all sacrificially stepped out in faith.[3]

If a plowman gets distracted, his furrow will not be straight. Jesus uses this illustration to emphasize that to successfully follow him will require focused concentration and devotion. Plowing techniques and equipment were not much different in Palestine in the early twentieth century, when this photo was taken, than in previous centuries.

Rejecting or Responding to Jesus

Big Idea *How people respond to Jesus and his ministry (and to his disciples' message) determines their spiritual destiny.*

Understanding the Text

The Text in Context

The mission of the seventy-two leads to reflections on the significance of Jesus's ministry and of the mission that he now shares with his followers. As in the earlier account of Jesus's transfiguration, we see again here that the drama being played out on the earthly level also has a supernatural dimension, both in the conflict with and the defeat of Satan (a theme that will be taken up again in 11:14–26) and in the intimate relationship of Jesus the Son of God with his Father. It is a privilege for the disciples to be involved in a game played with such high stakes, but it also puts a sobering onus on everyone to respond in the right way or face the consequences.

Historical and Cultural Background

God's judgment on Sodom (see 10:12) and that predicted by the prophets for the pagan cities of Tyre and Sidon (e.g., Isa. 23; Ezek. 28) were, in the Jewish mind, a potent symbol of the expected fate of those outside God's chosen people. To apply those models to ordinary Jewish towns in Galilee,

even to Jesus's own base of Capernaum, was profoundly shocking.

We have been introduced in 4:1–13 to "the devil" as the personal focus of opposition to the purposes of God. He appears now under what was probably his most common Jewish name, "Satan" (the "enemy" or "accuser"), familiar from Job 1–2, where Satan acts as a disaffected and destructive influence among the "sons of God." In postbiblical Jewish thought Satan (under a variety of names) and his associates (the "fallen angels" or "watchers") were regarded as the source of evil on earth.

Interpretive Insights

10:13 *Chorazin! . . . Bethsaida!* These towns are close to Capernaum. Chorazin had a predominantly Jewish population, as did the original village of Bethsaida, subsequently incorporated into a Hellenistic city by Herod Philip.

the miracles that were performed in you. Apart from one later (secret) healing recorded only by Mark (Mark 8:22–26), we have no records of miracles in these towns, though the feeding miracle in 9:10–17 is apparently located in the countryside near

Bethsaida. Jesus's assertion that both towns had in fact witnessed enough miracles to inspire faith shows how selective the Gospel accounts of Jesus's actual miracles are.

10:15 *And you, Capernaum.* For Jesus's miracles in Capernaum, see 4:23, 31–41. The specific miracle there recorded in 7:1–10 inspired the faith of a Gentile officer rather than that of the Jewish community (7:9). Even this town, so central to Jesus's ministry, is threatened with a fate comparable to that of Babylon (cf. Isa. 14:13–15).

10:16 *whoever rejects you rejects me; . . . him who sent me.* Jesus himself has met with rejection (10:13–15), and his disciples must expect the same (10:10–12). Underlying this delegation of Jesus's authority is the Jewish concept of the *shaliah*, the personal envoy of a king or other dignitary who is to be treated with the same respect as the king himself. The Mishnah states, "A man's agent is as himself" (*m. Ber.* 5:5). But the final clause of the verse extends the idea of delegation to a new level: the disciples' message comes with the authority not only of Jesus but also of God himself. That is

Key Themes of Luke 10:13–24

- There is no excuse for failure to respond to the clear work and word of God.
- Jesus's disciples carry the authority of Jesus himself, and even of God.
- There is a spiritual conflict underlying their earthly ministry.
- The uniqueness of Jesus is revealed in his special relationship with his Father.
- The way to God is through his Son, Jesus.
- To live in the time of the fulfillment of God's purposes is a priceless privilege.

why people's response to their preaching is of ultimate importance.

10:17 *even the demons submit to us in your name.* Jesus gave the Twelve power to cast out demons (9:1), but this has not been mentioned in relation to the seventy-two. Perhaps it was assumed as part of their commission to "heal the sick" (10:9). The delighted report of these latest envoys is in striking contrast to the failure of some of the Twelve in one case of exorcism (9:40). Does the addition here of "in your name" suggest that the earlier attempt had been undertaken with self-confidence rather than recognizing where the authority came from?

Chorazin was located about three miles north of Capernaum, close enough for its residents to have seen or heard or gone to Jesus for healing as he ministered and performed miracles throughout Galilee. This aerial view shows the third- and fourth-century AD reconstructed remains at ancient Chorazin. Earlier-period structures have yet to be found.

10:18 *I saw Satan fall like lightning from heaven.* For this imagery, compare the fall of the "morning star" (Lucifer) in Isaiah 14:12, from the same passage that Jesus alluded to in 10:15. The eviction of Satan and the other "fallen angels" from heaven (often associated with Gen. 6:1–4) became

Jesus tells his disciples to rejoice that their names are written in heaven (10:20). Lists of names were kept for various purposes in the ancient world. This papyrus scroll, written in Greek, contains a list of farmers (AD 196–98).

established in postbiblical Jewish thinking as an explanation for the origin of evil. It is graphically developed in Revelation 12:7–13. But here Jesus attributes that fall to his own ministry of deliverance, exemplified in the exorcistic ministry of his disciples.

10:19 *to trample on snakes and scorpions.* This is probably figurative language that refers to being under supernatural protection (cf. Ps. 91:11–13, quoted in 4:10–11), but it was perhaps taken more literally in the later conclusion added to Mark's Gospel (Mark 16:18).

10:20 *rejoice that your names are written in heaven.* A spirituality that focuses merely on earthly achievement, even if miraculous, has missed the main point of Christian salvation. Compare Matthew 7:21–23, where miracles and exorcisms are no guarantee of salvation. The idea of a heavenly register appears often in biblical and later Jewish literature (e.g., Exod. 32:32; Dan. 12:1; Heb. 12:23; Rev. 3:5).

10:21 *full of joy through the Holy Spirit.* This unusual expression may indicate a state of ecstasy (cf. Rev. 1:10). The mention of the Spirit introduces a trinitarian element to these key verses.

hidden these things from the wise . . . revealed them to little children. This recalls the contrasts of the Magnificat (1:51–53). Paul develops this theme in 1 Corinthians 1:18–31. Spiritual perception does not depend on intellectual capacity or education; indeed, these are more likely to prove a hindrance to the ability to "receive the kingdom of God like a little child" (18:17). As in 8:10, insight comes from special revelation by God, not from natural cleverness. "These things" is left unspecified; the reference is presumably to spiritual truth, especially the message of the kingdom of God.

10:22 *All things have been committed to me by my Father.* Jesus, as the Son of God, stands in a unique position between God and humankind. It is a position of supreme authority (cf. Matt. 28:18), but also a position of mediation. As the Son of God, he stands on the divine side of the human-divine divide, sharing with his Father a mutual knowledge that no one else can share by right. But as the Son of Man, he is also in a position to communicate this knowledge of the Father to other humans (the "little children" of 10:21).

No one knows who the Son is except the Father. It has been suggested that Jesus's statement here is to be taken not as a literal description of Jesus and God but rather as a parable: just as there is perfect mutual understanding between a father and a son, so there is between God and Jesus. It may be questioned whether that would in fact be a true generalization from human experience. But even if it were, the point of such a parable here (where Jesus has just addressed God as "Father") could only be to speak of the relation of Jesus to God, so the meaning would be the same.

10:23 *Blessed are the eyes which see what you see.* The disciples of Jesus have a privilege denied to even the holiest of the saints of Israel, that of being present at the realization of the fulfillment to which the prophets and kings could only look forward. Compare 1 Peter 1:10–12 (where even the angels are keen to get a look in!); Hebrews 11:39–40.

Theological Insights

Luke 10:22 (= Matt. 11:27) is perhaps the highest point in the Synoptic Gospels' presentation of the status of Jesus, the Son of God. Often described as a "Johannine moment," this verse has the same effect as, for instance, John 10:15, "The Father knows me and I know the Father"; John 10:30, "I and the Father are one"; and John 14:6, "I am the way and the truth and the life. No one comes to the Father except through me." Such passages raise acutely the issue of the exclusiveness of Christian salvation and stand firmly against a universalism according to which Jesus is only one among many ways to find God.

That is why it matters very much how people respond to the message of Jesus and his disciples. To reject that message is to forfeit the only means by which we humans can come to the knowledge of God. In the ministry of Jesus this salvation has now been made available to the Jews as God's people; for them to turn away from this ultimate way of salvation, now that it has been revealed in Jesus, is even more disastrous than the paganism of Sodom, Tyre, and Sidon and incurs an even more severe judgment.

But alongside the "wise and learned," who think that they know better than God, we see the disciples as the "little children," privileged to receive this ultimate message of salvation and commissioned to proclaim it to those around them with the authority not only of Jesus but also of God himself. There is thus an inevitable chiaroscuro, a blending of light and dark, in the coming of salvation to a world that is divided on the basis of how people respond to Jesus.

Teaching the Text

Three possible approaches for teaching this passage may be suggested:

1. *The authority and privilege of disciples*. Consider what 10:16, 17–20, 23–24 teach about the situation of disciples, with regard both to their own spiritual position and to their mission. How much of this applies specifically to the seventy-two, and how much to all disciples in all periods? Do these verses provide appropriate guidelines for mission in our modern society? Are there principles here that it would be inappropriate to try to put into modern practice? This passage can provide an opportunity for the teacher to show how we draw general principles from Scripture. Though these specific commands were given to the seventy-two, what can we learn here about the nature of God and our role as his servant sent out with his commission?

2. *The uniqueness of Jesus as the Son of God*. This passage, more than any other in Luke's Gospel, demonstrates the uniqueness of Jesus and the intimacy of his relationship with the Father. Encourage listeners to suppose themselves in debate with, say, a Muslim (or whatever group is most relevant in your context). How might 10:22 contribute to the debate? What objections should they expect to face? Is it still possible in this relativistic age to argue for the exclusiveness of the Christian way of salvation? How can such an argument be supported?

3. *The expectation of judgment*. What is meant by the judgment language of 10:13–15 (and of 10:12)? How might Jesus's condemnation of Chorazin, Bethsaida, and Capernaum be applied to our modern context? Can we still credibly use such language? You might challenge your audience by replacing the names of these towns with contemporary examples. Be careful in your selection. Notice that Jesus doesn't choose the great and decadent metropolitan centers of his day, but the "insider" villages that have heard his teaching and experienced his miraculous works.

You might also consider the question of whether judgment today may be more severe for some than for others, and if so, on what basis? How does the exclusive claim of 10:22 relate to those earlier verses?

Illustrating the Text

The seventy-two are to rejoice, not in the extraordinary powers passed on to them, but instead in the giver of that power and in their own eternal destiny.

Commentary: *Expositions of Holy Scripture: Luke I to XII*, by Alexander Maclaren. Maclaren (1826–1910), a renowned Scottish Baptist preacher and expositor, comments wisely about this principle, noting that "all personal service should be preceded by intense realization of the immense field and of the inadequacy of Christian effort, which vision will culminate in prayer for more toilers to be 'sent forth.'" Further, he says that the seventy-two returned with "a childish, surprised joy, and almost seem to have thought that Jesus would be as much astonished and excited as they were with the proof of the power of His name." Maclaren notes that "the contest between the personal Source of evil and Jesus was fought out by the principals, not by their subordinates, and it is already victoriously decided in Christ's sight." He concludes that what Jesus is saying is that "gifts and powers are good, and may legitimately be rejoiced in; but to possess eternal life . . . is better than all gifts and powers."[1]

The relationship of George MacDonald (shown here) with his earthly father helped him to understand the relationship of Jesus and God the Father.

There is no relationship as mutually empathic and as profound as the one between the Father and the Son.

Biography: George MacDonald. A gifted author of adult and children's novels, a poet, a literary critic, a creative theologian, and a beloved pastor, MacDonald (1824–1905) was held in high esteem by many luminaries in the literary world, including C. S. Lewis, who wrote, "I have never concealed the fact that I regarded him as my master; indeed I fancy I have never written a book in which I did not quote from him."[2] Lewis says that MacDonald had "an almost perfect relationship with his father" that was "the earthly root of all his wisdom."[3] From his father, Lewis adds, MacDonald "first learned that Fatherhood must be at the core of the universe," and this prepared him "in an unusual way to teach that religion in which the relation of the Father and Son is of all relations the most central."[4] While nothing on earth can adequately illustrate the relationship between the divine Father and Son, this human example certainly points toward its texture, dimension, and depth.

"Love Your Neighbor"

Big Idea *There are no limits to the disciple's duty to love other people, even the most unlikely.*

Understanding the Text

The Text in Context

On Jesus's journey to Jerusalem, which began in 9:51, much attention is focused on the nature and demands of discipleship. Here a question from someone outside the disciple group prompts Jesus to illustrate the central demand of discipleship by telling one of his best-loved parables. The famous "summary of the law" in the twofold demand to love God and to love one's neighbor occurs in all three Synoptic Gospels, but Luke's presentation of it is distinctive in two ways: first, it is the questioner, not Jesus, who first offers the summary; second, Jesus provides extensive comment on it in the form of the parable of the good Samaritan. The recent hostile reception of Jesus and his disciples by a Samaritan village (9:51–56) provides a telling backdrop to a parable that depends for its effect on the enmity between Jews and Samaritans.

Historical and Cultural Background

The mutual hostility between Jews and Samaritans goes back to the separation of Israel into the two kingdoms of Israel and Judah after the death of Solomon. It reached a peak in the attempts of the Samaritans to prevent the reestablishment of the kingdom of Judah under Ezra and Nehemiah. The separate Samaritan temple on Mount Gerizim was destroyed by the Jewish king Hyrcanus in the second century BC, and Samaritans had desecrated the Jerusalem temple during Jesus's boyhood. For the continuing standoff, see John 4:9. Luke's Gospel is remarkable in that both here and in 17:11–19 a Samaritan is favorably contrasted with Jews (compare Matt. 10:5, where that Gospel's only reference to Samaritans is wholly negative).

Rabbinic writings contain a number of attempts to summarize the demands of the 613 commandments of the Mosaic law in a few key texts (especially *b. Mak.* 24a, where surprisingly the chosen texts are not from the Torah itself, as here, but from the psalms and the prophets), but only Jesus (and his questioner here) seems to have brought together Deuteronomy 6:5 ("Love the LORD your God") and Leviticus 19:18 ("Love your neighbor as yourself") for this purpose.

Interpretive Insights

10:25 *an expert in the law.* This is perhaps a more highly trained professional than the normal scribes (NIV: "teachers of the law"), but the terms may be merely synonymous (see on 11:37–54). The question is probing ("to test Jesus") but not overtly hostile, and Jesus's acceptance of the lawyer's answer suggests a more positive rapport than in most such encounters.

what must I do to inherit eternal life? An identical question will be asked by the rich ruler in 18:18 (and will receive a similarly searching and pragmatic response). The actual phrase "eternal life" occurs elsewhere in Luke only in 18:30, but it goes to the heart of Jesus's message of salvation. This is not a legal nicety; it is a fundamental spiritual issue.

10:27 *Love the Lord your God . . . Love your neighbor as yourself.* Deuteronomy 6:5 was very familiar as part of the Shema, recited twice daily as a sort of creed by all pious Jews; it is its combination with Leviticus 19:18 that produces a potent new manifesto for godly living. The lawyer had asked for something to "do." His choice of texts does indeed provide a central ethical principle, but it goes far beyond mere ethics by prescribing the relationship with God that underlies all godly behavior. It is remarkable that Luke allows the lawyer, rather than Jesus himself (as in Matthew and Mark), to utter this innovative and far-reaching summary of the law.

10:28 *Do this and you will live.* Is eternal life therefore to be "earned" by how we behave? But to love God with all your heart, soul, strength, and mind is much more than adopting a code of behavior; it is a spiritual relationship that affects all aspects of our life.

10:29 *who is my neighbor?* The questioner, however, focuses only on the second,

more directly ethical, principle. As a lawyer, he wants his obligations spelled out with the limits clearly defined. In the Old Testament "neighbor" usually means a member of one's own community, a fellow Israelite (extended in Lev. 19:33–34 to include foreigners resident within Israel), and it was assumed that the same standards need not be applied to one's relations with people outside the community (cf. Matt. 5:43–47). So exactly who is it that I am commanded to love? Jesus has already given a provocative answer to this question in 6:27–36; now he puts it in the form of a story.

10:30 *A man was going down from Jerusalem to Jericho.* This steep descent of some seventeen miles through a desolate rocky area, connecting two wealthy cities, offered ample opportunity for bandits. The audience would assume that the unidentified traveler in this area is Jewish.

10:31 *A priest . . . passed by on the other side.* Coming away from the temple in a state of ritual purity, the priest perhaps was concerned to avoid contracting impurity by contact with what looked like (or might soon become) a dead body. In any case, it is always safer not to involve oneself in another person's problems—and besides, the bandits might still be lurking nearby.

10:32 *So too, a Levite.* This person is a temple helper, thus a lesser personage than a priest, but also perhaps concerned with ritual purity. Both priest and Levite represent the pious elite from whom exemplary behavior might be expected.

10:33 *But a Samaritan.* A Jewish audience, having heard Jesus poke fun at the religious professionals, would expect the next character to be a Jewish layman or local rabbi, whose more humane response would put the priest and the Levite to shame. That might have provoked an irreverent chuckle. The introduction instead of a Samaritan, far outside his own territory, was as deliberately shocking as if a Southern preacher before the Civil War had set up a black hero to shame the pillars of white society.

10:34 *brought him to an inn and took care of him.* A Samaritan had good reason to be cautious of the reception that he might meet in a Jewish inn (presumably in Jericho), but this traveler's evident familiarity with the innkeeper (10:35) suggests that he was a regular visitor whose wealth no doubt outweighed his dubious racial origin. Even so, he was a brave man, since to turn up with a badly wounded Jew thrown across his donkey was to invite dangerous misunderstanding.

10:35 *he took out two denarii.* This is about two days' wages (cf. Matt. 20:2), enough to pay for a few days in the fairly basic accommodation at the inn. But the traveler's care extends even to the possibility that a longer stay might be needed. His "compassion" (10:33) is not just impulsive; it is practical and thought through.

10:36 *Which . . . was a neighbor to the man?* In Leviticus 19:18 the "neighbor" is the one to be loved, and in that sense the "neighbor" in the story should be the wounded man. But Jesus sees the neighborly

The setting of Jesus's parable of the good Samaritan is the road from Jerusalem to Jericho. It was a seventeen-mile journey through the desolate Judean wilderness. Travelers went down to Jericho because the elevation drops approximately 3,300 feet. This photograph shows the rocky, barren wilderness through which the road passes.

relation as reciprocal. A Jewish audience would regard it as particularly humiliating to receive such extravagant love from a Samaritan, of all people, so that Jesus's concept of neighborliness goes far beyond a patronizing benevolence shown by the chosen people to those less fortunate.

10:37 *The one who had mercy on him.* Did the lawyer find the word "Samaritan" too uncomfortable to say directly? His words read literally, "the one who did the mercy with him," an unusual expression that draws out the essentially practical nature of "mercy" (the priest and Levite may have *felt* pity, but they did nothing) and leads directly into the powerful application: "Go and *do* likewise."

Theological Insights

Jesus's debates with religious leaders are usually hostile, but here we see him in essential agreement with a legal expert. This summary of the law, offered by the lawyer and approved by Jesus, could hardly be faulted (see the admiring response of the scribe in Mark 12:32–33). It is not in his basic understanding of the law that Jesus was out on a limb, but in the radical comprehensiveness of the way he applied it. This parable subverts not the ethical demand of the law, but the Jewish sense of ethnic superiority.

The two chosen texts (Deut. 6:5 and Lev. 19:18) suitably sum up the two main aspects of religious duty, as expressed in the two "tables" of the Decalogue, one's duty to God and one's duty to other people. For other New Testament statements of the primary importance of love in fulfilling the law, see Romans 13:8–10; Galatians 5:14; James 2:8 (all of which focus on Lev. 19:18), and compare Jesus's own summary in Matthew 7:12.

The parable of the good Samaritan, however, is not primarily a call to universal benevolence; rather, it is a challenge to social and ethnic stereotyping. For a Jew to be kind to a Samaritan might be unnatural, but such an act could afford a smug sense of superior goodness. But to be the recipient of unconditional love *from* a Samaritan would take a typical Jew far outside the comfort zone, since it challenges the very basis of Jewish identity as the true people of God. This parable, properly understood, is one of the most powerful challenges to racism in the Bible.

The expert in the law answers his own question to Jesus by quoting from the Shema and adding Leviticus 19:18. The Community Rule of the Dead Sea Scrolls and later the Mishnah record that the Shema (Deut. 6:4–9) was recited twice daily. It was also during this time that the practice of wearing phylacteries seems to have begun. The Shema is one of the biblical passages that is housed in phylacteries. These small boxes are held in place on the head and arm by leather straps like the ones worn by this Jewish man at the Western Wall in Jerusalem. Although there is still much discussion about the ancient practice of wearing phylacteries, today observant male Jews starting at age thirteen don them during morning prayer services.

Teaching the Text

Ask most people what the name "Samaritan" suggests, and you will probably get an answer about going out of your way to help people in need. Samaritans are by definition "good." That is precisely the opposite of what Jesus's original audience would have thought, and it is important to communicate the hostility that the term would arouse in a Jewish audience. The parable *is*, of course, a fine example of helping someone in need, but that is not its main point, and the teacher should aim to expand the listeners' awareness of its message. For this, it is important to read it in its context, as the answer to the lawyer's question, "And who is my neighbor?" Try to identify an analogous group or ethnicity that would provoke a similar response for your audience. Some possibilities include an avowed atheist, a Mormon missionary, or a radical Islamist.

It would be easy to let the parable dominate the discussion, but loving one's neighbor is only the second part of the love command in 10:27. Consider what it means to "love God." How does this work out in relation to the four aspects of human life listed: "heart," "soul," "strength," and "mind." And what are the implications of loving your neighbor "as yourself"? Is Luke 6:31 relevant? Can the way we use the word "love" in our modern climate of thought become a hindrance to grasping the full implications of the dual love command?

The congregation or group could be invited to consider how far Jesus's story reflects the nature of his own mission as

The Good Samaritan, 1633 (etching), by Rembrandt Harmenszoon van Rijn (1606–69), depicts the Samaritan leading the injured man to the inn. With the inclusion of the woman at the well and the dog, the image depicts the story against the backdrop of ordinary life.

Savior, coming to a lost and helpless world that has rejected him.

Illustrating the Text

Believers are called upon to show compassion to anyone who is in need.

Autobiography: *Radiance in the Gulag,* **by Nijole Sudanaite.** Sister Sudanaite, a Lithuanian Catholic, was arrested by the KGB for her work. This book, often compared to *The Diary of Anne Frank*, is her account of her arrest and exile in a Siberian labor camp, where she endured endless indignities and deprivations. Despite the hardship, her spirit remained strong and resolute, and she continually gave testimony to the God she believed in. While in the labor camps, people who knew her situation sent her care packages. In the camp, prisoners had to pay for many things out of their very limited wages, including housing and even to receive packages. Nevertheless, Nijole paid the fee, repackaged the things she received, and sent them to other Christians she perceived were suffering more than she was. As a believer in terrible circumstances she was still finding a way to show compassion to those in need.

Commentary: *Preaching the Parables: From Responsible Interpretation to Powerful Proclamation*, by Craig L. Blomberg. Blomberg writes,

> Obviously there is an example here that we are supposed to imitate. . . . But do *what* likewise? Jesus could hardly expect twenty-first-century Americans to find a donkey, secure some oil and wine, look for every needy person, transport them to the local innkeeper, and pay him with two silver coins. We have to ask what a contemporization, what a modern equivalent to this passage might look like.

He goes on to say that the first thing that comes to mind is helping someone whose car has broken down on the road. However, he also notes that he has no mechanical ability. Then he tells about the time when he and a friend were driving on a snow-packed road in Yellowstone Park, and their car spun off the road into a ditch. A man with a truck came along and hauled them back onto the road. "The road that Jesus describes," he writes, "was probably far more like that semi-isolated, snow-packed, slippery road in Yellowstone" than the streets and roads that he drives on most of the time. However, finally, what is crucial, he says, is that our attitude, no matter what a person's need, be like that of the Samaritan—full of compassion. We must not become calloused.[1]

Lessons on Devotion and Prayer

Big Idea *It is our personal relationship with God that should take priority in our lives; those who know God as Father can pray to him with full confidence.*

Understanding the Text

The Text in Context

Prayer, and especially Jesus's practice of prayer, is a prominent theme for Luke. He has portrayed Jesus at prayer already in 3:21; 5:16; 6:12; 9:18, 28–29, indicating that this was an important part of his way of life. Those passages record the fact of Jesus's frequent prayer rather than its content. But in 10:21–22 we have heard Jesus in prayer to his Father, and we have been told of the intimate relationship shared by the Father and the Son. The disciples have become aware of this special relationship expressed in Jesus's prayers, and they want to share it. Remarkably, without compromising the uniqueness of that relationship, Jesus now encourages them also to address God as Father and to draw on that relationship in what they pray for.

The story of Martha and Mary takes up the theme of the women who followed and provided for Jesus (8:1–3). While it does not refer to prayer to God, Mary's personal devotion to Jesus perhaps foreshadows what later becomes a central element in Christian prayer and devotion.

Historical and Cultural Background

Set forms of prayer were familiar among Jews at the time of Jesus, both in the synagogue service and in the recitation of the Shema (see on 10:27). An Aramaic synagogue prayer or doxology known as the Qaddish begins with the clause "Exalted and hallowed be his great name" and continues "May he let his kingdom rule . . . speedily and soon." The prayer that Jesus here teaches his disciples (a longer version of which appears in Matt. 6:9–13) would thus have had a familiar ring, though the Qaddish had no parallel to the petitionary second half of the prayer. There are, however, further parallels between the Lord's Prayer and the Eighteen Benedictions of the synagogue liturgy.[1]

Jewish thought had adopted from the Old Testament the idea that God is the Father of his people, but to approach him in prayer simply as "Father" (Aramaic "*Abba*," a familiar but respectful form of address) is less clearly evidenced in surviving Jewish records and apparently is a distinctive innovation by Jesus that became a treasured spiritual privilege among the early Christians (Rom. 8:15; Gal. 4:6).

Interpretive Insights

10:38 *a village where a woman named Martha opened her home to him.* According to John 11:1, the village was Bethany, just outside Jerusalem, and Jesus was already a friend of the family, known to them as "the Teacher" (John 11:28). Jesus and his disciples regularly depended on the hospitality of friends and well-wishers as they traveled (see Luke 8:1–3). Luke does not name the village. If he knows it was Bethany (near the end point of the journey that began in 9:51 and ends in chap. 19), he has placed this incident here, out of chronological order, for its contribution to the overall portrayal of discipleship.

10:39 *Mary, who sat at the Lord's feet, listening.* The Twelve were males, but here is a woman who fully fits the pattern of a disciple. Jewish society would not expect a woman to be so privileged, and neither did Martha!

Key Themes of Luke 10:38–11:13

- Two of Jesus's women disciples provide contrasting examples of devotion.
- Spiritual understanding takes priority over practical service.
- The Lord's Prayer is a model for a right balance in our prayers.
- We should pray with confidence, knowing that God is not reluctant to respond.
- Our heavenly Father will give us what is good for us.

10:40 *Lord, don't you care?* This displays the natural frustration of a busy woman who sees her sister "shirking," and she blames Jesus for encouraging her. Presumably, she has no objection to listening to "the Teacher" in itself; it is a matter of priorities.

10:42 *but few things are needed—or indeed only one.* Most English versions (including the earlier NIV) follow those manuscripts that read simply "but only one thing is needed," a more direct contrast with the "many things" (many chores or many items for the meal?) that Martha was busy with. On the latest NIV reading,[2] however, Jesus apparently asks for a simpler meal ("few things") rather than the more elaborate hospitality that Martha feels obliged to offer, and then he changes the subject by focusing on the "one thing" (listening to the word of God) that Mary has chosen. On either reading there is a

Martha opens her home to Jesus in 10:38, and Jesus tells a parable about prayer using the setting of a house locked up at night (11:5–8). Jewish village homes of the first century were typically single rooms where mats were rolled out for sleeping on the floor at night and put away to make space for daytime activities. Cooking may have been done inside or in the courtyard. Martha may have been tending to preparations both outside and inside the house while Mary sat at the feet of Jesus. Shown here is the interior of a first-century AD home in the Palestinian village of Taybeh.

deliberate word play on what is "needed" for the meal and what is spiritually most necessary.

Mary has chosen what is better. Spiritual food takes priority over physical food. Martha's desire to provide the best hospitality was not wrong in itself, but she had her priorities wrong.

11:1 *teach us to pray, just as John taught his disciples.* Here is one of several incidental indications of a continuing group of followers of John the Baptist, seen as an uneasy parallel to the Jesus movement (cf. 5:33; 7:18–23). John had taught his disciples to fast and pray often (5:33), but we are not told what form those prayers took. Note that the prayer that Jesus teaches is for disciples to use corporately ("Give *us* . . . forgive *us* . . . lead *us* . . .") rather than in individual devotion.

11:2 *When you pray, say.* This suggests a set form of words, but Matthew's equivalent introduction, "This is how you should pray," may indicate more a pattern of prayer than a set formula. The fact that the wording of the two versions differs indicates that the formulation was not rigid. In practice, Christian devotion has always found a place both for the verbatim repetition of the Lord's Prayer (in whichever version) and for its use as a template for more extended prayer.

Father, hallowed be your name, your kingdom come. On "Father," see "Historical and Cultural Background" above. This first part of the prayer (which closely resembles the Qaddish [see above]) focuses on God, before 11:3–4 addresses *our* needs. The additional third clause in the Matthean version ("Your will be done" [Matt. 6:10]) does not differ significantly from the coming of God's kingship—that is, his effective rule over human society. This whole first section is, quite simply, a prayer that God be God, and that he be seen and honored as such on earth.

11:3 *Give us each day our daily bread.* "Daily" represents a Greek word, *epiousios* (a term apparently coined by the Gospel writers to translate Jesus's Aramaic), that probably derives from a phrase meaning "for the coming day." On that basis some have argued that this is a prayer not for everyday sustenance, but for provision for the future (eschatological) "day of the Lord." But Luke's very precise phrase "each day" and the tense of the verb, which implies "keep on giving," make that view unlikely. The believer here recognizes that daily survival depends on God's gracious provision. We live, under his care, one day at a time (cf. the provision of manna in Exod. 16:4).

11:4 *Forgive us . . . for we also forgive.* Physical need is balanced by spiritual need, and we are as dependent on our Father for the one as for the other. The parallel between God's forgiving and ours may suggest that our forgiveness is "earned" by forgiving others, but the rest of Luke's Gospel (notably in the parable of the lost son [15:11–32]) emphasizes that forgiveness is by grace, not by merit. The point is rather that there is a fundamental insincerity in asking for forgiveness if we refuse also to forgive; the Father's grace should be mirrored, however inadequately, by his children.

everyone who sins against us. This is literally "everyone indebted to us," but the use of this metaphor in the second clause can hardly indicate a different sort of "forgiveness" (the verb is the same), since in the Matthean version the debt metaphor is used in both clauses.

lead us not into temptation. "Temptation" and "testing" represent the same word in Greek (see on 4:2), and the latter is perhaps the primary sense here, since God does not *tempt* anyone (see James 1:13–14). A weaker sense of "lead us not" is possible: "do not let us be tempted" (cf. 22:40, 46), envisaging an experience that, like that of Jesus, is both (negative) temptation and (positive) testing. Disciples, aware of their human weakness, naturally pray to be spared such an ordeal if possible. Luke's version of the prayer omits the balancing "worst-case scenario," appealing for rescue when things do get the better of us (cf. Matt. 6:13b).

11:5–8 *Suppose you have a friend.* This homely parable teaches that it is not a waste of time to ask God for what you need. If even a reluctant neighbor can be prevailed upon to help, how much more so we can count on help from God, who both knows and wants what is best for his people. Compare the similar parable of the persistent widow (18:1–8).

11:9–10 *Ask . . . seek . . . knock.* This explains the point of the parable. The present imperatives probably indicate repeated asking, seeking, and knocking. We should keep on praying with confidence that God will respond. This is the practical reality of our experience of petitionary prayer; the philosophical puzzle of why we need to ask at all if God already knows and cares is simply not raised.

11:11–13 *you fathers . . . know how to give good gifts to your children.* Jesus now draws on the opening word of the prayer, "Father," to encourage our confidence in prayer. Even human fathers, who are, by comparison, "evil," do good not harm to their children. The snake and scorpion, which might be superficially mistaken for a fish and an egg (the scorpion can roll itself into a protective ball), are symbols of evil (10:19).

give the Holy Spirit to those who ask him. Whereas Luke speaks of the Father giving the "Holy Spirit," Matthew's version uses the more obvious term "good gifts" (Matt. 7:11). Luke perhaps thinks of the Holy Spirit as the source of all that is good rather than envisaging a specific petition to be "given" the Holy Spirit (an idea that has no parallel in Luke's Gospel before 24:49, though it might anticipate what he will record in, e.g., Acts 1:4; 2:1–4).

Theological Insights

The story of Martha and Mary is one of the most prominent examples of Luke's concern to emphasize the role of women among Jesus's disciples. If 8:1–3 might have suggested that their sole function is to look after the material needs of Jesus and the disciples, Mary represents a less

Would a father give his son a scorpion if he was asked for an egg? Of course not! Even imperfect, sinful earthly fathers usually do not want to bring harm to their children. Shown here is a scorpion, with its venomous stinger at the end of its tail.

mundane calling; she is a disciple in the fullest sense, and she is a model for men as well as women.

In 11:1–13 the twin themes of prayer and of the fatherhood of God are brought together and are shown to be inseparable. Prayer that is merely a religious routine has missed the point. Prayer arises out of and expresses the confidence of those who know God as Father and therefore can rely on his loving care. It is not a "shopping list" of demands that need to be pressed on a reluctant deity. We persist in prayer not because we need to persuade God but in order to foster that relationship of dependent trust.

Teaching the Text

These two passages share the common theme of devotion to God, demonstrated through discipleship (10:38–42) and prayer (11:1–13), and so may be profitably taught together. They are distinct and important enough individually, however, that most will want to teach them independently.

1. *Martha and Mary*. Many will sympathize with Martha. So encourage listeners to consider or discuss Jesus's apparently one-sided response. What does it do to our sense of fairness? Why was Mary's choice "better"? Does

this mean that the many Marthas in the church are second-class disciples? Is it relevant to apply this passage to the question of differing vocations? How do we guard against the twin dangers of mere activism versus being so heavenly minded as to be of no earthly use?

Although the importance of discipleship and the priority and privilege of sitting at Jesus's feet as a learner are the primary points that ought to be developed in a lesson or sermon, Jesus's countercultural approach to women is also worth discussing. As throughout the Gospel of Luke, Jesus lifts up and treats as equals those who occupy the lower ("outsider") positions of society (the poor, the sick, lepers, tax-collectors, sinners, prostitutes, Samaritans, women, children, etc.).

2. *Prayer*. Every clause of the Lord's Prayer is a potential basis for teaching. The teacher may use it that way, encouraging listeners to consider what aspects of prayer each clause illustrates. But it is important also to see both the balance of the prayer as a whole and the importance of the focus on God as being prior to the focus on our needs. The first two petitions concern God's glory and kingdom, not our needs. And the whole thing needs to be set within the theme of God as our Father in heaven, which is illustrated especially in 11:9–13.

Jesus teaches his disciples to pray, using what has come to be known as the Lord's Prayer (11:2–4) as a model for the right balance in our prayers. The courtyard and cloister of the Pater Noster Church on the Mount of Olives in Jerusalem contains ceramic plaques on which the text of the Lord's Prayer is written in 140 different languages.

Another theme that could be considered and discussed is that of persistence in prayer. If God already knows and cares, what would be lost if we did not go on asking, seeking, and knocking?

Illustrating the Text

Let Jesus work on your heart before you work your heart out for Jesus.

Personal Testimony: Invite a "Martha" or two to share their testimonies of how their service to the Lord became more than just keeping busy or working hard. Have them tell about how they came to a "Mary moment" in which Jesus transformed their heart and freed them from keeping score, comparing to others, and feeling used when serving in church. The key here is to find a volunteer or staff member who is known for excellence *and* a great attitude. You want a testimony that shows how love absorbed while sitting at Jesus's feet frees them to scrub dishes joyfully and willingly. The illustration is to show that Mary and Martha need not represent irreconcilable tribes—they can be united within the same heart, as long as the Mary moments come first.

Prayer is not merely about airing a shopping list of needs and desires; it is an expression of childlike trust and gratitude.

Theological Reference: One sixteenth-century confession of the Protestant Reformation (the Heidelberg Catechism, question 116) declares that prayer is actually "the chief part of the gratitude which God requires of us." What this statement means is that in God's eyes, prayer is not really a matter of his creatures' narcissistic begging for selfish desires. The mere act of asking God for anything expresses faith and gratitude that pleases him in and of itself. When we pray, we are acting on a faith that declares that (1) God exists and is listening, (2) he is good, and (3) he can be trusted to answer generously and wisely now as he has in the past. Praying is thanking, then, regardless of the petitions being expressed.

The Lord's Prayer is not just a rote prayer—it is a template and teaching resource that can expand our heart's vocabulary and experience of conversation with God.

Theological Resources: Throughout the history of the church, the Lord's Prayer has been used as a model for praying and a pattern for teaching important aspects of prayer. Make use of it and teach your people to pray the pattern Jesus taught his disciples, not just a rote repetition of the Our Father. This could be in the form of a message series, Sunday school class, or handout. If your theological tradition has a teaching tool to help you flesh out the truth contained in the Lord's prayer, such as a catechism or classic teaching, this would be a key opportunity to draw on such a resource. One possibility would be to explore this truth using the Heidelberg Catechism's teachings on the Lord's Prayer (questions 116–129). If you are not familiar with its breakdown and explanation of the petitions in the Lord's Prayer, it may be worth your time to check it out.

Negative Responses to Jesus

Big Idea *Jesus has come not to collude with Satan but rather to confront and dispossess him. Jesus is far greater than any prophets or kings who have come before, bringing the light that we now must shine to the world.*

Understanding the Text

The Text in Context

There have been indications throughout Jesus's ministry in Galilee that not everyone is favorably impressed by him. Now the opposition is focused in two specific lines of attack (11:15–16). The first concerns his deliverance of those who were demon-possessed, a major theme of Luke's account of Jesus's ministry so far (see 4:31–37, 41; 6:18; 7:21; 8:2, 26–39; 9:37–43). An attempt to turn his exorcisms against him now leads to a "debate" in which the underlying spiritual significance of this ministry is explored. Jesus is not merely a successful village preacher and healer; he is God's agent in the decisive overthrow of the power of evil.

The second line of attack concerns Jesus's authority to present himself as God's messenger; they want a "sign from heaven." While refusing to give such a convenient "sign," Jesus's appeal to Old Testament precedent here adds a further significant dimension to his claim to a unique authority.

A cryptic comment on "light" is added, perhaps in contrast to the failure of Jesus's

contemporaries to embrace the light of God's truth, which he has brought.

Historical and Cultural Background

For demon possession, see "Historical and Cultural Background" on 4:31–44. It was believed that all these lesser demons were under the authority of the chief demon, whom we have met already as "the devil" (4:2–13) and as "Satan" (10:18). The name "Beelzebul" as an appellation for Satan appears in the Synoptic Gospels as well as in the pseudepigraphic *Testament of Solomon* (first to third century AD?), where he is referred to as the "ruler of demons" (3:1–6; 4:2; 6:1–8). In biblical thought Satan is a malevolent power, but never on a level of authority equal to God.

Interpretive Insights

11:14 *Jesus was driving out a demon that was mute.* The focus of attention in this passage is not on the actual exorcism but rather on the controversy for which it provides the spark. The demon is described as "mute" because that is how the possessed man was affected.

11:15 *Beelzebul, the prince of demons.* This name derives from the Canaanite term "Baal" ("lord")—perhaps "lord of the height" or "lord of the house." A pagan god Baal-zebub ("lord of flies") is mentioned in 2 Kings 1:2–16; hence the corruption of this name to "Beelzebub" in the Latin and Syriac versions.

11:18 *If Satan is divided against himself, how can his kingdom stand?* This is a commonsense argument: the idea of the devil driving out his own subordinates is ridiculous. On the devil as "the ruler of this world," see on 4:6; he is envisaged as exercising his rule through the lesser demons who possess people.

11:19 *by whom do your followers drive them out?* Exorcism was an accepted practice in Jewish circles. Jesus assumes that those other exorcists operated by the power of God. But in 9:49–50 Jesus has also implicitly approved the use of his own name by an exorcist outside the disciple group. For others, see Acts 19:13–16.

11:20 *the finger of God.* In Exodus 8:19 this vivid expression is used for the miraculous power available to Aaron, which the Egyptian magicians could not match. Jesus's exorcisms, by a simple command rather than using elaborate incantations and ritual, are likewise evidence of a superior authority.

the kingdom of God has come upon you. The destruction of Satan's "kingdom" (11:18) demonstrates that God's kingship is already in force (see on 10:9). The verb used here often has the sense of taking someone by surprise: it is a reality even though people have not yet recognized it.

11:21–22 *a strong man, fully armed.* This is an image for Satan, whose "possessions" Jesus is plundering through his exorcisms. However real Satan's continuing power, he is no match for God, operating through his Son.

11:23 *Whoever is not with me is against me.* Here we have the obverse of the comment in 9:50: "Whoever is not against you is for you." Both are in contexts relating to exorcism, the more positive declaration relating to a benign, if unaffiliated,

Jesus describes himself as overpowering Satan, using the image of Satan as "a strong man, fully armed" who has his protective armor taken away by someone stronger. This relief shows a well-armed Roman soldier carrying a spear, sword, and shield (second century AD).

exorcist, while this more negative version refers to those who attribute Jesus's own exorcisms to demonic power. Both exclude any middle ground; Jesus leaves no scope for neutrality.

11:24–26 *When an impure spirit comes out of a person.* This cautionary tale humorously depicts a demon as having human feelings. It is perhaps intended as a warning against half-measures. It is not enough to get rid of evil; it must be replaced by good. There is perhaps also (in the light of 11:19) a warning against exorcisms that do not lead to faith. For the "seven other spirits," compare 8:2.

11:27–28 *Blessed is the mother who gave you birth.* This is an impulsive comment by an enthusiastic supporter rather than a thought-out theological declaration about Mary (cf. 1:42, 45, 48). Jesus's deflating response recalls 8:21 (see comment there). Family pride is subordinated to the demands of true discipleship.

11:29 *It asks for a sign.* The second of the hostile approaches mentioned in 11:15–16 was the demand for "a sign from heaven." The Old Testament is familiar with the idea of miraculous events to authenticate prophetic utterances (e.g., Exod. 4:1–9; 1 Kings 18:36–39; Isa. 7:10–14; 38:7–8), though such signs alone are no guarantee (see Deut. 13:1–3). Such "signs" continued to be claimed by "prophets" in Jesus's day (see, e.g., Josephus, *Ant.* 20.97, 168, 170). But in view of all the miracles already recorded in Luke's Gospel, it is not obvious what more they wanted (as Jesus will point out in 12:54–56), and the demand looks more like an excuse for not responding to Jesus's message. Hence he describes

them as a "wicked generation" and refuses to give the sort of sign that they asked for.

except the sign of Jonah. Matthew 12:40 spells out the sign of Jonah as a reference to Jesus's resurrection (which, being still future, provided no sign yet for the people who were now asking). Jonah's miraculous deliverance from drowning was (and still is) the most memorable element in his story, and while this happened before Jonah went to Nineveh, Jewish readers generally assumed that the people of Nineveh knew about it, and that this influenced their response. There is no other obvious way in which "Jonah was a *sign* to the Ninevites." The alternative suggestion that Luke saw Jonah's preaching itself as the "sign" not only drives an unnecessary wedge between Luke and Matthew, but also makes it hard to explain why Luke (unlike Matthew) seems to have deliberately separated off the reference to Jonah's preaching and its effect (11:32) by first speaking of the Queen of Sheba. The "sign" that Jesus speaks of is still future (notice "*will* be" in 11:30).[1]

11:31 *The Queen of the South.* This is the Queen of Sheba, whose story in 1 Kings 10:1–13, like that of Jonah and the Ninevites, shows a Gentile responding to the word of the God of Israel, received through his chosen spokesman. She came to "test" Solomon (cf. 11:16 here), but unlike Jesus's opponents, she was willing to be convinced. The response of these pagans sets in unflattering relief the failure of Jesus's Jewish contemporaries to recognize God's messenger.

11:31–32 *something greater than Solomon . . . greater than Jonah is here.* The repeated formula asserts that Jesus is not merely on a par with the greatest of God's

Old Testament representatives; his coming brings "something greater." Jonah the prophet and Solomon the king (son of David) and sage represent (together with the priesthood and temple, to which the same formula is applied in Matt. 12:6) the principal means by which God communicated with and governed his people in Old Testament times; but in Jesus, God's kingship has come to his people in a new and decisive way, which supersedes all these Old Testament roles. Such a claim goes far beyond their request for a "sign."

11:33–36 *See to it, then, that the light within you is not darkness.* This little complex of sayings about light, with parallels in different contexts in Mark 4:21 (= Luke 8:16 [see above]); Matthew 5:15; 6:22–23, is difficult to interpret. In this context it probably reflects on the response of Jesus's contemporaries to the "light" that his ministry has now openly revealed (the "something greater" of 11:31–32?). The main point seems to be a warning against ignoring or distorting that light. Those who wish to please God must be fully open to his truth and guidance, and not all Jesus's hearers had proved to be so. But the details are less obvious. It is not clear how the eye functions as the "lamp of the body" (by letting in light from outside? by guiding the body's movement? by somehow itself providing light?), and there is a further word play in the idea of the eye being either

"healthy" or "unhealthy," literally "single" and "bad" (the same word as for the "wicked" generation in 11:29)—words that in another context (as in Matt. 6:22–23) can imply "generous" or "stingy."[2]

Theological Insights

Jesus's responses to the two hostile approaches (11:15–16) together serve to establish his unique significance in the fulfillment of God's purpose. First, his power over demons demonstrates that in his ministry God's kingship has now come, and Satan's power over the world has been decisively broken. So underlying the human encounters and proclamation of Jesus there is also a supernatural dimension to his mission. Second, that supernatural dimension, soon to be dramatically endorsed by his resurrection after death, marks him out as God's ultimate spokesman and representative, superseding even the most august authorities of Old Testament Israel. In Jesus the work of God has moved up a level; the endgame has begun.

Teaching the Text

What are apparently two unconnected statements—the accusation that Jesus casts out demons by Satan's power (11:15) and the request from him for a sign (11:16)—are linked together by Luke. The teacher or preacher will do well to show how these two objections/demands are related. What do they reveal about how people outside the

In 11:35 Jesus says that lighted lamps are not hidden under bowls but placed on a stand so that the light is visible. This is a first-century AD lampstand from Italy.

disciple group perceived Jesus? And how are Jesus's responses related? What do they reveal about his overall understanding of what he has come to do?

Different groups (and different members of the same group) may differ as to how this material about demons and supernatural conflict relates to our church life and mission today. Some may have relevant experiences of "spiritual warfare" to share. Consider how 11:20–22 applies to our discipleship today.

In our society many see no reason to make decisions for or against Christian truth. But 11:23 indicates that a nondecision is in fact a decision. You might discuss with your audience how this statement differs from the one in 9:50. In what situations do each apply?

The demand for a "sign" fits well with our modern preoccupation with authority and verification. Does Jesus's refusal of a sign apply only to that historical context, or does it have something to teach us still about the life of faith? Does it mean that we should not try to support our evangelism with historical evidence or the evidence of

miracles? Perhaps discuss with your audience the role miraculous signs have played in the past and whether (and under what circumstances) they may continue to have a role in provoking faith today. It may be helpful here to read some of the literature about mission contexts where spiritual "power encounters" have been important in the advance of the gospel.

Illustrating the Text

Jesus has the power to drive out demons.

Missionary History: Exorcism has always been part of the missionary experience in some parts of the world. Rowland Bingham (1872–1942), founder of the Sudan Interior Mission, wrote about the "constant invisible warfare" that has to be waged against the powers of darkness. "It is fashionable in the Western world to relegate belief in demons and devils to the realm of mythology, and when mentioned at all it is a matter of jest. But it is no jest in West Africa or any other mission field for that matter. One has not to

> The only sign Jesus will give is the sign of Jonah. This sarcophagus shows scenes from the book of Jonah (AD 300).

go far in the jungles of Nigeria, the Sudan or Ethiopia . . . to believe in devils and demons." Missionaries frequently have told "strange and macabre stories" of their "encounters with these sinister forces of evil."[3]

People can be for Jesus or against him; there is no middle ground.

Quote: *Chameleon Christianity: Moving Beyond Safety and Conformity*, by Dick Keyes. In this intelligent book, Keyes writes,

> The Christian who lives in the chameleon mode will bend to the currently respectable viewpoint. . . . Those who make all moral choices into black and white issues do reduce moral life to absurdity. But Christians who turn away from biblical moral absolutes altogether are also foolish. With no black or white there is only uniform, unbroken, medium gray. Without absolutes, relative good and evil is an illusion and a pretense, for they must be relative to something.[4]

Keyes reminds his reader that that "something" is, of course, Christ.

Bible: **Revelation 3:15–16.** "I know your deeds, that you are neither cold not hot. I wish you were either one or the other! So, because you are lukewarm—neither hot nor cold—I am about to spit you out of my mouth."

To demand signs of Jesus's authority is to misunderstand his work.

Quote: **"The World's Last Night,"** by C. S. Lewis. In this essay (1952) about the second coming of Christ, Lewis writes,

> He [God] could, if He chose, repair our bodies miraculously without food; or give us food without the aid of farmers, bakers, and butchers; or knowledge without the aid of learned men; or convert the heathen without missionaries. Instead, He allows soils and weather and animals and the muscles, minds, and wills of men to co-operate in the execution of His Will. . . . He seems to do nothing of Himself which He can possibly delegate to His creatures.[5]

The Failure of Israel's Leadership

Big Idea *Those who should be leaders of the people of God have lost their way spiritually, and judgment is inevitable and imminent.*

Understanding the Text

The Text in Context

In 5:17–6:11 Luke recorded a series of events that reveal how Pharisees and scribes disagreed with Jesus over matters of legal interpretation and religious practice (see also 7:30, 36–50). Now Jesus takes the initiative in criticizing these two groups. The resultant standoff, with Jesus denouncing the leaders as ripe for judgment and the leaders determined to destroy Jesus (11:53–54), sets the scene for the coming confrontation in Jerusalem, where (as has already been predicted in 9:22) scribes will play a significant role in the events leading to Jesus's death.

A fuller version of this critique appears in Matthew 23. That is set in Jerusalem, where the majority of Pharisees and scribes were based. Luke perhaps has transferred it into his loosely structured journey section so as to bring it together with the accounts of opposition to Jesus already recorded in 11:14–36. The distorted perspective of which Jesus here accuses the religious leaders is a stark illustration of the "unhealthy eye" against which he has just warned in 11:33–36.

Outline/Structure

The roughly parallel passage in Matthew 23:13–36 has a series of seven "woes" directed against the scribes and Pharisees together. Luke here has six "woes," three against the Pharisees (11:42, 43, 44) and three against the scribes (11:46, 47, 52), with 11:45 to link the two sets by showing that scribes and Pharisees belong together, and a conclusion in which the two groups make common cause against Jesus. In effect, 11:39–41 is a seventh "woe," though not explicitly so introduced.

Historical and Cultural Background

On the two groups of Jewish leaders addressed here, see the sidebar "Scribes and Pharisees" at 5:12–26. Here we find the term "lawyers" (NIV: "experts in the law") rather than "scribes" (NIV: "teachers of the law"), but the reappearance of "scribes" in 11:53 strengthens the view (see on 10:25) that the two terms may be virtually synonymous, especially when "lawyers" are combined, here and in 7:30, with "Pharisees."

The invitation to eat in a Pharisee's house is paralleled in 7:36 (see notes there) and 14:1: Luke wants his readers to know that Jesus enjoyed the respect of religious leaders, even though he disagreed with them, and his table talk must have made him an uncomfortable guest. Here, unlike 7:44–46, there is no indication that Jesus was first treated with disrespect; indeed, it is Jesus who causes offense both by his neglect of the expected ablutions and by severe criticism of his host.

Interpretive Insights

11:38 *Jesus did not first wash before the meal.* What may have begun as a simple matter of hygiene had become for the Pharisees a formal ritual requirement, extending to the home the purity regulations that had been prescribed for priests in their cultic duties (Exod. 30:18–21; Lev. 22:4–7). The Pharisee expects Jesus, as a religious teacher, to apply a stricter standard than was required of ordinary people. For a fuller debate on this issue, see Mark 7:1–23 (= Matt. 15:1–20).

11:39 *you Pharisees clean the outside of the cup.* The detailed Pharisaic rules for purity fill one of the six main sections of the Mishnah (*Teharot*, "Cleannesses"), though much of this elaboration is later than Jesus's time. Jesus sees this preoccupation with external cleanness as missing the point of true religious observance. His distinction between

When it says in 11:38 that "Jesus did not first wash before the meal," it may refer to the hand-washing ritual that religious Jews engaged in prior to eating. This stone cup may have been manufactured for ritual hand washing during the late Second Temple period.

"outside" and "inside" (using the literal utensils as a metaphor for the human person) recalls his radical pronouncement, recorded elsewhere (Matt. 15:11; Mark 7:15), that impurity comes from within, from the heart, not from what is touched or eaten.

11:40 *Did not the one who made the outside make the inside also?* An exclusive concern for "external" ritual betrays too limited an understanding of God. God did prescribe some rules of purity, but his law is even more concerned with ethical behavior and spiritual values. To miss that is to be "foolish" (one who lacks good judgment), a strong term of disparagement.

11:41 *as for what is inside you.* Ritual washing does nothing to change the "inside" attitude of "greed and wickedness" (11:39). Jesus instead summarizes internal purity in the single demand: "Be generous to the poor." It is by such ethical behavior, not by ritual observance, that the true orientation of the heart is revealed. Compare the parable of the good Samaritan, with its focus on love expressed in *doing*.

11:42 *you give God a tenth.* The principle of giving a tenth of all produce to God (to provide for the upkeep of the priesthood) was clear in the Torah (Lev. 27:30), and Jesus does not object to its observance ("without leaving the former undone"). In itself, such tithing does no harm. But what Jesus objects to is the distorted sense of priorities that puts all the emphasis on tithing even the most insignificant garden herbs but gives no attention to the fundamental principles of the Torah ("justice and the love of God").

11:43 *you love the most important seats.* The "outward" focus of many Pharisees meant that they were more interested in their own reputation for godliness than in actually living the way God wanted. The repetition of the word "love" in very different senses in 11:42 and 11:43 shows how they are out of kilter with God's scale of values.

11:44 *unmarked graves.* Graves were covered with lime plaster to make them visible, so that people would not inadvertently become defiled by touching them (Num. 19:16). But the Pharisees' outward respectability conceals behavior ("what is inside you" [11:39–41]) that is morally unclean, and there is nothing to warn other people of it.

11:45 *you insult us also.* Pharisaic behavior and values were governed by the scribal interpretation of the Torah. It is that whole system of interpretation that Jesus is implicitly attacking. In 20:46 he will make the same criticism of scribes that he makes here in 11:43 of Pharisees.

11:46 *you load people down with burdens they can hardly carry.* The aim of scribal elaboration of the law was, in theory, to make it easier to know what was permissible and what was not. But the increasingly detailed stipulations had the opposite effect, leaving people overwhelmed by legal demands and prohibitions.

11:47 *you build tombs for the prophets.* A Jewish work from about this period, *Lives of the Prophets*, identifies the burial place of each of the prophets and describes the elaborate tombs of some of them. Some prophets were persecuted and even martyred: Uriah (Jer. 26:20–23) and the Zechariah mentioned here in 11:51.

During the time of Jesus, tombs were built to honor the Old Testament prophets. The entrance to a large tomb with many burial niches is shown here. It is dated to the first century BC, but during the medieval period it was identified as the burial site of the prophets Haggai, Zechariah, and Malachi and became known as the Tomb of the Prophets.

Jewish tradition also attributed martyrdom to Isaiah, Jeremiah, Ezekiel, Amos, and Micah (see *Lives of the Prophets*; see also Neh. 9:26; Acts 7:52). The leaders of Jesus's day are heirs to that ignoble tradition.

11:49 *God in his wisdom said.* The "quotation," attributed to (literally) "the wisdom of God," cannot be clearly identified as coming from any extant literary source. In Matthew 23:34 Jesus speaks these words himself. He may have drawn on some unknown tradition, written or oral, but perhaps more likely he himself is acting as the spokesman for the divine wisdom. His words accurately depict the future experience of Christian preachers.

11:50 *this generation will be held responsible.* There is a sense of culmination in these verses. If "something greater" than God's spokesmen in the Old Testament has now come (11:31–32), the stakes have been raised. This is Israel's moment of decision, and to refuse God's initiative at this point is to face a culminating judgment. In Matthew these verses are immediately followed by Jesus's prediction of the destruction of the temple (which did in fact happen to "this generation," in AD 70).

11:51 *from the blood of Abel to the blood of Zechariah.* This represents a full catalog of Israel's martyrs; it is a happy coincidence that in English (not in Hebrew or Greek) these two names begin with the first and last letters of the alphabet! The murder of Abel is at the very beginning (Gen. 4:8), that of Zechariah near the end of the last book of the Hebrew Bible (2 Chron. 24:20–22). Neither was strictly a "prophet" (though "the Spirit of God came on" Zechariah), but both called out

for their blood to be avenged (Gen. 4:10; 2 Chron. 24:22).

11:52 *you have taken away the key to knowledge.* This would be a particularly wounding accusation because the scribes' role was to help people understand the Torah. But their distorted interpretations had the opposite effect, keeping people further away from knowing God's will.

Theological Insights

Jesus's challenge to the religious leadership of his day was partly over their self-importance, but mainly it involved their interpretation of the Torah. Their overriding concern for rules and regulations amounted to a preference for the "outside" over the "inside." They focused on the minutiae of ritual and conformity, whereas Jesus went back to first principles, "justice and the love of God." The Torah was not supposed to be a rulebook that could be used as a simple checklist, so much as a guide to the more demanding principles of living according to the will of God.

The strong note of judgment in this passage indicates that this was not just a matter of different preferences or of exegetical nuances but a fundamental shift on the part of the religious leadership away from the godly living that was the essence of Torah. We see here already the parting of the ways that would soon set rabbinic Judaism and the Jesus movement on irreconcilably different courses. And Jesus's claim to be in true succession to the prophets who had stood up for God's values and had suffered for it sets the scene for his own reception when he eventually comes to Jerusalem.

Teaching the Text

Jesus launches seven accusations at the religious leaders in this section. Encourage listeners to consider each in turn and to discern what are the basic principles that divide Jesus's approach to the law and to godly living from that of the leaders. How far are these separate issues, and how far is there a general pattern underlying them?

Where in our modern church life can similar dangers of distorting or ignoring the principles Jesus is here upholding be seen? "Let the person who is without sin throw the first stone"!

It may be appropriate to raise here the controversial issue of the continuing relationship between Judaism and Christianity. Is it fair to see modern Judaism as the heir to the scribal attitude that Jesus here criticizes? How far is the judgment that Jesus sees as imminent for his own generation relevant for our understanding of where the true focus of the people of God is to be found today?

Illustrating the Text

A concern for proper procedure may ignore the real dimensions of Christian discipleship.

Literature: *Pilgrim's Progress*, by John Bunyan. In this classic book (1678) Bunyan (1628–88) depicts how religious teaching can get in the way through two characters that his protagonist, Christian, meets on the way to the Celestial City. The characters arrive together, as do many of those whom Christian meets on his journey. Their names are "Formalist" and "Hypocrisy," and they

One of the accusations of Jesus against the Pharisees was that they cleaned the outside but not the inside. This may refer to the ritual cleansing by immersion in a *mikveh*. Many *mikvehs* were located close to the temple mount so that visitors could purify themselves outwardly with water before entering the temple courts. Here is a *mikveh* from the Second Temple period.

have been born in Vainglory. Instead of just appearing on the appointed path, they come tumbling over a wall on the left hand of the way, having avoided both the Cross and the Hill of Difficulty. Formalist is a stickler for correctness, a lover of ritual. He employs the forms of religion to quiet a dull conscience. He prefers form to substance. Hypocrisy takes this even further and finally lies—the inevitable end of emphasizing only form. Together, these two may get many people's attention, seducing them while their inner life and character are in decay. They are self-deceived, and they have taken the shortcut to holiness, over the wall instead of by the narrow gate. Christian cannot help replying, "I walk by the rule of my Master; you walk by the rude working of your fancies. You are counted thieves already by the Lord of the way; therefore I doubt you will not be found true men at the end of the way. You come in by yourselves without his direction, and shall go out by yourselves without his mercy."[1]

Religious teaching sometimes mistakenly makes it harder rather than easier for people to please God.

Biography: Emily Dickinson. American poet Emily Dickinson (1830–86) had a lifelong struggle with God, shown poignantly in many of her poems.

Biographers note that she had many "spiritual trials" that formed her later life while attending Mount Holyoke, a women's seminary. It is difficult to separate legend from reality, but it appears that there was some repressive expectation of the women there. Mary Lyon was the brilliant founder of the school; she believed in the advancement of women in a time when it was not encouraged. Nevertheless, she "worked for the conversion of every young woman under her charge," and the "rigors" of the place were substantial, most of the days filled with assigned tasks. In one account, Lyon separated the women into three groups: "the 'No-Hopers,' the 'Hopers,' and the 'Christians.'" The last group contained the largest number of women, ones who could give certainty to their profession of faith; a number more were "Hopers," "who believed themselves on the verge of conversion." A smaller group, which included Dickinson, was "without hope" and could not claim faith in Christ. They, of course, were Lyon's greatest concern.[2] Whatever the case, Dickinson remained ambivalent spiritually for the rest of her life.

In one poem she wrote about church,

Some keep the Sabbath going to church;
I keep it staying at home,
With a bobolink for a chorister,
And an orchard for a dome.

Divided Loyalties

Big Idea *Those who are preoccupied with immediate concerns are in danger of missing what ultimately matters.*

Understanding the Text

The Text in Context

The latter part of chapter 11 has been dominated by the theme of opposition to Jesus. That theme is now continued, but also it is developed to speak of the opposition that Jesus's disciples too must expect to meet, and that will challenge them to stand up for God in a hostile environment. A collection of sayings of warning and encouragement spells out the uncomfortable choices that disciples must make. This then raises the issue of the priority of spiritual over material concerns, and the parable of the shortsighted plutocrat then leads into the theme of the tension between God and mammon, which will run through much of the rest of chapter 12 (and will be resumed in chaps. 14 and 16).

Outline/Structure

In 12:1 a large crowd is introduced, but Jesus speaks "first" specifically to his disciples in 12:1–12. Then in 12:13 an interruption from the crowd leads into a more public parable. In 12:22 Jesus will return to addressing disciples, but then he will turn back to the crowd again at 12:54.

Historical and Cultural Background

While Jesus was with them, his disciples faced some criticism, but by and large it was on Jesus himself that the opposition focused. After his death, however, they would face sporadic persecution from both Jewish and pagan sources. Luke himself will provide ample evidence of this in Acts. We know from Josephus (*Ant.* 20.200) that the Sanhedrin contrived the death of "James the brother of Jesus the so-called Messiah," while rabbinic sources testify to the exclusion of the *minim* (heretics) from the synagogues and to the execution of some followers of Jesus (*b. Sanh.* 43a). Nero's violent persecution of Christians in Rome in AD 64/65 (Tacitus, *Ann.* 15.44) apparently was not widespread, but by the early second century it had become a capital offense to be a Christian (Pliny the Younger, *Ep.* 10.96–97).

Interpretive Insights

12:1 *A crowd of many thousands had gathered.* Luke's graphic description reminds us that, despite the opposition, Jesus still has a large following (cf. 9:14). But the disciples are carefully differentiated from the wider crowd, whose loyalties are not yet determined.

the yeast of the Pharisees, which is hypocrisy. Yeast (which actually refers to leaven, a small portion of dough that contains yeast), because of its pervasive quality, and because it was removed in preparation for the Passover festival, was sometimes (but not always [see 13:20–21]) a symbol for evil influence (cf. 1 Cor. 5:6–8; Gal. 5:9). For "hypocrisy," see on 6:42; the term has not been used in 11:37–52, but it sums up the distorted religious values exposed there (cf. its repeated use in the parallel passage, Matt. 23:13–36).

12:2–3 *There is nothing concealed that will not be disclosed.* In this context (for a similar saying with a different application, cf. 8:17) these two verses seem to be a warning against thinking that you can get away with pretending to be what you are not. That is the essence of hypocrisy. Our true nature, even if we succeed in hiding it from other people, will eventually be revealed by God's judgment.

12:4 *do not be afraid of those who kill the body.* Martyrdom makes sense only if there is a firm conviction of life after death. In that perspective, even physical suffering and death are the lesser evil.

12:5 *Fear him who . . . has authority to throw you into hell.* That is, of course, God (not the devil, as some have imagined). This is the only time

Key Themes of Luke 12:1–21

- Do not think that you can conceal your true self; truth will come out.
- Fear of human opposition must be outweighed by our ultimate loyalty to God.
- Our final salvation depends on our willingness to acknowledge Jesus, whatever the cost.
- Those who loyally speak God's word will know his protection and guidance.
- Those who give priority to earthly gain will find that they have forfeited true life.

Luke refers to "hell" (*geenna,* "Gehenna"), which is a more prominent theme in Matthew. The term derives from the Valley of Hinnom, outside the walls of Jerusalem, where the city's rubbish was burned, and it had become a standard Jewish expression for God's final destruction of the wicked. To "fear" God is to recognize him as the ultimate authority and judge, and so to put his will first. But that "fear" is carefully balanced here in 12:6–7 by trust in God's care for his people.

12:6 *Are not five sparrows sold for two pennies?* Small birds ("sparrows" is probably too precise) were sold as food for the poor and as pets for the rich. If something so cheap nonetheless matters to God, how

much more his people matter! Little birds still die, of course, and so do disciples; but this is not a matter of indifference to God.

12:7 *the very hairs of your head are all numbered.* Compare 21:18. The disciples' confidence derives from the fact that God knows everything about them and so also, by implication, about what happens to them.

12:8 *whoever publicly acknowledges me before others, the Son of Man will also acknowledge before the angels of God.* The verdict in the heavenly court depends on one's willingness on earth to be known as a disciple of Jesus. The temptation not to acknowledge Jesus, but rather to "disown" him (12:9), would be strong, especially in later times when to be a Christian was in itself a capital offense (see "Historical and Cultural Background" above). But the principle applies also at the lower level of everyday abuse and ostracism met by those who stand up for Jesus. The change from "me" to "the Son of Man" (as in the similar saying in 9:26) has led some to suggest that here (and in 12:10) Jesus is speaking of a "Son of Man" other than himself, but the use of the phrase in the Gospel tradition as a whole makes this

Jesus faced opposition during his ministry. After his death his followers would face persecution. For example, the Roman emperor Nero, who ruled from AD 54–68, ordered the horrific persecution of Christians during the last years of his reign. This is a sculptured head of the emperor Nero from the Julian Basilica, Corinth (AD 60).

highly unlikely. The term "Son of Man" here suitably recalls the imagery of the judgment scene in Daniel 7, from which it is derived.

12:10 *anyone who blasphemes against the Holy Spirit will not be forgiven.* There are different versions of this saying in Matthew 12:31–32; Mark 3:28–29. All agree that blasphemy against the Holy Spirit cannot be forgiven, and in Matthew and Mark the reference in context is specifically to the charge (already recorded by Luke in 11:15) that Jesus's exorcisms are accomplished by demonic power. To attribute the work of God to his enemy is an unforgivable perversion of truth and betrays a settled opposition to God (rather than a single impulsive utterance). But why is it less serious to slander the Son of Man? The point is probably that Jesus, in his "incognito" as the Son of Man, might not immediately be recognized for who he is. The Holy Spirit, by contrast, is the one who works in people's hearts to call forth a response. To "blaspheme" him is ultimately and finally to reject God's call and offer of forgiveness.

12:12 *the Holy Spirit will teach you . . . what you should say.* For a very similar promise, see 21:12–15. This is not an excuse for lazy preachers; it is an assurance that in the intimidating setting of a formal hearing, faithful disciples will not be left to their own devices. This is a very practical outcome of the gift of the Spirit promised in 3:16 (and cf. 11:13).

12:14 *who appointed me a judge or an arbiter between you?* The man (presumably the younger of two brothers) apparently was looking for a legal ruling or sanction relating to his father's will, and he thought that this "teacher" (rabbi) would be the ideal person to give it. We are not told whether he had a good case, but in any event, Jesus has a very different understanding of his own role.

12:15 *Be on your guard against all kinds of greed.* This is not a verdict on the specific case (though the word for "greed" may imply that the man was trying to get the better of his brother), but rather a general comment on human values. Spiritual wealth takes precedence over all earthly possessions.

12:16–20 *he told them this parable.* It is the story of a successful farmer, and Jesus's hearers no doubt would have envied the man's success and admired his good business sense. It is only in 12:20 that the trap is sprung: there is another dimension to life, which neither the farmer nor Jesus's hearers have taken into account. There is a play on words that is lost in translation: the man speaks complacently to his "self," but it is that very "self" that will be demanded from him. Even his own "self" is not his own, but God's ("demanded" is a term used for collecting a loan).

12:21 *This is how it will be with whoever stores up things for themselves but are not rich toward God.* The parable is not teaching that no provision should be made for the future; its message is that our relationship with God must take precedence over our selfish concerns. The story focuses on the farmer's thoughts about himself: note the repeated "I" and "my" and the advice to himself to enjoy life rather than use his wealth more constructively. But we are stewards, rather than outright owners, of our wealth, and we are accountable to God for how we use it.

Theological Insights

Various aspects of judgment feature in these verses:

- the future revelation of what is at present hidden
- the only mention in Luke of "hell" (though 16:19–31 will speak of punishment after death)
- repudiation in heaven of those who did not acknowledge Jesus on earth
- a sin (blasphemy against the Holy Spirit) for which there is no forgiveness
- a reminder that our life and death are in the hands of God

In all these aspects it is God who is in control. It is God, and only God, who can consign people to hell. But those who are loyal to God can face future judgment with confidence. It is only those who fail to acknowledge his lordship ("fear him") in this life, and especially those who take a clear stand against him ("blaspheme against the Holy Spirit"), who have cause to fear. For the true disciple, death is not something to be afraid of.

Teaching the Text

In 12:1–12 we find seven distinct sayings (12:1, 2–3, 4–5, 6–7, 8–9, 10, 11–12), which may originally have been independent before Luke brought them together here. Any or all of these can be a suitable unit for teaching, but it is probably fairer to Luke to treat them together and aim to draw out some of the aspects of judgment outlined in "Theological Insights" above.

Encourage listeners to focus on the contrasting exhortations "Fear him" (12:5) and "Don't be afraid" (12:7) and to reflect on the place of "fear" in the Christian life.

The "unforgivable sin" is often a source of worry to sensitive Christians. Here in 12:10 it lacks a clear context to define what "blasphemy against the Holy Spirit" might mean in practice. Consider the parallels in Mark and Matthew, where the context is much more specific, and discuss in what ways such a sin might be committed today.

The tension between 12:9 (those who disown Jesus will be disowned) and 12:10 (those who speak against the Son of Man may be forgiven) should be explored. Are they talking about different categories of people?

The parable of the successful farmer makes a sharp division between earthly prosperity and spiritual well-being. What does this mean in practice? Is there a clear dividing line between responsible provision and an unhealthy preoccupation with possessions? Is it possible to be a rich disciple? How might the message of this parable be applied to the "prosperity gospel"?

Illustrating the Text

Fear of human opposition must be outweighed by our ultimate loyalty to God.

Christian History: *Fox's Book of Martyrs.* This book, a renowned work of church history and martyrology, is an abridgement of *Acts and Monuments* (1563) and has gone through many editions. Also available are many recent accounts of those killed as a result of ministering and witnessing in the name of Christ.

Jesus discussed greed by telling a parable about a rich but foolish farmer who decided to build bigger storage facilities for his abundant grain harvest. This building at Ostia Antica, where the port of Rome was located, has been identified as the Horrea Epagathiana et Epaphroditiana. It was built as a warehouse in which foodstuffs, mostly grain and olive oil, were stored (AD 145–50).

Our final salvation depends on our willingness to acknowledge God.

Biography: *Here I Stand: A Life of Martin Luther*, **by Roland Bainton.** In the face of being called before the emperor who was threatening him, Luther (1483–1546) declared,

> You ask me what I shall do if I am called by the emperor. I will go even if I am too sick to stand on my feet. If Caesar calls me, God calls me. If violence is used, as well it may be, I commend my cause to God. He lives and reigns who saved the three youths from the fiery furnace of the king of Babylon, and if He will not save me, my head is worth nothing compared with Christ. This is no time to think of safety. I must take care that the gospel is not brought into contempt by our fear to confess and seal our teaching with our blood.[1]

Those who focus on earthly gain may find that they have missed the essence of true life.

Bible: Ecclesiastes 2:17–21. This passage is a powerful "commentary in advance" on the parable of the rich fool.

Poetry: "The Pulley," by George Herbert. In this poem Herbert (1593–1633), a Welsh-born English poet, orator, and pastor, expresses the necessity to hold blessings and riches with a loose hand.

When God at first made Man,
Having a glass of blessings standing
  by—
Let us (said He) pour on him all we
  can;
Let the world's riches, which dispersed
  lie,
Contract into a span.

So strength first made a way,
Then beauty flow'd, then wisdom, hon-
  our, pleasure:
When almost all was out, God made
  a stay,
Perceiving that, alone of all His
  treasure,
Rest in the bottom lay.

For if I should (said He)
Bestow this jewel also on My creature,
He would adore My gifts instead of
  Me,
And rest in Nature, not the God of
  Nature:
So both should losers be.

Yet let him keep the rest,
But keep them with repining
  restlessness;
Let him be rich and weary, that at least,
If goodness lead him not, yet weariness
May toss him to My breast.[2]

Priorities

Big Idea *Honoring God as king, and being ready for the return of the Lord, must take priority over the ordinary concerns of life.*

Understanding the Text

The Text in Context

Several themes from our last section are developed here: God's fatherly care, the absolute priority of serving God over all other concerns, and especially the tension between material concern and true discipleship—12:22–31 is a sort of commentary on 12:15 and the parable that illustrates it. This last theme of "God and mammon" will be picked up again especially in chapter 16. It reaches an uncomfortably radical climax in the demand to sell one's possessions here in 12:33, a demand that will be issued again in 18:22 to one particular potential disciple.

The call in 12:35–40 to be ready for the Lord's return introduces a new section (12:35–48) that sets out a further way in which disciples will stand out from the rest of society. It applies most obviously to the period after Jesus's earthly ministry is over and prepares for the fuller warning about "the days of the Son of Man," which we will meet in 17:20–37 as well as in Jesus's teaching about the future in chapter 21.

Historical and Cultural Background

Detachment from material concerns was an ideal preached by a number of ancient philosophies such as the Stoics and, most notably, the Cynics, whose founder, Diogenes, was famous for his ascetic lifestyle and rejection of social convention. But the Cynic ideal was of self-sufficiency and independence, not of trustful dependence on a higher power. Jesus does not here denigrate bodily concerns as unimportant or even evil (in the way later gnostic and Manichean thinking would do), but he puts them in perspective in relation to the service of the God who can be trusted to supply them.

The belief that Jesus would return in judgment after his death and resurrection belongs already in the tradition of Jesus's sayings. By the time Luke wrote his Gospel, it had been strongly developed in Paul's letters and had become a defining feature of the early Christian community.

Interpretive Insights

12:22 *do not worry.* "Worry" is the key term of 12:22–30. It has been used for the earthly concerns that choke the good seed (8:14) and for the domestic preoccupation that kept Martha from concentrating on "what is better" (10:41). It denotes not a proper responsibility in ensuring provision, but a distracting anxiety that closes the mind to higher concerns.

12:24 *Consider the ravens.* Birds, of course, do have to search long hours for their food; God does not drop it into their beaks. But the point is that food is there to be found because God makes provision for all that he has created.

And how much more valuable you are than birds! Compare 12:7; 13:15–16. Such comparative valuations depend on the belief that humankind is the peak of God's creation. They do not devalue the animal creation or justify human exploitation of animals; rather, it is because the birds really do matter to God that we can be sure that he cares for us even more.

12:25 *add a single hour to your life?* The alternative translation "add a single cubit to your height" hardly fits the context here. Not many people would want to be half a meter taller, and this would hardly be a "very little thing" (12:26). The "cubit" is used here as a metaphor for a period of life (compare "life*span*"). The passage is about

survival, not stature, and worrying about our survival changes nothing. It may even shorten our life.

12:27 *Consider how the wild flowers grow.* The birds illustrated God's care about food; now flowers indicate his care about clothing. The God who lavishes such extraordinary beauty on such short-lived and common things is hardly likely to ignore his people's need for proper clothing.

12:29 *do not worry about it.* A different verb is used for "worry" this time, giving us quite a vivid metaphor: "do not be up in the air."

12:30 *your Father knows that you need them.* This assurance separates the Christian from the secular world and eliminates any need for worry. In 11:9–13 it was the basis of an exhortation to persistent prayer; here not even prayer is mentioned, simply a confident expectation of God's provision.

12:31 *seek his kingdom.* "The kingdom of God" means his effective rule (see on 4:43). To "seek" that rule is to place oneself under God's control and to allow one's priorities to be molded by his values and

"Consider the ravens" (12:24). Ravens were considered unclean according to Old Testament law, and six species are common to Israel. The bird shown here is a hooded crow (*Corvus cornix*), a predatory and scavenging bird for which God provides food.

purpose. There may also be the sense of being eager to see God's rule effectively established in society (as in the Lord's Prayer [11:2]), but that seems a less central idea in this context.

these things will be given to you as well. "These things" are food and clothing, the necessities of life. The promise is that God will provide for the material needs of his loyal servants, not that they can expect to be more prosperous than others.

12:32 *to give you the kingdom.* The essentially active sense of the word *basileia* ("kingship, rule") suggests that this phrase means "to make you kings," an idea that will be developed more clearly in 22:28–30 specifically with reference to the Twelve. The "little flock" of those who seek God's kingship will also be privileged to share in it, as agents through whom his rule is to be exercised.

12:33 *Sell your possessions and give to the poor.* Compare the practice of the early Christians in Acts 2:44–45; 4:32–37. This radical ideal needs to be balanced against practical responsibility. Peter, for instance, seems to have retained his boat and fishing tackle, and even his home in Capernaum. The itinerant lifestyle of Jesus and his disciples depended on the hospitality and support of well-wishers who had the means (cf. 8:3). But material security is to be subordinated to spiritual priorities, as the parable in 12:16–21 has underlined. See further on 18:22.

treasure in heaven. The idea is not that giving to the poor automatically "buys" a heavenly reward, but that the disciples' orientation away from mere earthly security means that they are "rich toward God" (12:21). This is the only wealth that lasts. Compare 16:9.

12:35–36 *servants waiting for their master to return.* This is a parable from everyday life in a wealthy household. As the owner's slaves are not off duty while he is away, so disciples must be ready for their Lord's return. The point would be obvious to Christians after Jesus's death, resurrection, and ascension. At this point in the Gospel story there has been no indication to the disciples of Jesus's going away and coming back, and they may have seen in the parable no more than a general exhortation to be alert in God's service, just as the Old Testament prophets had warned people to be ready for a coming "day of the Lord."

12:37 *It will be good for those servants.* Literally (here and in 12:38), "Blessed are those slaves." This unexpected beatitude makes a startling shift away from normal life. Jesus himself will recognize in 17:7–10 that this is not how slaves are treated. But Jesus turns conventional ideas of status on their head (see also 22:26–27), as he will in a more practical way in John 13:3–17. The sheer generosity of God's reward for his faithful servants is breathtaking.

12:39 *If the owner of the house had known at what hour the thief was coming.* The need to be ready at all times for the Lord's coming, and the danger of being caught unawares, is reinforced by this separate parable, which caught the imagination of early Christians (see 1 Thess. 5:2; 2 Pet. 3:10; Rev. 3:3; 16:15). The point of the comparison is, of course, the burglar's choice of time, not his profession.

Theological Insights

The call to simple trust in God's provision for material needs in 12:22–31 is very attractive, but it raises serious problems in the light of experience: Christians, especially those in the less affluent parts of the world, do starve and suffer from homelessness and other hardships. Faith does not seem to be an absolute guarantee that even the bare necessities will be available, and it would be a very insensitive disciple who insisted that any fellow believer who is in need must have failed to seek God's kingdom. There seems sometimes to be an absolutism about Jesus's teaching that needs to be balanced against other elements. This idealistic passage does not obviate either the need for hard work to provide for one's own family or the importance of making practical provision for those less well-off.

The expectation of an eschatological coming of the Son of Man (12:35–40) will be spelled out more fully in 17:20–37, and similar language will recur in the latter part of chapter 21, though there it is woven together with the prediction of the destruction of the temple. Since the term "the Son of Man" has been used clearly and consistently in this Gospel (as in the other Gospels) as Jesus's own title for himself, such language would naturally be understood of a return of Jesus after his ascension to heaven, a future event that became known, especially in Paul's letters, as Jesus's parousia. Here there is no such technical term, and it must remain uncertain how Jesus's disciples during his ministry might have envisaged the "return/ coming" in these sayings.

Teaching the Text

The pressures of modern society—relationships, work, finances, health concerns—produce extreme stress and anxiety in many people, and the teacher or preacher should have no difficulty connecting Jesus's teaching in these verses to everyday life. How can we learn to live a life of peaceful rest in God's sustaining power?

The problems raised in "Theological Insights" above concerning 12:22–31 are also a suitable focus for teaching that section. Consider how this simple faith in God's material provision relates to the following:

- the fact of world hunger and poverty, from which Christians do not seem to be immune
- the need to make appropriate provision for our own and our families' future
- the complexities of modern socio-economic structures and lifestyle expectations

Are there examples of Christian attitudes toward material concerns that are distinctive from surrounding secular ("pagan" [12:30]) society? Discuss what sets Christians apart.

Jesus tells his hearers to "consider the wildflowers" (12:27), such as those shown in this landscape in Israel. Just as God clothes them beautifully he is able to provide for the material needs of his people.

The teacher should also discuss the implications for disciples today of Jesus's demand to sell one's possessions and give to the poor. Is it possible to have "treasure in heaven" while still retaining an affluent lifestyle? Where is the dividing line between normal responsible provision and ungodly affluence?

The parable in 12:35–36 suggests a state of constant "red alert." Is that realistic in normal life? This passage may provide an opportunity to consider whether and, if so, why modern Christianity has lost some of the urgency of first-century discipleship.

What relation, if any, is there between the "being ready" Jesus speaks of here and the attempts of some Christian groups to prove the imminence of the Lord's coming or even to predict its specific date?

Illustrating the Text

If we trust our heavenly Father, we will not worry about our material needs.

Hymn: "His Eye Is on the Sparrow," by Civilla D. Martin and Charles H. Gabriel. This hymn (1905) was immortalized by Ethel Waters (1896–1977), an African American blues and jazz singer, and the song title became the title of her autobiography. It could be very evocative to play a recording of Ethel Waters singing the song, as it is also a piece of American history. Interestingly, Waters's powerful voice and style enabled her to break into the previously white-dominated theater and performance world of the 1940s and 1950s before she eventually sang at Billy Graham rallies. The refrain of the song uses the image of a bird—in this case, a sparrow (see 12:6–7). The words to two of the verses are as follows:

> As a reward for their watchfulness, the master waits on his servants in this parable of Jesus (12:35–38). This frieze from the Nereid Monument shows men reclining at a banquet while a servant attends them (400 BC, Turkey).

Why should I feel discouraged, why
   should the shadows come,
Why should my heart be lonely, and
   long for heav'n and home,
When Jesus is my portion? My con-
   stant Friend is He:
His eye is on the sparrow, and I know
   He watches me;
His eye is on the sparrow, and I know
   He watches me.

[Refrain] I sing because I'm happy, I
   sing because I'm free,
For His eye is on the sparrow, and I
   know He watches me.

"Let not your heart be troubled," His
   tender word I hear,
And resting on His goodness, I lose my
   doubts and fears;
Though by the path He leadeth, but
   one step I may see;
His eye is on the sparrow, and I know
   He watches me;
His eye is on the sparrow, and I know
   He watches me.

Personal Stories: While great stories of
provision exist, such as George Mueller's
account of God's meeting the needs of the
orphanages that he established in England
in the nineteenth century, it might be very
valuable, in advance of preaching this passage, to ask members of the congregation
to turn in short testimonies to God's provision for them in specific situations through
the years. This exercise seems more likely
to bring encouragement than the more familiar and distant accounts because it will
represent the experience of the immediate
church family.

Nature: *The Birds Our Teachers,* **by John
Stott.** Besides being a renowned Christian leader, scholar, and cleric, John Stott
(1921–2011) was an avid birdwatcher. In
this book he notes that Jesus himself told
us to be birdwatchers (see Matt. 6:26; cf.
Luke 12:24) and to learn from them. Stott
quotes Martin Luther: "We have as many
teachers and preachers as there are little
birds in the air."[1] He includes a chapter on
sparrows (see 12:6–7) and one on ravens
(see 12:24), both of which contain helpful
illustrations and quotable comments.

Jesus's disciples must always be ready for his return.

Visual: A photograph could usefully illustrate the posture of expectancy: runners
waiting for the starting gun, military personnel on guard duty, a woman about to
give birth. The expectancy is physical as
well as mental—a posture of body as well
as of attitude. Jesus's disciples must always
be ready for his return, which may be at an
unexpected time.

Quote: *My Utmost for His Highest,* **by Oswald Chambers.** Reflecting on this passage,
Chambers (1874–1917) writes,

> The great need for the Christian worker
> is to be ready to face Jesus Christ at any
> and every turn. This is not easy, no mat-
> ter what our experience is. The battle is
> not against sin or difficulties or circum-
> stances, but against being so absorbed in
> work that we are not ready to face Jesus
> Christ at every turn. This is the one great
> need, not the facing our belief, or our
> creed, the question whether we are of any
> use, but to face *Him.*[2]

Interpreting the Times

Big Idea *God's true servants will not be caught unawares but will always be found doing their master's will.*

Understanding the Text

The Text in Context

The theme of readiness for the Lord's coming, begun at 12:35, now continues: 12:35–48 is a coherent unit of teaching, which has been broken up here simply to accommodate the commentary divisions. The collection of sayings that follows in 12:49–59 does not relate specifically to that theme, but it does add further to the sense of crisis: Jesus's arrival has confronted people with serious and difficult choices that will have eternal consequences. This theme will continue in the call to repentance in 13:1–9.

All this is to be understood against the background of 12:1: Jesus has attracted a very large crowd, but he speaks primarily to

his disciples. However, what he says has relevance to all who hear him, and the larger crowd is expected to take notice. In 12:54 that wider audience comes more clearly into focus.

Historical and Cultural Background

The setting presupposed in 12:41–48 (as already also in 12:35–38) is that of a relatively affluent household in which most of the work is done by a good number of slaves, owned by and responsible to their master. Such a large household would have a "steward" (NIV: "manager"), himself a

The setting for Jesus's parable about the faithful and wise manager reflected the current Roman social hierarchy illustrated on this funerary relief. The inscription indicates that the large figures shown in deep relief are a family of freedpersons, both male and female, whose former master may have been a Roman merchant. The smaller figures in shallow relief are the slaves that belong to the family (ca. 50 BC, Thessaloniki).

slave, to whom the householder delegates responsibility over the rest of the slaves, both for supervising their work and for looking after their material needs. Slaves were routinely kept in order by the threat of corporal punishment (12:47–48).

The family group presupposed in 12:52–53 is, however, apparently less affluent: no slaves are mentioned, just the immediate nuclear family and their spouses.

Interpretive Insights

12:41 *are you telling this parable to us, or to everyone?* Peter often is the spokesman for the disciple group. In view of the surrounding crowd (12:1) he wants to know whether all are equally called to vigilance. The answer is not clear from what follows. If "slaves" is a metaphor for disciples, then apparently they are the immediate target. But everyone in the crowd is a *potential* disciple, so perhaps the question does not really need an answer. If the shoe fits, wear it.

12:43 *It will be good for that servant.* This is another beatitude as in 12:37–38 above. The one so congratulated is the "faithful and wise steward," so called on the basis of his behavior in the first of two possible scenarios (12:42–44). The steward's behavior in 12:45–46, by contrast, is not "faithful and wise."

12:44 *he will put him in charge of all his possessions.* This slave receives not just the management of the other slaves. The reward for having been faithful in this less demanding area is not a relaxation of his duties, but rather a huge increase in his responsibilities, as in the parable of the minas in 19:16–19 (though no doubt he could also expect an enhanced status and

Key Themes of Luke 12:41–59

- To be ready for the Lord's coming means being faithful in fulfilling the tasks he has given us.
- There are rewards for those who are faithful and punishments for those who rebel.
- Punishment is more severe for those who knew what they should be doing.
- Jesus's mission is not a comfortable one, and it will leave people seriously divided.
- Those who fail to recognize the significance of his ministry and to respond to it face judgment.

lifestyle). The essence of discipleship is service rather than privilege.

12:46 *He will cut him to pieces.* This is a surprisingly vivid and violent image. The setting in an ordinary household has been left behind. The following clause, "assign him a place with the unbelievers," shows that the intended application has invaded the parable. This violent end represents the lot of those who have abused their Lord's trust and so have failed in their discipleship.

12:47–48 *The servant who knows the master's will . . . the one who does not know.* This is a separate saying but is appropriately added here because it too uses the imagery of master and slave. Both slaves are punished, but the one whose offense was unawares is treated less severely. The Old Testament distinguishes between intentional and unintentional sin, the latter (but not the former) being forgivable after atonement has been made (Num. 15:22–31). Here the fact that even the unwitting offender is punished, albeit more leniently, perhaps indicates that sin remains sin even when we are not aware of it, and it cannot simply be ignored.

12:48 *From everyone who has been given much, much will be demanded.*

Privilege brings responsibility. To be entrusted with "the knowledge of the secrets of the kingdom of God" (8:10) is to incur a much higher level of responsibility, and deliberate repudiation of that responsibility will have severe consequences.

12:49–50 *I have come to bring fire on the earth . . . I have a baptism to undergo.* The two images of baptism and fire have already been linked together in 3:16–17 in John the Baptist's prophecy of Jesus's mission. The fire indicates a mission that will purify and destroy and, like a wildfire spreading across the earth, leave no one unaffected. The baptism (being "plunged" into something) is not now about what Jesus will bring to others, but here (as in Mark 10:38) probably is an image for the personal suffering that will be an essential part of his own mission. Until all that is accomplished, Jesus feels "constrained," frustrated, longing to have it all completed. That the fire is not yet "kindled" suggests that he is thinking particularly of the coming judgment that will result from his mission (and which has been the subject of 12:45–48).

12:51 *peace on earth . . . division.* The angels spoke of the coming of peace on earth in 2:14 (and cf. 19:38), and Jesus's disciples have been sent to proclaim peace (10:5–6); he himself wants to bring peace to Jerusalem (19:42). Compare also the summary of Jesus's mission in Acts 10:36. This exclamation is therefore perhaps not so much a statement of Jesus's real purpose, but rather

a sad recognition that his message of peace will in fact prove to be one of division, as people take opposite sides in relation to him. This too was already predicted at his birth (2:34–35).

12:52 *there will be five in one family divided against each other.* Family solidarity was much valued, and so this is a particularly telling prediction: Jesus's divisive message will penetrate so deeply that even this basic loyalty is compromised. The specific relationships spelled out in 12:53 echo those of Micah 7:6, a poignant cameo of the dire state to which Judah's rebellion had brought its society.

12:56 *How is it that you don't know how to interpret this present time?* "Time" here translates *kairos*, often used of a time of special significance, even a crisis. Jesus is now speaking to those in the crowd who have not responded to his message by becoming disciples. The common sense that underlies elementary weather lore seems to have deserted them when it comes to interpreting the equally obvious signs of Jesus's ministry. Compare 11:20 for the visible evidence of the inbreaking of the kingdom of God. The "signs" that they had requested (11:16, 29) were already abundantly there. They are "hypocrites" in that

Just as they observed and interpreted the signs of nature, Jesus's listeners should have been able to "interpret this present time" (12:56). Here are clouds over the Mediterranean Sea near Acre with the potential of rain for Israel.

they are unable or unwilling to transfer their diagnostic skill from the natural sphere to the spiritual, and so they miss what is plain for all to see.

12:58 *As you are going with your adversary to the magistrate.* Here we have an everyday scene that illustrates the need to take timely action and not to let things drift. Once the legal process has been started, there is no way out. It is inappropriate to press the details of the cameo by asking who is represented by the "adversary," what the offense was, or what sort of "reconciliation" is in view. The point is in being alert to one's danger before it is too late. Sitting on the fence is not an option when the kingdom of God has dawned and God's judgment is imminent.

Theological Insights

There is an overriding sense of eschatological urgency in this whole section, which began at 12:35. The prospect of the Lord's return should concentrate the disciple's mind, and the fact that that return will be unannounced means that we can never be "off duty." But "being ready" is not a matter of calculating the possible date or of giving up the ordinary responsibilities of life. The steward's "readiness" consists in faithful service, in fulfilling responsibilities at all times, so as not to be caught unprepared.

So much for disciples who expect Jesus's return. But the rest of the world also needs to be alert and to avoid complacency. Jesus's ministry brings division and judgment, and no one is exempt. It is important to respond to the offer of salvation now, before it is too late.

The distinction between deliberate and unwitting sin in 12:47–48, with different levels of punishment resulting, raises interesting questions about the basis of God's judgment. Does this suggest a distinction between those who have heard and rejected the gospel and those who have never heard it?

The phrase "I have come to . . ." (12:49; cf. 5:32; 19:10) implies a mission that originated elsewhere, and it has been used to argue that the Synoptic Gospels also support the idea, familiar from the Gospel of John, of Jesus's preincarnate divine existence.[1]

Teaching the Text

There are three main sections in this passage, which may be taught either separately or together. If taught together, the focus should be on the necessity for believers to live a life of watchful readiness and service to the Lord, recognizing that this loyalty places us in opposition to the values and goals of the world. If taught separately, the following themes may be pursued:

1. *12:35–48* (including the last section of the previous passage). Consider the relationship between master and slave in a wealthy household, and reflect on why Jesus thought it suitable as a model for teaching about his return. Pick up the issues suggested in regard to 12:35–40 in the previous section, particularly the issue of what it means to "be ready." It might be helpful to think about how such imagery developed: its application to the later Christian expectation of the parousia is clear, but what might it have meant to the disciples when Jesus was still with them? A further lesson relates to 12:48b: invite listeners to consider what they themselves have been

"given" by God, and what therefore might be "demanded" of them.

2. *12:49–53*. This is a series of three rather loosely connected sayings. In your teaching consider in what way Jesus's ministry brought fire on the earth, the nature of his "baptism," and why division was inevitable. How does this relate to the Old Testament expectation of a "prince of peace"? And how far are Jesus's modern disciples expected to be dividers and fire raisers? Consider examples where Christian values are increasingly at odds with the values of the world. How can Christians both stand firmly for what is right and also be reconcilers and peacemakers?

3. *12:54–59*. Again, these apparently are two separate sayings. The first (12:54–56) raises the question of the nature of the "present time" that Jesus expects the crowd to interpret, and asks what signs should have given them the clue. In your teaching you might first point out the signs that Jesus's audience was failing to discern (the evidence of the in-breaking of the kingdom of God) and then raise the question of what signs our present generation may be missing. The second saying (12:57–59) similarly raises the question of the "right" (the word usually means "just, righteous") that they were meant to be able to judge, and what was the urgent action that

ought to result from this discernment. The "right" here relates to reconciliation with enemies or opponents. Consider with your group or audience how this issue of reconciliation represents the heart of the gospel message.

Illustrating the Text

We are to be ready for the Lord's coming, faithful to what he has given us to do.

Literature: *The Odyssey*, by Homer. This work (perhaps 850 BC, though its date is debated) is one of two great Greek epic poems (the other is *The Iliad*) attributed to Homer. The work chronicles the ten years that it took Odysseus (Ulysses in Roman mythology) to return to Ithaca after the ten-year Trojan War. He has many adventures

Using the parable of the faithful and wise manager, Jesus exhorts his followers to remain obedient while waiting patiently for his return. We find another illustration of faithfulness over a long period of waiting in the ancient Greek epic poem, *The Odyssey*. Penelope believes Odysseus has not died in the Trojan Wars and waits patiently for his return, despite pressure from many men who would take his place. This terra-cotta relief shows Odysseus, disguised as a beggar, standing before Penelope, as he learns that she has remained faithful (450 BC, Melos, Greece).

and mishaps but finally arrives home to his waiting wife, Penelope, and his son, Telemachus. While Odysseus has been gone, a group of suitors, really usurpers, have been taking advantage of his home and possessions on the assumption that he will never return. They have also aggressively sought Penelope's hand in marriage to further advance their intentions.

Penelope is aware that she could break her vows to her absent husband and choose a new husband who would be king and who would kill Odysseus. However, she remains faithful to Odysseus during his twenty-year absence, inventing reasons why she cannot choose a suitor, working hard to trick those who seek her hand. The device that works the longest for her is when she informs her suitors that she is weaving a burial covering for Odysseus's father, Laertes, and only when it is completed will she choose one of them to be her husband. Every day for a number of years she unravels part of the work that she has already finished, buying time. Because of Penelope's perseverance, her name has come to be associated with faithfulness in marriage.

Jesus's mission will leave people seriously divided.

Biography: Billy Sunday. Sunday was a baseball player who became a celebrated evangelist. His biographer, Elijah Brown, writes, "No one can doubt the absolute sincerity of the man. He is a Daniel come to judgment, a Savonarola denouncing the sins of the people, an Isaiah pointing to God as the solution of great public questions. . . . You cannot explain his marvelous success on any other basis than that God is with him." All this being true, Billy's plain talking and teaching of the Word divided people. Brown continues, "Of course there are some church members who will not go to hear Sunday. . . . They are living a dual life, and they do not want the sword of the Spirit as it is wielded by Billy to lay bare the rottenness of their lives."[2]

History: *A Legacy of Hatred*, by David A. Rausch. Rausch's fine book focuses on why Christians must not forget the Holocaust. In one chapter, Rausch asks, "What made the difference between the few Christians who helped the Jewish people and the multitude who did not?" Having studied the issue, he reflects that

> the reoccurring emphasis on established ethical patterns of Christian thought and practice looms large. They strove to be Christ-like in their attitudes toward other religions and races, seeking to unlearn the prejudice bolstered and sustained by the community around them. Because prejudice is a learned behavior, they geared their lives to immunize themselves from its infection. . . . Godly thinking provided personal enhancement and comprehension of the infinite value of a human life and God's love for *every* person.[3]

Clearly Christlike thinking can divide not only unbelievers from believers but also believers from other believers.

"Unless You Repent . . ."

Big Idea *God requires repentance before it is too late, but people are more concerned with keeping the rules than with God's agenda.*

Understanding the Text

The Text in Context

These are two separate pericopes, brought together here simply for the convenience of this commentary.

First, repentance has been at the heart of the message of both John (3:3, 8) and Jesus (5:32), and Jesus has rebuked his contemporaries for their failure to repent in response to his preaching (10:13–15; 11:32). In chapter 15 he will illustrate God's deep desire for sinners to repent. Here the theme is developed, but with a warning that judgment is also a reality, and the opportunity for repentance may not last forever. The message is reinforced with a short parable.

Second, we have seen in 6:1–5, 6–11 how Jesus's uninhibited approach to the observance of the Sabbath has put him in conflict with other religious leaders, and the issue will arise again in 14:1–6. Luke keeps this key issue before us as the tension builds up between Jesus and those who saw him as a threat to the authority of the law and of those who acted as its interpreters.

Historical and Cultural Background

Josephus records a number of incidents in which the insensitivity of the Roman prefect Pontius Pilate (already introduced in 3:1) led to brutal reprisals against his subjects' resistance (Josephus, *Ant.* 18.55–59, 60–62, 85–87; see also Philo, *Embassy* 299–305). The incident mentioned in 13:1 is not otherwise recorded, but clearly it is in character. Galileans

In 13:1 people bring news to Jesus about an incident involving Pontius Pilate, who was governor of Judea. This inscription found at Caesarea identifies Pontius Pilate with his title as prefect of Judea. He governed from AD 26–37.

were not under Pilate's jurisdiction, but the mention of "their sacrifices" indicates that this incident occurred in the temple in Jerusalem, which presumably the Galileans were visiting for a festival. The disaster at Siloam is also otherwise unattested; the Siloam reservoir was at the southern edge of Jerusalem, and the collapse may have been of part of the city wall, or perhaps of the new aqueduct that Pilate was constructing.

For the scribal conventions on Sabbath observance, and especially healing on the Sabbath, see "Historical and Cultural Background" on 6:1–16.

Interpretive Insights

13:1 *Galileans whose blood Pilate had mixed with their sacrifices.* Presumably, this is a vivid way of describing an act of violence targeted at a group of Galilean worshipers offering sacrifices in the temple. The report may have been intended as a warning to Jesus and his disciples as a group of Galileans bound for Jerusalem: it could be a dangerous place to be identified as a Galilean.

13:2 *worse sinners than all other Galileans.* The principle is more general, as may be seen from the following example in 13:4–5, which does not involve Galileans as such. The specific focus on Galileans here, however, may reflect a suggestion by some people that, as Galileans (sometimes regarded as potential rebels), this group of visitors to Jerusalem "had it coming to them."

13:3 *unless you repent, you too will all perish.* Not, of course, all in the same way (as the more literal translation "you will all perish similarly" might suggest, here and in 13:5), but the physical fate of this particular

group acts as a symbol of the spiritual fate of unrepentant sinners.

13:4 *who died when the tower in Siloam fell on them.* This seems to have been an accident (though perhaps caused by poor building standards), killing ordinary people in Jerusalem who happened to be in the wrong place at the wrong time. Jesus dismisses the common tendency in such circumstances to ask "Why them?" and to assume some hidden reason why they were "selected." Instead, he takes this too as a symbol of spiritual destruction. In view of human sinfulness, the surprising thing is not that this particular group suffered but that the rest of us have not yet faced judgment.

13:6–9 *Then he told this parable.* The word "repent" is not used in this parable, but the image of the fruitless fig tree that fails to change for the better is a clear symbol of failure to repent and to accept God's rule. Bearing fruit occurs frequently in the Gospels as a metaphor for the lifestyle that God requires (see 3:8–9; 6:43–45; 8:8). The prophets sometimes used the fig tree as a symbol for Israel's responsibility to God (Jer. 8:13; 24:1–10; Hosea 9:10, 16–17; Mic. 7:1), and most commentators regard Jesus's cursing of the fruitless fig tree outside Jerusalem (Matt. 21:18–19; Mark 11:12–14, 20–21) as an "acted parable" of the ripeness of the temple establishment for judgment. Luke perhaps omitted that incident because this parable already carried its message.

As with many parables, it is unwise to press the details to the point of allegorical correspondence. If God is the owner, who is represented by the worker who successfully deflects God's judgment for a time? It is better to see the story as a whole as enforcing Jesus's call for repentance and warning that there is a limit to God's patience with those who reject his grace.

13:11 *who had been crippled by a spirit.* Literally, "having a spirit of weakness." This phrase, together with the statement that the woman had been "bound" by Satan all this time (13:16), represents one of the few places in the Gospels where a physical ailment (here apparently a spinal deformity) appears to be attributed to demonic influence. This is to be distinguished from the story of the so-called epileptic boy in Matthew 17:14–20 and Mark 9:14–29, which is clearly described as an exorcism; the diagnosis as epilepsy is a modern "rationalization." Here there is no exorcistic language; in 13:12 Jesus refers to her condition simply as an "infirmity" (the same Greek word as in 13:11), and the healing is described in physical terms, by the laying on of hands (which is never used in Jesus's exorcisms). But even physical illness can be traced to the devil's influence, as in Acts 10:38, where Jesus's healing ministry in general is described as "healing those who were under the power of the devil."

13:14 *There are six days for work.* For scribal conventions with regard to healing on the Sabbath, see "Historical and Cultural Background" on 6:1–16. Clearly, after eighteen years this woman's condition,

however unpleasant, could safely be left to the next day. The synagogue leader's rebuke is, rather disingenuously, directed at the people rather than Jesus, even though it was Jesus who had taken the initiative when he saw the woman's condition. In bypassing Jesus, perhaps he is attempting to assert his own teaching authority, or perhaps he found Jesus too formidable a person to confront directly.

13:15 *untie your ox or donkey from the stall and lead it out to give it water.* "Tying" and "loosening" were among the acts forbidden on the Sabbath (see the sidebar "Rules for the Sabbath" at 6:1–16), but there was debate about what sort of knots were intended (*m. Shabb.* 15:1–2). There was, however, specific provision for cattle to "go out" on the Sabbath (*m. Shabb.* 5:1–4) and therefore presumably to be untied. Rabbis later formulated the principle that the necessities of looking after livestock overrode the strict observance of the Sabbath (*b. Shabb.* 128b), and apparently popular practice had already taken this for granted. For a similar argument from animal welfare, see 14:5 (cf. Matt. 12:11–12).

13:16 *should not this woman . . . be set free on the Sabbath day?* Jesus argues that not only is what he has done permissible, but also that the Sabbath is the most appropriate day for such an act. The Sabbath should be a day of joy rather than of suffering; it is the day to celebrate God's triumph over Satan, and it is a day for doing good, not harm (6:9; cf. Matt. 12:12). The woman's release from bondage echoes the sense (though not directly the wording) of the Messiah's mission of deliverance declared on an earlier synagogue visit in 4:18.

13:17 *all his opponents were humiliated.* Jesus's uninhibited stance on Sabbath observance struck a chord with ordinary people. The religious leaders, even if they themselves remained opposed to Jesus's "radicalism," could not afford to be cast as enemies of the people, and so they had to concede the argument, resulting in serious loss of face.

Theological Insights

Luke 13:1–5, together with John 9:2–3, takes an important stand against the common assumption (well exemplified by the arguments of Job's friends, and still commonly heard) that physical and material misfortune is "earned" by sin ("What have I done to deserve this?"). A simplistic solution to the problem of evil that attributes suffering to the sufferer's sin is sub-Christian. The popular tendency in the event of an accident to ask what the injured party did to deserve it must be resisted as essentially superstitious. An accident is an accident; however such events are to be reconciled with God's sovereignty over the world he has created, the moral culpability on the part of those affected should not be automatically assumed.

But this is not, of course, to make light of sin. This same passage teaches that all are equally sinful and deserve God's judgment. Hence comes the centrality of the call to repentance both in Jesus's message and in our proclamation of the gospel today. The parable of the fig tree reminds us that it is only by God's grace that we are not immediately destroyed, but that we must not therefore presume on his generosity: there is a limit to God's patience and therefore also a point of no return for the sinner who will not repent.

The story of Sabbath healing reinforces the message of 6:1–11: there are things more important than meticulous observance of religious conventions. The Sabbath is a day for "doing good" (6:9) even if it means bending the scribal rules. What to the scribes was a dangerously radical liberalism was for Jesus a joyfully positive affirmation of God's gift of a special day.

> The parable of the fruitless fig tree illustrates the limit to God's patience for those who ignore Jesus's call to repentance. The fig tree shown here has leaves but no fruit.

Teaching the Text

These are three separate pericopes, which may be taught either together or separately. If you teach them together, you might begin with the seemingly random nature of tragedy and loss, pointing out that these are clearly not the result of personal sin (13:1–4). Yet they *are* a result of sin and the fallen state of humanity and of all creation. The only solution to the sin problem is repentance (13:5), accepting the free gift of God, and then bearing the fruit that results from repentance (13:6–9). The route of legalism—seeking to earn salvation through one's own works—will only result in frustration and hypocrisy (13:15). If you teach the passages separately, the following themes could be stressed:

1. *13:1–5.* Consider recent accidents or atrocities that have led people to ask "Why me?" What does this passage have to teach about such situations? How do such events relate to God's control over his creation and to the different approaches that have been taken to the problem of suffering? Is there *any* place for the proposal that suffering is the result of human sin, and if so, how can this argument be put forward without suggesting the crass notion of individually earned suffering that Jesus here dismisses?

2. *13:6–9.* Consider what sort of "fruit" the parable of the fig tree is calling for. What are the implications of the parable for our evangelistic and/or pastoral approach to unbelievers and also to believers who are perceived to be unrepentant and/or unfruitful?

3. *13:10–17.* See "Teaching the Text" suggestions on 6:1–16, which are equally applicable here. Another point of discussion might be Jesus's attribution of the woman's deformity to Satan's "binding."

How far, if at all, is this perspective applicable to illness in general? In what sense is physical healing (rather than exorcism) a contest with Satan?

Illustrating the Text

Disaster and the suffering that follows are not necessarily the result of specific sins.

Bible: Job. Certainly this principle applies to the book of Job, in which Job's suffering is shown not to be a result of sin.

History: The year 2012 marked the centennial anniversary of the disaster of the famous ship that sank quickly into the icy North Atlantic, claiming 1,503 lives. The *Titanic* disappeared between 11:40 p.m. on Sunday night and 2:20 a.m. Monday morning.

Few disasters have so raised the question of cause and responsibility. The winter previous to the tragedy had been warmer; glacial ice in the Arctic Ocean had melted and broken up, pieces of it moving southward along the Labrador Current toward the popular transatlantic ship route that the *Titanic* traveled. It was also the time of the Industrial Revolution, when shipbuilders competitively began making their liners bigger and faster, setting travel records between Southampton in England and the United States.

In hindsight, the elements appear well placed for that fateful night. The Marconi wireless telegraph (1897) was beginning to appear on ships for passenger's convenience. The *Titanic* received a number of telegrams that fateful night, warning about the icebergs; however, they do not seem to have aroused the necessary caution in the crew. The number of lifeboats carried by the *Titanic* met the English board of regulation requirement; as it turned out, there were not nearly enough to accommodate the need. The President of the shipping line did order the use of a somewhat lower grade of steel than recommended, and there are those who thought the mechanical rivets should be one and a half inches long instead of the one-inch size used. Nevertheless, no one explanation can sum up the catastrophe. Walter Lord (1917–2002), author of the renowned *A Night to Remember*, writes that survivor Lawrence Beesley felt that they were "simply in the presence of something too big to grasp."[1] Few disasters have provoked more mystery and speculation than that surrounding the *Titanic*, cautioning us that tragedy is often beyond human reasoning.[2]

> The *Titanic*, ready for her maiden voyage on April 2, 1912 (photo by an unnamed English photographer)

There are things more important than religious observance of religious conventions.

Literary Essay: *Teaching a Stone to Talk*, **by Annie Dillard.** In a little piece on the people in church, Dillard wryly describes the way people keep their church life safe and manageable, conventional as it were. She writes,

> On the whole I do not find Christians, outside the catacombs, sufficiently sensible of the conditions. Does anyone have the foggiest idea what sort of power we so blithely invoke? . . . The churches are children playing on the floor with their chemistry sets, mixing up a batch of TNT to kill a Sunday morning. It is madness to wear ladies' straw hats . . . we should all be wearing crash helmets. Ushers should issue life preservers and signal flares; they should lash us to our pews. For the sleeping god may wake some day and take offense, or the waking god may draw us out to where we can never return.[3]

Ready for the Kingdom of God?

Big Idea *The kingdom of God brings many surprises: not all who think they belong to it really do.*

Understanding the Text

The Text in Context

In 13:22 we are reminded that this whole section of the Gospel (beginning in 9:51) is set on the journey to Jerusalem, and that destination comes into clearer focus in 13:33–35: as Jesus looks ahead to the way Jerusalem will treat its "prophet," we are prepared in advance for his eventual arrival there and his weeping over the unrepentant city in 19:41–44. Both Jesus (4:43; 8:1) and his disciples (9:2, 60; 10:9) have proclaimed the coming of the kingdom of God, and that proclamation now takes on a growing note of urgency, demanding a response.

Historical and Cultural Background

The Jewish expectation of an eschatological messianic banquet, derived ultimately from Isaiah 25:6–9, was much elaborated in later prophetic and apocalyptic texts (cf. also Ps. 23:5). In Isaiah's vision it was to be a banquet for all nations, but by the first century it was generally assumed that it was the Jews, as the chosen people of God, who were guaranteed a place there, with the exception of those few who had specifically forfeited their place through rebellion and unbelief. The idea of only a few finding the way to salvation (13:22–27) and of Gentiles coming in to replace Jews (13:28–29) was therefore by now a quite subversive notion.

The geographical sequence of Luke's journey narrative is unclear, but Jesus's eventual approach to Jerusalem by way of Jericho indicates that he, like most Galilean pilgrims, traveled down the east side of the Jordan to avoid going through Samaritan territory (see on 17:11). Most of his route would then have been through Galilee and Perea, the two areas under the political control of Herod Antipas, whose hostility toward Jesus, as a second John the Baptist, has already been noted (9:7–9, with 3:19–20). But Jesus is bound for Jerusalem, which is not under Antipas's jurisdiction.

Interpretive Insights

13:18–19 *the kingdom of God . . . is like a mustard seed.* For the meaning of "the kingdom (rule) of God," see on 4:43. "The kingdom of God is like . . ." therefore means, "This is how God's rule is being established." A mustard seed is proverbially tiny (see 17:6), but it produces a large plant: *Brassica nigra* can grow to more than two meters in height. "Tree" is a bit of an exaggeration, but the term is probably used to recall the great "tree" of Daniel 4:10–12, 20–21, whose branches provided shelter for animals and birds, representing the nations coming under the protection of Nebuchadnezzar's empire. So the kingdom of God, which as yet seemed quite inconspicuous, would one day grow to embrace all nations. Luke will record this expansion in the book of Acts.

13:20–21 *the kingdom of God . . . is like yeast.* The "yeast" is actually the small quantity of sour dough (leavened bread) that is inserted into the new dough and causes it to rise. The kingdom of God may be hidden at present, but its power is all-pervasive. Again the impact of the imagery is increased by exaggeration: sixty pounds of flour is far more than any household baker would use in one baking—enough to feed a small village!

13:23 *are only a few people going to be saved?* It is not clear what prompted this

- The kingdom of God is not obvious at first, but its power will be all-conquering in the end.
- Salvation must not be taken for granted; it demands that we give God our whole life.
- There are those who think they are God's people, but are deceiving themselves.
- The boundaries of the people of God will not be drawn where many people expect.
- Jesus knows that his mission is to end in death in Jerusalem.
- But he has a mission to Jerusalem, and he longs for the city to respond before it is too late.

question, but Luke has used "salvation" language to describe the coming of God's kingdom (1:69, 77; 2:30; 3:6; 19:9–10), and this questioner wants to know whether there is a limit to its scope.

13:24 *Make every effort to enter through the narrow door.* The question is not directly answered, but Jesus turns a speculative inquiry into a personal challenge. An answer is clearly implied, however: both the small size of the door (compare the fuller imagery in Matt. 7:13–14) and the effort (lit., "struggle") required to get through it indicate that only a minority will make it. You cannot simply drift into the kingdom of God.

13:25–27 *Away from me, all you evildoers!* Not only is the door narrow and difficult, but also it will not remain open forever. This little parable of the householder and his would-be guests adds a note of urgency to the exhortation of 13:24, and the repeated use of "you" enhances its challenge. But it also spells out the reason why some

Jesus compared the kingdom of God to a mustard seed that grew into a bushy plant in which birds could perch. The plant Jesus was referring to is probably the flowering black mustard plant (*Brassica nigra*) shown here.

will be unable to enter. The repeated charge "I don't know you or where you come from" tells us that the key to salvation is not simply a matter of lifestyle or of keeping the rules, but of relationship. We are not told whom the householder represents, but the parallel in Matthew 7:21–23 and the reference here to sharing meals with him and to his "teaching in our streets" indicate that it is Jesus himself who stands behind the door. The claim to have moved in the same social setting and even to have been in his audience carries no weight with him. All that matters for their salvation is that he *knows* them. Without that, they are simply "evildoers" (quoting Ps. 6:8). They may have *heard* his teaching, but they have not responded to it (cf. 6:47–49).

13:28 *you yourselves thrown out*. The motif of inclusion and exclusion continues from 13:24–27. The identity of "you" is not explicit, but the context, including the contrast with the many from all quarters of the world in 13:29, suggests that Jesus addresses those of his Jewish hearers who have not responded to the message of the kingdom of God. The presence of the patriarchs and the prophets shows, however, that not all Jews are excluded.

13:29 *will take their places at the feast in the kingdom of God*. Literally, they "will recline in the kingdom of God." The posture of reclining, as at a Roman formal meal, suggests that the scene is the messianic banquet (see "Historical and Cultural Background" above). The geographical listing recalls Psalm 107:3 and Isaiah 43:5–6, which speak of Jewish exiles being gathered back to Palestine. But the contrast with "you yourselves" in the previous verse indicates that here, as in Matthew 8:11–12, Jesus

is speaking of a more inclusive gathering that brings in believing Gentiles in place of unbelieving Israelites.

13:30 *there are those who are last who will be first*. Jesus uses this "slogan" on several occasions (Matt. 19:30; 20:16; cf. Mark 9:35) to highlight the radical effects of his mission and the "upside down" values of the kingdom of God. In this context it relates specifically to the issue of salvation; conventional ideas of who are God's true people need to be rethought.

13:32 *Go tell that fox*. The warning by Pharisees may have been kindly intended (for Pharisaic interest in Jesus, see "Historical and Cultural Background" on 11:37–54) or simply designed to scare him away, but Jesus does not regard Antipas as a serious threat and plans to ignore him and carry on regardless. "Fox" is a contemptuous term for someone without honor, perhaps also with the implication of being devious.

13:33 *today and tomorrow and the next day*. This repeated phrase emphasizes that Jesus's course is already set, and he will not deviate from it. Its goal is Jerusalem, beyond Antipas's jurisdiction, where Jesus has no illusions about his fate.

13:34 *you who kill the prophets*. Compare 11:47–51, and of course 13:33 here.

how often I have longed to gather your children together. Here we have one of the incidental indications that the Synoptic pattern of a single journey to Jerusalem does not tell us the whole story of Jesus's ministry. The Gospel of John records Jesus's repeated visits to the capital and documents the resistance that the Jerusalem establishment has put up against his mission.

13:35 *your house is left to you desolate*.[1] This could be simply a metaphor for coming judgment on the city, but in view of Jesus's specific prophecy in 21:6 (which in Matt. 24:2 follows on the heels of the present saying), it is more likely that the "house" referred to here is the temple (strikingly described as "*your* house" rather than God's). There is thus an explicit link between Jerusalem's rejection of Jesus and the destruction of the temple by the Romans in AD 70. If this is the correct interpretation, then the following sentence should be understood as referring not to the greeting that Jesus will receive from the disciples (not from the people of Jerusalem) in 19:37–38, but rather to the possibility of a subsequent change of mind by Jerusalem after the temple has been destroyed. But there is no assurance that such a greeting will ever be given, or therefore that Jerusalem will ever "see Jesus" again after it has rejected and killed him.

The desolation Jesus speaks about in 13:35 is probably the destruction of the temple that occurred in AD 70, during the successful siege of Jerusalem by the Roman army under the command of Titus. To celebrate this victory, an arch was erected in Rome at the southern entrance to the forum. This relief from the arch of Titus shows items taken in plunder from the temple in Jerusalem, including silver trumpets, the table for the showbread, and a menorah.

Theological Insights

The parables of the mustard seed and of the yeast draw out the tension between the "now" of the coming of God's kingship through Jesus's ministry and the "not yet" of its full implementation. Such tension runs throughout the New Testament's presentation of fulfillment in Jesus.

In 13:22–30 we are provided insights into the scope of the gospel. Its universal appeal is not matched by universal response, and there are those who regard themselves as God's people who are deceiving themselves (cf. 3:8). Complacency is a deadly enemy of salvation. The kingdom of God reverses human expectations, not least with regard to who are insiders and who are outsiders. The inclusion of Gentile believers (along with Jewish patriarchs and prophets) in the reconstituted Israel of the kingdom of God means that the whole concept of the "chosen people" must be reexamined.

Jesus's lament over Jerusalem maintains a balance between a deep desire for its salvation and a realistic appraisal of its liability to judgment. This has significant implications for the debate about how God's grace and sovereignty relate to human responsibility and choice.

Teaching the Text

The "kingdom of God" is illustrated in the two parables of 13:18–21 and is the focus also of 13:28–29. This provides an opportunity to teach what the phrase means, and to explore the wider implications of this dynamic term. In particular, discuss whether the kingdom is a "realm" or a "reign" (or both) and how far the "now and not yet" aspect of the two parables still applies to God's kingship today. Note that the kingdom of God is already present in the seed and the leaven but then expands and is transformed as the seed grows into a plant and the leaven permeates the dough.

"Are only a few people going to be saved?" (13:23) is a question still demanding an answer. What answers to it are suggested by Jesus's teaching in 13:24–30, 34–35? And what do these answers reveal to us about the basis of salvation? Are there people in our church communities today who could be surprised at the final verdict? (Comparison with Matt. 7:21–23 may be helpful.) What are the implications of this teaching for our own assurance of salvation, and for our pastoral and evangelistic approach to others?

In 13:28–30 Gentile members are envisaged as taking the place of members of the "chosen people" in a reconstituted Israel. This theme provides the teacher with a good opportunity to discuss the expansion of the church in Acts, Luke's second volume, where the gospel will be rejected by many in Israel and will be received with joy by many Gentiles. What are the implications of this for our understanding of the true people of God? Both these verses and Jesus's lament over Jerusalem (13:34–35) raise the issue of the place of Israel in God's plan of salvation. You might use this opportunity to discuss the difficult theological question of whether, and in what sense, Israel is still God's special people. Is there any hope for Israel's future in 13:35? A good cross-reference for this theme is Romans 9–11.

Illustrating the Text

The kingdom of God, at first inconspicuous, will grow to reach all nations.

Popular Culture: The fast-food restaurant chain McDonald's is an example of enormous growth from a small start. Ray

Jesus laments over the city of Jerusalem and the historic negative response that the city has given to God's messengers. This aerial view of the old city of Jerusalem was taken from the north. The temple of Jesus's day was located where the Dome of the Rock stands today.

Kroc, who worked as a salesman for various products, including multimixers, decided to visit a small but lively business run by the McDonald brothers, because they had bought several of his mixers. Seeing something unusual in their restaurant, he developed a vision for a nationwide chain bearing the brothers' name. The corporation started in 1955 in California, and one hundred million hamburgers had sold by 1958. Now, besides the over thirteen thousand restaurants in the United States, there are some thirty thousand locations in 120 countries abroad. One other notable example of spectacular growth is Facebook, which was started by a few college students but has expanded into a nearly universal enterprise.

The entrance into the kingdom is accomplished with purpose and rigor.

Literature: *Pilgrim's Progress*, by John Bunyan. Few writers explain the straight and narrow way more powerfully than does Bunyan (1628–88), or the dangers of laxness and straying from the path. In one passage from the classic book (1678) Christian is admonished by Evangelist to stay true to the appointed way and to refuse to listen to Worldly Wiseman. Evangelist says,

> Now there are three things in this man's counsel thou must utterly abhor:
>
> 1. His turning thee out of the way.
> 2. His labouring to render the Cross odious to thee.
> 3. And his setting thy feet in that way that leadeth unto the administration of Death. . . .

> "The Lord says, *Strive to enter in at the strait gate* [Luke 13:24], the gate to which I sent thee; *for strait is the gate that which leadeth unto life, and few there be that find it* [Matt. 7:14]. From this little wicket-gate, and from the way thereto hath this wicked man turned thee, to the bringing of thee almost to destruction; hate, therefore, his turning thee out of the way, and abhor thy self for hearkening to him.[2]

In Christ's lament one can see his suffering from loving those who rejected him.

Poetry: "The Incarnation and Passion," by Henry Vaughan. Vaughan (1621–95), a Welsh physician and metaphysical poet, was greatly influenced by George Herbert, to whom he attributed his conversion to Christ. A few verses from this poem are as follows:

> Lord! When thou didst thy self undress
> Laying by thy robes of glory,
> To make us more, thou wouldst be less,
> And becam'st a woeful story.
>
> Ah, my dear Lord! What couldst thou spy
> In this impure, rebellious clay,
> That made thee thus resolve to die
> For those that kill thee every day?
>
> O what strange wonders could thee move
> To slight thy precious blood, and breath!
> Sure it was *Love*, my Lord; for *Love*
> Is only stronger far than death.[3]

Table Talk

Big Idea *The kingdom of God reverses our conventional ideas of who really matters.*

Understanding the Text

The Text in Context

This is the third time Luke has depicted Jesus as an invited guest at a Pharisee's table (see also 7:36–50; 11:37–54), and on each occasion Jesus makes things uncomfortable, challenging the social conventions and the moral values of his hosts and fellow guests. In this case, the meal setting continues into 14:15–24, in which Jesus will use the motif of a special meal as the basis for a parable about the kingdom of God that picks up the theme of 14:12–14. But Jesus was equally at home in less respectable company, and the great parables of chapter 15 will be prompted by the objections that Pharisees raised to his eating with "sinners." So the Pharisees, despite their occasional hospitality to Jesus, are finding themselves increasingly at odds with his teaching and his style of ministry.

Historical and Cultural Background

For Jesus's relations with the Pharisees, and especially their invitations to him to eat with them, see "Historical and Cultural Background" on 11:37–54. The social importance of shared meals in ancient society is demonstrated by numerous examples in both Testaments of the Bible.[1] To eat together created a special bond (cf. Ps. 41:9), and whom you ate with, or whom you invited to eat with you, defined your place in society. In a society where shame and honor were central motivating factors, this mattered. Jesus's willingness to eat with and to accept invitations from both the respectable and the disreputable, the influential and the marginalized, was one of his most striking traits. Compare with these Pharisaic meals Jesus's meal in the house of Levi (5:29–30). It was this generous inclusiveness that aroused the disapproval of the more conventionally religious (cf. 15:1–2).

For scribal rules on Sabbath healing, see "Historical and Cultural Background" on 6:1–16.

Interpretive Insights

14:1 *to eat in the house of a prominent Pharisee.* Literally, he is "one of the leaders of the Pharisees." This time Jesus is moving in the highest circles. The subsequent table talk in 14:7–14 presupposes fellow guests for whom social status is important. The midday meal customarily followed the synagogue service on the Sabbath (Josephus,

Life 279), using food prepared the previous day. Jesus may have been the visiting preacher that day.

he was being carefully watched. The invitation may have arisen not from simple hospitality but rather from a desire to check the orthodoxy of this new popular preacher (cf. 11:53–54; 20:20). It is possible, though Luke does not explicitly say so, that the presence of the obviously deformed man at the meal was a deliberate test case. The fact that after healing the man was "sent on his way" (14:4) indicates that he was not there as a guest.

14:2 *suffering from abnormal swelling of his body.* This is the NIV's idiomatic rendering of Luke's *hydrōpikos* ("dropsy, edema"), a condition in which swelling occurs from an accumulation of fluids in the body's soft tissues. The condition itself can be uncomfortable and embarrassing, but usually it is not immediately life-threatening. However, it sometimes can be evidence of underlying heart or kidney failure.

14:3 *Is it lawful to heal on the Sabbath or not?* Jesus appears to take the initiative, though the very presence of the obviously affected man at the meal may already have been an unspoken challenge (see above).

14:4 *they remained silent.* The question of healing on the Sabbath was not directly answered in the law of Moses, but we have already seen that scribal development of the law had by now declared it illicit (6:7; 13:14). The issue here is much the same as in those earlier incidents, and perhaps their unwillingness to make a public statement, which will be repeated here in 14:6 ("And they had nothing to say"), reflects their earlier humiliation (6:11; 13:17).

Key Themes of Luke 14:1–14

- Jesus defends his Sabbath healings by asserting the priority of love over regulations.
- It is better to be honored by others (and by God) than to claim honor for yourself.
- "Pride goes before a fall."
- Hospitality is about giving, not expecting benefits in return.
- The values of the kingdom of God challenge conventional scales of value.

14:5 *a child or an ox that falls into a well.* In Matthew 12:11 the same argument is used with regard to a sheep falling into a pit, and a related argument from animal welfare in 13:15 has "your ox or donkey." This issue of animal safety in relation to Sabbath law was discussed both among the later rabbis (who allowed a rescue [*b. Shabb.* 128b]) and more contemporarily at Qumran (where it was forbidden [CD 11:13–14]). Many manuscripts here have "donkey" instead of "son" (the Greek words are not dissimilar), producing a more natural pairing. But the very unexpectedness of "son" (surely no one would leave their son in a well until sunset!) suggests that it may be the original text. The argument is, as in the two previous incidents, that human welfare takes priority over Sabbath rules.

14:7 *picked the places of honor at the table.* In 20:46 Jesus will single this out as a typical trait of scribes: they want to be noticed and admired (cf. also 11:43). To be placed close to the host was more prestigious, and one's place in the social pecking order was perhaps even more significant in the honor/shame culture of first-century Palestine than it is in our (supposedly) more egalitarian society. "Showing off" was not a social taboo.

he told them this parable. What Jesus says in 14:8–10 is a parable in that it depicts a specific situation from which one may draw more general conclusions. In particular, the social advice of the parable is interpreted in 14:11 in a way that suggests an application to our relationship with God rather than merely with other people on a social level.

14:8–10 *When someone invites you to a wedding feast.* This whole scenario could be read simply as prudential advice for social climbers: it is better to aim low and hope for promotion than to aim too high and risk loss of face (cf. Prov. 25:6–7). But human society does not usually work like that: in the real world it tends to be the assertive who are noticed and honored, whereas those who do not push themselves forward are more likely to be ignored. It is only in the kingdom of heaven that "the meek will inherit the earth" (Matt. 5:5). It seems more likely, therefore, that here Jesus is deliberately challenging the prevailing social system and commending an alternative scale of values in which honor is something given by God, not arrogated to oneself, and in which "Pride goes before a fall." This is the worldview of the Magnificat, in which the proud and mighty are humiliated and the humble are elevated to honor (1:51–53). It is a world upside down.

14:11 *all those who exalt themselves will be humbled.* This concluding summary (which will be repeated in 18:14; see also Matt. 23:12) confirms the subversive, rather than merely prudential, interpretation of the "parable" in 14:8–10. It repeats the sense of Jesus's maxim in 13:30: "There are those who are last who will be first, and first who will be last." The kingdom of God is full of surprises.

14:12 *Jesus said to his host.* His host was an important person, "one of the leaders of the Pharisees." As in 7:44–47; 11:39–52, Jesus risks the "bad manners" of embarrassing his host in front of the other guests in order to challenge conventional morality.

14:12–14 *When you give a luncheon or dinner.* Jesus turns from the guests' behavior at dinner to the host's motivation in inviting them. Normal society works on a basis of mutual obligation: the reward for hospitality is to be invited in return. The threefold repetition of "repay" emphasizes this reciprocal expectation. But God's kingdom is one of grace, not of quid pro quo, as the following parable will illustrate (see 14:21, mentioning the same four disadvantaged groups), and we are called to follow his lead by giving to those who cannot give back. For such hospitality there is a "repayment," but it is not in this life. There is a similar theme in 6:32–36, and compare Matthew 6:1–6, 16–18 for the

Many of the recorded conversations and teachings of Jesus in Luke occurred in the context of meals. Dining in the Roman style meant reclining on couches or benches, usually in an arrangement of three that were placed in a "U" around a central table. The places of honor would have been on the center couch. A Roman dining room, known as a triclinium, is pictured here on a third- or fourth-century AD mosaic from Sepphoris.

contrast between earthly (human) reward and the unseen reward that God gives.

14:14 *the resurrection of the righteous.* Compare 20:35–36, where Jesus refers to "those who are considered worthy of taking part in the age to come and in the resurrection from the dead." Such people are "God's children" and so are "children of the resurrection." Resurrection is not an automatic destiny for all, but only for those who belong to God's family and whose lifestyle has therefore shown the family resemblance.

Theological Insights

For Jesus's rejection of a rule-based approach to Sabbath observance and his prioritizing of human welfare over scribal regulations, see on 6:1–16; 13:1–17.

This section of the Gospel highlights one of Luke's primary interests: the apparently topsy-turvy scale of values in the kingdom of God. This is summed up in 14:11, and the message will be graphically reinforced by the parable of the Pharisee and the tax collector in 18:9–14. God reverses our conventional way of assessing who is important and who can be ignored, and in Luke's Gospel Jesus appears repeatedly as the champion of the underdog, the marginalized, and powerless; he is the preacher of "good news to the poor" (4:18). It was humble shepherds who received the announcement of the Messiah's birth, and a despised woman who left the Pharisee's house with a blessing, and an "unclean" Samaritan who played the role of hero in one of Jesus's parables. Examples of this "Magnificat principle" will be multiplied as we make our way through Luke's story. The primary emphasis is on acceptance by

God, on the "wrong" people being saved. But this passage reminds us also that God's people are expected to reflect his generous values, so that the topsy-turvydom of the kingdom of God is reflected in our social relationships, even at the level of our guest lists and seating arrangements, as well as in our expectation of salvation.

Teaching the Text

There are three separate themes in this section, even though all three (and also the parable that follows in 14:15–24) are set at the same meal table. It will be helpful to describe for your congregation or audience the nature of meals as rituals of social status in the first century (see "Historical and Cultural Background" above). You might think of parallel situations today where someone might break social norms. In all three of the following themes, Jesus breaks social norms and challenges the thinking of his day. The kingdom of God turns the world's values upside down. The poor and humble and oppressed are lifted up and the rich and powerful and influential are brought down.

1. *Healing on the Sabbath (14:1–6).* Much the same issues arise here as in 6:6–11; 13:10–17. See "Teaching the Text" on 6:1–16. God created the Sabbath for the good of human beings, not to control them or put oppressive burdens on them. Consider areas where we might put legalistic rules on others that are neither commands of God nor for the benefit of others. Are there aspects of our church or social life where there is a danger of regulations getting in the way of "doing good"? On the other hand, some people use their own rejection

of "legalism" as an excuse to live however they want, without discerning the harm that certain behaviors bring to themselves or their Christian witness. Consider where the right balance is here. How far should we be guided by the "instinctive" impulse to "do good" (6:9) by tackling the problem first before asking theological or legal questions? Can you think of circumstances in which this might be a bad precedent?

2. *Places at table (14:7–11)*. Some scholars speak of an honor/shame culture as being different from our own. To what degree is that true? You might suggest situations in which Jesus's advice here might be literally applied in our culture. What are examples of when pride has gone before a fall? And are there principles here that should be applied more widely to our (and our society's) sense of values?

3. *Whom to invite (14:12–14)*. It is particularly helpful when teaching this section to remind listeners of the role meals played in the culture of the first century. This passage is not just about inviting your friends over for a party. Rather, meals were the arena in which social status was established and maintained. People of that day would not think of inviting the lower members of society to their banquets, since these people could give nothing in return. So Jesus is calling believers to offer the same kind of undeserved and unconditional grace that God has given us. Encourage listeners to examine their own (and others') motivations for offering hospitality. Does 14:12 describe our typical behavior? Are there situations where 14:13 should be literally applied? Are there current examples of this happening? Consider what might be an analogous situation in your cultural context.

Illustrating the Text

Jesus put human need above religious rules.

Literature: *Les Misérables*, by Victor Hugo. Written in 1862, this novel by the French author Hugo (1802–85) is considered one of the greatest of that century. Few characters in great literature stand out so memorably as the dark, almost maniacal police inspector Javert, who relentlessly, legalistically pursues Jean Valjean through the years. All that Valjean has done is steal a loaf of bread to feed his family. He spends years in jail for this, growing embittered, and then manages to escape. His conversion experience is familiar and often told. Nevertheless, Javert pursues him, keeping to the letter of the law, never seeing the human component, never knowing mercy.

Humility is a primary component of great character.

Television: *Keeping Up Appearances*. This British television series (1990–95) features Patricia Routledge as Hyacinth Bucket (pronounced pretentiously "Bouquet"). In the absolute antithesis of this principle, Hyacinth is a working-class woman who has married a middle-class man, Richard, and becomes a hopeless snob, forever trying to impress her neighbors with money, always putting on airs, and also unwittingly making it very clear that she is not of the social standing that she pretends to be. Even watching one humorous episode of this series would render many examples of how not to be humble.

Literary Autobiography: *Good People: From an Author's Life*, by Jon Hassler. In this lovely book, novelist Jon Hassler (1933–2008) talks about an encounter he had with

since the first grade? But with this difference: Jackie wasn't being humble for God's sake . . . he was being simply himself.[2]

When we give, we should do it without drawing attention to ourselves.

Quote: *Extreme Righteousness: Seeing Ourselves in the Pharisees*, **by Tom Hovestol.** Hovestol points out the ways in which modern church giving can lack humility:

> Looking at Jesus's warnings, we should evaluate our own motives with three questions:
>
> 1. Are there ways that we 'sound trumpets' or 'toot our own horns' to advertise our giving?
> 2. Are we in danger of drawing inaccurate conclusions about ourselves and others by our level of giving?
> 3. Do we give for the praise of people? . . .

Still we may practice more subtle, culturally correct methods of announcing our giving. Many churches use pledge cards to set their annual budget and conduct capital campaigns and "faith promises" to increase giving for missions. Though such giving can honor God when pledged in faith, the motive also can be mixed. For obvious reasons, some people give more when they sign their name on the dotted line. Meanwhile, many are motivated to give at year-end to save on income tax. Others give, knowing the church treasurer and others will see our amounts. . . . Perhaps the most sinister financial practice of all is to evaluate our own godliness by the level of our financial contributions.[3]

a truly humble person, a bright, insightful boy named Jackie whom he calls "a twelve-year-old saint." Hassler was only a few years older, and during their acquaintance Jackie contracted a fatal illness. Hassler visited him regularly, and the "sweetness of [Jackie's] soul" stayed with him for a lifetime. Jackie remarked on the boys playing football outside his window without "a trace of envy in his voice," and when Jackie's brother-in-law, worried about his weight loss, often brought him a quart of ice cream, Jackie ate it, only to throw up when his brother-in-law left. Hassler writes,

> God knows how many quarts of ice cream Jackie forced down and brought up again to sustain his family's hope. I know only that the more I saw of Jackie's self-abnegation, the more fascinating it became. Wasn't this the sort of God-pleasing humility the church had been urging on me

The Cost of Discipleship

Big Idea *The kingdom of God demands our full commitment; you cannot be a half-hearted disciple.*

Understanding the Text

The Text in Context

Jesus's table talk in the house of a leading Pharisee continues with a parable about a similar banquet, which picks up the theme of 14:12–14, the challenge to invite those who cannot reciprocate. In the parable, however, the host represents God himself, whose open-hearted generosity is the model that we are called to follow. But the parable also highlights the obverse of that free grace, the fate of those who, having initially accepted the invitation, then failed to honor it. This raises the possibility of failed discipleship, and the following verses, 14:25–35, explore this theme, not now at the table, but as Jesus continues his journey toward Jerusalem. This paragraph therefore takes up the theme with which the journey began (9:57–62): the cost of following Jesus.

Historical and Cultural Background

For the significance of meals and who is invited to them, see "Historical and Cultural Background" on 14:1–14. This parable reflects the protocol followed for more formal meals, for which an invitation was issued and accepted some time in advance, so that the host would know how much food to prepare; acceptance of the initial invitation was thus a social commitment. A slave was then sent out on the day to tell the guests when the feast was ready (cf. Esther 5:8; 6:14). To back out at that stage would expose the host to serious embarrassment and loss of face.

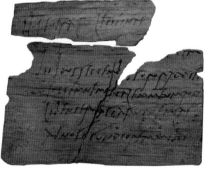

Jesus focuses on the social etiquette of the day as he tells his parable of the great banquet. Once an invitation to a banquet was issued and accepted, the guest was obligated to attend. Shown here is an invitation to a birthday celebration written AD 97–103 and found in the remains of a Roman fort at ancient Vindolanda (modern Chesterholm), Northumberland, England.

The banquet in the parable clearly represents the messianic banquet (see "Historical and Cultural Background" on 13:18–35), a traditional way of envisaging ultimate salvation.

For the challenge to accepted convention in Jesus's demand that his disciples put following him before family loyalty, see on 9:57–62.

Interpretive Insights

14:15 *Blessed is the one who will eat at the feast in the kingdom of God.* This reference to the messianic banquet perhaps invites Jesus to endorse the popular expectation of who will be on the guest list. Instead, as in 13:28–29, Jesus will turn it on its head.

14:16–20 *they all alike began to make excuses.* Parables often contain features that would be improbable in real life. It is most unlikely that the three "excuses" listed (especially getting married!) could have arisen unforeseen in the short time between the original invitation and the call to table, or that anyone would buy a field or oxen (let alone the considerable investment of five pairs) without first inspecting them. Such implausible excuses would be a calculated insult to the host, and his anger is understandable. But these excuses serve within the parable context to illustrate the sort of preoccupations (property, commerce, relationships) that (like the thorns in the field [8:14]) can get in the way of effective discipleship.

14:21 *the poor, the crippled, the blind and the lame.* These are the same four groups of people whom Jesus has exhorted his host to invite to meals in 14:13 (and who were excluded from the messianic banquet

Key Themes of Luke 14:15–35

- Initial enthusiasm for the kingdom of God can be lost under the pressure of competing interests or loyalties.
- Some surprising people will share in God's salvation, in place of those who should have been there.
- Following Jesus must take priority over even the most basic family loyalties.
- Do not set out on the path of discipleship until you have faced up to what it will cost.

as envisaged by the Qumran community [1Q28a 2.3–9]). These are the people least likely to be invited to a special meal because they will be unable to return the invitation and so fulfill the expected social convention. But it is these "losers" who represent the ultimate beneficiaries of the kingdom of God.

14:22 *there is still room.* In adding a second stage of recruitment (contrast Matt. 22:9–10), Luke is perhaps reflecting on the process that he will relate in Acts: the mission to Jews was followed by one to Gentiles (represented here by those outside the town). The repeated and pressing invitation emphasizes the host's determination that his provision not be wasted, and thus it expresses God's desire to welcome as many as possible into his kingdom.

14:23 *compel them to come in.* The verb "compel" (*anankazō*) conveys a sense of urgency, but is not a sanction for forcible conversion, still less for the excesses of the Inquisition. In the parable setting, these "no-hopers" would naturally be reluctant to believe that such an invitation could be serious, and so they would need to be persuaded.

14:24 *I tell you.* The "you" is plural, whereas in the parable the host has spoken to his slave in the singular; either he now addresses the newly assembled guests, or, perhaps more likely, this is Jesus's concluding comment. In the latter case, the messianic banquet has remarkably become *Jesus's* banquet.

not one of those who were invited will get a taste of my banquet. The parable balances the free grace of God with the reality of judgment for those who reject his salvation. Like the saying in 13:28–29, this parable speaks of the replacement of those who should have been at the banquet by a motley group of those who have no right to be there. The parallel parable in Matthew 22:1–14 is grouped with two others that speak of the loss of the privileged status of the Jewish religious leadership in favor of those whom they despised, and the setting here in the house of a leading Pharisee may indicate that Luke had a similar replacement theology in mind; but if so, it is less clearly marked by either the wording or setting than in Matthew.

14:26 *If anyone comes to me and does not hate father and mother.* Jesus often exaggerated in order to make a point forcefully, and few interpreters have supposed that actual hatred is meant here. It is a matter of priorities: even the most basic of human attachments must give way to the demands of God's kingdom (cf. 18:29). For a similar use of "hate" in the sense of "love less," see 16:13, and compare Genesis 29:31–33; Malachi 1:2–3. The Matthean parallel here has "love more than" (Matt. 10:37).

14:27 *whoever does not carry their cross.* See on 9:23. Jesus's own crucifixion will not be specifically referred to as such until the crowd shouts for it in 23:21, but the cross was well enough known and feared in the Roman world, and especially in Palestine, where it was regarded as a barbarous foreign punishment, to make the metaphor unmistakable.

14:28 *Suppose one of you wants to build a tower.* This is the first of two hypothetical scenarios designed to illustrate the danger of embarking rashly on discipleship without first recognizing the demands that it will make. The public humiliation of the failed tower builder illustrates the dishonor, as well as the personal tragedy, of a shallow commitment that, like the man who built without foundation (6:49), ends in spiritual disaster.

14:31 *Or suppose a king is about to go to war.* Here is another illustration of "biting off more than you can chew." The detail is not to be pressed to the point of finding here a recommendation to come to terms with the enemy (the devil? sin? the secular world?); rather, the point is that you should not get started on something that you do not have the resources to complete.

14:33 *those of you who do not give up everything you have.* Compare the instruction in 12:33 (and in 18:22) to sell everything, and see comments there. Like the saying in 14:26, this concluding summary sets up an absolute contrast, between the things of this world and the kingdom of God, which does not take into account the practical business of living. The point is again that God must come first.

14:34 *if it loses its saltiness.* Pure sodium chloride cannot be anything but salt, but the "salt" taken from the shore of the Dead Sea and sold in Palestine was not pure: the salt content might be washed out, leaving a useless deposit. Whether the thought is of salt as flavoring or as preservative, it is the distinctive "saltiness" that makes an effective disciple; one who is no longer "salty" (i.e., who is indistinguishable from the world around) is no good to anyone. For this metaphorical use of salt, compare Matthew 5:13; Colossians 4:6. "Loses its saltiness" is literally "is made foolish," possibly reflecting a pun on an Aramaic word that means both "tasteless" and "stupid."

Theological Insights

The parable of the banquet continues the theme of surprises in the kingdom of God: the "wrong" people finish up as the winners. Salvation is by grace, not by having the right pedigree. But if salvation cannot be gained by inherited privilege or by working to deserve it, it can, apparently, be lost

by failure to respond to God's call, and the host's dismissive words in 14:24 indicate that there is a point of no return. To have received and responded to the message of the kingdom of God is not enough if we then turn away from its demands and allow other concerns to supplant God's claim on our lives.

The sayings about the cost of discipleship in 14:25–35, though separated from the parable by a change of scene, have a similar focus and also envisage the possibility of ultimate failure. The kingdom of God is for the committed, not for the dilettante. For Luke's stress on this theme, see also 9:57–62; 18:24–30.

Teaching the Text

Before applying the parable to contemporary life, it is important for the teacher or preacher to set it in the context of Jesus's ministry. This is one of Jesus's more allegorical parables, where the banquet owner

Comparing effective disciples to salt, Jesus says, "Salt is good, but if it loses its saltiness, how can it be made salty again?" (14:34). One source of salt for the Jewish people was the Dead Sea, shown here with its crystallized salt clusters. But these salt clusters are a mixture of different mineral salts. Depending on the chemical composition, the salt obtained may be tasteless or bitter and therefore useless.

represents God, the invited guests represent the religious leaders and other "insiders" in Israel, and the second set of guests represent those "outsiders" (sinners, tax-collectors, Samaritans) who are responding positively to Jesus's proclamation of the kingdom of God. In the book of Acts, it will be the Gentiles in particular who are the "outsiders" who respond to the gospel.

After establishing this historical context in Jesus's ministry, it is appropriate for the teacher to contextualize the parable for today. How might it apply to contemporary church members as a call to full commitment?

Both the parable and the following sayings envisage the possibility that some who initially respond to God's call may ultimately fail to make the grade. This raises issues at two levels: (1) theologically, it seems to call in question the traditional understanding of the "perseverance of the saints"; (2) pastorally, it opens up the issue of assurance of salvation. Does our ultimate salvation depend on our continued faithfulness? Part of the answer here may be found in considering the historical context discussed above. In light of Luke's narrative strategy, the parable may be seen to relate especially to Israel's corporate response, rather than to the question of individual salvation. This is about Jewish rejection and Gentile reception of the gospel. The sayings that follow, then, encourage Jesus's hearers to consider the cost before responding. Though salvation is a free gift from God and costs us nothing, it ultimately costs us everything—our whole life given to God as a living sacrifice (Rom 12:1–2).

For issues arising from Jesus's demand to give up everything, see "Teaching the Text"

on 12:22–40. In the light of 14:26 here, listeners might be encouraged to consider the implications of discipleship for family life and loyalty, especially when not all members of a family share the faith.

In a discussion or small group setting, ask the group for examples from their own experience of the cost of following Jesus. In a sermon or teaching lesson, you might present examples from church history or more recent missionary accounts of those who have sacrificed all for the sake of the gospel.

Illustrating the Text

It is possible to lose one's enthusiasm for the kingdom of God to competing interests and loyalties.

Video: *The Great Feast*, by Tim Andrews. This interesting and amusing video is an animated short that puts the parable into the context of a barbeque. The host calls friends who have any number of excuses, believable and ludicrous, for not coming: marriage, taking care of their "paddock," sickness, and so on. The host then asks the less attractive and the infirm to the barbeque. This short film is funny and pointed and contemporary.

We must not overestimate or underestimate the call to discipleship.

Commentary: *Preaching the Parables: From Responsible Interpretation to Powerful Proclamation*, by Craig L. Blomberg. Blomberg articulates the problem of the modern interpreter, which is to overestimate the cost of discipleship. He writes,

> Jesus is not saying that we must know everything God will ever ask of us

throughout our entire lives and then agree to it in advance in order to become true believers. If that were his criterion, no one would ever qualify. Jesus is saying, however, that we must realize the amount that commitment could cost. . . . Surrendering every area means including the touchy areas of our lives that we don't do well talking about in Christian circles, most notably that famous triad of money, sex, and power.

He adds, "The straightforward interpretation of the command to 'give up everything' sounds as if we must become totally impoverished." Instead "every would-be Christian must give up whatever stands in the way of wholehearted discipleship."

Conversely, Blomberg talks about the importance of not underestimating the cost of discipleship. In a series of personal illustrations he talks about the decision that he and his wife made to practice a principle of "graduated tithe, which means that as [their] annual gross income increase[ed] above and beyond any simple cost of living increase," their giving went up as well. Besides that, he notes, he decided to pursue a theological career instead of one in mathematics, even though that meant a great difference in salary, because he wanted to "affect people's lives for eternity," and for him (he is careful to emphasize this), the math career would not have done that.[1]

Quote: *The Prodigal God: Recovering the Heart of the Christian Faith,* **by Tim Keller.** In this book Keller, a New York City pastor, talks about the nature of a feast and its importance and its practical application today. He writes, "When we invite someone to eat with us, it is an invitation to relax a bit and get to know one another. In many cultures, to offer to eat with someone is to offer them friendship." But, he continues, "We live in a culture in which the interests and desires of the individual take precedence over those of the family, group, or community."[2]

One of the excuses given for not keeping the commitment to attend the great banquet was "I just got married" (14:20). A bride and groom decorate this piece of Greek pottery (440–420 BC, Athens).

Luke 14:15–35

Lost and Found

Big Idea *"The Son of Man came to seek and to save what was lost" (19:10).*

Understanding the Text

The Text in Context

After the scene at a Pharisee's table in 14:1–24 (cf. 7:36–50; 11:37–54), the focus turns to the much less conventional meals that Jesus enjoyed with social and religious outsiders. This theme was earlier raised by the meal in Levi's house (5:27–39) and by the "sinful woman" who disrupted another more conventional meal (7:36–50), and it has been reflected in Jesus's subversive ideas about who should be at the messianic banquet (13:28–29; 14:15–24). The issue for Jesus is not simply a matter of table etiquette, but rather of God's plan of salvation, which will be gloriously summed up at the table of an arch-sinner in 19:10. So a trio of parables here challenges the reader to rethink who is ultimately acceptable to God. They not only justify Jesus's unconventional practice but also, in the person of the unbending older brother, draw attention to the danger of opposing and, ultimately, missing out on God's grace.

Historical and Cultural Background

Kenneth Bailey offers a wealth of cultural insights on these three parables,[1] some

of which will be picked up in the following comments.

Interpretive Insights

15:1 *tax collectors and sinners.* On tax collectors, see "Historical and Cultural Background" on 5:27–39, and for the standard pairing of "tax collectors" with "sinners," see 5:30; 7:34.

15:2 *the Pharisees and the teachers of the law.* See the sidebar "Scribes and Pharisees" at 5:12–26. These two groups (who for Luke effectively form a single body of religious purists) have been responsible for most of the expressed opposition to Jesus in the Gospel, even though we have noted a degree of (guarded?) openness to Jesus on the part of some Pharisees (7:36; 11:37; 13:31; 14:1). Here, as usual, they are concerned with following the rules of purity, for which they themselves were responsible, rather than with helping people. For the same group set over against tax collectors, see also 5:29–30; 7:29–30.

15:4 *Suppose one of you has a hundred sheep.* This would be quite a large flock, indicating a relatively prosperous owner. A hundred sheep would probably be too many for one man to look after, so the owner may have had an employee or a family member with whom he could leave the rest of the flock while he went in search of the lost one. But the owner cared enough to go himself rather than sending his assistant to search. In light of the way the scene was set in 15:1–2, it is probably right to see the shepherd's action as representing the rescuing mission of Jesus himself, but the shepherd is also the owner, who corresponds to the father in the third parable as representing God. There is no need to press the distinction: in the mission of Jesus God himself is seeking the lost, and the shepherd's joy over the rescue becomes the joy of "heaven."

15:6 *Rejoice with me.* The overwhelming note is one of joy, first at finding the sheep (15:5) and then at the homecoming.

15:7 *rejoicing in heaven.* The parallel in 15:10 speaks of "rejoicing in the presence of the angels of God." It is God's joy that is primary, but the summoning of the friends and neighbors in the parable points to a sharing of that joy: the whole angelic community has shared God's concern for the

Key Themes of Luke 15:1–32

- Jesus's practice of sharing meals with those outside respectable society is at the heart of his mission.
- God cares for the individual, not just for the community as a whole.
- Those who seem lost can still be restored.
- God's love will go to extraordinary lengths to welcome back the lost, and their return gives him great joy.
- God's people should share that joy rather than standing aloof and parading their own merits.

lost sinner and now rejoices at the happy outcome.

one sinner who repents. Repentance is at the heart of the message of John (3:3), of Jesus (5:32), and of the church (24:47). Jesus's favorable attitude toward "sinners" (15:2) did not mean that they had no need to change. It is only when repentance takes place that the kingdom of God has triumphed.

ninety-nine righteous persons who do not need to repent. Compare 5:32, where the term "righteous" was similarly ironical. No one is exempt from the need to repent (13:3, 5), but with some it is more obvious than with others.

15:8 *Or suppose a woman has ten silver coins.* Here a female scenario balances the story of the male shepherd (as in 13:18–21). The coins are drachmas, each of which would be roughly a day's wage, so that the loss of one was a matter of real concern in a peasant household. The story is making essentially the same point as that of the shepherd, though

"And when he finds [his lost sheep], he joyfully puts it on his shoulders and goes home" (15:5–6). This scene was captured in early Christian art as a portrayal of Jesus. This statuette, known as *The Good Shepherd*, is from the fourth century AD.

Luke 15:1–32

since the loss of the coin need not be as public as that of the sheep, the extravagant public celebration is more striking in this case.

15:11 *There was a man who had two sons.* In the third "lost and found" parable the stakes are much higher: the shepherd lost one sheep out of a hundred, the woman one coin out of ten, but this man one son out of only two. The story is much more fully developed, and in particular the son who stayed at home features strongly alongside his delinquent brother; in the end it is the former who is the loser. Indeed, this might be ironically called "the parable of the two lost sons": one was lost and found, the other kept and lost.

15:12 *Father, give me my share of the estate.* Culturally, this was a deeply insensitive demand to make while the father was still in good health: he cannot wait for his father to die! That the father complies is even more remarkable. The younger son's share would be one third of the estate (Deut. 21:17).

15:13–16 *he began to be in need.* In order to travel, the son had to convert his property into cash. His subsequent wastefulness and humiliation are graphically described; note especially the ultimate degradation for a Jew: feeding *pigs*. Bailey fills out the picture especially with details about the carob "pods" that the pigs were given.[2]

15:17–19 *he came to his senses.* These verses portray the "repentance" that was the subject of the first two parables (15:7, 10), even though that term is not used here. His motive was primarily a self-centered need to survive, but his decision still represents

The lost coin was a Greek drachma and, like a Roman denarius, was worth about one day's wage. The drachma pictured is from ancient Larissa in Thessaly, Greece (435–400 BC).

a total reversal of his previous attitude and an acceptance of his father's authority, which previously he had flouted. The inclusion of "against heaven" even suggests a genuine sense of wrongdoing.

15:19 *make me like one of your hired servants.* He cannot reclaim his privileges as a son, and he has no inheritance to go back to, but he still hopes for an independent and productive life as an employee (not one of the slaves [15:22]), which may eventually enable him to make some financial reparation to his father.

15:20 *while he was still a long way off.* This suggests that the father is on the lookout (Helmut Thielicke famously dubbed this parable "the waiting father"). Like the shepherd and the woman, he is searching. His undignified run down the road risks social humiliation, and his public embrace of the disgraced son declares to a potentially hostile village that the son is restored to the family. The son's rehearsed speech is interrupted before he can make his proposition of employment; he is "this *son* of mine" (15:24) again. Grace has ruled out the need for earning his way back to favor.

15:23 *Bring the fattened calf.* To kill so large an animal indicates that this is not merely a family celebration: the whole village is invited, as in the other parables (15:6, 9). The son's public rehabilitation is therefore complete.

15:25–30 *Meanwhile, the older son.* The older son's alienation is shown by the fact that he stays away from the house and only inquires from a distance. He has no intention of joining in the celebration. By refusing to take his expected place at the feast, he publicly snubs his father, and by speaking of "this son of yours" he refuses to acknowledge that he belongs to the same family as his brother. He represents a self-centered negativity that submerges the good news under his own sense of personal grievance. His father's "favoritism" leaves him full of self-pity: he has been nothing but a slave, and an unrewarded one at that.

15:31–32 *"My son," the father said.* Rather than stand on his dignity, the father has left the house (15:28) for a second time (15:20), and remarkably he overlooks his son's insolent rant. He appeals to his son's sense of fairness ("everything I have is yours"—his part of the inheritance is still intact) and his family loyalty ("this brother of yours"). His repetition of the declaration of 15:24 focuses the reader's attention on the key feature of the story, the recovery of the lost *one* rather than the "righteousness" of the ninety-nine, here represented by the older son. We are not told how the older son responded, but the signs are not encouraging. The listening Pharisees are left to reflect on which son represents them and which represents the sinners with whom Jesus ate.

Theological Insights

God loves sinners and calls them to repentance. His grace goes to extraordinary lengths to bring them back, and his joy is unbounded when the lost are found. So much is clear from all three parables.

The older brother adds a further dimension. God's "faithful" people are called on to share his outgoing love and his willingness to accept the repentant. If they fail to do so, it is they, rather than those whom they look down on, who will miss out on the blessings of salvation.

The parable of the prodigal son has often been called "the gospel in a nutshell." Yes and no. The shepherd's search and the father's run down the road speak eloquently of the hardship and humiliation that Jesus accepted in his mission to seek and save the lost, but the means of salvation through the cross are at best hinted at. The necessary correlative to repentance is atonement, and that must be sought elsewhere in Jesus's message.

Teaching the Text

In teaching the three parables it is important to set them first of all in the context of Jesus's ministry and its narrative progression in Luke. While all three parables describe God's great love for the lost and his joy when they return to him, the third represents a natural climax by containing additional allegorical elements: the father representing God, the younger son representing the sinners and tax collectors to whom Jesus is ministering, and the older son representing the self-righteous religious leaders who are rejecting Jesus's ministry to the lost. Only when this original context is understood can the parable be appropriately contextualized today.

In terms of application, it is helpful to point out in your teaching that each of us at times plays the role of each character: (1) wandering away from God or rejecting his authority, (2) joyfully seeking out and welcoming sinners, (3) arrogantly looking down on others as "too lost" to be reconciled to God.

There are other issues that could be taken up in a lesson or sermon:

1. Taking the three parables together, consider how far true repentance and restoration depends on (a) the sinner, (b) God, (c) the believing community.

2. Should Jesus's practice of associating with sinners be taken as a model for our own discipleship and mission? If so, how should it be applied in practice in our own social setting?

3. Are the other ninety-nine sheep just a minor element in the story, or whom might they represent? Their characterization as "not needing to repent" is intriguing. Is God not interested in the respectably religious? How do they relate to the older son?

4. Encourage listeners to consider how far the term "the gospel in a nutshell" fits the parable of the two sons (see "Theological Insights" above).

5. Kenneth Bailey lists the following five words as summing up the message of the parable of the two sons: **sin, repentance, grace, joy, sonship**. Do these accurately represent the content of the parable? Is there anything missing? (E.g., might "compassion" [15:20] be added?). In your teaching or study group, spell out the implications of each word.

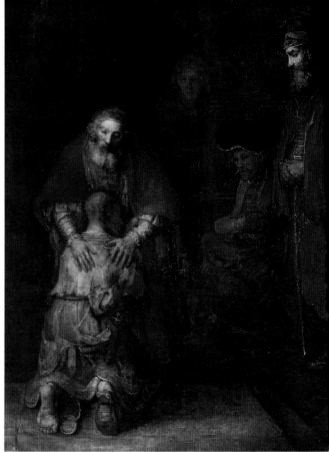

The Return of the Prodigal Son, ca.1668–69 (oil on canvas), by Rembrandt Harmenszoon van Rijn (1606–69)

Illustrating the Text

God will go to extraordinary lengths to rescue the lost, and he welcomes them back with joy.

Story: "The Runaway," by Philip Yancey. This is Yancey's modern retelling of the parable of the prodigal son, featuring a young girl who runs away from home. It is available on the *Christianity Today* website, followed by some valuable comments on the nature of God's grace.[3]

Song: "When God Ran," by Benny Hester. This song powerfully recounts the parable and especially the shocking display of love in the father's willingness to run to his son and offer him full and unconditional forgiveness. It is available online.

Quote: *What's So Amazing about Grace?*, **by Philip Yancey.**

> The story of the Prodigal Son . . . appears in a string of three stories by Jesus—the lost sheep, the lost coin, the lost son—all of which seem to make the same point. Each underscores the loser's sense of loss, tells of the thrill of rediscovery, and ends with a scene of jubilation. Jesus says in effect, "Do you want to know what it feels like to be God? When one of those two-legged humans pays attention to me, it feels like I just reclaimed my most valuable possession, which I had given up for lost." To God himself, it feels like the discovery of a lifetime.[4]

The restoration of the prodigal, while free and unconditional to him, came at a cost.

Christian Living: *The Prodigal God*, **by Timothy Keller.** In a remarkably fresh take on this familiar story, Keller writes,

> While Act I of the parable showed us how free the father's forgiveness is, Act 2 gives us insight into its costliness. The younger brother's restoration was free to him but it came at enormous cost to the elder brother. The father could not just forgive the younger son, somebody had to pay! The father could not reinstate him except at the expense of the older brother. There was no other way.

As Keller points out, "Every penny that remained of the family estate belongs to the older brother" since the father had said to him, "My son, everything I have is yours."[5]

God came not only to restore the prodigal son but also the angry and resentful elder brother.

Christian Living: *The Prodigal God*, **by Timothy Keller.** Keller continues his insightful treatment of this parable, "Jesus does not put a true older brother in the story, one who is willing to pay any cost to seek and save that which is lost. . . . The younger brother gets a Pharisee. . . . Either as elder brothers or as younger brothers we have rebelled against the Father." Keller concludes that Jesus is "our true elder brother," who "paid our debt, on the cross, in our place."[6]

God and Mammon

Big Idea *Our heavenly well-being depends on how we have handled the possessions entrusted to us here on earth.*

Understanding the Text

The Text in Context

Two more parables (16:1–8a, 19–31) follow the three in chapter 15. In the light of the interpretive comments on the first parable in 16:8b–9, both parables make a connection between life on earth and life in heaven, and the focus in both is on wealth and how we use it, a prominent theme in Luke that has already been given sustained attention in chapter 12 (summed up in the call to store up treasure in heaven in 12:33–34) and, more indirectly, in chapter 14. The same theme will recur especially in 18:18–30.

Between the two parables is a collection of sayings, with a change of audience (from the disciples to the listening Pharisees) in 16:14. Most of these sayings (16:8b–15) continue to relate to the theme of the responsible use of possessions, but the three sayings in 6:16–18, taking up issues of dispute between Jesus and the Pharisees, are on different subjects.

Historical and Cultural Background

A steward (NIV: "manager") was an employee given wide-ranging executive responsibility for running his employer's estate and dealing with his tenant farmers. The debts of oil and wheat represent the agreed rents, in kind, for land leased out by the rich man. The manager unilaterally reduces the rent on the assumption that his employer, having delegated his authority, would not know what amounts had been agreed.

An alternative view[1] is that the employer knew the agreed rents, but by the time he saw the altered contracts, he was unwilling to forfeit the reputation for generosity that had resulted from the reduced rents, wrongly assumed to have been authorized by him.

A different reading[2] assumes a financial rather than an agricultural

setting. The rich man (or the manager on his behalf) has loaned out large sums of money at interest, but the loans have been expressed in commodity terms in order to avoid the Jewish prohibition of "usury" (lending money at interest). The manager uses his unsupervised authority to remove the "interest" element from those debts, thus pleasing the debtors but leaving his employer unable to protest because that part of the bill could not be legally defended.

Numerous variations on these basic approaches have also been suggested. The following notes assume the first of these options.

Interpretive Insights

16:1 *accused of wasting his possessions.* The charge is not merely of incompetence but of dishonesty (16:8). The manager will not dispute the charge of misappropriation, and he takes it for granted that he will (justly) lose his job (16:3–4).

16:3–4 *people will welcome me into their houses.* Unable or unwilling to face the humiliation of earning or begging his living, he plans to use his present position of authority, while he still can, to curry favor with the tenant farmers. By putting them in his debt, he will have a cushion of goodwill to fall back on, possibly even another job to go to.

16:6–7 *Nine hundred gallons of olive oil . . . A thousand bushels of wheat.* The quantities are large, indicating relatively wealthy tenant farmers, who thus would be valuable friends for the dismissed manager to have on his side.

make it four hundred and fifty . . . make it eight hundred. No reason is indicated for the difference in treatment (one is given a 50 percent reduction, the other only 20 percent), and it would be inappropriate allegorization to look for a symbolic reason.

16:8 *The master commended the dishonest manager.* The commendation is not, presumably, for his dishonesty (for which he was firing him) or for having cheated him yet further by reducing the rents, but for his initiative and foresight, even at his employer's expense. If this seems an improbably objective assessment by the man who has been cheated, we should note that characters in a parable do not have to behave as in real life. An alternative reading, that this is Luke's editorial comment (saying that Jesus, the *kyrios*, expressed this opinion after finishing the parable), produces an incoherent sequence, since Jesus continues speaking in the next verse, with no indication of an editorial interruption.

One debtor owed nine hundred gallons of olive oil. Liquids such as olive oil and wine were stored and transported in clay vessels known as amphoras such as the one shown here from first-century BC Italy.

Luke 16:1–18

the people of this world . . . the people of the light. This is an unusual formulation of words for the contrast between disciples and the rest of society. "People" is literally "sons"; the Qumran community described themselves as the "sons of light" as opposed to the "sons of darkness." True disciples may have something to learn from worldly common sense, in this case the manager's canny instinct for self-preservation, however much they must distance themselves from the world's basic values.

16:9 *use worldly wealth to gain friends for yourselves.* "Worldly wealth" is literally "the mammon [Aramaic for 'possessions'] of unrighteousness" (cf. 16:11, where the Greek says "unrighteous mammon"). Money and possessions lend themselves to ungodly purposes, but they can also be used for good ends (the Aramaic translation of Deut. 6:5 has "Love the Lord your God with . . . all your mammon"). The mention of "eternal dwellings" indicates that the "friends" represent not earthly supporters but rather a heavenly reception committee. Just as the manager made sure he had a refuge after he lost his job, so disciples should ensure that they will be welcome in heaven when this life is over. A responsible and generous use of possessions is one way to make such preparation (cf. 14:14).

16:10–12 *Whoever can be trusted with very little.* This short complex of sayings may originally have been independent, but it follows appropriately from the comments on the message of the parable in 16:8–9. The way you use your possessions on earth shows whether you can be trusted with spiritual wealth.

16:13 *No one can serve two masters.* This saying is found also in Matthew 6:24,

linked to its context here by the catchword "mammon" (16:9, 11, 13). The NIV translation is misleading: many people do hold two jobs with different employers at the same time. But "serve" is literally "be a *slave* of," and one cannot be wholly *owned* by two slave owners. This pithy saying sums up the theme of the priority of God over any earthly interests that has run through much of the Gospel. It ensures that the parable is not taken as giving too positive an account of the value of possessions. "Money" here is "mammon," picking up the term translated "wealth" in 16:9, 11.

16:15 *What people value highly is detestable in God's sight.* "Detestable" is a word often associated with idolatry: their love of money is in effect worship of the false god "mammon." Like many of Jesus's sayings, this one is not to be pressed to the conclusion that God disapproves of all human aspirations. The literal sense, "what is exalted among people," perhaps indicates proud conceit (the Pharisees' self-justification and the admiration that they seek from others) rather than valuation in a neutral sense. Compare Isaiah 2:12–18. The saying possibly echoes Proverbs 16:5.

16:16 *everyone is forcing their way into it.* This is a new subject. Jesus's proclamation of the good news of the kingdom of God has brought to fulfillment what until the coming of John the Baptist had been merely a hope for the future. "Forcing their way into it" suggests enthusiastic response, but the wording is unusual, and in light of the clearly negative parallel in Matthew 11:12, it can also be taken to mean "is using force against it" (possibly a comment on the Pharisaic opposition just noted). Another option would be "is being forced into it," perhaps picking up the use of "compel" in 14:23. This is an obscure saying, but one that in some way underlines the climactic period of history inaugurated by John's mission.

16:17 *It is easier for heaven and earth to disappear.* This is another independent saying (cf. Matt. 5:18), which is perhaps intended here to balance the sense of a new beginning in 16:16. The law and the prophets are being fulfilled in the kingdom of God, but that does not mean that they are dispensable. Matthew 5:17–20 and especially the examples that follow in 5:21–48 tease out the tricky blend of continuity and discontinuity that result from the *fulfillment* of the Old Testament in the ministry and teaching of Jesus.

16:18 *Anyone who divorces his wife.* This is the only teaching about divorce in Luke. Matthew 5:31–32 and Matthew 19:3–12 = Mark 10:2–12 fill out the picture of Jesus's views, which were controversial in a Jewish society that generally accepted a man's right to divorce his wife (not vice versa) on the basis of Deuteronomy 24:1–4. Divorce carried an automatic right for both man and woman to remarry. Jesus's more rigorous teaching is based on the view that if God has made two people "one flesh" (Gen. 2:24) in marriage, that union cannot simply be set aside, so that a purported divorce with the remarriage that follows results in "adultery" by both parties, in that they are violating a one-flesh union that in God's sight is still unbroken.

Theological Insights

The parable and the sayings that follow it in 16:8–15 contribute several key insights with regard to the relation of worldly possessions to the kingdom of God:

- Despite its association with ungodly living ("the mammon of unrighteousness"), wealth can and should be used in God's service.
- The way we use our earthly wealth affects our heavenly well-being; compare the call in 12:33–34 to store up "treasure in heaven" by not clinging to earthly possessions.
- To love possessions for their own sake puts us in conflict with God's call on us: "You cannot be slaves of both God and mammon."
- The kingdom of God requires a reversal of the normal human scale of values.

Luke 16:18 is the only teaching of Jesus on divorce in the book of Luke. Shown here is a Jewish bill of divorce from AD 72. It was written in Aramaic and found in one of the caves located within the high walls of the Wadi Murabba'at.

The three brief sayings in 16:16–18 raise, but do not develop, important theological issues:

- the radical change, beginning with John, as the Old Testament is fulfilled (and the position of John as the "hinge" between Old and New)
- the balance of continuity and discontinuity between the Old and New Testaments, especially with regard to the continuing function of the law of Moses

- Jesus's rejection of divorce, with all the issues this raises for Christian ethics today

All these issues need to be filled out from other parts of the New Testament, noted above in "Interpretive Insights" on 16:16–18.

Teaching the Text

In view of the brevity of the independent sayings in 16:16–18, it is probably not appropriate to use them as a basis for teaching. If you do, you will need to range more widely than this passage to fill out the far-reaching issues that they raise (see "Theological Insights" above). This is a good passage to turn to when discussing the role of John the Baptist (see, e.g., 7:18–35).

The parable of the manager is a puzzle to many. Is Jesus really approving dishonesty? Why does he introduce and apparently commend such a disreputable character? These questions raise the issue of what parables are intended to achieve: they are not necessarily models for imitation (though of course some are [see 10:37]). So what is it about the manager's self-interested action that Jesus commends and calls us to emulate? While some may be tempted to skip this unusual parable when teaching through Luke's Gospel, in fact its strangeness can be a "hook" for gaining the interest of your audience. Read, narrate, or dramatize the parable, then ask, "What was Jesus thinking?! Why would he commend such a dishonest character?" Notice that in his teaching after the parable, Jesus himself draws out various applications:

1. Act shrewdly with the resources you have been given (16:8–9). This passage gives an opportunity to discuss our attitude toward and use of possessions. Too often Christians are so concerned with conservative and traditional ways of doing things that they do not use the creative and intellectual gifts God has given them. We should be as innovative and shrewd for the kingdom as our secular counterparts are in the marketplace. Encourage listeners to consider creative ways wealth may be used for heavenly benefit. While it is true that earthly riches can be an enormous impediment to our spiritual life (see 18:24–25), they can also be used greatly for God's purposes. Discuss what is good, and what is bad, about "mammon" (possessions).

2. Get an eternal perspective and plan ahead for the inevitable future (16:9). Life is short and only what has heavenly value will last. Notice that the parable of the rich man and Lazarus follows in 16:19–31. How might that rich man have found "treasure in heaven"?

3. Be responsible in the little things and God will use you for greater things (16:10–12). The manager acted shrewdly, opening up greater opportunities. Jesus says the same is true in our Christian lives.

4. Serve the only Master who really counts (16:13). In the end, the manager's loyalty to his earthly master counted for little. Our ultimate loyalty must be to God, who holds in his hands our eternal destiny.

Illustrating the Text

Wealth can be a tremendous hindrance to ultimate salvation.

Literature: *Paradise Lost*, **by John Milton.** In this great epic poem (1667) about the fall of Satan and his angels and the subsequent sin of Adam and Eve and their expulsion from the garden, Milton (1608–74) depicts one of the fallen angels as Mammon. The description of the viciousness of his fall is striking. In fact, the passage tells us that even in heaven Mammon was more caught up with the streets of gold than with the Divine (book 1, lines 678–90):

> Mammon led them on,
> Mammon, the least erected Spirit that
>   fell
> From Heav'n, for ev'n in Heav'n his
>   looks and thoughts
> Were always downward bent, admiring
>   more
> The riches of Heav'n's pavement, trod-
>   den gold,
> Than aught divine or holy else enjoyed
> In vision beatific: by him first
> Men also, and by his suggestion taught,
> Ransacked the centre, and with impi-
>   ous hands
> Rifled the bowels of their mother Earth
> For treasures better hid. Soon had his
>   crew
> Opened into the hill a spacious wound
> And digged out ribs of gold.[3]

Wealth can be an aid or a great hindrance to effective discipleship.

Quote: *Money and Power*, **by Jacques Ellul.** Ellul (1912–94), a French philosopher, law professor, and theologian, issues this warning:

> When we claim to use money, we make a gross error. We can, if we must, use money, but it is really money that uses us and makes us servants by bringing us under its law and subordinating us to its aims. We are not talking only about our inner life; we are observing our total situation. We are not free to direct the use of money one way or another, for we are in the hands of this controlling power. Money is not only a manifestation of this power, a mode of being, a form to be used in relating to man—exactly as governments, kings, and dictators are only forms and appearances of another power clearly described in the Bible as political power. . . . That Mammon is a spiritual power is also shown by the way we attribute sacred characteristics to our money. The issue here is not that idols have been built to symbolize money, but simply that for modern man money is one of his "holy things." . . . We understand then why money questions are not considered part of the moral order. They are actually part of the spiritual order.[4]

Anecdotes: There are many stories of people who, while wealthy, were also tremendously generous, giving away great quantities of money. R. G. LeTourneau (1888–1969), a renowned business magnate and inventor, known as the "man who moved mountains" for his expertise in designing and manufacturing earth-moving equipment, was also a Christian philanthropist who is said to have given away huge portions of his income without fanfare. Numerous other examples can be found, such as Christian doctors who have gone to impoverished countries to donate their services and resources or business people who have funded missionary endeavors.

Affluence and the Afterlife

Big Idea *Material wealth can go with spiritual poverty; in the end it is spiritual wealth that matters.*

Understanding the Text

The Text in Context

There has been no change of audience since 16:14: Jesus is still speaking primarily to the Pharisees. (He will return to teaching the disciples in 17:1.) Luke has characterized the Pharisees as lovers of money (16:14), so this parable is a warning to the affluent. It is thus the culmination of a theme, already set out in the blessings and woes of 6:20–26, that has run strongly through these middle chapters of the Gospel, especially in 12:13–34; 14:1–24, 33–34; 16:1–15: treasure in heaven is more important than wealth and comfort on earth.

Central to this teaching on wealth has been the assumption that this world is not the end, and that how we use our wealth here with respect to other people has consequences for our life after death (12:20–21, 32–34; 14:14, 15–24; 16:8–9). This parable focuses in on that theme, fills out the meaning of the "eternal dwellings" of 16:9, and offers the fullest portrayal of life after death in this Gospel. Indeed, this passage, together with Matthew 25:31–46, provides the essential data for understanding Jesus's teaching on the traditional "four last things" (death, judgment, heaven, hell).

Historical and Cultural Background

There is unmistakable anger in Jesus's description of the social inequality that was typical of first-century Palestine, as it has been of most cultures, ancient and modern. If the beggars are not literally at our gates, we know that they are out there if we dare to look. It was taken for granted in Jewish society that there would be rich and poor, but almsgiving was expected and highly valued. Rabbi Simeon the Just (third century BC) said, "By three things is the world sustained: by the law, by temple-service and by acts of generosity" (*m. 'Abot* 1:2). By the first century there was a well-organized relief system based on the synagogues, sustained by contributions from members of the community. This was partly regulated by the so-called tithe for the poor (Deut. 26:12), but there was also much private initiative, to the extent that the rabbis had to regulate to prevent a man impoverishing himself and his family by excessive giving.

The Pharisees, in disagreement with the Sadducees (20:27; Acts 23:6–8), believed in a life after death. In most of the Old Testament "Hades" represented the abode of the dead, a place of neither joy nor punishment, but a shadowy survival to which no one looked forward except as an escape from earthly suffering. But Daniel 12:2–3 shows a developing idea of differing fates after death, and by the first century the ideas of heaven and hell were widely accepted, though pictured in quite a variety of ways. In Jesus's teaching "hell" (*geenna*, "Gehenna" [see on 12:5]) is a place of destruction and/or punishment, but in this parable Hades seems, unusually in the New Testament, to have the same connotation. As in 13:28–29, heaven is again envisaged as a banquet (see below on 16:22).

An Egyptian folktale from around the same period also tells of a reversal of fortunes for a rich and a poor man in the afterlife, with the rich man tormented and the poor man placed close to Osiris.[1]

Interpretive Insights

16:19 *There was a rich man.* With no introduction to identify this as a parable, Jesus launches straight into a story of two individuals. As a (presumably) imaginary story designed to provoke reflection and response, it is rightly described as a parable, but the graphic description of the situation of the two men after death makes it also a lesson (in a vividly pictorial form) about the

> Key Themes of Luke 16:19–31
>
> - Those who have material wealth are expected to share it for the benefit of others.
> - A position of privilege or disadvantage on earth may be reversed after death.
> - In the afterlife there are two possibilities: happiness or suffering.
> - There is no possibility of a second chance after death.
> - The key to eternal happiness is repentance during this life.

afterlife, and the debate with Abraham about the rich man's family (16:27–31) adds a further moralizing conclusion. These features are too pronounced to be set aside as merely "scenery" incidental to a supposedly main point that there can be a reversal of fortunes after death, and that selfishness does not pay in the end.

16:20 *a beggar named Lazarus.* He is the only character in any of Jesus's parables to be given a personal name, a Greek abbreviated version of the Hebrew name "Eleazar," meaning "God has helped." (The medieval use of "lazar" for "leper" derives from this parable; it did not mean "leper" in ancient times.) The naming of the beggar here may simply serve the literary function of providing a name by which the rich man can identify him in 16:24, 27, but it is possible that Jesus expected his hearers to recognize the etymology of the name as reflecting the ultimate outcome of the story. Any link with the Lazarus of John 11 (who, unlike this Lazarus, *was* sent

Jesus's parable starts, "There was a rich man who . . . lived in luxury every day" (16:19). This mosaic floor excavated in the Jewish Quarter in Jerusalem would have decorated a house occupied by a wealthy family in the first century AD.

back from the dead) is unlikely; the name was very common.

16:21 *Even the dogs came and licked his sores.* This translation is misleading: the Greek says, "*But* also the dogs. . . ." This is not an escalation of his suffering, but a welcome (and therapeutic) relief. Dogs, unclean as they were in Jewish eyes, did their best for this beggar, whom the respectable company refused to help.

16:22 *the angels carried him to Abraham's side.* Literally, it is "to Abraham's chest." As in John 13:23–25, to recline at a formal meal "against the chest" of the host (i.e., in the place on the host's right) denotes the place of honor. Lazarus is taken straight to the messianic banquet, at which Abraham, Isaac, and Jacob preside (13:28), and is given the most prestigious place there. The contrast with his earthly condition could not be more marked. The role of angels in conveying a dead person to heaven is unusual, perhaps representing popular belief.

died and was buried. A starkly simple statement in comparison with the fulsome account of what happened to Lazarus. There is to be no further banquet for the rich man.

16:23 *In Hades, where he was in torment.* On Hades, see "Historical and Cultural Background" above. The "torment," by fire (16:24), fits the normal understanding of hell (*geenna*) rather than that of

Hades; the two ideas seem to be merged here. (An alternative view, that both men are in Hades, which is envisaged as divided into zones of bliss and of torment, reads less naturally here: Hades is specifically "this place of torment" [16:28], where the rich man now finds himself.) Compare 13:28 for the idea that the suffering of the lost is increased by being able to "see" the saved at the banquet.

16:24 *Father Abraham, have pity on me.* All Jews claimed Abraham as their "father" (cf. 1:54–55; 13:16; 19:9). In 3:8 John the Baptist envisaged Jews relying on this relationship for salvation, but this man seems resigned to his fate and begs only for palliative help. But he expects Lazarus to be at his beck and call—the habits of a lifetime die hard!

16:25 *in your lifetime you received your good things, while Lazarus received bad things.* The simple reversal of fortunes set out here is specific to this story. It would go beyond the parameters of the parable to find here a more general principle, that all who are privileged on earth will suffer after death, and vice versa. While there is no explicit statement that the rich man's suffering results from his callous treatment of Lazarus, the loaded way their respective situations were described in 16:19–21 invites the reader to make that assumption.

16:26 *a great chasm.* The geography of heaven and hell was variously pictured in Jewish writings, but the "chasm"

In 16:19–20 the rich man is "dressed in purple and fine linen" and has plenty to eat, all good things. Purple robes would have indicated his wealth because the dye used to create purple was very expensive, and usually only royalty could afford it. Shown here are the shells of the murex snail, from which the purple dye was obtained.

serves here not so much as a topographical feature but rather to picture the complete separation of the two, and thus to emphasize that the division after death is permanent. There seems no room here for any idea of purgatory or of a second chance after death.

16:27 *send Lazarus to my family.* The rich man assumes that all his brothers are bound for the same destiny, since presumably the whole affluent family shared the same lifestyle (they need to "repent" [16:30]). His altruism, which extends only to those in his immediate family circle, contrasts with his previous lack of interest in the plight of Lazarus.

16:29 *they have Moses and the Prophets; let them listen to them.* A Jew had no excuse for ignorance of the way of salvation. Being the "people of the book," they knew of God's bias toward the poor, to which both law and prophets give frequent expression. The permanent value of the Old Testament, just asserted in 16:17, is thus reinforced.

16:31 *they will not be convinced even if someone rises from the dead.* Within the story the point is simple: those who will not listen to Scripture are beyond help; even a miracle will not convince them. But it may also be read as a wry reflection on Jesus's own experience. Neither his fulfillment of the law and the prophets nor his miracles have convinced the Pharisees, and when the ultimate miracle of his rising from the dead takes place, many of those whom these Pharisees represent will remain unmoved.

Theological Insights

The basic story reinforces the conflict between God and mammon. Affluence can lead to self-sufficiency and to a callous unconcern for the less privileged, and that is the way to spiritual disaster.

But this parable also provides some of the New Testament's clearest teaching (albeit in pictorial form) about judgment and life after death. The following seem to be assumed:

- There is life after death for both good and bad.
- The afterlife provides an opportunity for the injustices of life on earth to be corrected (cf. the blessings and woes of 6:20–26).
- There is a clear and unbridgeable divide between heaven and hell.
- There is no second chance of salvation after death.
- Judgment is based on our response to God's will as set out in the Scriptures.

Like the other great judgment scene in Matthew 25:31–46, this parable may leave the impression that judgment is based solely on how we have treated other people. The gospel of salvation through the atoning death of Christ must be supplied from elsewhere in the New Testament.

Teaching the Text

This parable raises both ethical and theological issues that can be discussed in a sermon or lesson.

Ethically, it cries out against socioeconomic injustice. Encourage listeners to consider how far our affluent lifestyle today is complicit in a similar injustice, and what we can do about it both individually and corporately. Who are our Lazaruses, and where are they (internationally as well as locally)? This would be a good place to review this important theme of the rich and poor throughout Luke's Gospel (e.g., Mary's Magnificat [1:46–53], the beatitudes and woes [6:20–26], the parable of the rich fool [12:13–21], etc.). On the theme of the eternal consequences of one's concern for the poor and oppressed, compare Matthew's parable of the sheep and the goats (25:31–46).

Theologically, the parable provides an opportunity to discuss our understanding of judgment and of life after death, taking up the issues listed in "Theological Insights" above. Discuss how much is pictorial imagery (carried by angels, Abraham's bosom, fire, the cooling finger, visibility between heaven and hell, the great chasm, etc.), and what are the realities underlying the imagery. Remember that this is a parable and is not *necessarily* intended to describe the specifics of the afterlife.

Does it bother us that the parable says nothing about atonement as the basis of salvation? What might this teach us about our approach to Scripture as a source for theology (i.e., the danger of looking for the whole gospel in a single passage)? How does judgment on the basis of deeds (e.g., Rom. 2:6–11) fit into the gospel of grace?

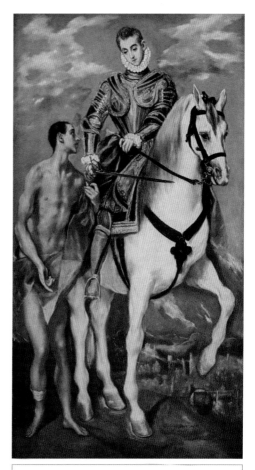

Saint Martin and the Beggar (ca. 1597–99), by El Greco

Illustrating the Text

Those who have material wealth are expected to help others.

Church History: St. Martin of Tours. Born in Hungary, Martin (316–397), while still a boy, attended a Christian church without his parents' permission at about the time when Christianity, though still looked down on by many in high society, was becoming a legal religion. At the age of fifteen, Martin fulfilled the requirement of joining the cavalry and was stationed in France, where he had the famous vision that is most often told in connection with his name. As the story goes, he ran into a beggar who, in need of clothing, touched Martin's heart. He then cut his military garment in half and gave the beggar the other part. That night he dreamed of Christ, who was wearing the half-garment that he had given away. According to the story (and there are several variations), Jesus said to him, "Here is Martin, the Roman soldier who is not baptized; he has clad me."[2]

Several great works of art show details of the story. Among the most famous is one by the Spanish painter El Greco (1541–1614), *St. Martin and the Beggar* (ca. 1597–99), which hangs in the National Gallery of Art in Washington, DC. In the painting, Martin is seated on a white horse and looks down at the partially clothed beggar, who looks up at him.

Judgment is based on our response to God's will as set out in the Scriptures.

Quote: *Mere Christianity*, by C. S. Lewis. In the following passage Lewis underlines the biblical reality that we will see eternal consequences for our choices.

> When the author walks on to the stage the play is over. God is going to invade, all right: but what is the good of saying you are on His side then . . . ? For this time it will be God without disguise; something so overwhelming that it will strike either irresistible love or irresistible horror into every creature. It will be too late then to choose your side. There is no use saying you choose to lie down when it has become impossible to stand up. That will not be the time for choosing: it will be the time when we discover which side we really have chosen, whether we realized it or not. Now, today, this moment is our chance to choose the right side. God is holding back to give us that chance. It will not last forever. We must take it or leave it.[3]

Literature: *The Inferno*, by Dante Alighieri. *The Inferno* (*Hell*) is the first part of the trilogy *The Divine Comedy* (1308–21), by the Italian poet and philosopher Dante Alighieri (1265–1321). It is about the specific judgments awaiting those who violate God's law. In one short passage he describes the punishment of one group of "souls."

> This miserable state
> Is reserved for the dismal souls of those
> Who lived their lives with neither
>   praise nor blame.
> They have been mingled with that
>   wicked choir
> Of heavenly angels who did not rebel
> Nor were they pledged to God, but to
>   themselves.[4]

Lessons in Discipleship

Big Idea *True discipleship cannot be undertaken casually; the service of God demands all that we can bring to it.*

Understanding the Text

The Text in Context

In 17:11 Luke reminds us that Jesus and his disciples are still on the journey to Jerusalem. Much of the journey narrative (9:51–19:44) consists of teaching given to the disciples. In the last few chapters this has largely taken the form of parables, and we will return to parables at the beginning of chapter 18. But in this section we find four separate units of teaching (17:1–2, 3–4, 5–6, 7–10), loosely connected in that all relate to the nature and demands of discipleship, followed by a brief exemplary story. The story involves a Samaritan, whose action, like that of the good Samaritan in 10:30–37, shows up the failure of the Jews in the story and so reinforces Luke's insistent challenge to accepted social conventions.

Historical and Cultural Background

For "leprosy" and the ritual associated with its cleansing, see on 5:12–26. For relations between Jews and Samaritans, see on 9:37–56; the term "foreigner" (lit., "of another race/kind") in 17:18 underlines the ethnic and religious divide. The remarkable situation here of a single Samaritan being in a group with nine Jews in this border region must presumably be accounted for by the dire situation of those ostracized because of their disease; ethnic prejudice has given way to the camaraderie of suffering and social exclusion.

There are echoes in 17:11–17 of the healing of Naaman (to which allusion has already been made in 4:27), a foreigner with leprosy, healed with a word, cured as he went away, and returning to offer thanks (2 Kings 5).

Interpretive Insights

17:1 *Things that cause people to stumble.* The word *skandalon* (lit., "stumbling block, trap") occurs often especially in Matthew to denote causes of spiritual failure, whether temporary or complete. The RSV translated it as "temptation to sin," but that is too limited. A disciple may be damaged spiritually by unkindness or malicious gossip (or even by simply being ignored) as well as by temptation and bad example. To be the cause of another person's spiritual failure is so serious that a quick drowning would be a merciful alternative to the judgment that it incurs.

17:2 *one of these little ones.* The reference is not only to children, though of course it includes them. For God's people as "little children," compare 10:21. In Matthew 18:6–14 (and 10:42) disciples are "little ones" and are to be treated with special consideration. In the kingdom of God the "little ones" are the ones who really matter. See above on 9:47–48.

17:3 *So watch yourselves.* This clause could be either the conclusion of 17:1–2 or the introduction to 17:3–4 (there is no "so" in the Greek text).

If your brother or sister sins against you. As in 6:41–42, the context indicates that the "brother or sister" is not just an actual family member, but more generally a fellow disciple. The best Greek manuscripts do not have "against you" here, but since it does occur in 13:4, it is probable that the thought throughout is of personal offense rather than a more objective awareness that a fellow disciple has gone astray. The "rebuke" is in context not a self-righteous condemnation but rather a realistic pointing out of the offense with a view to reconciliation. Once the rebuke has been effective in producing repentance, forgiveness is not an option but a duty.

17:4 *seven times in a day.* The partial parallel in

Matthew 18:21–22 makes it clear that this is not meant to be a specific limitation (seven, but no more) but instead a round number for unlimited forgiveness. A later rabbinic discussion concluded that three times was enough (*b. Yoma* 86b–87a).

17:5 *Increase our faith!* The imperative verb could be translated simply as "give," but the focus on smallness in 17:6 probably supports the sense "add to" (i.e., "increase").

17:6 *faith as small as a mustard seed.* For the mustard seed as a proverbially tiny amount (seven hundred seeds in one gram, according to one expert), see on 13:18–19. This response therefore brushes aside the request for *increased* faith: it is not the "amount" of faith that matters, but the power of the God in whom that faith is placed.

you can say to this mulberry tree. The Greek clause is indefinite, "you *could* say," which may imply that they do not have even this minimal amount of faith yet. Or perhaps the indefinite formulation is to draw attention to the exaggerated

To emphasize the seriousness of causing someone to stumble, Jesus said it would be better to be thrown into the sea with a millstone around one's neck. This would bring certain death since millstones were quite heavy, needing donkeys to turn them. Shown here are several millstones on display at Capernaum.

example chosen: "You *could* say, but of course you would not." To uproot a mulberry tree and plant it in the sea by a mere word (in itself a rather pointless, if spectacular, exercise) represents doing what is humanly impossible.

17:7–10 *We are unworthy servants; we have only done our duty.* The NIV's regular use of "servant" for the Greek word for "slave" has unfortunately reduced the impact of this little parable. If the behavior depicted on the part of the master in 17:7 is socially unthinkable with a (hired) "servant," how much more so with a (wholly owned) slave! (That was the point of the similar imagery in 12:37.) A slave, however tired he may be, does as he is told and expects no thanks for it. This may seem a bleak model for discipleship: is our God a slave driver? But the point is that the best we can do is still less than what we owe to God as our sovereign Lord; there is no place for preening and complacency in discipleship. "Unworthy" could also be translated "useless"; the same word is used in Matthew 25:30 for the slave who gained no profit for his master. We can never put God in our debt. Compare a similar saying by Rabbi Yohanan ben Zakkai: "If you have worked hard in keeping the Torah, do not claim merit for yourself,

since that is what you were created for" (*m. 'Abot* 2:8).

17:11 *along the border between Samaria and Galilee.* In 9:51–56 Jesus had tried to set off through Samaria. If Luke's travel narrative represents only a single journey, he seems to envisage Jesus now following instead the traditional route for Galilean Jewish pilgrims to festivals in Jerusalem, which skirted Samaria and went down the east side of the Jordan, recrossing to the west bank at Jericho (where he will arrive in 18:35).

17:12 *They stood at a distance.* This is what would be expected, rather than the boldly unconventional approach of the man with leprosy in 5:12. They did not approach Jesus, and this time we are not told that he

Jesus told the lepers, "Go, show yourselves to the priests" (17:14). Because lepers were considered unclean they would need to be seen by the priest to be declared clean. In order to become ceremonially clean they had to participate in a complicated ritual. The ritual, described in Leviticus 13 and 14, involved offering sacrifices, shaving the entire body, washing one's body and clothes, and waiting for a period of days, after which the procedure would be repeated. During the Second Temple period, part of this process took place at the temple complex. In the northwest corner of the court of the women was the chamber of the lepers, where those who had been cured would come to bathe on the eighth day of their purification process and wait for their guilt, sin, and burnt offerings to be sacrificed by the priests.

chamber of the lepers

court of the women

touched them. As in 7:7, a word of healing was enough.

17:14 *as they went, they were cleansed.* Here we see another difference from the previous curing of leprosy. In that case, the healing was instant, and the command to go to the priest followed. To set off for Jerusalem (see on 5:14) before the healing was visible suggests a remarkable faith in Jesus's power and the reliability of his word.

17:16 *He threw himself at Jesus' feet and thanked him.* Now that the disease is cured, the man can be declare "clean." His gratitude to the healer is natural, even though Jesus will correctly attribute the praise rather to his Father (17:18).

17:18 *Has no one returned to give praise to God except this foreigner?* Presumably the priest to whom he, as a Samaritan, must show himself would be in Samaria, not in Jerusalem, hence his separation from the other nine. Samaritans worshiped the same God, but Jews did not expect them to be truly pious. But this Samaritan, like the Gentile army officer (7:9), has shown faith that puts Israel to shame.

17:19 *your faith has made you well.* This formula is often a "performative utterance," but not here, since the cure of the ten has already taken place, all of them presumably through similar "faith." But this man's overt praise of God is evidence of a spiritual health that Jews would not expect to find in a Samaritan.

Theological Insights

Each of the four sayings in 17:1–10 has a different focus. Some key insights are as follows.

1. *The centrality of repentance and forgiveness.* A saving relationship to God depends on our repentance and his forgiveness (3:3; 5:32; 13:3–5; 15:7, 10; 24:47; and note especially the parable of the lost son [15:11–32]), but here we see also the ethical implications, in that we are equally obliged to forgive each other in response to repentance, to "be merciful, just as your Father is merciful" (6:36).

2. *Faith and miracle.* Jesus's dismissal of the request to "increase" faith disallows the notion that we can contribute (by the quantity of our faith) to what is God's work, not ours. Everything is possible to those who call on God's power, but that does not mean that the person who prays has *carte blanche*, irrespective of the suitability of what is prayed for.

3. *The danger of spiritual pride.* The medieval idea of "works of supererogation" was fundamentally wrong. There is nothing that "goes beyond" our duty to God (not even the Samaritan's return to give thanks), and therefore there is no place for spiritual pride and self-satisfaction.

The story of the grateful Samaritan is a further contribution to Luke's ongoing portrayal of God's concern for the outsider and the presence of grace in the most unlikely places. See "Teaching the Text" below for more on this.

Teaching the Text

The sayings of 17:1–10 raise several pastoral issues that should be considered in a lesson or sermon:

- What sort of "stumbling blocks" to another's discipleship might Jesus have had in mind? What are examples of people whose Christian journey has been derailed by what other Christians have done or said (or not done or said)? Are there things in our own lives, individually or corporately, of which Jesus would say, "Watch yourselves" (17:3)?

- Discuss the damage that results from an unforgiving attitude. Why do we find it so hard to forgive? It might help to draw attention to the parable that explores this issue in Matthew 18:23–35, and to the relevant clause in the Lord's Prayer (Matt. 6:12; Luke 11:4). If repentance is a prerequisite of forgiveness, what do we do with someone who is apparently unrepentant?

- Is 17:6 an encouragement to "adventurous" praying? Are there limitations that should be observed? How should we seek to encourage those who feel they do not have the faith to "expect great things from God"?

- Does 17:7–10 mean we can never relax in our service for God? Is there a danger of discouragement through feeling that we can never do enough? Why may Jesus have felt it necessary to make this point about always being "useless slaves"?

The story of the ten lepers is often taught as a lesson on gratitude. Only one man returned to thank Jesus and we should act with similar gratitude. While this is certainly one point, in the context of Luke's Gospel (and Acts) the parable's greater message centers on the fact that this gratitude is shown by an "outsider," a Samaritan rather than a Jew. In the overall scheme of Luke-Acts, the self-righteous in Israel reject the gospel, while outsiders receive it—sinners, tax-collectors, and eventually, Gentiles. In

this sense the story parallels 7:36–50, where the sinful woman who anointed Jesus's feet shows more love than Simon the Pharisee because she has received much greater forgiveness.

On the fact that the man is a Samaritan, remind listeners of Luke's other references to Samaritans (9:51–56; 10:30–37; Acts 8:4–25), and contrast them with Matthew's only such reference (Matt. 10:5). Why was this theme so important to Luke? There are at least two important reasons. First, the Samaritans—like sinners, tax collectors, lepers, prostitutes, and other outsiders—are among the "lost" that Jesus came to save (19:10). Second, in Acts, Luke's second volume, the proclamation of the gospel in Samaria (Acts 1:8; 8:4–8) is essential for the outward expansion of the good news. Luke's Gospel is quintessentially the "gospel for the outsider."

Illustrating the Text

It is a serious matter to be the cause of a fellow disciple's failure.

Film: *Days of Wine and Roses*, directed by Blake Edwards. This film (1962), though not a Christian one, shows powerfully the horror of leading someone astray and then being unable to restore them. In this well-acted film, Joe Clay, an alcoholic, falls in love with a beautiful girl, Kirsten, who is pure-hearted and loving. Soon, he begins to tempt her to drink with him.

After they marry, she gradually is drawn into the drinking because she wants to be with him, and his addiction is separating them. It is only a matter of time before both of them begin to spiral downward. Finally, Joe hits rock bottom, submits his life to a path of addiction recovery, realizes the terrible thing that he has done, and sets about trying to get Kirsten help. At the end of the movie, she is not on the path of healing. This is a chilling metaphor for the seriousness of prompting another's failure.

We should be ready to forgive someone who is truly repentant.

Anecdote: *The Gift of Peace*, **by Cardinal Bernardin.** In these personal reflections (published in 1997) as he was dying of pancreatic cancer, the devout Chicago cardinal Bernardin (1928–96) tells about being falsely accused by a troubled young man, Steven. Bernardin, full of compassion, reaches out to him and hears his repentance and says a mass for him, noting, "In every family there are times when there is hurt, anger, or alienation. But we cannot run away from our family. We have only one family. . . . So, too, the Church is our spiritual family. Once we become a member, we may be hurt or become alienated, but it is still our family. Since there is no other, we must work at reconciliation."[1]

In gratitude for his healing, the Samaritan leper returned to Jesus, knelt down, and thanked him. Other examples of thankfulness for healing are found in the ancient world. Healing gods like Asklepios existed in Greek and Roman culture, and replicas of body parts, like the feet shown here, were often presented at their shrines as thank offerings or petitions for cures (fourth century BC).

One must develop a habit of gratitude, refusing to take God's blessings for granted.

Popular Culture: The thank-you note is a last bastion in what journalist Mary Killen has called an "epidemic of discourtesy." Even with the ease of communication via email or text messages, fewer and fewer people seem to be taking the time to thank others. And often, if thanks are given at all, it is only in a quick message that can hardly be described as articulate, memorable, or a product of much effort.

Quote: "God and a Grateful Old Man," by Lewis B. Smedes. Smedes (1921–2002), a renowned author, ethicist, and theologian, wrote, "I have never met a grateful person who was an unhappy person. And for that matter, I have never met a grateful person who was a bad person. . . . All we need to be grateful is the insight to recognize a real gift when we get one. A gift is not just something we get for nothing."[2]

The Coming of the Kingdom of God

Big Idea *The kingdom of God is already here, but there will be a future appearance of the Son of Man for which people will be unprepared.*

Understanding the Text

The Text in Context

The kingdom (reign) of God has been at the heart of the preaching of Jesus and his disciples since 4:43 (see note there). In 10:9, 11 it was said to "have come near" (cf. 11:20), while in 11:2 Jesus taught his disciples to pray for it as apparently something still future (cf. 9:27). Now a question from Pharisees invites Jesus to clarify this central aspect of his teaching. But in his response and his following teaching to the disciples Jesus moves away from the kingdom of God to speak instead of "the days of the Son of Man" in a way that clearly goes beyond the present scene to a climactic moment of history.

In Mark 13 and Matthew 24–25 all such teaching about the future is gathered together into a single discourse that begins with the destruction of the temple but then apparently goes on to speak of a more ultimate eschatological event, described in Matthew 24 as the *parousia* (visitation) of the Son of Man. Luke will also include such a discourse in 21:5–36, though with

less clear reference to the parousia, as we will see; but Luke is the only Gospel writer who also includes this separate eschatological discourse that is not linked to the specific earthly event of the destruction of the temple, even though most of the content of this section (17:23, 24, 26–27, 31, 34–35, 37) has parallels in Matthew 24. These verses therefore stand apart from their immediate context but prepare the way for chapter 21.

Historical and Cultural Background

On the title "the Son of Man," see the sidebar "The Son of Man" at 5:12–26. The concept here of "the days of the Son of Man" or "the day when the Son of Man will be revealed" probably derives from Daniel's vision of the enthronement of the "one like a son of man" in Daniel 7:13–14. In view of Jesus's persistent use of "the Son of Man" as a self-designation, it cannot now refer to a figure other than himself (and 17:25 here confirms this), but the expectation of an eschatological revelation of Jesus himself as Son of Man is (apart from one tantalizing hint in 12:40) a new concept in Luke's presentation of Jesus's teaching. It seems to take the place of the general Jewish expectation of a climactic "day of the Lord," when evil will be defeated and God's people ultimately vindicated.

The two great disaster narratives in Genesis, the flood (Gen. 6–8) and the destruction of Sodom (Gen. 19) provide, respectively in 17:26–27 and 17:28–29 with 17:32, well-known Old Testament models for this future act of judgment. The same two events are cited together in this way in a number of Jewish sources (cf. also 2 Pet. 2:5–8).

Interpretive Insights

17:20 *when the kingdom of God would come.* The Pharisees express the misunderstanding, shared by too many modern interpreters, that "the kingdom of God" denotes a specific, identifiable future event

rather than the more general concept of God's effective reign. Jesus's reply refuses to allow God's kingship to be tied down in that way. It is not the sort of future "happening" whose timing can be calculated by looking for signs and preparatory events.

17:21 *the kingdom of God is in your midst.* The traditional rendering "is within

Jesus compares the revelation of the Son of Man to the day when judgment rained down on Sodom. Shown here is the site known as Bab edh Drha, one possible location of ancient Sodom.

you," though a possible translation of the Greek phrase, has led to the erroneous idea that God's kingdom is somehow internal to people's minds, a matter of *our* attitudes and values. The more likely sense is "among you (corporately)"; that is, God's kingship is already a reality, that it has established itself even without your having noticed it (cf. 11:20; see also the parable of the mustard seed [13:18–19]).

17:22 *one of the days of the Son of Man.* Even though the "kingdom of God" is not to be understood as simply a future event, there is a future event for disciples (notice the change of addressees) to look forward to (see "Historical and Cultural Background" above). But it may not come as soon as they would wish. The phrase "*one of* the days" is puzzling. "Days" (plural) here and in 17:26 designates an extended period (cf. the "days" of Noah and of Lot [17:26, 28]), but it is not clear why just "one of" those days (rather than simply "the day") is singled out. The use of the singular "day of the Son of Man" (17:24, 30) better suits the Old Testament background of the (singular) "day of the Lord."

17:23 *Do not go running after them.* The reference is perhaps to the sort of prophetic or messianic pretenders who were a feature of Jewish life in the period leading up to the war with Rome in AD 66, some of whom called their followers out into the desert to await a miraculous deliverance from Roman power (see Acts 5:36–37; 21:38).

17:24 *the Son of Man in his day will be like the lightning.* It will be suddenly and universally obvious when "the Son of Man is revealed" (17:30). That is why they should not, in their eagerness to see that

day, give credence to charlatans who claim that the Son of Man has already appeared, but only in secret (17:23).

17:25 *But first he must suffer.* They should not hope for a premature glorification of the Son of Man that bypasses the destiny that Jesus has already clearly spelled out in 9:22, 44. This verse rules out any suggestion that Jesus's language about the "day(s) of the Son of Man" refers to anyone other than himself; it is the same Son of Man who is to suffer and be rejected who will then be revealed in glory.

17:27 *People were eating, drinking, marrying.* The Genesis account does not describe the lifestyle of Noah's contemporaries, but these are everyday activities. Popular tradition had also developed the idea that Noah warned others of the flood to come and was mocked for his efforts (cf. 2 Pet. 2:5: "a preacher of righteousness"; Heb. 11:7: "he condemned the world"). So only Noah's family was prepared; others simply carried on as normal until it was too late.

17:28 *People were eating and drinking, buying and selling, planting and building.* As in 17:26–27, the description is of normal life, rather than the specific wickedness of Sodom. Again, Lot and his family were the only ones who were warned and rescued before the disaster struck.

17:30 *the day the Son of Man is revealed.* The verb *apokalyptō* suggests something more dramatic than mere visibility; Paul refers to Jesus's parousia as an *apokalypsis* (2 Thess. 1:7; 1 Cor. 1:7; cf. the *apokalypsis* of the antichrist [2 Thess. 2:3–10]), and that seems to be the sense here too.

17:31 *no one . . . should go back for anything.* Similar language is used in Matthew

24:17–18 to underline the urgency of flight when Judea is invaded by the Romans. Here there is no invading army, and it is not clear why flight should be so urgent when the Son of Man is revealed, but the general sense is that the eschatological emergency allows no scope for gathering up possessions. As so often in Luke, earthly possessions are seen as a hindrance to spiritual salvation.

17:32 *Remember Lot's wife!* This is another reference to the destruction of Sodom, when Lot's wife disastrously ignored the angels' command not to look back as they escaped from the city (Gen. 19:17, 26); her looking back represents an unwillingness to let go of possessions and of the old life.

17:33 *Whoever tries to keep their life will lose it.* A parallel saying in 9:24 depicted the radical choice demanded of those who commit to following Jesus on earth. Here it seems less appropriate, but the idea is presumably that a preoccupation with earthly goods (as exemplified by Lot's wife) is in conflict with the spiritual commitment of those who will be saved rather than lost when the Son of Man appears.

17:34–35 *one will be taken and the other left.* Two cameos (one male, one female) represent normal life suddenly disrupted. It is not stated where or for what purpose the one is "taken." The analogies of Noah and Lot may suggest that it means being rescued from disaster (hence perhaps the notion of a "rapture" of God's people from the earth before judgment falls),

but it could equally mean being "taken" for destruction such as befell those who were unprepared in 17:27, 29. The point is that the judgment when the Son of Man appears will divide people who until that time have been indistinguishable.

17:37 *Where there is a dead body, there the vultures will gather.* This is a proverbial saying (cf. Job 39:30) for which many interpretations have been proposed. In this context it may mean "Keep your eyes peeled" (you can always spot where a carcass is by watching where the vultures congregate). In that case, it would be a call to spiritual alertness, to avoid being caught unawares by the day of the Son of Man.

Theological Insights

This is a remarkable section, found only in Luke. If, as the comments above have assumed, there is a deliberate link between the address to the Pharisees in 17:20–21 and that to the disciples in 17:22–37 the thought moves from the kingdom of God (already a present reality) to the future "day(s) of the Son of Man." The implication seems to be that there is a continuity

When the Son of Man is revealed, if two women are together grinding grain, one will be taken and the other left (17:35). If bread or flour was not purchased commercially, grinding grain for the bread needs of a family was done daily by hand. Shown here are two women operating the tools used for hand milling. The woman at the top is using a grindstone, while the woman at the bottom is using a rotary hand quern.

Luke 17:20–37

between the two, and that therefore the future authority of the Son of Man (Jesus) is the fulfillment of God's reign.

For comments on an earlier pointer to a future coming of the Son of Man, see "Theological Insights" on 12:22–40. The word "*parousia*" is again not used (it is used in Matt. 24:3, 27, 37, 39), and the language is of revelation rather than of "coming" (unlike 12:40), but this is now the clearest account in the Gospels of what we speak of as Jesus's "second coming," uncomplicated by any link with the destruction of the temple as it will be in the later Synoptic discourse (Matt. 24–25; Mark 13; Luke 21). The Old Testament echoes here emphasize that the parousia, like the prophetic vision of the "day of the Lord," is a time of judgment and division, and one for which people will be found unprepared.

"For the Son of Man in his day will be like the lightning, which flashes and lights up the sky from one end to the other" (17:24).

Teaching the Text

This is a good opportunity to return to people's understanding of what "the kingdom of God" means. In your teaching be sure to bring out both the present and the future dimensions of the kingdom. In what sense is it present? In what sense is it future? How does the Pharisees' question indicate that they misunderstood what Jesus was talking about? Why does Jesus's reply (after first correcting their misunderstanding) shift the focus instead to the "day(s) of the Son of Man"? What then is the link between the Son of Man and the kingdom of God?

Encourage listeners to imagine themselves in the place of Jesus's disciples. What would they have made at that time of his talk about future "days of the Son of Man"? And how might their understanding have developed after the period of his earthly ministry?

How does what Jesus says here relate to what is generally taught in our churches about the "second coming"? Do we place the emphasis where Jesus did? This might be a good time to teach about obsession with setting dates and the "signs" of times. When Jesus talks about the end times, he does not give specific signs or encourage speculation. Instead he calls his followers to live a life of spiritual readiness at all times.

This text could also provide an opportunity to discuss dispensationalist teaching about a future "rapture," whereby believers are taken up from the earth to be with Jesus at his return (see 1 Thess. 4:13–18). Consider to what extent 17:34–35 provides a secure basis for such an idea. Is this its main scriptural support?

Illustrating the Text

Jesus teaches that his second coming will occur when no one is expecting it.

News Story: Any number of natural and manmade disasters have occurred when no one was expecting them, completely disrupting the lives of those who suffered through the events. These serve as metaphors for this principle. Examples are the many tornadoes and hurricanes that have come at night. In February 2012 the town of Harrisburg, Illinois, was hit by a tornado, packing winds of 175 miles per hour, at 4:50 in the morning. Authorities were only able to issue a thirteen-minute warning, which few heard because of the early hour. Several devastating tsunamis and tidal waves have occurred in recent history, among them the one that hit Sri Lanka in 2004, and the one in Japan in 2011, horrifying in its speed and intensity, leaving in its wake unimaginable disaster.

Unforgettably, the 9/11 disaster came blasting into the life of New York City, arriving so quickly that thousands had no way to escape. In the history of WWII, both the aerial assault on Pearl Harbor and the atomic bomb dropped on Hiroshima are other examples of unexpected calamity. Other current events are the bombings of commuter trains in Spain in 2004 and England in 2005, as well as the bombings at the Boston Marathon in 2013. So much can happen in life that we cannot prepare for, but the coming of the Lord is one event that we can be ready for.

As Christians, we should be alert and travel light.

Human Metaphor: In the 1970s and 1980s, when overseas flights and Eurail passes were inexpensive, thousands of American and European young people took advantage of the bargains, trying to see as many countries as possible on their passes. Their secret to traveling well was a backpack or portable luggage. They could grab lunch at the train station and climb on board easily. They had less baggage to monitor and the freedom to move around with facility. The contrast between the light travelers and those traveling with full sets of luggage was striking.

Sermon: "The Weight of Glory," by C. S. Lewis. In this beautiful address, Lewis speaks eloquently of the temptation of Christians to confuse the delights of the world with what is ahead in heaven, to travel heavy by trusting things instead of looking through them to their source. This is "all a cheat," he says. "The books or the music in which we thought the beauty was located will betray us if we trust to them; it was not in them, it only came through them, and what came through them was *longing*. . . . If they are mistaken for the thing itself, they turn into dumb idols, breaking the hearts of their worshippers." He goes on, "philosophies of Progress . . . want to convince you that earth is your home," and they will try to "persuade you that earth can be made into heaven."[1]

Two Parables about Prayer

Big Idea *We should pray with confidence that God will respond, but our confidence should be in God's mercy, not in our own merits.*

Understanding the Text

The Text in Context

Parables have been a prominent feature in Luke's narrative of the journey to Jerusalem, especially in chapters 14–16. The two parables in the present section, together with one further one in 19:11–27, will round out the collection before Jesus reaches Jerusalem. The first of these two parables is linked to the preceding section in that it finishes with a comment on the coming of the Son of Man. Its focus, however, is on present discipleship, and in particular on prayer, which has been a recurrent theme in Luke (see especially 11:1–13) and in his frequent mention of Jesus's own prayers (3:21; 6:12; 9:18, 28–29; 11:1). The second parable continues the theme by depicting two people at prayer, though its introduction and conclusion point to a wider truth about the reversal of values in the kingdom of God. This truth will then be graphically exemplified in the stories of the children and the rich man, with Jesus's comments on the latter, in 18:15–30.

Historical and Cultural Background

Local justice normally was administered by a council of elders, a significant part of whose role was to arbitrate in property disputes. The "judge" in this parable is acting alone, however (as apparently in 12:58; and cf. the request to Jesus in 12:13–14), and there is later evidence that a full council was not required for monetary arbitration. Widows are frequently mentioned in the Old Testament as typically vulnerable members of society, to whom therefore special consideration should be given.

Jewish men who were ritually pure, like the Pharisee in the parable Jesus tells in 18:10–14, could stand in the court of the Israelites. This was a narrow area just inside the Nicanor Gate (shown here from the model of first-century AD Jerusalem), which was next to the courts of the priests. This is one place the Pharisees would have gathered during the customary hours of prayer. The tax collector probably remained in the outer court (the court of the Gentiles), which was open to all.

In this case the widow turns out to be far from helpless!

Both Pharisees (see the sidebar "Scribes and Pharisees" at 5:12–26) and tax collectors (see "Historical and Cultural Background" on 5:27–39) are by now familiar categories in this Gospel. There is a danger that the modern reader, familiar with the Gospel stereotypes (Pharisees as opponents of Jesus, tax collectors as his friends) may miss the radically subversive message of this parable when addressed to ordinary status-conscious Jews (18:9) at that time, for whom Pharisees were admirable for their serious observance of God's law and tax collectors represented the irreligious underclass. The scene of this parable is the temple in Jerusalem, where Israelite men stood to pray in the court of Israel overlooking the court of the priests, where the sacrificial ritual took place (cf. 1:10).

Interpretive Insights

18:1 *to show them that they should always pray and not give up.* Luke sometimes gives an introductory "steer" to guide his readers' interpretation of a parable (cf. 18:9; 19:11). This one is expressed in quite general terms; it does not relate specifically to praying for the coming of the Son of Man, which has been the subject of the preceding section and will return in 18:8b.

18:2 *who neither feared God nor cared what people thought.* The judge in the story represents God, but this initial description makes it clear that his character is not to be seen as a reflection of what God is like. Rather, he is shown as a selfish scoundrel in order to set up the "how much more" argument of 18:6–7. If even a man like this can be prevailed on, how much more so will a

Key Themes of Luke 18:1–14

- We should persist in prayer and not give up.
- God shares our longing for justice, and he will not deny it.
- There is no place for self-satisfaction before God.
- God prefers a repentant sinner to a self-righteous "good" person.
- In the kingdom of God human values and expectations are reversed.

response be obtained from God, who really does care for his people's good.

18:3 *Grant me justice against my adversary.* We are not told the nature of the dispute, but it may well have been about property. The root term for "justice" (*edik-*) used here and in 18:5, 7, 8 focuses on the vindication of someone who has been wronged, though it may also include the punishment of the wrongdoer (cf. the use in 21:22). A widow who fights her own case must have been without male support that she could rely on, and so she would more easily be exploited.

18:5 *I will see that she gets justice, so that she won't eventually come and attack me!* His eventual compliance is purely selfish, to get rid of a personal nuisance ("keeps bothering me"). The unusual verb here translated as "attack" is literally "give a black eye to." Some interpreters treat it here merely as a metaphor for "subdue" (cf. 1 Cor. 9:27, using the same verb), but in this none-too-serious parable context it is better taken literally: the poor man is afraid of being "handbagged" by the feisty little widow!

18:6 *the unjust judge.* There is a delicious irony in the (literally) "judge of injustice" going against his own nature to give the widow "justice." But it is precisely this emphasis on his corrupt character that gives force to the "how much more" argument.

18:7 *justice for his chosen ones.* The Old Testament idea of Israel as a "chosen nation" gives rise in the New Testament to the description of God's people as his "chosen ones" (only here in Luke, but see Mark 13:20, 22, 27; Rom. 8:33; Col. 3:12). The term suggests a strong contrast between them and the ungodly world out of which they are "chosen," so that the "justice" spoken of here may be understood as the vindication of a persecuted minority. In the end God will make sure that his people do not lose out.

Will he keep putting them off? Various translations have been suggested for this obscure clause. The more usual sense of the verb would give "and he is patient with them," hence, for example, the REB translation "his chosen, to whom he listens patiently while they cry out to him day and night." But by different routes these contrasting translations reach the same essential sense: God takes notice of persistent prayers and can be trusted to answer them, even if not immediately.

18:8 *when the Son of Man comes, will he find faith on the earth?* This sentence does not link directly to the parable, and the reintroduction of the hope of the coming of the Son of Man (see 12:40; 17:22–37) shifts the focus from present discipleship into the future. Perhaps the coming of the Son of Man is understood as the time of the vindication of God's people. In context, the "faith" that is referred to must be the persistence in prayer that the parable has inculcated, and the challenge is to maintain it until vindication comes.

18:9 *To some who were confident of their own righteousness.* This is another clear interpretive "steer" given by Luke. The preceding parable was told to disciples, but this is apparently for a wider audience. The description fits the "righteous" who stand over against repentant sinners in 5:32, and the attitude that has been displayed by Pharisees throughout the

The parable Jesus told in 18:10–14 begins, "Two men went up to the temple to pray." The main staircase used to gain entrance to the various courts around the temple is shown here and is known as the monumental staircase. Much of it has been reconstructed, but the lowest steps seen in the foreground are from the first century AD.

Gospel, especially in their disdain for the sinful company that Jesus kept (5:30; 7:39; 15:2); compare also Jesus's comment on the Pharisees in 16:14–15. But to conclude that the parable applies *only* to Pharisees is to miss its point entirely: if the shoe fits, wear it!

18:11 *The Pharisee stood by himself and prayed*. Assuming a large number of men praying, we are to envisage two men standing separate from the crowd, but for opposite reasons: this man because he was too good to mix with others, the other keeping "at a distance" because he was too bad. An alternative reading changes the word order to read, "The Pharisee stood and prayed this to (about?) himself."

God, I thank you that I am not like other people. There is no reason to think that this prayer is insincere: most Pharisees would have been able to claim truthfully to have avoided the sins listed, and to be living a life more strictly governed by God's law than those of most ordinary people. But the smug self-congratulation is what stands out. It reminds one of the later rabbi who instructed Jewish men to thank God that they had not been born a heathen, a woman, or a slave. If, as was normal, he is praying aloud, the insensitivity is even greater, and an element of self-advertisement is added to his smugness.

18:12 *I fast twice a week and give a tenth of all I get*. These too represent a normal Pharisaic lifestyle (cf. 5:33; 11:42). The (possibly first-century) Christian manual the *Didache* instructs Christians to fast on Wednesdays and Fridays, not on Mondays and Thursdays as "the hypocrites" do. Both his fasting and his tithing go well beyond the demands of the Old Testament law, but

to be a Pharisee was to be committed to a much more rigorous ritual code.

18:13 *God, have mercy on me, a sinner*. The description of the tax collector's attitude conveys a sense of personal unworthiness, which, in view of Jesus's comment in 18:14, we should probably take to include not merely low self-esteem but active repentance (as with the real-life tax collector in 19:1–10). "Have mercy on" is more literally "be propitiated toward"; he is seeking a new relationship with God.

18:14 *justified before God*. The Greek text has simply "having been justified." In the original setting of this parable it would be reading too much into this verb to find here the whole Pauline theology of the acquittal of the sinner before God through the atoning sacrifice of Christ. The point is rather that the repentant tax collector was regarded by God as more "just" than the self-satisfied Pharisee. Such a conclusion challenges every conventional notion of "justice." The basis of God's assessment of the two men is not a simple record of what they have done but their current attitude toward him.

for all those who exalt themselves . . . and those who humble themselves. Here we have a repetition of 14:11; see comments there.

Theological Insights

1. *The unjust judge*. This parable raises the paradox that God knows and cares about our needs and yet expects his people to be persistent in praying for them. The "how much more" argument of the parable indicates that God is not like the judge, who needs to be badgered or cajoled into taking action, but the parable does not explain why, then, we still need to pray. The

likely answer, that prayer, like all aspects of discipleship, is a partnership involving our will and action rather than a unilateral work of God that overrides our freedom and responsibility, must be supplied from elsewhere.

2. *The Pharisee and the tax collector.* This is not so much a "how to pray" parable as a sharp challenge to our conventional understanding of "goodness" in relation to God. Like so much in Luke's Gospel, it turns accepted values upside down. The kingdom of God is the realm of grace, not of achievement. God's love is not earned; it is freely given to those who are conscious of their need of it and yet their unworthiness for it.

Teaching the Text

These two parables can be taught together as a message on prayer, or separately with emphases on their respective themes of persistence in prayer and humble contrition before God.

1. *The unjust judge.* Remind listeners of the parable of the dishonest manager (16:1–9). Why did Jesus choose such disreputable characters for his stories? What is achieved by contrasting God with a selfish scoundrel? It is important to stress the "how much more" aspect of the parable. If such an unrighteous judge will respond to persistence, how much more will our loving Father respond. Share from your own experience or solicit others to share experiences of persistent prayer and its results. Were those prayers answered? In what way does it encourage persistent prayer? What would have happened if they had given up praying? This passage also provides an opportunity

to discuss the frustration people experience when their prayers are not answered as they hope or expect. It is important to stress that the "justice" God's people get in the end may not be in this life, but in eternity. Persistent prayer means persistent faith, even to the end. This helps to explain the reference, seemingly out of place, to the Son of Man at the end (18:8). Those who pray persistently even to the end will experience vindication at the coming of the Son of Man.

2. *The Pharisee and the tax collector.* In your teaching be sure to highlight the fact that, although we think of Pharisees as hypocrites, the original audience would have had great respect for them and complete disdain for the tax collector. Bring the parable into the present day by thinking of highly respected pillars of your society, and of those considered the lowest of the low. Do we still need this message? Is there something deep in our psyche that makes people ask, "What have I *done* to deserve . . . ?" Is grace still an alien concept for most people? Compare the Pharisee's attitude with Jesus's teaching in 17:7–10. How can a religious person get it all so wrong?

Illustrating the Text

Jesus enjoins us to persist in prayer and not give up.

Church History: Augustine of Hippo. For years Augustine's (354–430) mother, Monica, prayed for him as he lived licentiously, shunning God. Eventually, in response to those prayers, Augustine was wonderfully converted. In his famous work *The Confessions*, which has been translated into more languages than any Latin writings except those of Virgil, he writes,

> "You put forth your hand from on high," and you drew my soul out of that pit of darkness, when before you my mother, your faithful servant, wept more for me than mothers weep over their children's dead bodies. By that spirit of faith which she had from you, she saw my death, and you graciously heard her, O Lord. . . . You did not despise her tears when they flowed down from her eyes and watered the earth beneath, in whatsoever place she prayed. Graciously you heard her. . . . For almost nine years passed, in which I wallowed "in the mire of the deep" and in the darkness of error, and although I often strove to rise out of it, I was all the more grievously thrust down again. But all the while, that chaste, devout, and sober widow . . . ceased not in all her hours of prayer to lament over me before you. Her prayers entered into your sight.[1]

Autobiography: *Out of a Far Country: A Gay Son's Journey to God, a Broken Mother's Search for Hope*, by Christopher Yuan and Angela Yuan. Christopher Yuan, now an adjunct faculty member at Moody Bible Institute in Chicago, lived for years as a gay man, a central figure in St. Louis's gay community and also heavily involved in selling and using drugs. Arrested for his involvement in drugs, he spent a number of years in jail. For seven years his heartbroken mother prayed faithfully for him, learning how to love him in godly ways and letting God change her. Finally, Christopher submitted his life to the Lord and has spent the years since basing his identity on Christ and living out this testimony before the world. This book (2011), written by both the son and the mother, is a story of hope and persistence.

The conversion of St. Augustine of Hippo (AD 354–430) was an answer to his mother's persistent prayers. The painting of Augustine shown here is by Antonello da Messina (AD 1472–73).

God prefers a repentant sinner to a self-proclaimer of goodness.

Poetry: "The Apologist's Evening Prayer," by C. S. Lewis. In this poem the apologist asks God to deliver him from pretentiousness. At one point the poet prays, "Lord of the narrow gate and needle's eye, / Take from me all my trumpery lest I die."[2]

Story: "Revelation," by Flannery O'Connor. Few writers expose the heart of pride and hypocrisy as does American author Flannery O'Connor (1925–64). In this story (published posthumously in 1965) a very self-absorbed, proud, middle-class, Southern woman, Ruby Turpin, is always thanking God that he has made her who she is, "a neat clean respectable white woman,"[3] overweight but with a good complexion and disposition. The story takes place in a doctor's office, where she experiences a violent encounter that teaches her who will be first in the kingdom of heaven. The story illustrates well this principle.

The Revolutionary Values of the Kingdom of God

Big Idea *In the kingdom of God accepted human values of status and importance are turned upside down.*

Understanding the Text

The Text in Context

As the journey to Jerusalem nears its end, encounters with others on the way illustrate the principle expressed in 18:14b, and in so doing they reveal how far those around Jesus still are from grasping the true nature of God's kingdom and the necessary pattern of Jesus's own mission. Their incomprehension focuses especially on the issue of wealth, and thus it provides an opportunity for some far-reaching teaching on this theme, which has been so prominent on the journey (see especially 12:13–34; 14:1–24, 33–34; 16:1–15, 19–31). A final, and more detailed, prediction of the specific fate awaiting Jesus in Jerusalem (18:31–33; cf. 9:22, 44; 12:50; 13:32–33; 17:25) prepares the reader for Jesus's arrival in the city in chapter 19 and the narrative of confrontation, suffering, death, and resurrection that is to follow.

Historical and Cultural Background

This passage presupposes a socially graded society (like most human societies, then and now) in which children, as those with no rights of self-determination, were at the bottom of the heap, and the successful and affluent at the top. It was generally assumed, as indeed much of the Old Testament wisdom literature had taught, that wealth was a sign of God's blessing and of a life lived according to his standards, and thus was a goal to be eagerly pursued. The wealthy deserved respect and exerted social influence over those less successful.

The specific reference to "the Gentiles" in 18:32 reminds us that Judea, unlike Galilee, was directly subject to Roman power, and that the Jewish leadership in Jerusalem had only limited powers of government; they did not have the right to impose a death penalty (see John 18:31).

Interpretive Insights

18:15 *bringing babies to Jesus for him to place his hands on them.* Children were sometimes brought to religious leaders for blessing; compare Simeon's blessing of Jesus in 2:28. The term that Luke uses here indicates babes in arms.

they rebuked them. We are not told why. Did they think that Jesus must have more pressing concerns and more important people to meet? But Jesus's response to this unwelcoming attitude turns this little pericope into an account of the disciples' failure to grasp God's values.

18:16 *the kingdom of God belongs to such as these.* For the wording, compare 6:20. People like this fall within the sphere of God's rule and his blessing. "Such as these" points beyond actual babies to others who share their status at the bottom of the pecking order of human society (such as the tax collector of 18:9–14?). The point is more fully spelled out in 9:46–48.

18:17 *receive the kingdom of God like a little child.* This could mean either "receive it as one receives a child" or "receive it as a child does." A roughly parallel saying in Matthew 18:3 speaks of "becoming like children" in order to enter the kingdom of God, and that is probably the sense here: the true members of the kingdom of God are those who are no more self-important than little children. This carries a rebuke to the disciples: their "grown-up" sense of importance puts them out of tune with God's value scale.

18:18 *a certain ruler.* This indicates a leading member of society, perhaps a synagogue leader.

what must I do to inherit eternal life? Have Jesus's comments about entering the kingdom of God worried him in view of his much higher place in the social order? The same question was asked by the lawyer in 10:25 (see comments there). Note the assumption that eternal life depends on *doing* something. Jesus's reply will be equally practical (18:22), but it will go far beyond conventional ethical rules to demand an all-embracing personal commitment.

People were bringing babies to Jesus for his blessing. This third-century AD relief from Palmyra, Syria, shows a well-dressed woman holding a baby in her left arm.

18:19 *Why do you call me good?* The man's address to Jesus as "good teacher" was simply polite (or flattering?), but Jesus turns it into a theological challenge. The statement that only God is good puts a question mark against any idea that eternal life can be "earned" by being good. Later Christians were embarrassed by the apparent suggestion that Jesus is not good and is not God, but that is to take Jesus's words woodenly out of context.

18:20 *You know the commandments.* The five items selected from the Decalogue are those that relate to how we treat other people and thus can most easily be used as a practical ethical checklist. Literally interpreted, all five can be "ticked off" as duly observed by a conventionally moral person, and there is no reason to doubt the sincerity of the man's claim to have done so (18:21). But for a more radical perspective on two of them, see Matthew 5:21–30.

18:22 *You still lack one thing.* Just keeping the accepted rules is not enough. Jesus's demand goes beyond ethical conformity. The command to sell and give is also something to "do," but it is so extraordinary and far-reaching that it goes to the heart of the man's spiritual commitment. It would destroy his conventional life of wealth and influence and require him to put God before mammon. "Come, follow me" then sets this demand in the context of a personal discipleship that would in effect turn his cozy world upside down. For the command to sell and give and the prospect of "treasure in heaven," compare 12:33–34 and see the notes there;

Jesus says that it is easier for a camel to go through the eye of a needle than for the rich to enter God's kingdom (18:25). These bone needles from the Roman period were found at Sepphoris.

here "treasure in heaven" picks up the man's inquiry about eternal life.

18:23 *he became very sad.* Luke does not say (as do Mark and Matthew) that the man "went away" at this point, so here he remains as the direct target of Jesus's caustic comment in 18:24. As there is no indication of his continuing presence with the disciple group, however, we are left to assume that his "sadness" proved insurmountable.

18:24–25 *it is easier for a camel to go through the eye of a needle.* What is declared "hard" in 18:24 becomes impossible in 18:25; a camel (the largest animal in Palestine) *cannot* go through the eye of a needle. The response in 18:26 draws the right conclusion, as Jesus's reply in 18:27 acknowledges. A frequently repeated attempt to evade the rhetorical force of Jesus's saying is the claim that "the eye of the needle" was a name for a small gate in the city wall. But there is no historical evidence for such a gate in Jesus's time. A later rabbinic saying uses an elephant going through the eye of a needle to illustrate an impossibility.

18:27 *What is impossible with man is possible with God.* The stark simplicity of 18:25 is modified not by suggesting ways in which the impossible might exceptionally be made possible but by shifting the whole discussion away from human possibility to the dimension of divine grace. Nobody "enters the kingdom of God" through their own efforts or assets, but only as God does for them what they cannot do for themselves.

18:28 *We have left all we had to follow you!* Like so many of Peter's interventions in the Gospels, this one partly misses the point even though it relates to what has just been said. The disciples have done what the rich man refused to do. So does this mean that they have "earned" a place in the kingdom of God? Has the impossible become possible for them?

18:29–30 *Truly I tell you.* Jesus remarkably overlooks the self-congratulation in Peter's claim. No one who gives things up for God will be the loser in the end. The "many times as much in this age" need not be of quite the same nature as what has been given up (home and relatives; it can hardly be a promise of multiple wives!), but it will be a more than adequate substitute for them. The thought presumably includes the new "family" of the disciple community (see 8:21). The ultimate reward, however, is not in earthly benefits, but in the "eternal life" that the rich man sought but failed to grasp.

18:31 *everything that is written by the prophets about the Son of Man will be fulfilled.* Jesus's title "the Son of Man" derives from a passage (Dan. 7:13–14) that speaks of glory rather than suffering, but Jesus has already used the title more widely for his total mission, including the suffering designated for God's servant in Isaiah 53 (to be cited in 22:37). His rejection and death will not be a political accident but the working out of a pattern declared long ago; see 24:25–27, 44–47.

18:32 *He will be delivered over to the Gentiles.* Previous predictions have spoken of Jesus's coming death (9:22; 13:33),

after he is rejected by the Jewish leadership (9:22; 17:25). Now he spells out more clearly what is to happen in the subsequent Roman trial and execution (chap. 23); Luke will not there specifically mention spitting and flogging, but see Mark 15:15, 19.

18:34 *The disciples did not understand any of this.* See the equally emphatic three-fold statement, though in different words, after the previous passion prediction in 9:45. The disciples' privileged insight (8:10) has not yet extended to grasping the reality or the purpose of Jesus's death in Jerusalem.

Theological Insights

The fact that the phrase "the kingdom of God" occurs five times in this passage alerts us again to the theology of the Magnificat (1:51–53), whereby those who have power and influence in this world's structures must give way to the insignificant and powerless, so that in the kingdom of God the first become last, and the last first. To be a disciple of Jesus is to be committed to a value revolution that not only demands our own total commitment to God's cause but also challenges our most basic assumptions about how society should operate.

The phrase "treasure in heaven" (18:22) raises the issue of rewards. The outcome of true discipleship is eternal life (18:18, 30), not as a remuneration earned by faithful service (for the exclusion of that idea, see 17:10), but as God's gracious gift to those who enroll under his kingship. But it is not just "pie in the sky when you die"; there is compensation, and much more, even in this life (18:30) for those who have given up earthly security for the kingdom of God.

Teaching the Text

This passage provides another good opportunity to consider the meaning of "the kingdom of God." While it certainly entails eternal life (18:18), it is much more than this. How has this passage filled out that understanding?

In 18:15–17 what is it about children that makes them (here and in 9:46–48) a suitable model for understanding the kingdom of God? In our culture, many people will think of children as "innocent" or "pure," but this is not Jesus's point. Rather, children in first-century culture were socially marginalized, lowly, and totally dependent (see "Historical and Cultural Background" above). We receive the kingdom of God by humbly admitting our total dependence on God. In your teaching consider who Jesus would have used in our culture as an example of this kind of vulnerability and dependency.

This point helps us to interpret the account of the rich ruler that follows, which many find discomforting. Should they obey the command of 18:22 to sell all they have? One common response is that this instruction was specific to this man rather than being a general pattern for discipleship. But this is often used as an excuse today. People breathe a sigh of relief that they won't have to sell their possessions! But what about the similar statement in 12:33? Does Peter's claim in 18:28 indicate that 18:22 expresses a universal demand? Don't be afraid in your teaching to dwell on the shocking nature of Jesus's radical demand. These words were meant to be provocative and they should be for us today. In the end, Jesus demands our whole life, including *all* our possessions. While this may not mean selling everything we have (see comments on 19:8 below), it *does* mean that everything we own is to be used for God's purposes and glory. Challenge your audience to consider personally what kind of radical change in their lifestyle Jesus's words should provoke.

In the light of 18:24–27, why are there so many rich Christians? (It might be good to define or have a group discuss the meaning of "rich," first in terms of your audience's own social context, and then in terms of living standards in the world as a whole.)

The disciples did not understand when Jesus said that the Son of Man will be delivered to the Gentiles to be mocked, insulted, spat upon, flogged, and killed (18:33). These fourteenth-century AD marble statuettes depict the flogging of Christ.

How does observation of modern church life relate to Jesus's claim that you cannot be a slave of both God and mammon?

Why was it so difficult for the disciples to grasp the nature of Jesus's own mission (18:34; cf. 9:45)? Should "what is written by the prophets about the Son of Man" not have been obvious to them, well-brought-up Jews?

There are many important issues in this section!

Illustrating the Text

Children are vitally important to God.

Theological Reflection: David Garland warns against imposing our modern Western ideas of children on this passage. The ancient world did not have a romantic notion of children as innocent, creative, playful, or spontaneous. In the Greco-Roman world in general children were viewed as lowly and without social status. Unwanted infants were sometimes "exposed"—literally thrown away. Others were raised as prostitutes or as gladiators. Some were even disfigured to enhance their value as beggars.[1] Modern parallels would be the exploitation of children in some parts of the world as low-income factory workers in dangerous or unhealthy conditions—practically a slave trade—and the abuse of children in the sex-trade industry. In a countercultural manner, Jesus welcomes children and exalts their status. The kingdom of God is made up of those who are lowly, humble, and totally dependent on God.

God wants all that we are and have.

Spiritual Autobiography: *The Gift of Peace*, **by Cardinal Bernardin.** As he was dying, Bernardin (1928–96), cardinal of the Chicago diocese, reevaluated his relationship to money and realized that while having made a vow only to keep a checking account and to put any gifts he received into special charities and project funds, he had slipped and begun saving the generous gifts he got. At the time of his writing this book (published posthumously in 1997), he notes, "I have now reexamined all this and ensured that I am free from things so that I am no longer distracted in my relationship with the Lord."[2]

Wealth can be the enemy of salvation.

Film: *Born Rich*, **directed by Jamie Johnson.** In this documentary film (2003),[3] Jamie Johnson, heir to the Johnson and Johnson wealth, looks at the children who are born to the very wealthy, among them the Vanderbilts, the Trumps, and the Bloombergs. He talks about the difficulty that these children have in coming to personal identity, as their sense of their selves can be compromised or lost by their wealth. Unfortunately, this creates a chasm between their lives and those of others, only deepening the problem and making it less likely to be resolved.

A Blind Beggar and a Rich Scoundrel

Big Idea *Two incidents at Jericho demonstrate Jesus's mission to save the lost, whatever their place in society, whether oppressed or oppressor.*

Understanding the Text

The Text in Context

The journey that began in 9:51 is near its end, as Jesus and his disciples cross the Jordan and enter Jericho before the final climb up to Jerusalem. Two events in Jericho illustrate again the deep social divisions that came to our attention in 18:14–30, and the issue of the salvation of the rich (18:18–27) is explored further in the story of Zacchaeus, which provides a poignant contrast to that of the rich ruler. It also takes up again, and brings to a climax, the recurrent theme of Jesus's willingness to mix with "tax collectors and sinners" (5:27–32; 7:29–35, 36–50; 15:1–32) in order to bring them his message of salvation. The salvation here again of a man whom other Jews would regard as beyond the pale forms the setting for an epigram (19:10) that sums up Luke's understanding of the mission of Jesus, already powerfully illustrated in the parables of chapter 15.

Historical and Cultural Background

The ancient city of Jericho was by this time an affluent settlement, recently elaborately expanded by Herod; its warm winter climate made it a favored place for leading citizens of Jerusalem to have a second home. Such an administrative center was a suitable location for a "chief tax collector" (the term occurs nowhere else), not an ordinary local official like Levi and his

Jesus healed a blind beggar as he approached Jericho and met Zacchaeus as he entered Jericho. Few excavations of the New Testament town have been done because the modern town lies above any remains. Archaeologists have uncovered the ruins of Herod the Great's elaborate winter palace, which are shown here.

friends (5:27–29), but probably the head officer for the region, hence his affluence. As such, he may be expected to have been a familiar, if very unpopular, figure in the community. His choice of a fig-mulberry tree (which has large leaves) indicates a man who feels safer out of the public eye.

Interpretive Insights

18:35 *sitting by the roadside begging.* A blind person had little alternative for making a living. Giving alms to the poor was a recognized part of Jewish religious duty, and pilgrim crowds on the way to Jerusalem for the Passover festival might be expected to be especially amenable.

18:37 *Jesus of Nazareth is passing by.* "Jesus" was a common name and so required a descriptive "surname," particularly in this Judean area where Jesus was not a local. But his reputation is now such that a stranger, even in Jericho, may be expected to know who he is. For "of Nazareth" as Jesus's public title, compare 4:34; 24:19.

18:38 *Jesus, Son of David, have mercy on me!* This is the only time in Luke that Jesus is addressed as "Son of David," and the repetition of the title in the next verse shows that it is meant to be noticed. To the crowds he is simply Jesus of Nazareth, a noted teacher and wonder worker, but this blind man seems somehow to have grasped the deeper truth about Jesus: he is the Messiah. The fact that, when cured, he will "follow" Jesus (18:43) suggests that this was more than just flattery to gain attention. His insight prepares for the more general acclamation of Jesus in 19:38 as "the king." For Jesus's own comments on the title "Son of David," see also 20:41–44.

- Jesus goes out of his way to help a beggar whom the crowd wants to ignore.
- The healing of the beggar's blindness leads to his becoming a disciple.
- Jesus takes the initiative to make contact with a powerful but unpopular man.
- Even a chief tax collector can be saved.
- Zacchaeus's salvation involves massive financial restitution.
- "The Son of Man came to seek and to save the lost" (19:10).

18:39 *Those who led the way rebuked him.* We are not told that they were disciples, but the use of the same term as in 18:15 ("rebuke") invites us to compare these two attempts to keep unimportant people from gaining Jesus's attention.

18:40 *Jesus stopped.* Perhaps the use of the messianic title made it clear that the man was not just begging for money. At any rate, Jesus, unlike his associates, will not turn away the socially insignificant and vulnerable.

18:41 *Lord, I want to see.* This seems obvious to us, but a beggar who was no longer blind would lose his chief asset for begging and thus an uncertain future. It was a prospect that required real "faith" (18:42).

18:42 *Receive your sight; your faith has healed you.* This is the only specific account of the healing of the blind in Luke (though see 7:21–22), a direct fulfillment of the Nazareth manifesto (4:18). For the healing formula involving "faith," compare 7:50; 8:48; 17:19. The Greek word for "healed" (*sōzō*) here (as in 8:48; 17:19) is the normal word for "saved," hence the appropriateness of this same formula in 7:50, where it refers to spiritual rather than physical healing. The use of the same verb (and the noun "salvation") in 19:9–10 links these two stories of salvation, one primarily physical, the other spiritual.

18:43 *followed Jesus, praising God . . . they also praised God.* "Followed" probably means that he took up the life of discipleship in place of a life of begging, and he would be among the crowd that will accompany Jesus to Jerusalem. The double mention of praising God prepares us for the arrival of this group in Jerusalem in 19:37, where the praise will relate to "all the miracles they had seen."

19:2 *Zacchaeus.* On his status, see "Historical and Cultural Background" above.

19:4 *climbed a sycamore-fig tree to see him.* This is not a very dignified thing for a socially prominent man to do, but he may have hoped to be hidden by the large leaves. The "sycamore-fig" is a "fig-mulberry" (*sykon*, "fig" + *morea*, "mulberry"), a luxuriant fruiting tree of the Mediterranean unrelated to the tree of the maple family for which "sycamore" is normally used.

19:5 *I must stay at your house today.* For Jesus to invite himself to stay in the house of such a man was an even more blatant social outrage than his acceptance of Levi's hospitality in 5:29–30 and also a slight to the more worthy citizens who might have welcomed him. For Jesus, the work of "salvation" took precedence over social protocol, and he recognized in this powerful but despised man someone "lost" needing to be found.

19:8 *Look, Lord! Here and now I give . . . pay back.* This translation gives a performative sense to the Greek present tenses underlying "give" and "pay back." Alternatively, it has been suggested that Zacchaeus (like the Pharisee in 18:12) is boastfully claiming that these are already his regular habits, but not only is it difficult to see how one could *regularly* give away half of one's possessions, but also the sequence of the story better suits a performative sense: this is a decisive, one-time response to the presence of Jesus. Luke records no explicit statement of repentance, but the reader assumes, and Jesus's comments in 19:9 will presuppose, that so radical an act of restitution must spring from a fundamental change of heart and a determination to avoid unjust exploitation in the future.

It is interesting to compare Zacchaeus's declaration with what Jesus demanded of the rich man in 18:22. Zacchaeus gives half of his possessions, not all, though the additional restitution of

Zaccheus climbed a sycamore-fig tree in order to see Jesus. These trees can reach sixty feet tall when fully grown, but their low, thick branches make them easy to climb. Here is a sycamore-fig tree growing in Ramat-gan, Israel.

400 percent of his ill-gotten gains (the law required only 120 percent [Lev. 6:5; Num. 5:7]) would probably make a sizable hole in the other half. And we are not told that he left home and followed Jesus as a disciple (as the blind man has done [18:43]). But there is no hint that his response is insufficient; rather the opposite. Does this suggest that 18:22 may not be intended as a rigid rule so much as a diagnostic test of the depth of a person's commitment, and that its practical outworking may differ in different situations?

19:9 *Today salvation has come to this house.* "Today" indicates that Zacchaeus's declaration, just made, is the evidence of salvation. It indicates so radical a change that it can be understood as the sort of "repentance" that causes joy in heaven according to 15:7, 10. Zechariah and Simeon sang of God's "salvation" coming to the people as a whole (1:69, 71, 77; 2:30), but now it is brought down to the individual level.

this man, too, is a son of Abraham. Jesus issues this riposte to the grumblers in 19:7. To some Jews, a tax collector (and especially a chief tax collector), even if Jewish by birth, had forfeited any right to be counted among the chosen people. But Zacchaeus's repentance has restored his birthright. It was to Abraham that God's promises to his people had especially been made (1:55, 73), and it was in association with Abraham that his people were to enjoy God's salvation (13:28; 16:22–30).

19:10 *The Son of Man came to seek and to save the lost.* The words echo Ezekiel 34:16, where God is seen as the good shepherd of his people, rescuing them from neglect and exploitation by their failed rulers.

God's mission is now fulfilled through the Son of Man, whose concern for "the lost" was graphically portrayed in the parables of chapter 15.

Theological Insights

Several scholars, notably I. H. Marshall,[1] have located the focus of Luke's message in the term "salvation" (and its verb "save," which tends to be obscured in English versions by the use of "heal" instead of "save" where the problem is physical). This emphasis is well summarized in 19:10, but so also in these two stories, representing two men who were "lost" in different ways, but who found salvation through Jesus. The fact that they come from opposite ends of the social spectrum underlines again Luke's depiction of the wide scope of Jesus's ministry, which does not defer to worldly status or advantage. It is right to speak of a "bias toward the poor" in Luke's portrayal of Jesus, and it may have seemed at times that the rich are regarded as irredeemably bad (16:19–31; 18:18–27); but here is a rich man who also finds salvation. Even he can be a true son of Abraham.

Teaching the Text

The preceding comments[2] have attempted to treat this pair of stories as deliberately placed side by side for comparison, showing that Jesus is here to save both the oppressed and the oppressor. Is this is a valid insight? What other points of comparison and contrast might be drawn out? What contribution does their juxtaposition make to Luke's overall agenda of presenting Jesus as the Savior?

Both stories can be approached by encouraging listeners to put themselves in the place of an onlooker: in the first, as a member of the crowd traveling with Jesus; in the second, as an inhabitant of Jericho. Both groups discourage Jesus from acting on behalf of these two men. In your teaching, try to reconstruct the social expectations and constraints, and note how Jesus overrode them. What people in our society today might correspond to the blind beggar and to Zacchaeus? How would we react to seeing them treated as Jesus does here?

Since in Luke the Zacchaeus story is the climax of Jesus's journey to Jerusalem or "gospel to the outcast" (Luke 9–19), it may be helpful when teaching this passage to review some of the key texts in Luke that carry forward this theme. Notice especially these three: the call of Levi (5:27–32), the parables of lost things (chap. 15), and the Zacchaeus episode. The call of Levi concerns a tax collector and opposition to Jesus's dining with sinners. It climaxes with Jesus's claim that, as the great physician, he has not come to call the self-righteous,

but sinners (5:31–32). The parables of the lost and found in chapter 15 begin with this same theme of opposition to Jesus's dining with sinners (15:1–2) and climax with the "lost" being found. Now, climactically, Jesus is criticized for dining with a *chief* tax collector (19:7)—the worst of the worst—and concludes by announcing that he has come "to seek and to save *the lost*" (19:10). These connections can reveal to your audience that in Luke Jesus is portrayed especially as the Savior of lost people everywhere.

The Zacchaeus story also invites us to think again about wealth, its dangers, and its proper use, themes we have seen again and again in Luke's Gospel. What makes this rich man a possible subject for salvation

The ancient city of Jericho was important because it had a strategic military location, an abundant water supply, and a tropical climate. It was known as the "city of palms" (a modern view can be seen here). Major roads ran through it, agricultural products were grown near it, and archaeological evidence indicates that a large Jewish population occupied it, all of which would have made it a prosperous location for a tax collector.

in contrast to the rich man in 18:18–25? How does Zacchaeus's massive "redistribution of wealth" relate to Jesus's demands in 12:33; 18:22? In what ways might God be looking for a similar response from rich people today?

Illustrating the Text

In stopping to heal the blind man, Jesus shows his concern for the lowly and outcast.

Christian Fiction: *In His Steps: What Would Jesus Do?*, by Charles Monroe Sheldon. Among the top-selling books of all time, this novel (1897) is set in a small railroad town and has as its premise the imitation of Christ, which in this case means doing instead of just talking. The novel begins when a poor, jobless man shows up at the office of Rev. Henry Maxwell on a Friday to present his need when the pastor is busily composing his Sunday sermon. The preoccupied pastor is dismissive.

On Sunday morning, the same man appears at the church while the congregation is singing "All for Jesus, all for Jesus, / All my being's ransomed powers," and he proceeds to walk down the aisle until he reaches the open space in front of the pulpit. He faces the people, confronting them directly but inoffensively, telling them the story of his job loss, of the death of his wife, and of his having "tramped" through the city without finding any "word of sympathy or comfort except from your minister here, who said he was sorry for me and hoped I would find a job somewhere." He says about himself, "I'm not an ordinary tramp, though I don't know of any teaching of Jesus that makes one kind of a tramp less worth saving than another. . . . What do you mean when you sing, 'I'll go with Him, with Him, all the way'? Do you mean that you are suffering and denying yourselves and trying to save lost, suffering humanity just as I understand Jesus did?"

At the end of his moving talk, he falls over and later dies, precipitating the pastor's reevaluation of his whole life. Rev. Henry Maxwell then begins to live in light of Christ's model.[3]

True conversion results in profound change, including a change in relationship to past sin and to one's possessions.

All people need to turn to Jesus and be saved.

Film: *Regarding Henry*, directed by Mike Nichols. This 1991 film shows how a person can completely reform his or her life when shocked into awareness, a metaphor for what this passage is saying. Henry is an ambitious, self-focused, arrogant, even ruthless, highly successful Manhattan lawyer who has a beautiful wife and a troubled adolescent daughter, both of whom he sacrifices to his ambition, workaholism, and a secret affair. One evening, as he is buying a pack of cigarettes, he interrupts a burglary at a corner store and is shot and seriously wounded. Having been shot in the frontal lobe of his brain, he suffers some brain damage and is unable to move or talk. In time, with therapy, he regains his speech and mobility and begins to see how wrong his life has been in every way. With this growing awareness, he starts to change everything: the way he lives and relates to his wife and child.

Use It or Lose It

Big Idea *We have opportunities to serve God while we wait for his kingdom to be fulfilled, and he expects us to use them well.*

Understanding the Text

The Text in Context

As Jesus approaches Jerusalem, expectations are high. He has recently been hailed as "Son of David" (18:38–39), and soon he will be acclaimed "king" (19:38). He has declared that salvation has come "today" (19:9). Is this then the moment for the "kingdom of God" that he has preached to be brought in, with Jesus as its king in his capital, Jerusalem? This parable takes up that issue and prepares the reader for the paradoxical way things will work out in Jerusalem. It warns against expecting too much too soon, but at the same time it warns against indifference. The king *will* return, and those who have disobeyed or opposed him will be the losers.

There is a similar parable in Matthew 25:14–30. The story is constructed in the same way, but the details are very different, drawing out different applications, and Matthew's version lacks the "political" elements of Luke's. The Matthean parable is set at the end of the period of teaching in Jerusalem, in the context of teaching about the parousia, whereas Luke's version is linked more closely to the immediate situation of Jesus's arrival at Jerusalem. As with the parables of the great supper (Matt. 22:1–14; Luke 14:16–24), we seem to have the same basic story line differently developed for different contexts. Each should be interpreted on its own terms.

Historical and Cultural Background

Under the Roman Empire "kings," even if hereditary rulers in their own culture, had to be officially appointed by Rome as local client rulers. Such appointment was not automatic. When Herod died in 4 BC, two

Archelaus and Antipas, two sons of Herod the Great, went to Rome to petition for the position of king after their father's death. Their requests were denied, and they returned to rule the territories they had originally been given. This coin (both sides are shown) was authorized by Herod Archelaus (4 BC–AD 6).

of his sons, Archelaus and Antipas, both claimed the kingship and went to Rome to lobby for it. Neither was successful: they remained "ethnarch" and "tetrarch" of their respective territories. An official Jewish delegation had followed Archelaus to Rome, requesting his deposition, and it was in response to them that the title "king" was refused. Similar representations from his subjects eventually led to his deposition in AD 6.

As usual, the NIV's "servants" represents the Greek for "slaves." Slaves in a rich household, while remaining the "property" of their masters, might be given great responsibility, sometimes rising to senior administrative positions with considerable influence.

Interpretive Issues

19:11 *the kingdom of God was going to appear at once.* This is the same issue that the Pharisees raised in 17:20 (see comments there). Jesus's determined approach to the capital seems to have led some to assume a political objective. We are not told who "the people" (the Greek text has simply "they") were who thought this; in view of Jesus's clear statements (as recently as 18:31–33) of what was to happen, his disciples at least ought not to have had such ideas, but Luke has twice noted their failure to grasp what Jesus meant (9:45; 18:34). In giving this interpretive "steer" to the parable, Luke may reflect concern in his own days about the delay of the parousia. The parable depends on the master being absent for a period, but its focus is on responsible service rather than on the question of timing as such.

19:12 *to have himself appointed king and then to return.* See "Historical and

Key Themes of Luke 19:11–27

- God's kingdom will be fully implemented in his good time, but not at Jesus's entrance into Jerusalem.
- In the meantime, he expects each of us to make full use of our opportunities.
- The reward for faithful service is greater responsibility.
- To fail to use our opportunities is to risk losing everything.
- Doing nothing is not neutral; it is punishable disobedience.

Cultural Background" above; the fairly recent Archelaus incident would still have been a sensitive issue in Judea.

19:13 *ten minas.* The mina was a Greek coin worth a hundred drachmas, so roughly a hundred days' wages. There were about sixty minas to a talent, so that the sums here are very modest compared to those in the Matthean parable. Unlike in Matthew, all ten receive the same amount to start with.

19:14 *We don't want this man to be our king.* Although this delegation reflects the historical reality of the Archelaus incident, it seems less relevant to Jesus's story, and its denouement in 19:27 provides a rather incongruous ending. Is it here to remind us that during the period of Jesus's absence not everyone will be working for him or looking forward to his return?

19:16, 18 *your mina has earned ten more . . . your mina has earned five more.* The two successful slaves have achieved different levels of success starting from the same endowment (by contrast, in Matthew the amounts entrusted vary, but the rate of success is the same). Is this feature intended, like the different levels of yield from the seed in Mark's and Matthew's versions of the parable of the sower (Mark 4:8, 20), to recognize that disciples may vary in their capacity for success? God expects and rewards faithful service, even though not all will be able to reach the same level.

19:17, 19 *take charge of ten cities . . . take charge of five cities.* The reward for faithful service is increased responsibility! The successful slaves now receive administrative charge of substantial districts of the newly established kingdom. Compared to this political responsibility, the previous commercial enterprise was indeed a "very small matter." But the levels of success in trading have revealed each slave's individual capacity, and the new task is tailored to what each has shown himself capable of (cf. 16:10–12). The kingdom of God is not a totally egalitarian regime.

In the parable of the ten minas (19:12–27), ten servants are each given a mina. The mina is a monetary weight. This is a bronze half mina from the third to second century BC and is the equivalent to 30 shekels or 120 denarii.

19:20 *I have kept it laid away in a piece of cloth.* "Banks" in the ancient world were rudimentary and not much trusted. It was better to keep the sum intact than to risk losing even what he had received. The third slave's failure was due to fear rather than laziness. He knew that he would not be forgiven for losing what had been entrusted to him, and so he played it safe.

19:22 *I am a hard man.* As we have seen in 18:1–8, a parable character who represents God need not be like God in every respect. God is not "hard" and exploitative, but he does expect his people to make an effort on his behalf and to take risks rather than give up in fear.

19:23 *put my money on deposit.* Lending at interest was illegal between Jews. Here the master either expected his slave to bend the rules (thus reflecting his master's alleged business attitudes!) or wanted him to do business with a Gentile.

19:24 *Take his mina away from him and give it to the one who has ten minas.* As the other slaves recognize (19:25), this is a surprising move. For one thing, it is unexpected to find the first slave still in possession of the proceeds of his trading, which had been done for his master's benefit, not his own. But the response indicates also a sense of unfairness: why should he have yet more?

19:26 *to everyone who has, more will be given.* The same principle was expressed in 8:18 in a comment following the parable of the sower, apparently relating there to people's capacity to understand Jesus's teaching. Here it seems more general in its application. Success breeds success, and failure is compounded. As an observation on economic and social life, ancient and modern, this would be true, though many would find it regrettable. But it relates here to spiritual success and failure; it is those who are committed in their discipleship who make progress, but failure to take responsibility is a slippery slope to spiritual disaster. Use it or lose it!

19:27 *But those enemies of mine.* This final twist to the story seems to have little to do with the main theme; it simply rounds off the scenario set out in 19:14 with a savage reprisal typical of an ancient Near Eastern monarch. Did Luke include it as a warning to anyone inclined to defy the kingdom of God? There is a serious escalation between the punishment of the timid slave (loss of his mina) and that of the rebels: a failing disciple is not the same thing as a deliberate enemy of the kingdom of God.

Theological Insights

Luke's version of this parable involves two theological themes, the question of the timing of the coming of the kingdom of God, with which it opens, and that of the responsibilities and rewards of discipleship, which is the central theme of the story proper.

To the question whether the kingdom of God was to appear at once, the answer seems to be no. The absence of the one who is to be king in "a distant country" provides a period of delay, during which it is the responsibility of disciples not to calculate and watch for his return, but rather to get on with the job that he has entrusted to them. They must also, of course, resist the overtures of those who dispute his kingship. All this will be food for thought in a period when the parousia, the return of Christ, initially assumed to be imminent, turns out to be indefinitely delayed.

The parable does not spell out what is represented by the financial trading that is at the heart of the story, but the imagery seems broadly applicable to all areas of responsibility that God expects of his people. The parable indicates that he expects those responsibilities to be fulfilled to the best of our ability, with the recognition that those abilities may vary between individual disciples. It also teaches that the proper exercise of such responsibility will be rewarded, but that to back out of such responsibility is the way of spiritual ruin.

Teaching the Text

Luke apparently has two main purposes in placing this parable here, one "theological" and one related to practical Christian living. It will be helpful in your teaching to highlight both. The first is to show that the kingdom will not be fully revealed at Jesus's entrance into Jerusalem (see 19:11). Jesus will instead depart (at his ascension) to receive his royal authority (19:12, 15), later returning to judge and reward his subjects (19:15). The second (and primary) point is the need for good stewardship during his absence (19:13–27).

I have noted above the need to interpret each of the two Synoptic versions of this parable on its own terms. But in your teaching it may be helpful to read both side by side, and to identify the differences, so as to highlight more clearly what is distinctive to Luke's version. What does he intend us to conclude from the fact that all slaves receive the same amount but their results differ? Or from the different levels of reward given to the two successful slaves?

The way the slaves are treated also raises the issue of fairness and inequality. Are we comfortable with the principle of compounded inequality expressed in 19:26, even purely as a matter of secular economics? And in what way can it be transferred to the spiritual world? Why is the slave who hid his mina not treated with grace rather than with dismissal and deprivation? You might stress here that, although we are saved wholly by God's grace, recipients of the gift of salvation have a responsibility to serve faithfully as God's servants.

Or do all these questions assume too allegorical a function for the parable? Are we meant to press such details, or simply to focus on the main point? How would we define what that "main point" is?

Do the more "political" elements in Luke's introduction (19:11) and in the inclusion of the rebels (19:14, 27) unnecessarily complicate a story that would work well without them? What might Luke have hoped to achieve by including them? Is there a possible allegorical meaning with regard to Jesus's own kingship and the resistance to it by the Jerusalem authorities?

Does this parable have a message for those in our own day who also think that "the kingdom of God is going to appear at once"?

Illustrating the Text

A truly committed disciple must be responsible with the gifts that God has given.

Theological Book: *Pensées*, **by Blaise Pascal**. This complex work (published posthumously in 1669) by Pascal (1623–62) in itself is a testimony to an unusual discipleship and would be worth pursuing as background to the quotation that follows. A scientist and mathematician, Pascal received an illumination from God and was converted in 1654. *Pensées* was to have been a careful and thorough defense of Christianity, a work that would convict the intellect, but what we read are, says T. S. Eliot in his introduction, "the first notes for a work that was far from completion."[1]

Nevertheless, the collection of what has been described as "fragmentary writings" has endured, beloved and revered. In one of these fragments Pascal writes about the nature of discipleship:

> I love poverty because he loved it. I love riches because they afford me the means of helping the very poor. I keep faith with everybody. . . . I try to be just, true, sincere, and faithful to all men. I have a tender heart for those to whom God has more closely united me; and whether I am alone or seen of men, I do all of my actions in the sight of God, who must judge of them, and to whom I have consecrated them all.[2]

Film: *Saving Grace*, **directed by Robert M. Young**. In this engaging film (1985) the pope, a bit weary of the state of the church and dressed in ordinary clothing, finds himself accidentally locked out of his papal estate and not easily recognizable as he is. He decides then to travel to a very poor, rural village where he discovers the true meaning of discipleship, what it means to personally reach out to help in practical and not always easy ways, to resist temptation and live his faith, and to have his life vitally intertwined with people. When he returns to his estate, he can address with more passion what it means to be a disciple of Christ. Many scenes could be shown, but particularly interesting is his speech when he returns home.

Faithfulness in small things is significant in God's view.

Poetry: "Am I Thy Gold?" by Edward Taylor. In this poem Taylor (1642–1729), a pastor, poet, and doctor in the American colonial period, asks the Lord to become for him "spectacles that [he] may read," so that he can serve the Lord. The last verse follows, indicating that the Lord can use those devoted to him in extraordinary ways.

> Lord, make my soul Thy plate; Thine image bright
> Within the circle of the same enfoil.
> And on its brims in golden letters write
> Thy superscription in an holy style.
> Then I shall be Thy money, Thou my hoard;
> Let me Thy angel be, be Thou my Lord."[3]

The Coming of the King

Big Idea As Jesus approaches Jerusalem, his disciples hail him as king, but he weeps over the city's failure to grasp its opportunity for salvation.

Understanding the Text

The Text in Context

At last the journey that began in 9:51 has reached its goal. From here on the story will be set in and around Jerusalem. At its heart will be the confrontation between Jesus, the expected Messiah, and the Jerusalem authorities, who reject his claim, and that confrontation is already symbolized here by the contrasting reactions of the disciples and the Pharisees to his deliberately symbolic mode of arrival. The sense of impending judgment on Jerusalem and specifically on its temple in 19:41–46 prepares for the more detailed prediction of its destruction in chapter 21. The material in 19:47–48 leads into the following narrative by not only setting the scene for Jesus's teaching in the temple but also highlighting the contrast between the murderous intentions of the authorities, which will eventually lead to his death, and the popular enthusiasm for Jesus.

Historical and Cultural Background

As the Passover festival approached, large crowds poured into Jerusalem, swelling the city's population to perhaps six times its normal size. The temple courtyards would be crowded with these pilgrims from all over the Jewish world. The temple was much more than a building for religious worship; it was the cultural heart of Judaism. Its vast outer court of the Gentiles was a natural gathering place for traders, teachers, and sightseers, and it was from this courtyard, rather than the temple building proper (which only priests could enter), that Jesus drove out the traders.

Jesus's prediction of the fate of the city in 19:43–44 recalls prophetic descriptions of Nebuchadnezzar's capture of Jerusalem in 586 BC (e.g., Jer. 6; cf. Isa. 29:1–4).

Interpretive Insights

19:29 *Bethphage and Bethany at the hill called the Mount of Olives.* The road from Jericho goes through Bethany, on the far side of the ridge (the Mount of Olives) that overlooks Jerusalem from the east, and

As Jesus headed west toward Jerusalem up the Jerusalem Jericho Road, he passed the towns of Bethany and Bethpage as he neared the Mount of Olives. Shown here is a photo taken in the late 1930s showing the approach to the Mount of Olives that passes Bethany.

at the probable site of Bethphage comes into sight the city (see 19:41) across the Kidron Valley.

19:30 *a colt tied there, which no one has ever ridden.* Matthew and John specify that it was a donkey, and both quote Zechariah 9:9 in explanation. Luke follows Mark in using the Greek word for "(new) colt," which occurs (for the Hebrew for "donkey") in the LXX version of that verse, and the disciples' response in 19:38 makes it clear that they took this as a deliberate enactment of the Zechariah prophecy. After walking some one hundred miles from Galilee, Jesus, who is never recorded as riding elsewhere in the Gospels, hardly *needed* a ride for the last mile downhill! Besides, there is rabbinic evidence that Passover pilgrims were normally expected to arrive on foot. This way of approaching Jerusalem was, then, a conspicuous and deliberately acted claim to be the "king" of Zechariah 9:9–10. The mention of a donkey's colt tied up might remind some also of the messianic vision of Genesis 49:10–11.

19:31 *The Lord needs it.* Luke often refers editorially to Jesus as "the Lord," but it would be unparalleled in Luke to have Jesus

Key Themes of Luke 19:28-48

- Jesus rides toward Jerusalem on a donkey in order to illustrate his messianic claim.
- His disciples get the point, and they hail him as king.
- But Pharisees, and the Jerusalem authorities, continue to oppose him.
- Jesus weeps when he sees that the city is about to refuse its last chance to escape judgment.
- He declares, in deeds and words, God's judgment on the misuse of the temple.

use that title of himself. The natural meaning is "God needs it." The ready response of the villagers to this cryptic message delivered apparently by total strangers suggests that it may be a prearranged password that Jesus had agreed on with known supporters in the village.

19:36 *spread their cloaks on the road.* For a similar gesture of homage to one proclaimed king, see 2 Kings 9:13.

19:37 *the whole crowd of disciples.* Matthew and Mark say that the messianic acclamation was uttered by the crowds accompanying Jesus. All three Synoptic writers therefore make clear that it was not the people of Jerusalem who hailed Jesus as king; he will not reach the city until 19:45. Jesus's words in 19:42–44 show that Jerusalem's reaction to the Galilean prophet would be very different (cf. also Matt. 21:10–11).

19:38 *Blessed is the king who comes in the name of the Lord!* The traditional Passover greeting from Psalm 118:26 is given a special focus by the addition of "the king," alluding to Zechariah 9:9. Jesus is not just any Passover pilgrim. The messianic fervor is unmistakable, as the Pharisees' objection in 19:39 makes clear. But this is not the fulfillment of 13:35; the

greeting is uttered by Jesus's disciples, not by the people of Jerusalem.

Peace in heaven and glory in the highest! Luke uses (for the benefit of Gentile readers?) "glory" in place of the Jewish shout "hosanna" (Mark and Matthew). The resultant acclamation echoes the angelic chorus that greeted the first announcement of the Messiah's birth (2:14).

19:39 *Some of the Pharisees.* Hitherto they have been Jesus's main opponents, but they are now mentioned for the last time. Once Jesus is in Jerusalem, he will be confronted instead by the Jerusalem authorities, especially the priests with their headquarters in the temple (see 19:47).

19:40 *if they keep quiet, the stones will cry out.* Perhaps a proverbial saying (cf. Hab. 2:11): there are some things that cannot be hushed up.

19:41 *he wept over it.* Luke has already recorded a similar lament, uttered while still on the way, at 13:34–35. Now the crisis is closer, and the prophecy more detailed.

19:42 *If you, even you, had only known.* A better translation in context is "If you too had known"—if the city had been able to share the disciples' understanding of the climactic importance of the Messiah's coming, as they have expressed it in 19:38. The "peace" offered to Jerusalem (note the repetition of the same word as in 19:38), but about to be rejected, is that of the king of peace (Zech. 9:9–10). The name "Jerusalem" was

Jesus wept over the city of Jerusalem because it would reject him, resulting in judgment at the hands of the Romans in AD 70. This coin with the inscription "Judea capta" was a sestertius minted by Vespasian (AD 69–79) to commemorate the victory by his son Titus over the First Jewish Revolt. This military conflict occurred from AD 66 to 70 and resulted in the destruction of the temple and the city of Jerusalem.

popularly understood to mean the place of peace, *shalom* (cf. Heb. 7:2 with Ps. 76:2).

19:43 *The days will come upon you.* In 13:35 Jesus has already predicted the destruction of the temple, and he will do so again more forcibly in 21:6, but here he goes further and predicts the Roman siege of the city as a whole, as well as its devastation that was to follow in AD 70; this theme too will be more fully developed in 21:20–24.

19:44 *you did not recognize the time of God's coming to you.* Literally, this is "the time of your visitation," which in this context seems to refer to Jesus's messianic arrival, the coming of the king to his capital. If Jerusalem had joined in welcoming its king (saying, "Blessed is he who comes in the name of the Lord" [13:35]), there would be hope for its salvation, but Jesus already knows that whatever some individuals may decide, the city and its leadership will not recognize him as the Messiah.

19:45 *he began to drive out those who were selling.* Traders in sacrificial animals and supplies were allowed by the temple authorities to set up their stalls in the court of the Gentiles. For Jesus, this indicates that the whole institution has lost its way as a center for the worship of God ("my Father's house" [2:49]) and has become a human commercial enterprise. But now his own teaching of "the way of God" (20:21) in the temple courts (19:47) will supplant commerce; God will triumph over mammon.

19:46 *It is written.* Two specific Old Testament texts are cited, the first (Isa. 56:7) expressing the temple's intended role as a religious focus for all nations (an especially appropriate allusion in the court of the Gentiles), the second (Jer. 7:11) drawn from Jeremiah's great temple sermon, which had similarly denounced the people's sinful behavior while still claiming God's presence among them (Jer. 7:1–15). Other texts, not cited, that would come to mind for those well versed in Old Testament prophecy would be Malachi 3:1–4 (the Lord coming to purify his temple) and Zechariah 14:21 (the elimination of commerce from the house of the Lord), both understood to be part of the eschatological judgment.

19:47 *were trying to kill him.* The preceding verses suggest that this hostility on the part of the Jerusalem authorities (here listed in a way similar to 9:22; 20:19) arose from Jesus's high-handed attitude toward the temple establishment. They could hardly ignore his action, especially if they had become aware that the messianic authority that it implied had already been flaunted in his dramatic approach to the city.

19:48 *all the people hung on his words.* The crowds in the temple courts would by this time be largely made up of Passover visitors, who would likely be more favorable to the Galilean Messiah. The solution to the authorities' problem will be related in 22:2–6.

Theological Insights

Jesus's actions in approaching Jerusalem on a donkey and driving out traders from the temple courts carried obvious messianic implications. He was in effect throwing down the gauntlet to the Jerusalem authorities, as their immediate response in 20:2 will show. The manner of his arrival has therefore set up a confrontation of authority that will lead eventually to Jesus's trial and execution, and in the longer term to Jerusalem's own destruction.

But alongside the settled hostility of Jerusalem's leadership is the enthusiastic promotion of Jesus's messianic claims by his own disciples (19:37–38) and the wider approval with which the crowd of ordinary pilgrims in the temple courts will respond to Jesus's teaching (19:48). The division within Israel that Simeon predicted (2:34–35) is now taking place. The question is therefore sharply posed as to who represents the true Israel: Is it the official leadership in Jerusalem or those who have welcomed the promised Messiah? The insistent reference to a disastrous end for Jerusalem (13:34–35; 19:41–44; 21:5–6, 20–24; 23:27–31) suggests a radical answer to that question.

Teaching the Text

Each of the three main incidents in this section (the messianic arrival, the weeping over Jerusalem, the demonstration in the temple) raises important issues for teaching. But the notes above have attempted to show that all three are part of a carefully compiled whole, and teaching on these verses should bring that out.

The donkey ride is often described as Jesus's "entry" into Jerusalem, but in fact he does not reach the city until later (19:45). People often wrongly assume that the messianic welcome was uttered by the people of Jerusalem. But all the evangelists in different ways indicate a contrast between the attitude of the disciples and pilgrim crowd outside the walls and that of the city. This should be teased out by careful analysis of what each of the Gospel writers actually says.

Encourage listeners to put themselves in the position of Passover pilgrims arriving from Jericho with Jesus. What would they make of the acclamations? And of the demonstration in the temple? How does the Passover season contribute to the total effect?

By contrast, how might ordinary people who lived in Jerusalem react to this Galilean visitor and his remarkable claims?

Discuss how far Jesus's predictions of the destruction of the city and temple are merely statements of fact, and how far they carry a theological message. What might that message be? Note that Jerusalem plays an ambivalent role in Luke's Gospel. On the one hand, it is the city of God, the place where his salvation will be accomplished and from where the gospel message will go to all nations (Acts 1:8). On the other hand, it is symbolic of Israel's rejection of God's messengers. It is Jerusalem that in the past has rejected and killed the prophets and will now reject the Son (13:34–35; 19:9–19). For this rejection the city will be destroyed.

The whole crowd of disciples began to praise God when they reached the place where the road went down the Mount of Olives, across the Kidron Valley, and into the city of Jerusalem. This is the view from the Mount of Olives into the Kidron Valley, with the walls of the Old City of Jerusalem and the modern Temple Mount in sight.

Illustrating the Text

Jesus's triumphal entry was a carefully planned act of "glorious defiance and superlative courage."[1]

Film/Television: In many westerns, whether film or television, the cowboy hero (such as in the movies *Shane* or *Pale Rider*) or lawman (such as Wyatt Earp) often find themselves in situations beset by oppression and injustice, often at the hands of powerful ranchers or a group of villains. These heroes are bent on righteousness above all and often show tremendous courage, defying the forces arrayed against them. Shane, the main character in a movie and a popular novel by that name, is often seen as a Christ-type. Westerns could provide useful parallels to Jesus's entry into Jerusalem in the face of opposition.

Bible: 1 Kings 1:33. This verse refers to the importance of Solomon's riding David's mule in order to be recognized as king.

Hymn: "All Glory, Laud, and Honor," by Theodulf of Orléans. This beloved hymn was composed in Latin by Theodulf (760–821) around 820. Some of the verses are as follows:

All glory, laud, and honor
To you, Redeemer, King,
To whom the lips of children
Made sweet hosannas sing.

You are the king of Israel
And David's royal Son,
Now in the Lord's name coming,
Our King and Blessed One.

The multitude of pilgrims
With palms before you went,
Our praise and prayer and anthems
Before you we present.

To you before your Passion,
They sang their hymns of praise.
To you now high exalted,
Our melody we raise.

Jesus's most poignant and unrestrained wailing was over Jerusalem's stubborn unbelief.

Hymn: "O Patient Christ," by Margaret Wade Deland. This more recent hymn, by the American poet Deland (1857–1945), highlights Jesus's patience and compassion and calls on him to "rouse us" to live for him, even as he is patient still.

The intensity of Jesus's language demonstrates his absolute indignation over the defilement of God's house.

Quote: "The Emotional Life of Our Lord," by B. B. Warfield. The renowned Princeton theologian Warfield (1851–1921) writes in this chapter of his Christology,

> Perhaps in no incidents recorded in the Gospels is the action of our Lord's indignation more vividly displayed than in the accounts of the cleansing of the Temple. . . . The form in which it here breaks forth is that of indignant anger towards those who defile God's house with trafficking, and it thus presents us with one of the most striking manifestations of the anger of Jesus in act.[2]

Popular Culture: It would be good to ask in what ways people are prone to defile the temple today. It seems possible to suggest that the casual, thoughtless use of technology such as texting, using the internet, or leaving the sanctuary to answer a call during a church service or school chapel is a defilement of sacred space, an act of disrespect to God little noted today. Such behavior is not tolerated in secular environments such as opera productions and symphony recitals.

Challenge and Counterchallenge

Big Idea *Jesus's dramatic arrival in Jerusalem provokes the religious leaders to question his credentials, but Jesus in turn uses a parable to challenge their legitimacy.*

Understanding the Text

The Text in Context

After the long journey southward (9:51–19:44) Jesus has deliberately entered Jerusalem as the Messiah, and his actions and teaching in the temple have thrown down the gauntlet to the religious authorities of Jerusalem (19:45–48). Now they take up the challenge, and the rest of chapter 20 will continue the public confrontation. While the authorities remain hostile, the larger crowd in the court of the Gentiles remains at least potentially open to Jesus's appeal. It is only when they are able to detach Jesus from his popular support that the authorities will be able to carry out their plan to silence him, in chapters 22–23. Meanwhile, Jesus proves more than a match for them in open debate.

Historical and Cultural Background

The whole of chapter 20 is set in the court of the Gentiles, a vast public area (some thirty-three acres) surrounding the temple building, which at Passover time would be crowded with pilgrims from

When Jesus came to the temple complex, he taught the people in the public area known as the court of the Gentiles. It was here that he drove out the merchants selling animals for sacrifice, and it was here that he was challenged by the chief priests and elders. This drawing shows the court of the Gentiles viewed from the royal stoa, which was on its south side.

all over the Jewish world, and in which a teacher could gather a crowd.

The chief priests, scribes, and elders (the same three groups Jesus has predicted will reject him in Jerusalem [9:22]) were the three groups that made up the Sanhedrin, the ruling council of Israel, which under Roman occupation had been granted authority to regulate local affairs as well as strictly religious responsibilities. The temple area was their power base.

Jesus's parable reflects the agrarian situation in Palestine where absentee landlords let out estates to tenant farmers in return for an agreed share of the produce. A vineyard was a long-term investment in that new vines would not produce a significant harvest (and therefore any profit for either owner or tenants) until the fourth year.

Interpretive Insights

20:2 *Who gave you this authority?* The question of legitimate authority runs through this whole Jerusalem phase of the story that leads up to Jesus's arrest and trial. From the point of view of the official leadership, a Galilean visitor with no formal rabbinic training had no right to set himself up as an authority in "their" temple, as Jesus has done both by his high-handed action in 19:45–46 and by his teaching. The group that now approaches Jesus looks like an official delegation from the Sanhedrin, fulfilling their duty to regulate religious affairs. This self-appointed "messiah" seemed determined to cause trouble. For Jesus, of course, the temple was not theirs, but simply "my Father's house" (2:49).

20:4 *John's baptism—was it from heaven, or of human origin?* What looks like an evasive changing of the subject

Key Themes of Luke 20:1–19

- Jesus is now in serious confrontation with the leaders in Jerusalem.
- When they question his authority, he implicitly claims the same divine authority that John the Baptist had.
- His parable accuses them of failing in their duty as leaders of God's people and threatens the end of their tenancy.
- He predicts that they will kill him, and they plan to do so.
- But in the end God's purpose will triumph over all opposition.

(especially when Jesus will go on to refuse a straight answer to their question) in fact implies a bold claim. John also had no formal authorization, but his ministry (here referred to by its most memorable feature, John's innovative rite of baptism) had made a profound impression. If John's mission had been from God, so was that of Jesus (whom John had described as "more powerful" than himself [3:16]). Even if the Jerusalem authorities did not know of the connection between John and Jesus that Luke has established in chapters 1–2, the analogy between the two prophetic and popular preachers holds good.

20:6 *all the people will stone us.* Luke has already told us (7:29–30) that the religious leaders, unlike "all the people," had not approved John's ministry. But they dare not confront the popular enthusiasm for John directly, just as now they are inhibited by popular support for Jesus (19:48; 20:19; 22:2). People were comparing Jesus to John (9:19).

20:8 *Neither will I tell you.* Jesus will make no formal answer. But we have seen that his counterquestion clearly implies a claim to the same divine authority that John had, and the following parable, portraying him as the son of the vineyard owner, will reinforce that claim.

20:9 *A man planted a vineyard.* Although Luke does not include the direct echoes of Isaiah 5:1–2 with which Mark and Matthew begin this parable, the imagery of Israel as God's vineyard was well known from several Old Testament passages, and the motif of fruit denied would probably call Isaiah 5:1–7 to mind even without explicit allusion. This, then, is a story of God's dealings with Israel, but especially with its leaders, represented by the tenant farmers.

20:10–12 *beat him . . . treated shamefully . . . wounded him and threw him out.* The sequence of abused slaves represents the prophets, whose maltreatment at the hands of Israel's leaders was a familiar theme (see 11:47–51; 13:33–34).

20:13 *my son, whom I love.* The repetition of the same words used in the divine declaration at Jesus's baptism (3:22) ensures that Luke's reader cannot miss the reference to God sending his son Jesus as his last appeal to rebellious Israel. In this context, where the son is about to be killed, there is also a poignant echo of Abraham's intended sacrifice of Isaac (Gen. 22:2).

20:14 *the inheritance will be ours.* It is most unlikely that in reality the murder of the owner's son would allow the tenants to take possession as long as the owner himself was still alive (as indeed the sequel in 20:16 makes clear). But a parable does not have to reflect real life, and the tenants' scheme prompts the reader to recognize that the confrontation in Jerusalem represents the climactic showdown between the present leadership and God himself as represented

in his son Jesus. There is no room for both of them.

20:15 *They threw him out of the vineyard and killed him.* Here we have a veiled but unmistakable indication that Jesus is expecting to be executed. The site of crucifixion was outside the city walls (John 19:17; Heb. 13:12–13).

20:16 *He will come and kill those tenants and give the vineyard to others.* This clearly indicates the end of the present leadership of Israel. But who are the "others"? At a political level the thought could be of the coming Roman destruction of Jerusalem and the dissolution of its ruling Sanhedrin. But Matthew's version of this parable speaks of the kingdom of God being taken away from "you" and given to "a people who will produce its fruit" (Matt. 21:43), which seems to envisage a new Israel (not just a new leadership). Luke is less explicit, but the people's response, "God forbid!" (lit., "May it not happen!"), may suggest that such a radical idea is implied here too.

20:17 *The stone the builders rejected has become the cornerstone.* These words are quoted from Psalm 118:22 (where they precede the words of greeting quoted in 19:38). In the psalm they refer to the king (probably) rescued from his enemies and established by God as ruler. So also Jesus, rejected and crucified by those who saw him as a threat to their power, will be restored and will have the ultimate authority. This use of the psalm makes sense only in the light of an anticipated resurrection.

20:18 *Everyone who falls on that stone.* The quotation from Psalm 118:22 has introduced the new metaphor of a "cornerstone," which is probably to be understood as the key stone at the top of a corner of the building. Two prophetic allusions develop the metaphor of a significant stone (though not in the same architectural setting): in Isaiah 8:14–15 God himself will be a stone on which people will stumble and be broken, while in Daniel 2:34–35, 44–45 God's final triumphant kingdom is a rock that will strike down and pulverize all preceding powers. New Testament authors enjoyed collecting "stone" prophecies to illustrate the triumph of Christ (see Acts 4:11; Rom. 9:32–33; 1 Pet. 2:4–8). The first allusion here puts Jesus in the place of God in Isaiah's vision and reminds the reader of Simeon's prophecy that the child will be the cause of many falling in Israel (2:34).

Jesus ended his parable of the vineyard tenants by quoting Psalm 118:22, which speaks about a rejected stone becoming a capstone or cornerstone. In this photograph, Herodian cornerstones hold up the southeast corner of the Temple Mount. They average over seven feet long and three feet wide, and weigh approximately eighty tons.

20:19 *They knew he had spoken this parable against them.* The parable was spoken openly to "the people" (20:9), and although it is not explicitly applied, the imagery was too obvious to miss. In the setting where they have just challenged Jesus's authority, this was clearly a deliberate and public counterchallenge, calling on the people as a whole to support Jesus against their official leadership. If they had any doubts whether Jesus really was a serious threat to the status quo, and to their public authority, this parable has removed them. This is going to be a fight to the death.

Theological Insights

Jesus's question in 20:4 contrasts two types of authority, human and God-given. The prophetic ministries of Jesus and John

the Baptist represent the latter, but by implication the institutional status of the official leadership of Israel in Jerusalem is a merely human authority. That is why Jesus's parable can envisage them being deposed because of their failure to supply the "fruit" that God expects. That fruit is not specifically identified in the parable, but "fruit" is a familiar metaphor for living in conformity with God's will (3:8–9; 6:43–45; 8:1–21; 13:6–9), and the reader who has followed Luke's story so far will find it easy to contrast Jesus's proclamation of the kingdom of God with the leaders' hostility to that message. Theirs has become a self-serving leadership, shutting God out of his own vineyard. So it is time for a radical change, and the quotation from Psalm 118:22 sums up the coming regime change, when the kingdom of God will triumph over human opposition, even if it comes from those in supposedly religious authority in Israel.

Teaching the Text

These two pericopes belong together, as challenge and counterchallenge. The key issues are Jesus's identity and authority, which are challenged by the religious leaders.

In your teaching, you might raise the question of why Jesus did not give a straight answer to his opponents' question in 20:2. Did his counterquestion in fact imply a clear answer? And if so, was it more or

less effective by being conveyed in this cryptic form? Throughout chapter 20 the religious leaders are trying to trap Jesus in his own words. Yet he always outsmarts them, revealing their hypocrisy and hardness of heart. What is Luke teaching us about Jesus in these debates?

When teaching the parable of the vineyard, it can be enlightening to take your audience first through Isaiah's song of the vineyard, which begins as a love song and then turns into a judgment oracle (Isa. 5:1–7). Jesus's hearers would have recognized the echo immediately and identified God as the vineyard owner and the vineyard as Israel. Yet Jesus's retelling changes the focus from the vineyard to the tenant farmers (representing Israel's religious leaders),

Jesus starts his parable, "A man planted a vineyard." The audience listening to Jesus, especially the teachers of the law, would have recognized the parable's allusion to Old Testament imagery where Israel is God's vineyard. Grapes were a valuable agricultural crop in Israel, so vines were grown where soil was available, like those planted among the olive trees in this photograph.

who abuse the servants (the prophets) and eventually murder the son (Jesus). Discuss how Jesus retells an old story to make it relevant to his own ministry. What does the parable imply about Jesus's own role in the fulfillment of God's purpose for Israel? How radical is its conclusion meant to be? Would Luke have agreed with Matthew's version, which speaks of a new "people" inheriting the vineyard (Matt. 21:43)? Or is his version intended to speak only of a change of leadership in Jerusalem? (Consider here what will happen in Acts.)

Following on from the "in your face" style of Jesus's arrival at Jerusalem, these two pericopes show him in confrontational mood, prepared to antagonize powerful people. Is this a model for our own presentation of God's truth? When is there a place for the "gentle answer that turns away wrath" (Prov. 15:1)?

Illustrating the Text

Christ knows how to effectively confront a difficult situation in order to establish his authority and thwart the opposition.

Film: *A Time to Kill*, directed by Joel Schumacher. This film (1996) is based on the novel by John Grisham. Set in the deep South, this is the story of a small black girl who is brutally raped and left to die (she does not) by a group of drunken white men, members of the Ku Klux Klan. Her father, expecting their acquittal, takes vengeance and shoots the men. A young lawyer (played by Matthew McConaughey) defends the father at great danger to his own life. Nevertheless, he persists in the face of what looks like a losing battle. This young lawyer's closing speech is memorable and moving. In it, not only does he ask pertinent questions, but also he leads the jury in imagining a scene that turns the tide of the trial.

While claiming clearly to be the Son of God, Jesus demonstrates in his vulnerability that he knows what is coming, and that he will ultimately triumph.

History: Kenneth Bailey tells a remarkable story about Jordan's King Hussein that illustrates what should have been the tenant farmers' response to the vineyard owner's authority.

One night in the early 1980s, the king was informed by his security police that a group of about seventy-five Jordanian army officers were at that very moment meeting in a nearby barracks plotting a military overthrow of his kingdom. The security officers requested permission to surround the barracks and arrest the plotters. The king refused and said, "Bring me a small helicopter." A helicopter was brought. The king climbed in with the pilot and himself flew to the barracks and landed on its flat roof. The king told the pilot, "If you hear gun shots, fly away at once without me." Unarmed, the king . . . appeared in the room where the plotters were meeting and quietly said to them: "Gentlemen, it has come to my attention that you are meeting here tonight to finalize your plans to overthrow the government, take over the country and install a military dictator. If you do this, the army will break apart and the country will be plunged into civil war. Tens of thousands of innocent people will die. There is no need for this. Here I am! Kill me and proceed. That way, only one man will die." After a moment of stunned silence, the rebels as one, rushed forward to kiss the king's hand and feet and pledge loyalty to him for life.[1]

Luke 20:1–19

Two Testing Questions

Big Idea *In response to two questions designed to trap Jesus, he gives replies that not only avoid the traps but also convey important teaching.*

Understanding the Text

The Text in Context

Once Jesus has reached Jerusalem, he has set himself up as a regular teacher in the court of the Gentiles (19:47; 20:1). This has quickly provoked the temple-based leadership into challenging his authority (20:1–8), to which Jesus has responded with a parable that in turn questions their legitimacy as leaders of Israel (20:9–19). The two encounters in these verses are with different groups within the "coalition" that makes up the Sanhedrin. Their theological and political agendas were different, but they were united in the desire to discredit Jesus in the eyes of the crowd and to find a basis for destroying his challenge. In these two incidents the Jerusalem authorities take the initiative, but from 20:41 on it will be Jesus who directs the debate.

Historical and Cultural Background

The imposition of direct Roman rule over Judea and Samaria in AD 6 was followed by a census in order to impose a capitation (poll) tax on all citizens of the area. This particular tax was therefore a symbol of their political subjection, and so it was violently opposed by many Jews on patriotic grounds. The census provoked a significant armed uprising led by Judas of Galilee. His rebellion was crushed, but his ideology of "No king but God" (and therefore no taxes paid to a pagan power) was the inspiration for the later Zealot movement, which eventually led to war with Rome and the destruction of Jerusalem in AD 70. The question posed to Jesus was therefore politically very sensitive.

Sadducees, the "party" that controlled the temple priesthood, accepted as authoritative only the written law of Moses, and so they rejected such "newfangled" ideas as resurrection and life after death. The test case that they propose in order to ridicule the idea depends on the law of levirate marriage (Deut. 25:5–6). There are only two examples of this law being applied in the Old Testament (Gen. 38:6–11; Ruth 4:5–10), in both of which the surviving relative proves reluctant. But a large body of rabbinic legislation on the subject shows that the law remained in force, at least in theory. The imaginary story of a woman's seven marriages may be loosely based on a story from the apocryphal book of Tobit,

Key Themes of Luke 20:20–40

- Jesus declines to align himself explicitly with either side of a heated political debate.
- His answer disputes their presupposition that there is a necessary conflict between loyalty to God and civil obedience.
- Jesus defends the reality of life after death.
- But life in heaven is not to be imagined as being just like life on earth.
- God's covenant with his people cannot be terminated by death.

where a woman, Sarah, marries seven husbands in turn but each is killed by a demon before the marriage is consummated (Tob. 3:7–8; 6:14–15). Sarah eventually marries Tobias, son of Tobit, who survives the wedding night through prayer and by repelling the demon with the help of the angel Raphael (Tob. 8:1–18).

Interpretive Insights

20:20 *they sent spies.* In context "they" must be the members of the Sanhedrin with whom Jesus has just been disputing. Luke uses strongly pejorative language to describe these *agents provocateurs* and their political purpose. The question that they pose is not a sincere inquiry, but rather an attempt to get Jesus to incriminate himself. It is the more remarkable, therefore, that Jesus, well aware of their intention, nonetheless takes the issue seriously in his reply.

20:21 *you do not show partiality.* The fulsome opening address is, of course, flattery designed to get under Jesus's guard. But it also recognizes that Jesus, as a Galilean, was not subject to the controversial Roman tax in Judea. His opinion is therefore ostensibly being sought as a respected neutral authority in matters of religious duty.

20:22 *Is it right for us to pay taxes to Caesar or not?* Note the "for us": Jesus, they imply, can afford as a non-Judean to be objective about what was for them a fraught existential issue. The trap is clear

"Show me a denarius. Whose image and inscription are on it?" (20:24). The image on this denarius is that of Tiberius. The inscription reads *"TI CAESAR DIVI AVG AVGVSTVS,"* which is translated "Tiberius Caesar, Son of the Divine Augustus, the Augustus." Tiberius was the Roman emperor from AD 14 to 37 and therefore was ruling during the time of Jesus's ministry.

enough: to answer yes would be to alienate a large part of Judean public opinion, which saw this as a matter of patriotic principle; to answer no would make Jesus a dangerous radical in the eyes of the Romans.

20:24 *Show me a denarius.* The Roman silver coin, used for paying the tax, bore the portrait of the emperor and an inscription describing him as "son of God" and "high priest." Strict Jews therefore regarded it as idolatrous and so refused to use it; copper coins without such a portrait were available for daily commerce. By getting his questioners to produce a denarius, Jesus exposed their supposed patriotism as phony: they themselves were using the emperor's coinage, so they had no grounds for refusing to pay his tax.

Whose image? The word may be intended to suggest an analogy with the "image of God" in Genesis 1:27: as the coin belongs to Caesar, so we belong to God.

20:25 *give back to Caesar what is Caesar's, and to God what is God's.* This answer cleverly avoids a simple yes or no. But it does more. "Give *back*" suggests that taxation is a proper return for the benefits received through good government; this is far from the Zealot ideology, which saw Rome as simply the enemy of Israel and of God. But the second clause sets civic duty in the broader context of the kingdom of God. For the rebel Judas the Galilean and his followers, Rome was diametrically opposed to God, but Jesus implies that there may be good government under God (as there was at this time while Tiberius was emperor); there is no necessary conflict. But Jesus's formula does not address the question of how God's people should respond when Caesar sets himself up against God, as would happen under later emperors.

20:26 *they became silent.* Jesus has won the debate. Their discomfiture leaves the field open for a different faction within the Sanhedrin to try a more theological question in 20:28–33. When Jesus is judged to have won that debate as well, the tactic of public questioning will be abandoned (20:40). But the authorities have not dropped the issue: in 23:2 the same matter of Roman tax will be raised, and Jesus will be accused of the very radicalism that here he has carefully avoided.

20:28 *raise up offspring for his brother.* The verb suggests that the only "afterlife" that the Sadducees envisage is through progeny. If there was an expectation of personal resurrection, why need Moses have made such provision?

20:29 *Now there were seven brothers.* The story is meant to ridicule the idea of the resurrection. Could the woman be the wife of all seven in the afterlife? But even if the question was not meant seriously, it raises a real pastoral issue. Many people are married more than once, whether through death or divorce (or, these days, through serial relationships even without marriage). What becomes of such relationships in heaven?

20:34–36 *The people of this age marry.* Heaven is not to be envisaged as a simple continuation of life as we know it now. In that deathless (and birthless) existence ("like angels") there is no place for the procreation that is the basis of earthly marriage, and so perhaps Jesus is suggesting that the exclusiveness that is so important to earthly marriage

The Sadducees and the Pharisees differed in their views about the resurrection and life after death. Jesus addressed this issue using Exodus 3:6, where the Lord is called the God of Abraham, Isaac, and Jacob. Jesus argued that God would not identify himself with the dead, so they must still be alive or will be at the resurrection. Cenotaphs ("empty graves"—memorials to persons whose remains were elsewhere) to honor Abraham and Isaac had been commissioned by Herod the Great in the first century BC, along with an enclosure wall (shown here) to protect them. This building was constructed at the site of Machpelah, where Abraham had purchased a cave as a burial site for his wife Sarah. Her cenotaph as well as cenotaphs to Rebekah, Joseph, and Leah can also be visited here. This complex is known as the Tomb of the Patriarchs. Underground tombs exist beneath the building, but they have not been extensively excavated.

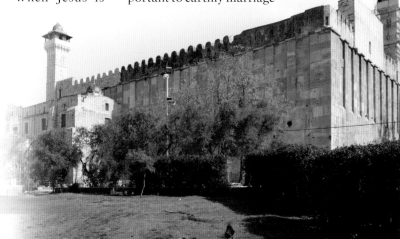

will be transcended in heaven. At any rate, he warns against any attempt to depict the life of "children of the resurrection" as being just like life on earth.

20:35 *those who are considered worthy.* Jesus does not teach a universal resurrection to "the age to come"; it depends on God's verdict, not on inherent "immortality."

20:37–38 *even Moses showed that the dead rise.* Jesus has answered the specific question asked, but now he turns to the basic issue it was intended to highlight: Is there life after death at all? That question might more easily be answered from texts in the poets and prophets of the Old Testament (e.g., Job 19:25–27; Ps. 16:9–11; Isa. 26:19; Dan. 12:2), but the Sadducees gave priority to the law of Moses. So Jesus argues instead from a pentateuchal passage, Exodus 3:6. If Moses can describe God as identifying himself as the God of people who have died, they must still be living (or will be raised). Underlying this assertion is God's covenant with the patriarchs. If God has committed himself to them in a covenant, he cannot allow that relationship to be simply terminated by death. It is an argument from the character of God, not simply from the way that text is expressed.

20:39 *Well said, teacher!* Scribes, who were mostly of the Pharisaic school and so believed in an afterlife, were pleased to see their ideological opponents silenced.

Theological Insights

The issue of how religion should affect civil responsibilities was important in the first-century church, and it has been controversial ever since. Jesus's answer here is not just "clever," for it also teaches that it is possible to be both a faithful Christian and a responsible citizen; the kingdom of God can coexist with the empire of Rome. Paul expresses a similar view in Romans 13:1–7 (cf. 1 Pet. 2:13–17) that even pagan rulers have a God-given function. Paul wrote in the earlier part of Nero's reign, when the imperial government was still relatively benign. A very different picture emerges in the book of Revelation, written at a time when Rome had apparently become a persecuting power, demanding religious submission in direct opposition to Christian loyalty. The principle of the two complementary jurisdictions of God and Caesar remains valid in theory, but when Caesar challenges God, there are uncomfortable decisions to be made.

Jesus's argument for life after death in 20:37–38 is so brief as to be quite cryptic. As an *ad hominem* argument addressed to Sadducees, it apparently carried its point, but a full theological defense of resurrection belief must take in the whole gamut of Scripture, the Old and New Testaments. The separate argument in 20:34–36 concerning the *nature* of resurrection life sounds an important warning against simplistic assumptions based on earthly experience. There is an inevitable and proper element of mystery about life after death.

Teaching the Text

These two pericopes are related in that they represent challenges to Jesus from various groups within the leadership of Israel. They can therefore be taught together with the rest of chapter 20 around the theme of Jesus's successful debates with his opponents. Ideally, however, they should be taught separately, since they have different themes and raise unique theological questions.

1. *The tax question.* Make sure that people have grasped the political situation underlying this question and how sensitive it was in Judea at the time. Discuss the possible repercussions if Jesus had answered with a straightforward yes or no. How would bystanders have evaluated what he in fact said? Where might they have placed him on the scale between patriotic insurgents and traitorous collaborators?

This passage of course raises the difficult question of the relationship of the Christian to the state. Discuss what sorts of issues in our society raise the same question of God versus Caesar. Who or what is "Caesar" in our political system? Are there limits to the principle that both God and Caesar have legitimate claims? How should Christians today react when these claims seem to be in conflict? Would Jesus have answered differently if he had been living at the time of the book of Revelation?

2. *The resurrection question.* This passage can raise many questions when you consider how many of our acquaintances can expect to meet more than one former spouse/partner in heaven. What are the pastoral issues involved? Does Jesus's teaching about "no marriage in heaven" sound bleak and unattractive? Why is this? How far are our subconscious ideas about heaven simply modeled on life as we know it on earth? How can we avoid this pitfall? While these questions are important and may be addressed in a sermon or lesson, be sure to focus on Jesus's primary point, which is the reality of resurrection and the afterlife.

Some of your listeners may find Jesus's argument from Exodus 3:6 obscure or unconvincing. His point is that long after the patriarchs were dead, God still identified himself as their God. They must therefore have a continuing existence with him. In your teaching you might suggest other arguments for the afterlife from Scripture, especially if not constrained by the Sadducean focus only on the law of Moses. Tease out in what way Jesus's argument depends on the character of God and his relationship with his people; how could we develop that argument more fully for our generation?

Illustrating the Text

A necessary conflict exists between loyalty to God and civil obedience.

Biography: Dietrich Bonhoeffer. Bonhoeffer (1906–45) was a German theologian and pastor who grew into his understanding of the need for civil disobedience. When he was twenty-seven, he wrote an essay entitled "The Church and the Jewish Question" after the Nazi regime had effected a boycott of Jewish businesses. He contended that the church had to defend and stand with the Jews; they could not sit by in neutrality, which would be simply cowardice and passivity. He paid for his civil disobedience with his life. The Nazis executed him in 1945. A very fine documentary called *Bonhoeffer* is available, and there are a number of excellent biographies, including *Bonhoeffer: Pastor, Martyr, Prophet, Spy*, by Eric Metaxas.

Quote: "Letter from Birmingham Jail," by Martin Luther King Jr. This eloquent letter (August 1963) is addressed to eight white Alabama pastors who argued that the racial battle had to be fought in the

Tribute Money, ca.1516 (oil on panel), by Titian (Tiziano Vecellio) (ca. 1488–1576)

justice denied." We have waited for more than 340 years for our constitutional and God-given rights. . . . But we still creep at horse-and-buggy pace toward gaining a cup of coffee at a lunch counter. Perhaps it is easy for those who have never felt the stinging darts of segregation to say, "Wait." But when you have seen vicious mobs lynch your mothers and fathers at will and drown your sisters and brothers at whim; when you have seen hate-filled policemen curse, kick and even kill your black brothers and sisters; . . . then you will understand why we find it difficult to wait.[1]

courts and not on the streets, a response to King's participation in the Birmingham campaign. The document is worth knowing thoroughly because it addresses the church's sin in being, in King's words, a "thermometer instead of a thermostat"— a striking metaphor. The following paragraph shows the spirit of King's thinking.

> We know through painful experience that freedom is never voluntarily given by the oppressor; it must be demanded by the oppressed. Frankly, I have yet to engage in a direct-action campaign that was "well timed" in the view of those who have not suffered unduly from the disease of segregation. For years now I have heard the word "Wait!" It rings in the ear of every Negro with piercing familiarity. This "Wait" has almost always meant "Never." We must come to see . . . that "justice too long delayed is

Current Trends: Today, there are an increasing number of such conflicts. For example, the announcement of a mandate for all businesses and institutions to perform abortions and supply contraceptives in their facilities and through their insurance plans created a dilemma for the Catholic Church and its hospitals.

The resurrection is of fundamental importance to the Christian faith.

Quote: A. W. Tozer. Tozer (1897–1963), a well-known pastor, preacher, and author, wrote, "Let no one apologize for the powerful emphasis Christianity lays upon the doctrine of the world to come. Right there lies its immense superiority to everything else within the whole sphere of human thought or experience. . . . We do well to think of the long tomorrow."[2]

Jesus Takes the Initiative

Big Idea *The pretentious religiousness of scribes and wealthy worshipers and of the magnificent temple buildings contrasts with the simple devotion of a poor widow.*

Understanding the Text

The Text in Context

In place of the question-and-answer scenario of the first part of Jesus's public ministry in the temple (20:1–40), we now have a series of pronouncements by Jesus that bring that phase of the Jerusalem story to an end. They begin with a response to the leaders' hostile questioning, in which Jesus raises the question of the nature of messiahship. But that is the end of Luke's record of Jesus's encounter with the religious leaders, and thereafter Jesus speaks rather to his disciples (though with the crowd still listening for 20:45–47 and possibly also for 21:1–6). His comments about the future fate of the temple will lead into a lengthy account of future events (21:7–36), before the drama reaches its climax in the events of the Last Supper and of the trial, death, and resurrection of Jesus.

Outline/Structure

This section consists of four pericopes that I have grouped together more for convenience and to avoid breaking up the continuous discourse that will form our next section than because they naturally belong together. The first pericope (20:41–44) more properly belongs with the preceding controversies, to which it forms the conclusion. Although they are independent traditions, 20:45–47 and 21:1–4 are suitably juxtaposed in order to display the contrast between false and true religion; they also share the theme of the contrast between people of importance and poor widows. The renewed focus on the temple in 21:1–4 then provides a suitable lead-in to the verdict on the temple in 21:5–6, but the latter pericope functions primarily as the basis for the following discourse.

Historical and Cultural Background

In the court of the women, the first of the exclusively Jewish courtyards in the temple area, beyond which women were not allowed to go, stood thirteen large chests to receive monetary contributions, six of which were designated for "freewill offerings." Giving was thus a public activity, and it may have been something of a tourist attraction.

The massive rebuilding and expansion of the whole temple complex begun by Herod in 19 BC was not completed until AD 64, but by this time the main structures were complete. Their magnificence was proverbial and no doubt was awe-inspiring for Galilean visitors. The part of the substructure that still survives (including the Western Wall) is made up of carefully dressed stones up to five meters in length. The temple buildings themselves that stood above this would have been even more splendid and filled with luxurious ornamentation and lavish offerings, but in AD 70 they were gutted by fire and then deliberately razed to the ground by the Roman conquerors (Josephus, *J.W.* 6.249–66; 7.1–3).

Interpretive Insights

20:41 *Why is it said that the Messiah is the son of David?* The one debating point raised by Jesus himself is surprising. Luke has made a point of Jesus's descent from David (1:27, 32, 69; 2:4; 3:31), and Jesus has not objected to being addressed as "Son of David" in 18:38–39 and subsequently as "king" (19:38). The issue is raised without a specific claim by Jesus to be either the Messiah or the Son of David, but in the light of his arrival in Jerusalem, it could

Key Themes of Luke 20:41–21:6

- The Messiah is not to be understood simply as a "son of David."
- Jesus denounces religious leaders who are all show and no substance.
- It is not the amount of a gift to God that counts, but the spirit in which it is given.
- The temple, for all its magnificence, is heading for destruction.

hardly be understood as simply an objective theological question.

20:44 *David calls him "Lord." How then can he be his son?* Jesus's argument depends on the view that David was the author of Psalm 110, and that its subject is the Messiah. Both points would be disputed by most modern scholarship (which sees the psalm as the words of a court prophet celebrating the enthronement of David himself or one of his successors) but would probably have been widely accepted at the time. (A rabbinic tradition that the psalm was about Abraham appears from the second century AD, perhaps as a defense against Christian use of it as a messianic testimony.) Jesus will use Psalm 110:1 again in 22:69 to speak of his own future authority.

But why does Jesus query the title "Son of David"? It can hardly be that he believes it to be untrue, since Luke has so carefully established it in the Gospel so far. More likely he regards it as inadequate: he is more than just another David; he is David's lord. Perhaps too the title risks giving the

The disciples of Jesus remarked about the beautiful stones that adorned the temple. Now all that remains from that time are the Herodian dressed stones that were part of the Temple Mount substructure during Jesus's day. One place to view them is along the lower course of the Western Wall (shown here), a place long revered by Jews.

Luke 20:41–21:6

impression that his mission is a political one, as David's was, and so misleading popular expectation of what he had come to do. But the motivation for the question is left tantalizingly unexplained.

20:46 *Beware of the teachers of the law.* This verse is an expanded version of the accusation that Jesus has made against Pharisees and scribes in 11:43 (cf. 11:45), though now it is addressed to his disciples (and to the listening crowd?) rather than directly to the scribes themselves.

20:47 *They devour widows' houses.* This time Jesus not only criticizes their search for human approbation but also exposes its hypocrisy. Their actions are the opposite of the reputation that they cultivate. The vulnerability of widows is a frequent biblical theme (cf. 18:2–5); God's people are expected to share his concern for them, not to exploit them. Exactly how the scribes might have taken material advantage of widows is a matter of speculation: perhaps it was through abusing their hospitality, or persuading them to part with money for "religious" causes, or by accepting and then exploiting commissions to manage their property. Their "lengthy prayers" were their supposed mark of authenticity as religious professionals.

The widow's offering was two small copper coins. These were probably leptons, such as the one shown here.

21:1–4 *this poor widow has put in more than all the others.* This is a typically Lukan theme: a very poor widow, at the bottom of the social scale, is praised above the more affluent majority, even though their gifts were objectively much greater. This is the theology of the Magnificat (1:51–53): the first are last, and the last first. It is the devotion of the heart, and the cost to the giver, that count rather than the amount of money. The contrast with the scribes in the preceding pericope is obvious: they cultivated a reputation for holiness, but it was a sham; she had no public profile, but she was the one who most pleased God.

That is the traditional reading of this story, but a suggested alternative interpretation proposes a different link with what precedes. This poor woman's offering is an example of how the scribes "devour widows' houses": the excessive demands of the temple treasury that they promote have forced this widow into making herself destitute, and Jesus is shocked at their callous demands and lack of compassion. That interpretation, which takes "all she had to live on" very literally, might be derived from 21:4 alone, but 21:3 is more naturally understood as praise for the widow's gift rather than as saying that she should not have had to give it.

21:5 *Some of his disciples were remarking.* The words "of his disciples" are not in the Greek text, so that this pericope and the following discourse could be read in Luke as being addressed to the wider crowd. The NIV addition derives from the clear statements of both Matthew and Mark that it was specifically disciples who both expressed their admiration for the temple and then formed the audience for the long address about its future. Luke does not make the audience so clear.

21:6 *not one stone will be left on another.* When Jesus first arrived in Jerusalem, he expressed his anger at what the temple had become (19:45–46). Since then it has been the scene of his teaching, and its authorities have been his chief opponents. But to speak of its total destruction goes far beyond anything that he has said or done so far. The temple has ceased to be the focus of God's rule, and it is now dispensable. This prediction echoes prophetic predictions of the destruction of Solomon's temple, which had led to the imprisonment of Jeremiah and the death of Uriah (Jer. 26:1–23). Jesus's words about the temple were a powerful additional reason for the authorities to determine to eliminate him. But the prophecy was to be literally fulfilled by the Roman general Titus a generation later.

Theological Insights

Two theological themes stand out from these rather disparate scenes.

1. *The status of Jesus as the Messiah.* Luke has made this a central theme of his Gospel from the infancy narratives on. The messianic role has come to expression in a variety of ways in Jesus's own words and actions and has been recognized by his disciples. His recent arrival in Jerusalem has been in an unmistakably messianic style, and a royal, Davidic status has been a prominent element in that. Jesus's questioning here of the title "Son of David" therefore forces the reader to rethink the nature of Jesus's messiahship. He is not just a son of David; his authority is on a higher level than earthly kingship. Matthew's version of this pericope includes the question "Whose son is he?" If he is not the Son of David, the reader may be expected to supply the answer "the Son of God." That is less openly implied in Luke's version, but it may well be what he had in mind.

2. *The theological significance of the temple.* The temple had been for Jesus "my Father's house" (2:49), but it had become degraded into a "den of robbers" (19:46), and now it had no future. Luke will record Stephen's alleged threat that Jesus would "destroy this place," and Stephen's own dismissal of the temple as God's house (Acts 6:14; 7:48–50). The book of Hebrews will declare the whole temple ritual obsolete, superseded by the climactic sacrifice of Jesus himself. The early Christian movement thus distanced itself from the temple, so that when Jesus's prediction was eventually fulfilled, it had for them already ceased to matter as a religious symbol. In its place was a temple "not made with hands" (Mark 14:58), constructed with "living stones" (1 Pet. 2:5).

Teaching the Text

In your teaching you will want to discuss traditional Jewish expectations concerning the Messiah from David's line (the "Son of David") as a conquering king who would reestablish the glories of the Davidic dynasty. Discuss what Jesus was aiming to achieve by disputing this traditional "Son of David" language. How might the title have misled people in their understanding of Jesus, or have been misused by those who opposed him? What does the description of the Messiah as David's "lord" imply about who Jesus really is? You might also point out the cryptic nature of Jesus's reply and the need for his hearers to fill in the blanks.

The Jewish concept of the messiah as the "Son of David" was focused primarily on a political leader who would reestablish the dynasty of David and regain Israel's independence. Shown here is an Aramaic inscription from 840 BC that refers to "the house of David." It is the only ancient text outside the Bible that mentions David and his dynasty.

Jesus is more than the traditional Son of David Messiah; but who is he? And who is he *for me*? This is the ultimate question in life and one that every person in the world will eventually need to answer.

In your teaching be sure to note the juxtaposition and contrast between the denunciation of the teachers of the law in 20:45–47 and the widow's offering (21:1–4), two contrasting descriptions of spiritual piety. The scribes are greedy, hypocritical, and prideful, while the widow is generous, authentic, and humble. Consider what sort of situation in our own setting might offer a parallel to this episode. What opportunities does our church or social life offer for ostentatious giving, and who might now play the role of the scribes (20:46–47) and the affluent (21:1, 4)? Who are now the people at the bottom of the social ladder, like the widow? Do our attitudes toward who matters and who deserves praise need to be adjusted in the light of Jesus's comments? What practical situations today might provoke Jesus to a similar response?

The prediction of the destruction of the temple also follows naturally from Jesus's denunciation of the scribes, since it is the failure of Israel's religious leaders that will lead to its destruction. In your teaching, discuss the significance of the temple in Jewish ideology at the time. What institution (or combination of institutions) might carry a similar significance for us? Try to weigh up the shock and patriotic horror that would greet Jesus's prediction of its destruction. You might also discuss the historical and theological consequences for this coming destruction and the radical implications of a temple-free religion. What did the destruction mean theologically for first-century Jews? For the early Christians? What should we make of the suggestion in some Christian circles today that the Jerusalem temple should be rebuilt?

Illustrating the Text

The Messiah is far more than the Son of David, a power figure; he is the Lord.

Quote: *The Trivialization of God: The Dangerous Illusion of a Manageable Deity*, by Don McCullough.

God knows we need to be lifted far higher than the ladder of success reaches; we need to be raised above petty desires for money and power and social status. A trivial god can sponsor only the most trivial forms of success. But the holy God, transcending all things and unhindered by a limited perspective, can discern and deliver authentic success. To lift us to this level, to help us become all that we can be, calls for a radical redefinition of "success." The God who sent the beloved Son to reveal abundant life and let him die poor, powerless and despised on a Roman cross has done precisely that: by declaring this death a victorious ending to a perfect life, God has not only redefined success for all time but has sent the god-of-my-success tumbling to the bottom of the ladder.[1]

Christract Christ condemns those with responsible positions who, knowing better, use that position to get ahead and be comfortable.

Literature: *Jane Eyre*, **by Charlotte Brontë.** This novel (1847) is based on the experiences of the English novelist and poet Charlotte Brontë (1816–55) and her siblings. The protagonist, Jane, is an orphan mistreated by her relatives. She is sent to an "evangelical" boarding school where the abuse continues. The girls are undernourished, cold, and unloved except by the occasional teacher. The headmaster, Mr. Brocklehurst, who lives very comfortably and parades his exquisitely dressed daughters in front of the orphans, provides this harsh treatment in the name of God. He says to the headmistress,

You are aware that my plan in bringing up these girls is, not to accustom them to habits of luxury and indulgence, but to render them hardy, patient, self-denying. Should any little accidental disappointment of the appetite occur, such as the spoiling of a meal, the under or the over dressing of a dish, the incident ought not to be neutralised . . . ; it ought to be improved to the spiritual edification of these pupils, by encouraging them to evince fortitude under temporary privation. A brief address on those occasions would not be mistimed, wherein a judicious instructor would take the opportunity of referring to the sufferings of the primitive Christians; to the torment of the martyrs; to the exhortations of our blessed Lord Himself, calling upon His disciples to take up their cross and follow Him; to His warnings that man shall not live by bread alone . . . ; to His divine consolations, "If ye suffer hunger or thirst for My sake, happy are ye." Oh, madam, when you put bread and cheese, instead of burnt porridge, into these children's mouths, you may indeed feed their vile bodies, but you little think how you starve their immortal souls![2]

Several film adaptations of the book have been made, including a well-reviewed version in 2011.

"When Will These Things Happen?"

Big Idea *The coming destruction of Jerusalem and its temple will mark a new phase in the establishment of God's kingdom under the vindicated Son of Man.*

Understanding the Text

The Text in Context

Since Jesus's arrival in Jerusalem it has become clear that his messianic authority is in irreconcilable conflict with the existing power structure in Jerusalem. His prediction of the destruction of the temple (21:5–6) now leads to an extended explanation (addressed to his disciples) that looks beyond his own imminent death and resurrection to a time when that conflict will be resolved. The power of the present Jerusalem establishment will be destroyed, and the risen Jesus will enter into his destined authority as the Son of Man. The reader's awareness of this ultimate prospect will provide a vital counterpoint to the apparent "defeat" of Jesus in Jerusalem that will be narrated in chapters 22–23.

Outline/Structure

The interpretation of this discourse is hotly disputed. My own view is a minority one: the focus of the discourse at least until 21:33 is consistently on the question from which it springs, the future destruction of the temple. Others believe that at some earlier point (and it is disputed at what point) Jesus changes from answering the disciples' question to talking about a quite different subject, his parousia, and thus shifts the focus from the events of the coming generation to an indefinite time in the eschatological future (despite the explicit statement of 21:32). Space does not allow me to do justice here to other people's views (or indeed to my own),[1] but the reader should be aware that some will disagree with the following exegesis.

Historical and Cultural Background

Josephus's account of the four decades leading up to the destruction of Jerusalem provides plenty of examples of the sort of events outlined in 21:8–11 in the area around Judea: messianic claimants, wars (both international and civil), earthquakes, famines, epidemics, and reported heavenly signs. His account of the siege and eventual capture of Jerusalem also fully justifies the graphic language of 21:20–24.

The meteorological and astronomical upheaval described in 21:25–26 recalls several of the Old Testament prophets who used similar metaphorical language to describe the destruction of earthly political powers, especially foreign nations such as Babylon (e.g., Isa. 13:10; 34:4, the passages more explicitly alluded to in the parallel Mark 13:24–25).

Interpretive Insights

21:7 *when will these things happen? And what will be the sign?* This question, which sets the agenda for Jesus's reply, is exclusively concerned with the prediction that he has just made of the destruction of the temple. It does not (as the equivalent question in Matt. 24:3 does) prompt any reference to the second coming (the parousia).

21:8 *many will come in my name.* These are not necessarily people claiming to be Jesus himself, but people who claim the messianic title that is properly his. Josephus (e.g., *Ant.* 20.97–99, 102, 160–72) tells of several such Jewish "impostors" who claimed to be prophets or kings before the war began in AD 66.

21:9 *the end will not come right away.* The "end" in context must mean the predicted destruction of the temple. These various supposed "signs" are too general. It will be time to panic only when the siege begins (21:20–24).

21:12 *they will seize you and persecute you.* "They" are not identified, but the scope seems wide, including both Jewish ("synagogues") and pagan ("kings and

governors") opposition. Acts will provide examples of both types of persecution of disciples in the decades following Jesus's ministry.

21:13–15 *you will bear testimony to me . . . I will give you words and wisdom.* Note that Jesus not only is the subject of their proclamation, but also is still actively involved with his disciples after the end of his earthly ministry. The promise of supernatural help in speaking relates to response under persecution (it is not an excuse for lazy preachers!). Note that a similar promise is made in 12:11–12, but with the Holy Spirit as subject.

21:16–17 *Everyone will hate you because of me.* The family hostility and the threat even of martyrdom fit the Jewish context, in which Jesus (and therefore his followers) was quickly branded a deceiver who "led Israel astray." For an example of the traditional Jewish response to such people, see Deuteronomy 13. Acts will record the martyrdoms of Stephen and James.

21:18 *not a hair of your head will perish.* Compare 12:7. In the light of 21:16 this can hardly mean total physical protection; is the reference more to spiritual survival?

That is probably also the sense of the "life" promised in 21:19 (cf. 9:24).

21:20 *When you see Jerusalem being surrounded by armies.* Mark and Matthew at this point speak cryptically of seeing "the abomination that causes desolation," but Luke makes the cause of the "desolation" more explicit. For the horrors of the Roman siege, see Josephus, *J. W.* 5.424–38, 512–18, 567–72; 6.193–213.

21:22 *this is the time of punishment in fulfillment of all that has been written.* These events are not simply a political catastrophe; they are to be understood theologically. Note the echo of Hosea 9:7. Such language, together with the phrase "wrath against this people" (21:23), implies that underlying the imperialistic power of Rome is the judgment of Israel's God on his people's spiritual rebellion, as Jesus has himself foreseen in 13:34–35; 19:42–44.

21:24 *until the times of the Gentiles are fulfilled.* "The times of the Gentiles" is not known as a phrase with a distinct meaning at the time. To speak of "times fulfilled" suggests a divine control of history, and so in context the phrase seems to mean "for as long as God permits the Gentiles to have the upper hand." No specific cutoff point for the period of Gentile dominance is stated.

21:25–26 *There will be signs in the sun, moon and stars.* Nothing in the text indicates a change either of time or of subject matter. Jesus's reply to the question about the destruction of the temple has so far brought us to the Roman capture of Jerusalem, and in the light of prophetic use of cosmological metaphors for political change (see "Historical and Cultural Background" above), that seems the most likely sense here too. The end of Jerusalem as the power center for God's people is an event of "earth-shattering" significance, which will leave people bewildered and terrified.

21:27 *they will see the Son of Man coming in a cloud with power and great glory.* The language is closely modeled on Daniel 7:13–14, where the prophet sees "one like a son of man" coming in clouds before God's throne to be given universal sovereignty. We have seen similar language used in 9:26 for Jesus's ultimate role as judge. In this context, in response to a question about the destruction of the temple, it is best understood as envisaging that event as an act of judgment by the now vindicated and enthroned Son of Man, rather than referring to the more eschatological "day/days of the Son of Man" that Jesus spoke of in 17:22–37.

21:28 *When these things begin to take place.* Jesus is speaking of events that his

In 21:25 Jesus said of the destruction of Jerusalem, "There will be signs in the sun, moon and stars." Just as Isaiah used cosmic imagery to describe the coming judgment on Babylon, Jesus employs this imagery to symbolize political changes within world history. In the ancient world, the positions of the sun, moon, planets, and stars were often seen to be portents of events on earth. This cuneiform tablet from Babylon, one of seventy in the corpus of Enuma-Anu-Enlil, records omens involving the position of Venus and a "wandering star" (Uruk, Mesopotamia, end of the first millennium BC). Jesus, following the Old Testament, transposes these portents into symbolic descriptions of coming judgment.

disciples themselves will witness (as 21:31–32 will also make clear), so the reference is still to the events of the siege and destruction of Jerusalem. The triumph of the Son of Man spells also their "redemption," the deliverance of his people from the power that has attempted to suppress him.

21:31 *the kingdom of God is near*. The vindication of the Son of Man brings in the fulfillment of God's purpose. For the prediction of "seeing the kingdom of God" within the living generation, compare 9:27.

21:32 *Truly I tell you, this generation will certainly not pass away until all these things*. This is a solemn declaration (as in 9:27) that all that has been predicted in the discourse so far will occur while some of "this generation" are still alive. This makes perfect sense if, as I have argued, the discourse as a whole, including the coming of the Son of Man, relates to the destruction of Jerusalem in AD 70. It is more difficult to explain for those who claim that 21:25–31 relates to the parousia. Some who hold this view claim that "this generation" refers back to 21:8–24, but not to the return of the Son of Man in 21:25–31. Others understand "this generation" to refer to the last generation before Christ returns, not to the disciples' generation. Still others take "generation" to mean "ethnicity" and to refer to the Jewish nation as a whole. None of these is a very satisfactory solution.

21:33 *my words will never pass away*. Jesus's prediction is as indestructible as God's word (cf. Isa. 40:8).

21:34–36 *Be always on the watch*. The parallel discourses in Matthew and Mark mark a clear change of subject at this point, turning to "that day or hour" which, in contrast to Jesus's explicit prediction of the destruction of the temple within "this generation," cannot be known (Matt. 24:36; Mark 13:32), and Matthew then goes on to speak at length about the parousia (using that Greek word) of the Son of Man. There is no such clear change of subject here in Luke, and these verses can be read as still warning the disciples to be ready for the destruction of Jerusalem; the continuing direct second-person address suggests this. But the idea here of a sudden event that catches people unprepared also recalls 12:39–40; 17:26–35, and it may be that the thought in Luke, as in Mark and Matthew, here moves on to the eschatological "day of the Son of Man." The universal scope of "all those who live on the face of the whole earth" suggests as much, and "to stand before the Son of Man" would be appropriate language for the final judgment (cf. 12:8–10). It is not easy to decide which Luke intended.

Theological Insights

The coming destruction of the temple is here set within the context of the establishment of the kingdom of God and the authority of the vindicated Son of Man. The temple represents the discredited old regime, and Jesus the Son of Man, rejected and executed by the priestly and scribal establishment, nonetheless represents the future for the people of God. Daniel 7:13–14 envisaged the dominion of the "one like a son of man" superseding the pagan empires represented by the four beasts of Daniel's vision, but Jesus now applies Daniel's imagery to the demise even of the Jewish power structure focused on the temple. Note the explicitly theological comment on the judgment on Jerusalem in 21:22–23, echoing the repeated declaration by Old Testament prophets that God used pagan nations to carry out his judgment on Israel.

All this prepares the disciples for what is about to happen. They will soon see Jesus condemned to death by the Jerusalem establishment, and it may seem that his message of a new kingdom of God has failed. But the resurrection and exaltation of Jesus will change all that. They have only to wait and watch for the fulfillment of God's purpose, when the Son of Man will reign supreme.

Teaching the Text

As noted above, Jesus's eschatological discourse in chapter 21 raises some of the most difficult interpretive questions in the Gospels and the teacher must decide whether to adopt the line of exegesis outlined above or to follow the more traditional reading that understands 21:25–28 to refer to the parousia (and then must see "this generation" of 21:32 either as referring to an earlier part of the discourse [21:8–24] or as having an unusual meaning, such as "the last generation" or "the Jewish people"). This issue in itself may be a suitable basis for teaching the passage, assessing the strengths and weaknesses of these different approaches.

But it would be a pity if this preliminary issue prevented sufficient attention being given to the main point, which is the dramatic reversal of the status quo with the loss of the temple and the triumph of the Son of Man. Get listeners to put themselves in the place of Jesus's (Jewish) disciples when they heard this and to imagine the mental and spiritual upheaval involved. What would this have meant for their orientation during

the coming days in Jerusalem and in the decades leading up to AD 70?

Teaching this passage might also lead to a larger discussion of the end times and Jesus's predictions related to the end (eschatology). If you choose to teach eschatology with reference to this discourse, be sure to focus on Jesus's primary points whenever he talks about the end. As believers we are not to set dates or obsess about the specific "signs" or historical events that herald the end. Rather, we are to remain always faithful and vigilant, living a life of godliness and spiritual maturity.

Illustrating the Text

We are called to maintain a fearless witness in the face of fierce opposition.

Church History: John Wesley. *Fox's Book of Martyrs* reports the persistent witness of the Wesley brothers.

> The successes won by Methodist preaching had to be gained through a long series of years, and amid the most bitter persecutions. In nearly every part of England it was met at the first by the mob with stonings and peltings, with attempts at wounding and slaying. Only at times was there any interference on the part of civil power. The two Wesleys faced all these dangers with amazing courage, and with a calmness equally astonishing. . . . Not only the germs of almost all the existing zeal in England on behalf of Christian truth and life are due to Methodism, but the activity stirred up in other portions of Protestant Europe we must trace indirectly, at least, to Wesley.[2]

We are to live in a constant state of personal readiness, whether for the return

of Christ or for any other crisis that might come our way.

The Roman destruction of the temple in Jerusalem in AD 70 is dramatically captured in this painting by Francesco Hayez (1867).

Literature: *The Lion, the Witch and the Wardrobe,* **by C. S. Lewis.** Readiness is illustrated memorably when Peter, one of the four children who come into Narnia, fights his first battle against a monstrous wolf who is threatening all the creatures and the children. Not feeling brave, Peter nevertheless rushes at the monster and, after a fierce encounter, kills him. Out of breath but relieved, Peter turns and sees Aslan "close at hand." Aslan says immediately, "You have forgotten to clean your sword." Blushing, Peter sees that the sword is "smeared with the Wolf's hair and blood," and he stoops down to wipe it clean. After this, Aslan knights him and says, "Rise up, Sir Peter Wolf's-Bane. And whatever happens, never forget to wipe your sword."[3]

Quote: D. L. Moody, "The Second Coming of Christ." "The moment a man realizes that Jesus Christ is coming back again to receive His followers to Himself, this world loses its hold upon him. Gas stocks and water stocks and stocks in banks and railroads are of very much less consequence to him then. His heart is free, and he looks for the blessed appearing of his Lord, who, at His coming, will take him into His blessed kingdom."[4]

Quote: *Mere Christianity,* **by C. S. Lewis.** "I must keep alive in myself the desire for my true country, which I shall not find till after death; I must never let it get snowed under or turned aside; I must make it the main object of life to press on to that other country and to help others to do the same."[5]

History: Josephus's vivid descriptions of the siege and capture of Jerusalem provide a great deal of illustrative material. See especially books 5–6 of his *Jewish War.* In one account, Josephus tells of a man who predicted the coming turmoil:

> But, what is still more terrible, there was one Jesus, the son of Ananus, a plebeian and a husbandman, who, four years before the war began, and at a time when the city was in very great peace and prosperity, came to that feast whereon it is our custom for everyone to make tabernacles to God in the temple, began on a sudden to cry aloud, "A voice from the east, a voice from the west, a voice from the four winds, a voice against Jerusalem and the holy house, a voice against the bridegrooms and the brides, and a voice against this whole people!" This was his cry, as he went about by day and by night, in all the lanes of the city. However, certain of the most eminent among the populace had great indignation at this dire cry of his, and took up the man, and gave him a great number of severe stripes; yet did not he either say anything for himself, or anything peculiar to those that chastised him, but still went on with the same words which he cried before.[6]

Getting Ready for the Passover

Big Idea *It is at Passover time that Jesus is to die, and he is determined to have a last Passover meal with his disciples before his death occurrs.*

Understanding the Text

The Text in Context

In 21:37–38 Luke rounds off the account of Jesus's teaching in the temple courtyard, which began at 20:1. With the mention of the Passover in 22:1 the long-anticipated climax of the story (see 9:22, 31, 44, 51; 13:31–35; 18:31–33) begins, as these verses relate the plotting of the Jerusalem authorities, the fateful decision of Judas Iscariot, and Jesus's own preparations for a last Passover meal with his disciples. The Passover setting will underlie, and provide a theological context for, the events of the

next few days. The protagonists of the drama of chapter 22 are here introduced; it will be an all-Jewish process, until the necessary transfer to the Roman occupying power in chapter 23.

Historical and Cultural Background

Passover was the most important of the three annual pilgrimage festivals in Jerusalem. For its special meaning, see "Theological Insights" below. The influx of Jews from across the Mediterranean world swelled the population of Jerusalem

This map shows the city of Jerusalem and its surrounding area during the time of Jesus. Jesus has been teaching daily in the temple courts (probably in the area of the royal stoa and the court of the Gentiles, where rabbis regularly gathered with their disciples) and then spending the night on the Mount of Olives. The traditional location of his Last Supper with the disciples is also labeled.

Luke 21:37–22:16

to several times its normal size, and the patriotic associations of the festival made it a time of great enthusiasm, but also potentially, under Roman occupation, of political disturbance.

At its heart was the slaughter of the Passover lambs and the ritual meal that followed. On the afternoon of the fourteenth day of the Jewish month of Nisan (April–May), the Passover lambs were killed in the temple courtyards, after which people ate the Passover meal in family groups during the night that began Nisan 15 (the Jewish day began at sunset). Scholars debate whether Jesus's last meal with the disciples was at the time of the regular Passover meal or on the previous night (the beginning of Nisan 14). This commentary takes the latter option,[1] that Jesus deliberately anticipated the official date for the meal, knowing that by the time Nisan 15 began, he would be already dead. In intention it was "the Passover" (meal), but it was held a day early, presumably without a lamb, which would not have been killed until the following afternoon (no lamb is mentioned in any of the Gospel accounts of the Last Supper).

Interpretive Insights

21:37 *to spend the night on the hill called the Mount of Olives.* At Passover time Jerusalem was massively overcrowded, and pilgrims from outside the city camped in the surrounding area. The west slope of the Mount of Olives, overlooking the city, was counted as within the extended city boundaries for the period of the festival. That is the traditional site of Gethsemane (though Luke does not use that name) where Jesus will be arrested (22:39–53).

This verse explains how Judas knew where to take the arresting party.

22:2 *the chief priests and the teachers of the law were looking for some way to get rid of Jesus.* Ever since Jesus arrived in Jerusalem, these two groups, together with other members of the Sanhedrin, have been determined to suppress this uncomfortable visiting preacher with radical views (19:47; 20:1, 19). The chief priests, who will take the lead in his trial, would be particularly incensed by his brazen repudiation of the temple system and his prediction of its destruction, while the scribes would be smarting after his blanket denunciation of them in 20:45–47. But a public arrest would risk a popular backlash because many ordinary people and festival pilgrims were on Jesus's side (19:48; 20:6, 19). They needed to catch Jesus away from the crowds. And that was where Judas came in (22:6).

22:3 *Satan entered Judas, called Iscariot, one of the Twelve.* "Iscariot" may mean "man of Keriot," referring to a town in southern Judea; if so, Judas probably was the only non-Galilean among the Twelve. Luke here gives a theological explanation of Judas's surprising about-face (cf. John 13:2, 27). The payment agreed upon offers a more secular explanation, but it may be doubted whether a month's wages (Matt. 26:15 mentions the sum of thirty silver coins) alone would be enough to persuade a man to betray the cause in which he has invested so much of his life. Perhaps more likely, Judas the Judean had become disillusioned with this northern movement, and now that he was in Jerusalem, he wanted to distance himself from it. He may even have come to share the authorities' view of Jesus as one whose radical ideas threatened to "lead Israel astray."

22:4 *officers of the temple guard.* In ordinary circumstances the Romans allowed the Jewish leadership to police the temple area with their own Jewish security force. The involvement of this armed security force at this stage already shows that the priestly leaders mean business. It will be they who carry out the arrest of Jesus (see 22:52).

how he might betray Jesus. The Greek verb regularly used in the Gospels to describe Judas's action (it will recur in 22:6, 21, 22, 48) literally means "hand over," but in a context where a supposed friend "hands over" Jesus to his enemies, "betray" is a valid interpretation. Luke has used the more specific term "traitor" for Judas in 6:16.

22:7 *the day of Unleavened Bread on which the Passover lamb had to be sacrificed.* Strictly speaking, the seven-day feast of Unleavened Bread followed immediately after the Passover day, but the term had come to be used more loosely for the whole festival period (cf. 22:1). Luke's words here appropriately denote the beginning (at sunset) of Nisan 14, which would close with the killing of the lambs the next afternoon; hence the phrase "had to be sacrificed" for an event still in the future (see "Historical and Cultural Background" above).

22:8 *Go and make preparations for us to eat the Passover.* Jesus and his band of

A room had already been prepared in which Jesus and his disciples would eat the Passover meal. To be furnished as a dining area it would have had couches on which the guests would recline to eat. Shown here is a couch and footstool from the first to second century AD.

followers formed a suitable "family" group for the celebration. It was a formal meal, and so needed a proper dining room rather than an informal picnic on the hillside.

22:12 *He will show you a large room upstairs.* The careful instructions for the rendezvous, the precise form of words to be used (including the title "the Teacher" used without explanation), and the fact that the room was available at this crowded period and already suitably "furnished" suggest that this provision had been agreed in advance with a supporter in Jerusalem. This meal was important to Jesus, and he had not left it to chance.

22:14 *When the hour came.* The Passover meal was eaten at night (Exod. 12:8). The two disciples have made the necessary preparations during the early evening, and now after dark the rest of the group join them.

reclined at the table. For the protocol for formal meals, where diners reclined on three sides of a central table, see on 7:36. Rabbinic sources indicate that reclining was specifically required at the Passover meal. The traditional depiction of the Last Supper (e.g., the famous painting by Leonardo da Vinci), with the diners sitting along one side of a long table, may be artistically convenient but is culturally inaccurate.

22:15 *I have eagerly desired to eat this Passover with you before I suffer.* It was important to Jesus that their last meal together be a Passover meal, even if held a day in advance. The explanation of his coming death in 22:17–20 will depend on the Passover theme for its symbolism, and it will be this that enables them eventually to understand his death, which he now clearly says is imminent, not as a political disaster but as redemptive.

22:16 *I will not eat it again until it finds fulfillment in the kingdom of God.* A similar statement will be made about the drinking of wine in 22:18. The kingdom of God, already established in principle through Jesus's ministry on earth, is yet to be fully realized (see, e.g., 13:18–21). The Passover meal itself, which in Israel looked back to God's great act of deliverance from Egypt, is now to be seen instead as a pointer forward to a greater deliverance that is now imminent. It will be "fulfilled" when God's saving purpose is ultimately achieved (his kingdom comes) through Jesus's death and resurrection. This is to be Jesus's last meal before that fulfillment takes place.

Theological Insights

The Passover commemorated that great act of deliverance, the exodus, which inaugurated Israel's existence as the special people of God. Jesus's death and resurrection are to take place in this setting, and his explanatory words over the bread and wine, uttered at a Passover meal, will draw on the Passover symbolism of redemption. All this, we learn from these verses, was not a matter of happy coincidence, but of Jesus's deliberate planning. He intended his saving death to be seen as the focus of a new exodus (cf. 9:31: "departure," *exodos*), and so the inauguration of a new basis for the people of God. Israel is to be reborn.

Teaching the Text

These verses are preliminary to the actual account of the Last Supper, but their strong focus on the Passover setting offers the opportunity to explore the theological

significance of the fact that Jesus died at Passover, and what this means for our understanding of the Christian church in relation to the people of God in the Old Testament. In your teaching, tease out the significance of the exodus events and discuss how Jesus's death and resurrection "fulfill" that pattern.

The exodus typology poses important questions about the identity of the Christian church. While the actual phrase "the new Israel" does not occur in the New Testament, there is much that points that way (especially in Rom. 9–11; cf. Paul's provocative phrase "the Israel of God" in Gal. 6:16). Discuss how radical a change resulted from the death and resurrection of Jesus. What are the elements of continuity and of discontinuity between the Israel of the Old Testament and the international people of God now to be constituted through their faith in Jesus? How does the Passover imagery help us in clarifying this issue?

The fateful decision of Judas remains a puzzle to many Christians, and there are (especially since the publication of the apocryphal *Gospel of Judas* in 2006) some scholars who try to rehabilitate Judas as a genuine supporter of Jesus whose plan to force Jesus to declare his hand went disastrously wrong. Luke does not provide us with a psychological answer to such questions; rather, he gives us the theological statement "Satan entered Judas." Is this explanation satisfying? Is anything to be gained by further speculation on Judas's motivation?

Illustrating the Text

Jesus intentionally used the Passover to connect the exodus to his death on the cross and establish a new and eternal Israel born by his blood.

Contrasting Concept: Tell the story (now quite well-known) of a woman who was asked by her husband why she always cut the ends off her roast. She didn't know, and began asking her mother and grandmother, neither of whom knew the reason for the practice—they had each inherited it from the previous generation. Finally, the woman asks her great-grandmother, who explains that the roast was cut down because the roasting pan she used seventy years before was too small to fit a full roast. Point out that the Passover celebration was like this old story, but in reverse—the people of God kept the traditions for years, remembering clearly how they got started, but never fully understanding them until a future moment when a distant descendant would finally reveal the real purpose and meaning behind the Passover. The Jewish people kept the tradition for generations until the one it spoke about could be revealed and could finally show what the tradition was actually about.

Jesus carefully prepared for his last meal with the disciples.

Personal Experience: Careful preparation often can communicate the importance of an event. Share a story of a time when you or someone else went to great effort to prepare for something because of its importance. This may be preparation for a romantic dinner, prayerful preparation for a sermon, scheduled rehearsal for a wedding ceremony or church service, study for a test, and so on. You might also relay how you or others perceived this preparation. What did it communicate about the event?

Jesus was betrayed by someone close to him.

Film: *The Sound of Music*, **directed by Robert Wise.** In this enduring musical (1965) about a family that escapes the Nazi takeover of Austria before WWII, there is a scene in which a young Austrian, Rolf, who has been courting the oldest von Trapp daughter, Liesl, surrenders to the seduction of the Nazi message and, against his better instincts, betrays the family. They have taken refuge on the roof of a convent when the soldiers, including Rolf, come after them. All goes well until Liesl gasps upon seeing him, and Rolf hears her and decides to show his power. Captain von Trapp appeals to him, and one can see, momentarily, the conflict in the young man until he blows his whistle, alerting the guards.

Jesus's Last Meal with His Disciples

Big Idea *Jesus uses the symbolism of the Passover meal to teach about the saving significance of his coming death.*

Understanding the Text

The Text in Context

This is the central part of Luke's account of the Last Supper, which began at 22:7 and runs through to 22:38, and which should be read as a whole, despite the divisions required by the format of this commentary. Jesus's words at the table prepare the reader directly both for his own arrest and death and for the failure of his disciples to stand by him. We are thus assured that in the tragic events to follow Jesus will not be taken by surprise, but that the whole sequence of events follows as his Father has "decreed" (22:22).

Outline/Structure

Luke's account of the supper is distinctive in that it mentions two cups of wine. A few ancient manuscripts omit 22:19b–20, thus eliminating the second cup, but most scholars now agree that this reading (which results in the surprising order of cup followed by bread [though there may be a parallel to this order in *Did.* 9:1–3]) is a rather clumsy "correction." Jesus's words over the bread and cup in 22:19–20 correspond to the eucharistic formula in Matthew 26:26–28; Mark 14:22–24; 1 Corinthians 11:23–25. But only Luke also mentions, in 22:17, another of the four Passover cups (see below). The saying thus introduced (22:18) corresponds to Matthew 26:29 // Mark 14:25 (which do not mention a second cup), and this then forms a balancing parallel to 22:16, referring to food and drink respectively.

Historical and Cultural Background

Probably already by the first century the Passover meal had developed into a set sequence of questions and answers drawing out the symbolism of the different parts of the meal in recalling the events of the exodus (see *m. Pesah.* 10).[1] Four cups of wine were prescribed to be shared among the diners before, during, and after the meal, each also with its appropriate form of words. Jesus's words over the bread and wine at the Last Supper take up this pattern to speak symbolically not of the past but rather of what is about to happen. The two cups mentioned by Luke probably correspond to the second and third Passover cups, the latter ("the cup of blessing") being drunk after the meal.

Interpretive Insights

22:17 *divide it among you.* The wording suggests a single cup passed around among the participants rather than the individual cups of later Passover ritual.

22:18 *I will not drink again from the fruit of the vine until the kingdom of God comes.* See comments on 22:16, which makes a parallel statement about eating. The coming of the kingdom of God is closely linked with Jesus's imminent death and resurrection. "Fruit of the vine" is a traditional term used in the formal thanksgiving for wine: "Blessed are you, Lord God of the universe, who created the fruit of the vine."

22:19 *took . . . gave thanks . . . broke . . . gave.* See comments on the same sequence of verbs used in 9:16 (and in all the other Gospel accounts of that event) and also in 24:30.

This is my body given for you. In the setting of the Passover meal, where foods symbolized historical events, the verb "is" is naturally understood as meaning "represents" rather than suggesting a transformation of the bread into another substance (especially as Jesus was bodily

Key Themes of Luke 22:17–34

- The broken bread and poured-out wine represent Jesus's saving death for his people.
- By sharing the bread and wine, Jesus's followers will continue to participate in that sacrifice.
- Jesus both knows who is going to betray him and foretells Peter's lapse under pressure.
- He commends humble service as the model for leadership.
- His faithful followers will share his kingship.

present, holding the bread). The "giving" of his body, together with the "pouring out" of his blood (22:20), points to his sacrificial death; in effect he himself takes the place of the Passover lamb. But exactly how this giving and pouring out are "for you" is not spelled out in Luke's version; Matthew 26:28 adds that Jesus's blood is poured out "for the forgiveness of sins," and compare Mark 10:45, where Jesus says that he gives his life "as a ransom for many."

Do this in remembrance of me. The Christian celebration of the Lord's Supper derives from this instruction, repeated also after the cup in the fuller version in 1 Corinthians 11:24–25. Whatever other significance the Lord's Supper may carry, it remains in essence, like the Passover, a memorial of a historical saving event.

22:20 *This cup is the new covenant in my blood, which is poured out for you.* This very condensed declaration both identifies the wine as representing the blood of Jesus shed "for you" and also connects his death

After supper Jesus took the cup, which may have looked like one of these first-century AD stone drinking vessels found at Masada.

345

with the exodus event, when God's covenant with his people at Sinai, ratified by the blood of sacrifice (Exod. 24:8), was the basis of Israel's new status as the people of God. The word "new" signals the fulfillment of Jeremiah's prophecy of a new covenant to replace that of Sinai, a covenant distinguished by a law now written on people's hearts, by the personal knowledge of God, and by the forgiveness of sins (Jer. 31:31–34).

22:21 *him who is going to betray me.* On the verb "betray," see on 22:4. Jesus knows Judas's plans, and he wishes to prepare the other disciples for the shock, but in Luke's version he does not specifically identify the traitor.

22:22 *The Son of Man will go as it has been decreed.* "Decree," used only here by Luke in his Gospel (he uses the same verb in Acts 2:23), would be more familiar to non-Jewish readers than "prophesied in Scripture." But in 18:31 Luke has spelled out what it means: this is the pattern already laid down in Scripture (cf. 22:37; 24:25–27, 44). The thought here may be specifically of Psalm 41:9 (cf. John 13:18) but probably embraces the whole scope of Jesus's destined suffering and death. The paradox of divine sovereignty and human responsibility is sharply set out in the two clauses of 22:22.

22:24 *A dispute . . . as to which of them was considered to be the greatest.* This issue, already raised and answered in 9:46–48, intrudes uncomfortably in this solemn setting. Does it arise from the shocking idea of a traitor among their number, and the speculation about who that might be? Or are they at last taking seriously the idea that Jesus will soon not

be with them, so that someone else will have to take the lead? At any rate, the dispute reflects little credit on Jesus's closest followers, whose "commitments remain surprisingly unreconstructed."[2]

22:25–27 *you are not to be like that.* The kingdom of God reverses the conventions of human self-importance (cf. 13:30) and the world's style of leadership. The disciples' model must be Jesus, their acknowledged leader, who is willing to take the place of a servant. Luke does not record Jesus's washing of his disciples' feet at this meal (see John 13:2–17), but it vividly illustrates his teaching here.

22:28–30 *I confer on you a kingdom.* In contrast to humanly achieved greatness, loyal disciples can look forward to a different kind of kingship. The present Passover meal is a foretaste of the ultimate heavenly banquet, where Jesus will again be the host. But there, when the kingdom of God is finally established (22:16, 18), God's royal authority will be delegated not only to Jesus himself but also, through him, to his chosen leadership team, the Twelve. (Nothing is said about Judas; perhaps Luke looks forward to the reconstitution of the Twelve after Jesus's resurrection, which he describes in Acts 1:15–26.) For "judging the twelve tribes of Israel," see on 6:13. In the light of 22:20, the reference is presumably to exercising authority (the Old Testament sense of "judge") within the reconstituted Israel of the new covenant rather than in relation to the old national community.

22:31–34 *I have prayed for you, Simon, that your faith may not fail.* Note the emphatic use in 22:31–32 of Peter's personal name, "Simon," not used by Luke since he was introduced in 5:1–11; 6:14. The NIV rightly distinguishes the singular "you" of 22:32, 34 from the plural "you" of 22:31. All of them will face an ordeal (for "sifting like wheat" as a metaphor for a testing ordeal, compare Amos 9:9) that could be fatal to their discipleship, but Peter is to be the key to their restoration after failure. This is ironical in that, despite Peter's estimate of his own loyalty (22:33), Jesus knows that he too will be unable to resist the pressure (22:34). But Jesus prays that this temporary lapse will not be terminal for Peter's faith (or "faithfulness," loyalty), and that there will be a "turning back" (the word often suggests repentance or conversion) after the failure, in contrast to Judas's decisive apostasy. The repentant Peter will then be in a position to "strengthen" the others. The history of the early church in Acts testifies

to the efficacy of that prayer. For Satan's initiative in testing God's servants, see Job 1:6–12; here too Satan's request has apparently been granted, but Jesus is taking the necessary remedial action by his prayer.

Theological Insights

Jesus's words over the bread and wine convey three main points:

- His death is to be vicarious (his body given and his blood shed "for you").
- It will inaugurate the new covenant, marking a new beginning for the people of God just as the exodus, commemorated at Passover, marked the emergence of Israel as the people of God.
- It is to be commemorated by his followers as they share bread and wine "in remembrance of me."

The theme of a new beginning for the people of God is also developed in the saying in 22:28–30 about the future reign of his disciples over "the twelve tribes of Israel." At this stage, the future kingdom of God is envisaged within the confines of Israel, but in 24:47 it will become clear that all nations are now invited to share the benefits of Jesus's saving death; Luke will go on to explore in Acts how this international

Jesus warns his disciples about the opposition they will face when he tells Peter that Satan will "sift all of you as wheat" (22:31). Sieves were used as grain was processed, the first time to separate the straw and larger impurities from the wheat grains and then a second time with smaller openings to remove the smaller particles of dirt, stones, and dust. In this photo from Israel in the early twentieth century, a woman is performing the first sifting step as grain falls and larger particles are retained in her sieve.

Luke 22:17–34

dimension of the reconstituted people of God would be achieved.

Both the prediction of Judas's betrayal and the warning to Peter about his imminent failure highlight the interplay between the grace and purpose of God and the reality of human agency (and satanic influence [cf. 22:3]). This theological tension is succinctly captured in 22:22.

Teaching the Text

This passage provides the teacher with the opportunity to explore the meaning and significance of the Lord's Supper. Compare the account here with the other Synoptic Gospels (Matt. 26:26–28; Mark 14:22–24) and especially with Paul's account in 1 Corinthians 11:23–25. Explore not only the Passover imagery but also the ritual as a celebration of the inauguration of the new covenant (22:20; 1 Cor. 11:15; Jer. 31:31–34) and as a preview of the messianic banquet (Isa. 25:6–9). Challenge listeners to consider their own understanding and experience of the Lord's Supper as an act of Christian worship. Compare this with the disciples' experience at the Last Supper; what might they have made of Jesus's extraordinary symbolic acts and words? Are we in danger of losing sight of what Jesus intended? Are there elements in the significance of the Passover setting that have been lost as the church has become predominantly Gentile? Of course it can be profoundly significant to partake together of the Lord's Supper in the context of teaching about its meaning and significance.

The prediction of Peter's denial provides the teacher with an opportunity to compare Judas and Peter. Why was Judas's act of betrayal a point of no return, whereas there was still hope for Peter? Do we need to develop a "theology of failure"?

Discuss Jesus's self-characterization as "one who serves" and its relevance as a model for our discipleship. How should such a model work out in practice in our church life and in our relations with the wider world?

In the light of our understanding of the "kingdom of God," is it surprising that Jesus is also a king, and that the Twelve are to share that kingship (see also 12:32)? What might the Twelve have made of 22:29–30 at the time? Are these verses expressing what is to be true only of them, or is there some sense in which it is true of all disciples? Compare, for example, Ephesians 2:6; 1 Peter 2:9; Revelation 3:21; 5:10.

Illustrating the Text

Jesus's words over the bread and wine inaugurate a new covenant to be commemorated faithfully by his followers.

Hymn: "We Gather Together to Eat the Lord's Supper." This Dutch hymn expresses the ethos of this important gathering.

> We gather together to eat the Lord's
>   supper:
> By eating and drinking, our oneness we
>   show.
> His presence possessing, our oneness
>   confessing.
> 'Tis thus we eat and drink, and His
>   blessing we know.[3]

It is the one who serves who is truly great.

Autobiography: Charles Colson. When Charles Colson (1931–2012) went to prison

This fresco is one of the rare artistic portrayals of Christ reclining with his disciples as they partake of the Passover meal that will be their last supper together. It can be seen at the church of the Sant'Angleo in Formis Abbey, Capua, Italy, and is one of many biblical scenes that line the wall of the nave (eleventh century AD).

in the wake of the Watergate scandal, he learned in complex ways the meaning of powerlessness. His lowly position as a prisoner stood in stark contrast to the great power he had once possessed as a special counsel to Richard Nixon. He writes,

> I was blind. Indeed, only in the "breakdown of power" did I finally understand both it and myself. For my view of life was through such narrow openings as the elegantly draped windows of the White House and my vistas were of lush green lawns, manicured bushes, and proud edifices housing the corridors of power. But looking at the world from the underside through the bars of a dark prison cage and the barbed wire of forced confinement, I could, for the first time, really *see*.

He saw what he had done and realized the rest of his life needed to be lived out in serving others. He continues, "I began to understand why God views society not through easily corrupted kings but through peasant prophets who in their own powerlessness could see and communicate God's perspective."[4]

Literature: "Matryona's House," by Alexander Solzhenitsyn. In this story by the Nobel Prize–winning Russian author Solzhenitsyn (1918–2008), a young man finally sees the beauty of a peasant woman's tenacious struggles against cold and hunger and the selfishness of those around her. She retains compassion and unquenchable good humor, and she is sacrificial to the end. The narrator concludes,

> She never tried to acquire things for herself. She wouldn't struggle to buy things which would then mean more to her than life itself. All her life she never tried to dress smartly in the kind of clothes which embellish cripples and disguise evildoers. . . . She never accumulated property against the time of her death when her only possessions were a dirty-white goat, a crippled cat, and rubber plants. We all lived beside her, and never understood that she was that righteous one without whom, according to the proverb, no village can stand.
> Nor any city.
> Nor our whole land.[5]

Luke 22:17–34

On the Mount of Olives

Big Idea *Jesus dreads what is to come, but he nevertheless accepts his Father's will and does not resist when he is arrested.*

Understanding the Text

The Text in Context

The action moves from the supper table to the place on the hillside where Judas knows Jesus is to be found, and to which he will lead the arresting party. Jesus's refusal to hide or evade capture by going elsewhere and his prohibition of armed resistance show that he has fully accepted the violent fate that he has repeatedly predicted to the disciples on their way to Jerusalem. Everything is happening as Scripture has indicated, and Jesus's agonized prayer confirms his acceptance of that divinely ordained pattern. The endgame begins with this scene on the Mount of Olives, and it will play out through the rest of chapters 22–23, with Jesus offering no resistance to those determined to execute him. It is only with chapter 24 that another side to the picture will emerge.

Historical and Cultural Background

The place of Jesus's prayer and arrest on the Mount of Olives is named by Matthew and Mark as "Gethsemane" ("oil press") and is described by John as a "garden" on the other side of the Kidron Valley. The traditional site of Gethsemane in olive groves on the western slope of the Mount of Olives fits the description of all four Gospels, and it was within the area designated for temporary residents during Passover week. Luke has made it clear in 21:37 that this was where Jesus and the disciples regularly spent the night (note "as usual" [22:39] and "the place" [22:40]). That was what Judas was relying on.

The garden of Gethsemane on the Mount of Olives (shown in the background) was the place where Jesus went to pray after dinner and was later arrested. He would have walked out of the city of Jerusalem and across the Kidron Valley (visible in the foreground) to reach this quiet place.

Interpretive Insights

22:36 *if you have a purse, take it.* The previous missions of the disciples (9:1–6; 10:1–4) were in Galilee, where they could travel light and rely on the hospitality of supporters. But now that they are in Jerusalem, and Jesus's enemies are moving against him, they should expect hostility and rejection. They will need to look after themselves.

if you don't have a sword, sell your cloak and buy one. In 22:49–51 Jesus will forbid his disciples to use their swords in his defense, and his words in 22:52 make sense only if his movement was known to be nonviolent. Most interpreters therefore conclude that the instruction to buy a sword was not meant literally, but rather is a vivid but metaphorical way of warning them of hostility ahead (as predicted more literally in 9:23–26?). Jesus's repudiation of a literal understanding in 22:38 suggests as much. In recording this saying, Luke was perhaps thinking not only of the immediately impending crisis, but also of the church's continuing experience of persecution that he will chronicle in Acts.

22:37 *he was numbered with the transgressors.* This is the only direct quotation from the portrait of God's servant in Isaiah 53 in the Gospel accounts of Jesus's passion, though most interpreters regard Isaiah 53 as a major source of Jesus's conviction that his suffering and death were foretold in Scripture (cf. 18:31); note the emphatic fulfillment formula here. The predicted endgame has begun, and when Jesus is arrested and tried as a criminal, his disciples too will be in danger.

22:38 *"That's enough!" he replied.* The disciples have taken his warning literally

Key Themes of Luke 22:35–53

- Jesus warns his disciples of dangerous times ahead and urges them to be prepared.
- In prayer he asks to be spared the ordeal, but he puts his Father's will above his own desire.
- The disciples sleep when they should be praying.
- Judas deliberately hands Jesus over to those sent to arrest him.
- Jesus does not resist arrest, and he forbids his disciples to use violence on his behalf.

and so have produced two swords (though we are not told where from). The NIV rendering of Jesus's cryptic response (lit., "It is enough") apparently takes it as exasperation at their literalness ("Enough of that!"). It is hard, in the light of 22:49–51, to suppose that he meant that the two swords would suffice (for what purpose?).

22:40 *Pray that you will not fall into temptation.* This instruction, repeated in 22:46, takes up the final petition of the Lukan Lord's Prayer (11:4). On the range of meaning of *peirasmos* ("temptation, testing"), see comments there (and at 4:2). Jesus has already predicted their ordeal and attributed it to Satan (22:31), the tempter. They need God's strength if they are to withstand the test, but instead they will fail to stay awake and pray.

22:42 *Father, if you are willing, take this cup from me.* Luke has reduced to a single prayer the threefold prayer and return to the disciples related by Matthew and Mark. The Old Testament prophets spoke of a "cup" of God's judgment (e.g., Isa. 51:17–23; Jer. 25:15–29), and Jesus saw his coming suffering in that light (Mark 10:38–39; John 18:11). The cup is given by God, and the metaphor perhaps is used to indicate that Jesus's coming death will involve for him a vicarious experience of God's judgment. It was this prospect, not only the physical suffering of death, that appalled him. But if that was the only way, Jesus will not allow his natural revulsion to overcome his commitment to his Father's purpose of salvation.

22:43–44 *An angel from heaven appeared to him.* The whole of 22:43–44 is not found in the other Gospels or in the earliest Greek manuscripts of Luke. It appears to be an early expansion of the Gethsemane story,[1] current at first primarily in the Latin-speaking church, designed to underline the seriousness of Jesus's mental conflict ("like drops of blood" does not necessarily mean that Jesus literally sweated blood, but that he sweated so profusely that the sweat fell like dripping blood). It combines human vulnerability with supernatural support.

22:45 *he found them asleep, exhausted from sorrow.* The contrast between Jesus's earnest prayer and the disciples' lethargy prepares us for what will happen when the arresting party arrives. Unlike Matthew and Mark, Luke will not specifically mention their running away, but all except Peter will disappear from the story until after Jesus's death.

22:47 *a crowd came up.* It soon becomes clear that this is no ordinary crowd. The mention of the presence of chief priests and elders with officers of the temple guard and the carrying of swords and clubs (22:52) indicate that this is not a disorganized rabble but rather an armed posse sent specifically to arrest Jesus, as planned in 22:4–6.

22:48 *Judas, are you betraying the Son of Man with a kiss?* In Matthew and Mark the infamous kiss is a prearranged signal to identify Jesus, for in the darkness one Galilean visitor would look much like another. Luke does not explain this; for him, the kiss, normally a mark of loyalty and affection, simply underlines Judas's treachery. Jesus's rhetorical question is heavily ironic. In the Greek text the word "kiss" is placed at the start for emphasis: "With a kiss do you . . . ?"

22:49–51 *one of them struck the servant of the high priest, cutting off his right ear.* The attempt at armed resistance follows from the cryptic exchange about swords in 22:35–38. Jesus's response in 22:51 (lit., "Allow [plural] this far," perhaps meaning "Let it go" or "Stop, that's enough") indicates that in 22:36 he had not meant to condone armed resistance. Jesus's healing of the servant (mentioned only by Luke) displays the opposite approach, more reminiscent of the principle that he expressed in 6:27–28. "The [not just "a"] servant of the high priest" perhaps

> In 22:50 one of the disciples, whom the Gospel of John identifies as Peter, drew a sword and cut off the ear of the high priest's servant. The word used to describe the weapon means a long knife or a short sword. It may have looked like the iron knife shown here.

designates a senior aide, in charge of the arresting party.

22:52 *the chief priests, the officers of the temple guard, and the elders.* Presumably, a few leaders had come to supervise the arrest; we can hardly suppose that the entire Sanhedrin had come out to the Mount of Olives.

Am I leading a rebellion? More literally, Jesus says, "As if against a bandit [*lēstēs*] have you come out . . . ?" The term *lēstēs* was later used for those who led nationalistic uprisings against Rome, but it had also the more general sense of a violent, armed man, a robber or thug. The NIV may be too much influenced here by the later usage, especially as Jesus is here addressing a Jewish, not Roman, force. Unlike a furtive criminal, Jesus has taught openly in broad daylight. The manner of his arrest shows that it is they, not he, who represent the forces of darkness. Since Judas has led the arresting party, the reference here to "darkness" may reflect Luke's attribution of Judas's action to Satan (22:3 [cf. John 13:2, 30]).

Theological Insights

This passage sometimes is appealed to in discussion about Christian attitudes toward war and pacifism. Unfortunately, it does not provide unequivocal support for either side. Taken alone, 22:35–38 might provide an argument for military preparation, but 22:49–51 speaks against violence even in response to force. The cryptic nature of Jesus's two brief responses in 22:38, 51 provides an insufficient basis for using this passage to apply to any situation beyond the specific occasion of Jesus's arrest.

The scene of Jesus at prayer provides one of the most powerful illustrations of the tension between his real humanity and his supernatural resources as the Son of God (cf. Heb. 5:7–9, likely a comment on this story). His unanswered request and his obedient submission to his Father's will represent two sides of the paradox of the incarnation. It was debated in the early church whether Jesus had both a divine and a human will; that formulation may be overly pedantic, but a truly biblical theology must make room for the tension displayed in this episode.

It is sometimes suggested that Jesus's desire to escape death compares unfavorably with the willing martyrdom of some of his followers or of a noble pagan such as Socrates. But this is to ignore not only the peculiarly horrible form of death by crucifixion but also the uniquely revolting prospect that the Son of God himself should vicariously experience his Father's judgment for the sins of all humanity.

Teaching the Text

Teaching on the Gethsemane account should focus on its central theme: Jesus's steadfast endurance and obedience to the Father to fulfill his suffering role despite the agony he experienced in anticipation of his suffering. This obedience can serve as a model for us as we face testing, temptation, and suffering in our Christian lives.

Here are some other themes that might be pursued by the teacher:

1. Encourage listeners to consider the meaning of Jesus's instruction to buy swords, and whether the disciples'

response was appropriate. Does the NIV's phrase "That's enough!" convey the right sense of Jesus's reaction, and what might he have meant? In the light of what happened in 22:49–51 (and even more of Matt. 26:52), what did Jesus mean in 22:36? Is there anything to be gained from this enigmatic passage for Christian discussions of pacifism and of nonviolence?

2. Reflect on the failure of the disciples. It may help to ask listeners to put themselves in the place of the disciples and attempt to relive their rollercoaster of reactions and emotions as they moved from the supper to the Mount of Olives, failed to stay awake with Jesus, and then watched his arrest. How might things have been different if they had been able to obey Jesus's repeated injunction in 22:40, 46?

3. Jesus's prayer in 22:42 invites us to consider our own petitionary prayer: What is the balance between praying in faith (and being confident of what we ask) and the recognition that God's will may be different from what we want? Should all specific petitions be qualified by "if it is your will"? Is it right to think of such prayer as a two-way conversation, and if so, how may this be achieved?

Luke (22:40–46) tells of Jesus's anguished time of prayer on the Mount of Olives on the night of his arrest. This grove of ancient olive trees adjacent to the Church of All Nations is one of the traditional sites of the garden of Gethsemane.

Illustrating the Text

Even the most well-intentioned disciples misunderstand and misapply some of Jesus's more mysterious words.

Comedy: Play a little bit of Abbott and Costello's classic bit, "Who's on First?" In this masterpiece of miscommunication, two men debate the base positions of a team populated with players named "Who," "What," "I Don't Know," "Why," and "Because." Play as much of it as time allows, and give your listeners a flavor for the bit. (You could also have some folks memorize the script and do some of it live, in costume.) After the laughter dies down, explain that even though the words of Jesus are absolutely true and reliable, we sometimes get confused like Costello and fail to connect the dots. The disciples made this same mistake with Jesus's words about swords. The good news is that Jesus is willing to keep explaining patiently, and sends his Spirit to help us interpret his Word.

More than anyone, Jesus understands the agony of choosing the right thing, even when it could cost everything.

Church History: Polycarp, the bishop of Smyrna and disciple of John the Apostle, became an early Christian martyr. He was called before a Roman proconsul in a stadium and ordered to deny Christ publicly or be executed. He responded, "Eighty and six years have I served Him, and He never did me any injury: how then can I blaspheme my King and my Savior?" The proconsul then threatened to throw Polycarp to the beasts, to which he replied, "Call them then, for we are not accustomed to repent of what is good in order to adopt that which is evil; and it is well for me to be changed from what is evil to what is righteous." Finally, seeing that Polycarp was unfazed by these threats, the proconsul told him he would be burned at the stake. Polycarp replied, "You threaten me with fire which burns for an hour, and after a little is extinguished, but are ignorant of the fire of the coming judgment and of eternal punishment, reserved for the ungodly. But why do you tarry? Bring forth what you will." Polycarp was able to submit to God's will and do what was right, even in the face of death—this is because he knew the One who had done the same thing in the garden of Gesthemane and on the hill of Calvary.

Jesus models the value of praying our heart's desires even when we know and accept that the answer may be "no."

Everyday Life: Describe the sight of a person exercising on a treadmill. The person will never get anywhere, nor is he or she really moving. If running were only about getting somewhere, a treadmill would be a ridiculous and even torturous device. If, on the other hand, running can also be about building stamina, developing muscles, fellowshipping with other runners, burning fat, releasing stress, and enhancing balance, a treadmill can be an incredibly useful device. In the same way, if prayer is only about getting somewhere—like into a blessing, or out of a crisis—it can seem like a wasted or even torturous exercise. If, on the other hand, prayer can also be about fellowship with God and other believers, building character, learning about God's voice, learning patience, grieving loss, and expressing hope, it is an incredibly blessed and useful activity.

The Trials of Peter and of Jesus

Big Idea *While Peter gave in to pressure and disowns Jesus, Jesus maintains his claim before the highest Jewish authority.*

Understanding the Text

The Text in Context

Matthew and Mark relate Jesus's trial before the Sanhedrin at greater length, as the central element in the condemnation of Jesus. Luke's account is much briefer (briefer even than his account of Peter's ordeal) and less decisive, so that the emphasis in this Gospel falls rather on the Roman trial and verdict, which follow in chapter 23.

Both main parts of this section are in clear fulfillment of Jesus's earlier predictions, that Peter would disown him (22:31–34), and that he himself would be rejected and condemned by the Jewish leadership (9:22). The confrontation that has been building up since Jesus's dramatic and provocative arrival in Jerusalem now reaches its climax. Political reality demands that Jesus's ultimate condemnation and execution should be a Roman verdict, but as far as Israel is concerned, the issue is already decided by the end of chapter 22.

Historical and Cultural Background

There has been much debate over the process followed in Jesus's Jewish trial, and over its legal status. Luke's brief account does not allow the sort of detailed comparison that has led many interpreters of Matthew and Mark to charge the Jewish leaders with flouting the rabbinic rules for a capital trial. But in any case, these rules were not formulated in the Mishnah until after Jesus's time and may not represent the practice in the early first century. It is also questionable how far any of the Gospel accounts should be understood as describing a formal trial as such, rather than a preliminary examination/interrogation with a view to formulating a charge to bring before the Roman prefect (who alone had the power to pronounce a death sentence).

Matthew and Mark speak of a hearing at night, leading to a decision reached early in the morning. They recount Peter's denial between the two phases, but it should probably be understood as happening concurrently with the examination of Jesus, which therefore may be understood as a single, continuous process. Luke's abbreviated account speaks only of the final stage of that process in the morning.

Interpretive Insights

22:54 *seizing him, they . . . took him into the house of the high priest.* The actual arrest is mentioned only at the conclusion of the scene on the Mount of Olives. Matthew and John tell us that the high priest was Caiaphas, whom Luke has mentioned in 3:2 (cf. Acts 4:6) but does not name again now. As chairman of the Sanhedrin, he would supervise the action taken against Jesus.

Peter followed at a distance. True to his boast in 22:33, Peter is apparently the only one of the disciples who has not deserted Jesus, though he wishes to remain incognito. John 18:15 says that another disciple, presumably John himself, went with him.

22:55 *a fire in the middle of the courtyard.* It can be very cold at Passover time in Jerusalem. We should probably envisage the open-air courtyard of a large house, in one part of which Jesus was held by guards (22:63), able to see and hear what was going on by the fire (22:61). Those around the fire would have been members of the household and visitors, probably including members of the returned posse.

22:56 *A servant girl.* The first challenger is a person of low social standing, but Luke's emphasis on her careful scrutiny of Peter

Key Themes of Luke 22:54–71

- Peter, isolated from the other disciples, fulfills Jesus's prediction that Peter would disown him before daybreak.
- Jesus is forcibly arrested and physically abused.
- Brought before the Sanhedrin, Jesus declines to answer their questions directly, but he makes his claims clear in his own terms.
- The Sanhedrin concludes that this is enough to render him guilty.

suggests that she may have been with the posse and recognized him as someone who had been with Jesus when he was arrested. The other two accusers are male and probably were members of the arresting group (note 22:59: "this fellow was with him").

22:57–60 *"I don't know him" . . . "I am not!" . . . "I don't know what you're talking about!"* In Matthew and Mark there is an escalation in the vehemence of Peter's denials, culminating in his oath (according to some interpreters, a curse on Jesus himself). Luke is content to record three parallel negative statements in which Peter denies both his knowledge of Jesus and his own discipleship. What is important is that there are three denials, thus directly fulfilling Jesus's prediction (22:34) and triggering Peter's remorse as he recognizes his predicted failure.

22:59 *for he is a Galilean.* Peter was obviously a stranger in this company, and his accent marked him out among these Judeans as, like Jesus, a northerner (cf. Matt. 26:73).

These ancient Roman steps connected the southern end of the city of Jerusalem with the Kidron Valley. Jesus may have traveled up steps such as these when he was led from the Mount of Olives to the house of the high priest.

22:61 *The Lord turned and looked straight at Peter.* For the setting, see on 22:55. This emotive touch would not fit the accounts of Matthew and Mark, for whom Jesus has already been brought before the leaders, but for Luke, he is still in the courtyard. His accusing (or pitying?) look, following immediately after the cockcrow, was enough to bring Peter to his senses.

22:62 *he went outside and wept bitterly.* In the light of 22:32, we should probably understand this as the moment of Peter's "turning back." It is this repentance that differentiates his "betrayal" of Jesus from that of Judas. For Peter, there is still a future.

22:63–65 *The men who were guarding Jesus.* In Matthew and Mark it is Jesus's Jewish judges who abuse him as a false messiah, after they have reached their verdict, but Luke's version does not directly implicate the leaders. This abusive treatment of Jesus the "prophet" by his Jewish guards takes the place of the violent mockery of the Jewish "king" by Roman soldiers in Matthew 27:27–31; Mark 15:16–20; John 19:2–3. Underlying their cruel sarcasm may be a popular belief, based on Isaiah 11:3, that the true Messiah should be able to identify his assailant without being able to see him. The reader, however, recognizes that what they say in jest is in fact true: Jesus the prophet has rightly predicted both Peter's denial and his own treatment, including mockery and abuse (18:32).

22:66 *the council of the elders of the people, both the chief priests and the teachers of the law.* For this listing of the constituent parts of the Sanhedrin, compare 9:22; 20:1. Luke's wording suggests a formal Sanhedrin meeting, perhaps in the council chamber rather than the high priest's house; Jesus is now answerable to Israel's highest court. In Luke's abbreviated account the proceedings consist of only two questions, which go to the heart of Jesus's claims and authority. No doubt the high priest, as chairman, spoke for the whole Sanhedrin (so Matthew and Mark), but Luke presents the questions as coming from the council as a whole.

The temple guard came to arrest Jesus in the garden of Gethsemane carrying swords and clubs. Later, at the house of the high priest, the men guarding Jesus mocked and beat him. This Greek vase shows a club-bearing bodyguard (530–524 BC).

22:67 *If you are the Messiah, . . . tell us.* The single question that forms the climax of the trial as recorded by Matthew and Mark ("Are you the Messiah, the Son of God?") is divided into two in Luke's version, resulting in an elusive dual response from Jesus. Neither answer is a straightforward yes, but both at least imply it, while avoiding giving them a firm legal handle to use against him.

22:67–68 *If I tell you, you will not believe me, and if I asked you, you would not answer.* Jesus questions his interrogators' openness; their attitude is such that neither a straightforward answer nor a counter-question (such as Jesus often used [cf. 20:3]) can expect to be taken seriously. The overall effect of this first part of Jesus's response is therefore "No comment." In Luke Jesus has not explicitly spoken of himself as "messiah," but in view of the blatantly messianic style of his ride to the city (19:28–40), it may seem surprising that he does not now declare that messiahship openly. But he is well aware of how "messiah" language can be used against him (as it will be in 23:2), and he prefers to choose his own terms.

22:69 *But from now on, the Son of Man.* Instead of the loaded term "messiah," Jesus uses his preferred title for himself and his mission, "the Son of Man" (see the sidebar "Son of Man" at 5:12–26). Combined with language about reigning at God's right hand, it is clearly not less than a messianic claim, but this bold declaration (drawing on Ps. 110:1; Dan. 7:13–14) shifts the focus from an earthly role to a future heavenly status. "From now on" indicates that, far from getting rid of Jesus, they will soon see his authority established and, by implication, their own destroyed. They may succeed in having him killed, but his execution will be the beginning, not the end. The prisoner at the bar will become the judge.

22:70 *Are you then the Son of God?* In Matthew and Mark this title appears together with "Messiah," almost as if it were a synonym. Luke's separation of the question gives it a special weight of its own, drawing out the implications ("then") of his claim to heavenly authority in 22:69. Jesus has not called himself "Son of God" publicly, though the title is at least implied in his parable in 20:9–18, but Judas may have briefed them on such private declarations as 10:22.

You say that I am. This reply is positive, without being quite straightforward, as in 23:3 (cf. Matt. 26:64; 27:11; Mark 15:2). It should probably be taken as a "Yes, but . . .": Jesus accepts the words that they have used, but not the meaning that they might read into them.

22:71 *Why do we need any more testimony?* From the point of view of Jewish orthodoxy, a man who accepts the title "Son of God," and who makes the outrageous claim to share God's heavenly authority, is dangerous. Despite Jesus's careful wording, they have enough to justify their already decided intention (22:2) to eliminate him, even though a less theological charge will be needed to persuade the Roman governor to pronounce sentence.

Theological Insights

This is a climactic moment. Before the highest court of Israel Jesus's identity as the Messiah and the Son of God is disclosed, albeit with the qualifications demanded by the polemical nature of the confrontation. By deliberately shifting attention from earthly messiahship to the heavenly authority of the Son of Man, Jesus decisively repudiates any notion of the Messiah as a merely nationalistic, political figure. The "king" who rode on the donkey to Jerusalem will reign not in Jerusalem but at God's right hand.

Even before his birth Jesus was designated "Son of God" (1:35), and he has been confirmed as such both by God himself (3:22; 9:35) and by demons whose supernatural insight could see what was as yet hidden from humans (4:3, 9, 41; 8:28). Now the secret is out. Paradoxically, the title that is the basis of Jesus's condemnation declares the ultimate truth about him. His imminent death, which was supposed to put an end to his claims, will in fact mark the inauguration of his reign at God's right hand, "from now on."

Teaching the Text

Luke has placed side by side the ordeals of Peter and of Jesus, which prompts us to compare and contrast their reactions under examination. Encourage listeners to consider the differences and the similarities in their circumstances, and in the way each of them responded. Why was Peter unable to withstand the social pressure? What may we learn from his fall and subsequent restoration? Do we need a "theology of failure" (with Peter as its patron saint!)?

Luke's account of Jesus before the Sanhedrin is so brief as to be quite cryptic. In your teaching, tease out the unspoken assumptions behind the questions posed by Jesus's examiners. What has Luke achieved by dividing the question into two? What might this tell us about the significance they found in the titles "Messiah" and "Son of

These scenes of Christ before the high priest and the denial of Christ by Peter, painted by Duccio di Buoninsegna from 1308 to 1311, decorate the restored altarpieces of the Siena Cathedral, Italy.

God"? Why was Jesus so apparently evasive in Luke's version? Compare the clear declaration of Mark 14:62a (though immediately followed by the same qualifying explanation). And what was it about Jesus's replies that the Sanhedrin took to justify their action against Jesus?

Illustrating the Text

Though Peter was finally loyal to Jesus, he had first betrayed him, even after having been warned.

Literature: *The Lion, the Witch and the Wardrobe*, **by C. S. Lewis.** One of the memorable story lines in this familiar and moving children's tale is Edmund's refusal to believe his sister Lucy's tale of what has happened in Narnia and his subsequently falling prey to the seductions of the Queen (also the White Witch), who is the enemy of Aslan. In the process of this seduction—which appeals to his gluttony, his vanity, and his illusions—Edmund betrays his siblings and creates the need for Aslan to die in order to satisfy the witch's demands for blood so that Narnia will not "be overturned and perish in fire and water." Having come to the recognition of what he has done, "Edmund was . . . looking all the time at Aslan's face. He felt a choking feeling."[1] Edmund is never the same again. We are told instead that he is sober and wise. Lewis wrote the story as an analogy to the biblical account.

Literature: *To Kill a Mockingbird*, **by Harper Lee.** This Pulitzer Prize–winning novel (1960), or the film based on it (1962), provides a good source for illustrating this passage. Particularly relevant for illustrative purposes is the trial of Tom Robinson, a black man falsely accused of raping a young white woman, Mayella Ewell. Everything that happens during the trial is a betrayal of the American system of justice and of the humanity of Robinson. The trial is a sham. The terribly racist community, prosecuting attorneys, and jurors are fixed in their ideas, and they violate the ideals and rules of law in order to convict a good man, even in the face of overwhelming evidence. Tom's attorney, Atticus Finch (played by Gregory Peck in the film version), confronts the prejudice in an articulate and moving defense, in which he declares,

> The defendant is not guilty. But somebody in this courtroom is. Now, gentlemen, in this country our courts are the great levelers. In our courts, all men are created equal. I'm no idealist to believe firmly in the integrity of our courts and of our jury system—that is no ideal to me. That is a living, working reality. . . . I am confident that you gentlemen will review without passion the evidence that you have heard, come to a decision, and restore this man to his family. In the name of God, do your duty.[2]

Atticus Finch's words are ignored. Robinson is convicted, and he is shot while trying to escape from prison.

The Roman Verdict

Big Idea *The Roman governor, under pressure from the Jewish leaders and crowd, reluctantly condemns Jesus to death.*

Understanding the Text

The Text in Context

In 18:32–33 Jesus predicted that he would be handed over to "the Gentiles" for execution, and that prediction also now comes true. Hitherto, the whole move against Jesus has come from the Jewish leaders and has taken place within Jewish circles, but now the political reality demands that, in order to have Jesus executed, they must involve the Roman governor. But while the governor is clearly in formal charge in this section, it is the Jewish leaders who are orchestrating things. Note their presence and initiative at each stage of the subsequent proceedings (23:1–2, 5, 10, 13); thereafter we hear of "the crowd" or a less specific "they," but Luke clearly intends us to see the Jewish leaders as orchestrating Jesus's condemnation, to which the governor weakly agrees.

Only Luke mentions the additional hearing before Herod Antipas. This does little to advance the legal process, other than further confirming Jesus's innocence, but it does add to the sense of the comprehensive rejection of Jesus by all those in power.

Historical and Cultural Background

Pontius Pilate, prefect of Judea and Samaria from AD 26 to 36, is mentioned in Jewish records as a harsh governor with a history of offending Jewish cultural and religious sensibilities. His weakness as Luke here portrays it seems uncharacteristic but probably derives from political expediency: he could not risk another riot. It would be his response to another such nationalistic uprising that eventually led to his removal from office (Josephus, *Ant.* 18.85–89).

In John 18:31 the Jewish authorities acknowledge that the Jews did not have the right to execute, and this would be consistent with Roman imperial policy generally. The few recorded cases of judicial killing by Jews in this period (Stephen, James the Just) are probably to be explained as, in effect, lynchings to which the Roman authorities turned a blind eye.

Crucifixion was a particularly barbaric form of execution normally employed for slaves and

Pontius Pilate was the Roman prefect over Judea and Samaria from AD 26 to 36. Local officials could authorize bronze coins; the one shown here was minted in Jerusalem during Pilate's administration.

political insurrectionists. Most Jews (and Romans, for that matter) found it repulsive, which makes the demand in 23:21 even more striking.

Barabbas (for the possibility that his full name was "Jesus Barabbas," see Matt. 27:16–17) is portrayed as a political insurrectionist. Mark 15:7 speaks of "the uprising" of which he had apparently been a leader. No other record of this specific insurrection has survived, but it is not surprising in the turbulent period that led up to the great Jewish revolt of AD 66 and that saw other such insurrections in Palestine (e.g., Acts 5:36–37; 21:38). As a nationalist freedom fighter, Barabbas would be a popular hero.

Interpretive Insights

23:2 *He opposes payment of taxes to Caesar and claims to be Messiah, a king.* These are two specific examples of the more general charge of "subverting our nation" (which will recur in 23:5, 14). The charges are well tailored for the ears of a Roman governor. The refusal of the poll tax had been the trigger for the revolt of Judas of Galilee in AD 6 (see on 20:20–40), and while Jesus's answer in 20:25 had carefully avoided a direct repudiation of the tax, his assertion of God's rights alongside Caesar's could be portrayed as treasonable. As for the title "Messiah," Jesus had earlier forbidden the disciples to use it (9:21), but he has not directly repudiated it in 22:67–69, and to Roman ears the status of the Messiah as Son of David (and the disciples' use of royal language in 19:38) would naturally suggest a political ambition.

23:3 *You have said so.* See on 22:70. "King of the Jews" might serve as a Gentile

translation of "Messiah," but Jesus's conception of that messiahship was quite different from what was being suggested to Pilate. Despite Jesus's caution, this is the charge on which he would be officially condemned (23:38).

23:4 *no basis for a charge.* Pilate will repeat this finding twice more (23:14–16, 22). Luke does not explain how Pilate (and Antipas [23:15]) came to this conclusion, but the dialogue recorded in John 18:33–38 reflects the sort of issues likely to have been in mind: Jesus's "kingship" was nonpolitical.

23:5 *He stirs up the people all over Judea.* "Judea" may be used here in the broader sense of the land of the Jews (and so including Galilee), but even so, this is something of an exaggeration, at least as far as Luke's record goes. But it was as a teacher with a following of enthusiastic disciples, whom he had also sent out to recruit others, that Jesus had come to the notice of the authorities in Galilee. An unpopular occupying authority cannot afford to ignore such popular movements.

23:7 *he sent him to Herod.* It is historically plausible that Herod Antipas, who was at least nominally Jewish, would go to Jerusalem for Passover, though none of the other Gospels mention his involvement (Luke will, however, presuppose it in Acts 4:27). As tetrarch of Galilee, Antipas had capital jurisdiction within his own region, but Jesus had been arrested in Judea, and it was there that execution was being demanded. If Pilate hoped that this move might relieve him of judicial responsibility, he was to be disappointed. But perhaps, like Festus in Acts 25:13–22, he was simply seeking a second opinion on the charge that he had found so unconvincing.

23:8 *he had been wanting to see him.* For Antipas's earlier interest in Jesus as a miracle worker, see 9:7–9, though 13:31–33 shows that this interest had taken a more threatening turn.

23:9 *Jesus gave him no answer.* After his guarded declaration to the Jerusalem leaders in 22:69–70, and the necessary but noncommittal response to Pilate's charge, Jesus had no more to say to those in authority; he simply allowed events to take their course.

23:11 *Herod and his soldiers ridiculed and mocked him.* Luke will not record the abuse of Jesus by Roman soldiers immediately before the crucifixion (though see 23:36–37), but the "elegant robe" here suggests a parody of royal dignity similar to that in Matthew 27:28; Mark 15:17; John 19:2–3. Antipas's troops probably were auxiliaries (see "Historical and Cultural Background" on 7:1–17).

23:12 *Herod and Pilate became friends.* We probably should think of a political rapprochement of these rulers of adjoining provinces rather than a personal friendship. Pilate's involvement of Antipas in the proceedings was a welcome diplomatic gesture of recognition and cooperation, and Antipas has obligingly endorsed Pilate's opinion (23:15).

23:13 *the chief priests, the rulers and the people.* This grouping constitutes the "crowd" that will be the dominant force in the rest of this scene (cf. 23:4). The hearing would be held in public, and the citizens of Jerusalem who gathered there made common cause with their leaders against Jesus.

23:16 *Therefore, I will punish him and then release him.* "Punish" translates a word for "discipline," and here it probably denotes an admonitory whipping less serious than the sometimes lethal scourging that accompanied crucifixion (e.g., Mark

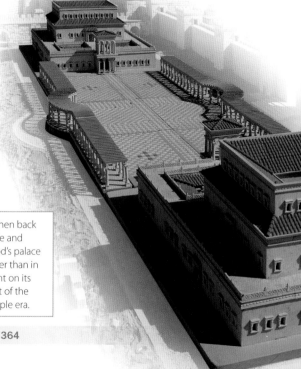

Jesus was taken to Pilate, then to Herod Antipas, and then back to Pilate, who surrendered him to the will of the people and crucifixion. Scholars feel that Pilate was staying at Herod's palace complex on the west side of the city of Jerusalem rather than in the Antonia Fortress that overlooked the Temple Mount on its north side. Shown here is Herod's palace complex, part of the model of the city of Jerusalem during the Second Temple era.

15:15). The punishment of an admittedly innocent man sounds cynical, but it was perhaps Pilate's way of trying to satisfy the Jewish leaders, short of actually having Jesus executed.[1] Luke does not explain that it was expected that one prisoner would be released under a festival amnesty designed to placate popular feeling (so Matt. 27:15; Mark 15:6; John 18:39), but that expectation will be presupposed in 23:18, 25.

23:18 *Away with this man! Release Barabbas to us!* On Barabbas, see "Historical and Cultural Background" above. For the Jerusalem crowd, there was no comparison between a known local resistance hero and a visiting preacher from the north who had been decisively repudiated by the Jerusalem religious leadership.

23:21 *Crucify him! Crucify him!* On crucifixion, see "Historical and Cultural Background" above. The Jewish crowd would know that this would be the method of execution that the Romans would use for an alleged insurrectionist (as presumably it would have been for Barabbas), but the apparent enthusiasm to see a Jewish religious teacher killed in this barbaric foreign way indicates the extent to which Jesus the Galilean had failed to win the support of the Jerusalem crowd. Luke does not say explicitly that the Jerusalem priests instigated this "popular" demand (so Matt. 27:20; Mark 15:11), but in the flow of his narrative the crowd and the religious leaders seem by now to have merged into one united opposition.

23:22 *I have found in him no grounds for the death penalty.* This third declaration of Jesus's innocence by the man who is shortly to pronounce the sentence of execution serves two purposes in Luke's narrative. On the one hand, it makes it clear that

the initiative in the condemnation of Jesus comes from the Jewish leaders, not from an objective Roman assessment of the evidence. This was probably a point of some importance to Christians as they sought to maintain the integrity of the Christian message in the Roman world. But on the other hand, it underlines Pilate's personal and/or political weakness: he recognized Jesus's innocence but was unable or unwilling to stand up to the pressure of the Jewish leaders with their supporting crowd.

23:25 *surrendered Jesus to their will.* Luke does not actually say that Pilate pronounced the death penalty, but in context that is all that "to their will" can mean. For all his formal authority, Pilate remains a reluctant accomplice in an execution already determined by the Jewish leaders. It will be, necessarily, a Roman execution, but it is what the Jewish leaders wanted. The suggestion of some commentators that Luke depicts the Jews as themselves carrying out the crucifixion lacks historical plausibility; the soldiers and the centurion in 23:36–37, 47 are clearly Roman, and Pilate remains responsible (23:52). Later attributions of responsibility to the Jewish leadership (e.g., 24:20; Acts 2:23) do not negate the necessary role of the Roman military authority in the execution.

Theological Insights

In response to the question of who was responsible for Jesus's execution, the formal answer is that it was the Roman governor, since only he had that power. But in his telling of this part of the story Luke seems to have gone out of his way to ensure that his readers see the Jewish leadership as ultimately responsible. Theologically, Jesus died not as a rebel against Rome but rather as one whose message of the kingdom of God conflicted with the interests of the current leadership in Jerusalem.

The contrast between Jesus, the preacher of peace and love (even for one's enemies), and Barabbas, the protagonist for armed resistance to Roman occupation, highlights the strongly countercultural nature of Jesus's message of the kingdom of God. The fact that it was Barabbas whom the crowd wanted released underlines Jesus's earlier perception that Jerusalem would not respond to God's call to repentance and so faced the inevitable judgment (13:34–35; 19:41–44).

The substitution of the admittedly innocent Jesus for guilty Barabbas memorably fulfills Jesus's prediction that he would be "numbered with the transgressors" (22:37). That fateful choice will be commented on again in Acts 3:13–14.

Teaching the Text

Jesus's hearings before Pilate and Herod bring out various themes, but the two most important for the teacher are the innocence/ righteousness of Jesus and the fulfillment of prophecy. Be sure to bring these out in your sermon or lesson. Four times Pilate declares Jesus to be innocent (23:4, 14, 15, 22; cf. Acts 13:28) and Herod confirms this (23:15). In the following scenes, the repentant criminal on the cross will say Jesus has done nothing wrong (23:41) and the centurion at the cross declares Jesus "innocent" or "righteous" (23:47). In Acts Jesus will be called "the Righteous One" (Acts 3:14; 7:52), a term that also means "just" or "innocent." This is significant for Luke not only because it shows that Jesus was not a criminal, but especially because it confirms that Jesus is the Suffering Servant of Isaiah 53 ("my righteous servant"; Isa. 53:11). The silence of Jesus (23:9) also confirms this identification, since it is said of Isaiah's Servant that "he was oppressed and afflicted, yet he did not open his mouth . . . like a sheep before its shearers is silent, so he did not open his mouth" (Isa. 53:7). Jesus has repeatedly predicted his death (9:21–22, 44; 17:25) and identified it with the fulfillment of Scripture (18:31). These predictions are now coming true.

Here are some other themes that could be highlighted in your teaching:

1. Compare this scene with Jesus's approach to Jerusalem (19:28–40), and in particular the shouts of the two crowds. Why the difference? Who

According to Luke, Barabbas had been imprisoned for murder and because of his involvement in an insurrection in the city of Jerusalem (23:19). Roman troops were stationed in Jerusalem to keep order especially during festival times when the city was crowded with visitors. The Antonia Fortress provided barracks for the soldiers as well as a commanding view of the activities occurring in the temple courts. Shown here is a view of the Antonia Fortress from the Second Temple–period model of Jerusalem.

made up these two different crowds? See above on 19:37. Try to disentangle the various vested interests of different groups in their response to Jesus.

2. Discuss what this scene (in the light of all that has led up to it) may be intended to convey concerning who is now the true Israel, and what this may mean for the future of Israel in relation to the coming kingdom of God. Luke does not include the chilling "self-incrimination" of the Jerusalem crowd (Matt. 27:24–25), but how far does his account here tally with such a reading of history?

3. Perhaps use the Barabbas episode to tease out what was distinctive about Jesus's message. How might ordinary "Jews in the street" have compared the two, and what is likely to have determined their choice as to which they should prefer?

Illustrating the Text

Pilate shows how sometimes the most powerful person in the room is also the weakest and least free.

Film: Mention a movie that looks at the life of a superhero. Superman, Spiderman, and Batman—almost all of them carry the theme of the burden the hero bears to serve others. Peter Parker (Spiderman) was once told by his Uncle Ben, "With great power comes great responsibility." Even though he or she bears unusual power, the responsibility to use that power and please different interest groups can often be crushing and isolating. This is true for political figures, who often have to place their own consciences at odds with public expediency. We see this in Pilate's dilemma. He seems to want to steer away from pronouncing judgment against Jesus, yet the need to maintain peace and order gets the best of him and he attempts to wash his hands of responsibility for Jesus's fate. Pilate's power was given by a world system opposed to the Christ, and that same system demanded that Pilate use it against Jesus, no matter what his conscience told him. Pilate's great power actually came with great helplessness and obligation.

The cry for crucifixion reveals the full depth of humanity's depravity and upside-down values—apart from God's grace, we would all have joined in shouting it.

Literature: Aesop's Fables. One of Aesop's fables is the story of the scorpion and the frog. The two meet on the bank of a river, and the scorpion asks the frog for a ride across the stream on his back. The frog asks, "How do I know you won't sting me?" The scorpion says, "Because if I do, I will also die." The frog is satisfied, and they set out across the river. Midstream, the scorpion stings the frog. As they both begin to drown, the frog gasps out, "Why?" The scorpion simply replies, "It is my nature." Fallen humanity has a sin nature that so distorts our minds that we can kill the author of life, even as he willingly bears our burdens in love. Our twisted desire to receive a murderer and condemn the sinless Son of God reveals just how far we have fallen—it is in our nature. The good news is that Christ is able to bring a new nature to life in us.

The Death of Jesus

Big Idea *Jesus dies on the cross, mourned by some and mocked by others, but confidently placing himself in his Father's hands.*

Understanding the Text

The Text in Context

The crowd demanded Jesus's crucifixion in 23:21, 23, and that now takes place, cruelly embodying Jesus's earlier warning that to follow him would mean to "take up the cross" (9:23; 14:27). A variety of reactions on the way to "the Skull" and at the cross reflect the different ways people have responded to Jesus and his claims within the Gospel. But as the scene progresses, a sequence of positive notes offsets the official rejection of Jesus (the faith and salvation of one of the criminals, the supernatural darkness and tearing of the temple curtain, Jesus's own calm demeanor in death, and the surprised reaction of the centurion) and so enable the reader to look forward to the triumphant climax of chapter 24.

Historical and Cultural Background

The condemned man usually was forced to carry the crossbeam, which would then be fixed to an upright already erected at the execution site. A placard stating the crime of which he was convicted was sometimes hung around his neck for the walk to execution, and then it might be attached to the top of the cross. The condemned man was fastened to the cross either by ropes or by nails through the wrists and ankles; John 20:25 shows that the latter, more cruel, method was used for Jesus. Most victims of crucifixion took longer to die than is recorded of Jesus, sometimes several days.

Interpretive Insights

23:26 *they seized Simon from Cyrene.* This is an apparently arbitrary imposition, since Luke does not mention either that Jesus was physically weakened by flogging (cf. Mark 15:15) or that Simon had any connection with him; Simon just happened to be in the wrong place at the wrong time. But the preservation of his name (and those of his two sons [Mark 15:21]) suggests that he may subsequently have become a disciple; his carrying the cross "behind Jesus" provides a surprisingly literal fulfillment of 9:23; 14:27.

23:27 *women who mourned and wailed for him.* Since Jesus addresses them as "daughters of Jerusalem," these were probably not the women disciples who will be mentioned in 23:49, but rather local people expressing, in typical Middle Eastern fashion, their revulsion at Roman brutality and perhaps (unlike the crowd in 23:16–23) still reflecting the popular support for Jesus noted in 19:48; 20:19; 22:2.

23:28–30 *weep for yourselves and for your children.* Jerusalem's fate will affect them much more seriously than that of Jesus; compare 13:34–35; 19:41–44; 21:20–24. The quotation from Hosea 10:8 in 28:30 compares Jerusalem's fate with the destruction of Samaria in the eighth century BC.

23:31 *when the tree is green . . . when it is dry?* This is proverbial language (cf. Ezek. 17:24; 20:47), probably comparing the present time of (relative) political security with the coming period of insurrection when the whole city will be ready to go up in flames; or perhaps it contrasts the execution of an admittedly innocent man with the deserved destruction of the rebellious city.

23:32 *Two other men, both criminals.* These men are never explicitly linked with Barabbas, but their crucifixion suggests a political crime, such as that of Barabbas described in 23:19. Luke uses a broad term, "wrongdoers," but Mark and Matthew use the more politically loaded term that we noted at 22:52. Jesus is placed between two "transgressors" in fulfillment of Isaiah 53:12 (see 22:37).

23:33 *the place called the Skull.* The other Gospels use the Aramaic term "Golgotha," but Luke simply translates it for Gentile readers. It was a known place

Key Themes of Luke 23:26–49

- On the way to the cross, Jesus is mourned by women of Jerusalem.
- He is crucified between two criminals, one of whom joined in mocking him, but the other seeks and finds a saving relationship with Jesus.
- He is mocked by Jewish leaders and Roman soldiers, and by Pilate's notice that ironically proclaims him "King of the Jews."
- The supernatural events at his death and the manner of his dying cause the centurion to recognize his innocence.

of execution, outside the city wall, and is probably the site where the Church of the Holy Sepulchre now stands.

23:34 *Jesus said, "Father, forgive them, for they do not know what they are doing."* The absence of these words from most of the earliest Greek manuscripts and some early versions leads most scholars to conclude that they were an early addition to the text (perhaps influenced by Isa. 53:12), since there seems no good reason for them to have been omitted if they were original.[1] But they eminently suit the demeanor of Jesus, and the similar prayer of the martyr Stephen in Acts 7:60 probably reflects this early tradition about Jesus's death, perhaps preserved independently.

23:35 *He saved others; let him save himself.* Luke makes a deliberate play on the word that he has used for Jesus's ministry of healing and deliverance (e.g., 7:50). But Jesus has made clear in 9:24 that "saving" life is not always the right course. The salvation that he bestows in 23:43 will be of a quite different order.

if he is God's Messiah, the Chosen One. Political necessity had demanded a less theological term in accusing Jesus to Pilate (repeated by the Roman soldiers in 23:37 and in the official charge in 23:38), but it was as a purported messiah that the Jewish leaders had rejected him, as did one of his Jewish fellow victims in 23:39. For "the Chosen One," compare 9:35.

23:36 *They offered him wine vinegar.* This probably was the cheap, dry wine brought there for the soldiers' use. Luke's spare account develops neither the theme of Jesus's thirst (John 19:28) nor the allusion to vinegar in Psalm 69:21 (Matt. 27:34, 48), but the mocking words that follow suggest an act of cruelty rather than of kindness.

23:41 *this man has done nothing wrong.* This declaration, together with the words

A sign saying "This is the King of the Jews" (23:38) was hung at the top of the cross on which Jesus was crucified. For this, Jesus was mocked by the soldiers and by one of the criminals crucified next to him. (The inscription is represented here by "INRI," which abbreviates the Latin phrase *Iesus Nazarenus Rex Iudaeorum*.) Shown here is an artist's interpretation of the crucifixion of Jesus (attributed to Jacopo della Quercia, AD 1420, Siena).

of the centurion in 23:47, stands in stark contrast to the mockery and rejection of Jesus by the majority, both Jewish and Roman, as the testimony of a neutral observer.

23:42 *when you come into your kingdom.* The man apparently takes seriously the sarcastic placard on Jesus's cross; as a Jew, he (unlike his colleague [23:39]) recognizes Jesus's messianic claim. We are not told whether he really thought that Jesus might escape the cross, or whether he was thinking in terms of otherworldly authority following Jesus's death. Jesus's reply assumes the latter.

23:43 *today you will be with me in paradise.* "Paradise" (cf. 2 Cor. 12:4; Rev. 2:7) is a less Jewish term used in the LXX for the garden of Eden but also applied more generally to an unworldly state of blessedness, "heaven." This imminent experience of heaven, both for Jesus and for the believing criminal, puts the reality of physical death and the horror of crucifixion in perspective. It also puts a significant question mark against the later tradition of Jesus's "descent into hell" after he died. In earthly reality the resurrection and subsequent ascension are still to come, but in the perspective of eternity Jesus goes straight from the cross to his heavenly throne.

23:44 *darkness came over the whole land*. A solar eclipse is not possible at the time of the Passover full moon, and in any case it would not last for three hours, so we must think of a special, supernatural darkening as an expression of God's displeasure (cf. Amos 8:9–10).

23:45 *the curtain of the temple was torn in two*. The temple had two massive curtains (Heb. 9:2–3), one screening the entrance to the sanctuary building from the courtyard, the other separating off the holy of holies inside. Many symbolic meanings have been suggested (such as the opening of a way into God's presence), but Luke does not explicitly endorse any of them. In context, the reader is perhaps most likely to think of Jesus's prediction of the temple's destruction, which is here foreshadowed.

23:46 *Father, into your hands I commit my spirit*. This expression of trust is drawn from Psalm 31:5; note the confident address to God as "Father." The Greek word translated "breathed his last" echoes "spirit," but (like the English word "expire") it is a natural euphemism for dying and should not be pressed here to denote the "spirit" as a distinct part of the person, still less to refer to the Holy Spirit. It means simply that Jesus died.

23:47 *Surely this was a righteous man*. In Matthew and Mark the centurion speaks of Jesus as "Son of God." Luke's formulation avoids the Jewish theological associations of that term and perhaps represents what such a phrase might have meant to a pagan. It is a wholly positive verdict, even if not carrying the theological weight that later

Christian reflection would find in "Son of God." It reinforces the conclusions of Pilate, Antipas, and the criminal (23:4, 14–15, 22, 41) that Jesus was innocent.

23:49 *all those who knew him*. These may include some or all of the Eleven (Luke has not told us what happened to any of them except Peter after Jesus's arrest) but probably also a wider circle of supporters (such as Joseph [23:50]) and perhaps also family members; we will hear of disciples additional to the Eleven in 24:9, 13, 33 (cf. Acts 1:13–15). The special mention of the women (whom we met earlier at 8:2–3) prepares us for their important role as witnesses in 23:55–56; 24:1–10.

Theological Insights

Like the other evangelists, Luke says little about the physical aspects of crucifixion. His account focuses instead on the rejection of Jesus (Jewish rulers, Roman soldiers, Pilate's sarcastic placard, one of the criminals) contrasted with support and recognition coming from unexpected sources (mourning women of Jerusalem, the other criminal, the centurion) as well as from his silent followers, while "the crowd," whose attitude is unclear in 23:35, will join in mourning Jesus in 23:48. The whole is given theological depth by the supernatural signs of the darkness and the tearing of the temple curtain. Jesus's suffering is not minimized, but his recorded words focus not on his own agony of abandonment (as in Matt. 27:46; Mark 15:34) but rather on compassion for others (the women and the believing criminal) and confidence in his Father (23:46). The tradition of his prayer for the soldiers in 23:34, even if not an original part of Luke, comes from the same mold.

Repeated echoes of Psalm 22 (dividing clothes and casting lots [Ps. 22:18], mocking [22:6–7], the saving of God's chosen one [22:8]) establish Jesus's death as fulfilling the Old Testament role of the righteous sufferer (which underlies also Jesus's last words, drawn from Ps. 31).

For a theological interpretation of the tearing of the temple curtain (taking it as the inner curtain), see Hebrews 6:19–20; 9:6–14; 10:19–22.

Teaching the Text

There are various ways to teach the crucifixion scene in a sermon or lesson. Contrast, for example, Luke's brief and restrained account of the actual suffering associated with crucifixion (he simply says, "they crucified him there") with the lurid depiction by some preachers and in, for example, the

2004 film *The Passion of the Christ*. Neither Luke nor the other Gospels dwell on the gruesome and bloody details. What does this teach us about how we should respond to the story, and how it may best be presented to people today? It might be noted that Jesus's greatest agony on the cross was not the physical suffering of crucifixion (others have suffered greater and more prolonged torture and physical agony), but the supreme suffering he experienced by taking on the penalty of the sins of the world.

Another approach to the crucifixion is to analyze the different attitudes toward Jesus and his death set out in this section. What do you think Luke was aiming to achieve by this blending of negative and positive attitudes? Notice, for example, the irony in the mocking of Jesus to save himself if he is truly the Messiah. Ironically, it is by *staying on the cross* that Jesus confirms he is the Messiah and brings salvation to the world. Notice, too, that even on the cross Jesus continues to offer forgiveness and salvation (23:34, 43). He is truly the Savior of the world.

Another traditional teaching method for this passage is to focus on Jesus's words from the cross. Seven "last words" (sayings) of Jesus appear in the four Gospels. Three of the seven come from Luke (and only from him; 23:34, 43, 46). When teaching through Luke (or another Gospel), it is important to maintain the integrity of the author's narrative by focusing on the sayings that appear

Just before Jesus died, the curtain of the temple was torn in two (23:45). In the temple, a curtain separated the most holy place, or holy of holies, from the holy place. Another curtain separated the holy place from the porch of the temple. Shown here is the curtain protecting the holy of holies in the tabernacle model at Timna, Israel.

here, rather than introducing others that may distract from each Gospel's theological purpose. What impression of the death of Jesus do these three sayings convey? Notice that the three in Luke (23:34, 43, 46) all pick up themes that have been important throughout his Gospel.

Illustrating the Text

Though he does not ignore Christ's suffering, Luke's focus is not so much on Christ's agony of abandonment as on his compassion for others.

Film: *Jesus*, directed by Peter Sykes, John Heyman, and John Krisch. Called by some "the best kept secret" in Christian missions, and described by one prominent Christian leader as "the best evangelistic tool ever invented," *Jesus* (commonly known as "The Jesus Film") is based on the book of Luke. It is shown worldwide on a continuing basis and has been instrumental in thousands of conversions. Much more restrained than the more recent and acclaimed *Passion of the Christ* (2004, directed by Mel Gibson), the clips of the crucifixion in this film are truer to the spirit of Luke than many other films. It is available online for full viewing.

The compassion of Jesus under great suffering is an inspiration for reflection on our own suffering as something that can be used to bless others.

Christian Living: *A Passion for Pilgrimage*, by Alan Jones. Reflecting on the death of Jesus, Jones writes, "In the end the Crucifixion is not a spectator sport. I cannot simply watch it on the sidelines. Something bursts within me—revulsion, hatred, disappointment—but I am not left untouched. The cross, acknowledged or not, leaves its own kind of wound in us. It sets us voyaging within ourselves."[2]

Hymn: "When I Survey the Wondrous Cross," by Isaac Watts. Watts (1674–1748), a well-educated, prolific English poet, composed this familiar hymn in 1707. It is said that Charles Wesley would have given up all his hymns to have composed this one. It captures the sorrow and compassion of Christ ("did e'er such love and sorrow meet") and the personal response of the hymn writer to that sacrifice ("demands my soul, my life, my all").

> When I survey the wondrous cross
> On which the Prince of glory died,
> My richest gain I count but loss,
> And pour contempt on all my pride.
>
> Forbid it, Lord, that I should boast,
> Save in the death of Christ my God!
> All the vain things that charm me most,
> I sacrifice them to His blood.
>
> See from His head, His hands, His feet,
> Sorrow and love flow mingled down!
> Did e'er such love and sorrow meet,
> Or thorns compose so rich a crown?
>
> His dying crimson, like a robe,
> Spreads o'er His body on the tree;
> Then I am dead to all the globe,
> And all the globe is dead to me.
>
> Were the whole realm of nature mine,
> That were a present far too small;
> Love so amazing, so divine,
> Demands my soul, my life, my all.

Luke 23:26–49

At the Tomb

Big Idea *Jesus is given a respectful burial, but two days later the tomb is empty, and angels say that Jesus is alive.*

Understanding the Text

The Text in Context

This is the point at which the whole story turns around. The apparently inexorable process of Jesus's arrest, trial, and execution has now run its course, but that is not to be the end. Earlier in the Gospel we heard Jesus's predictions of resurrection "on the third day" (9:22; 18:33), but these seem to have barely registered with the disciples, who are taken by surprise both in this section, by the discovery of the empty tomb and the angels' message, and in the next sections, by meetings with the risen Jesus.

There are well-known differences between the ways the four evangelists relate the discovery of the empty tomb (and still more in their selection and location of meetings with the risen Jesus). But while not all the details fit well together, all four accounts of the women and the angel(s) convey the same sense of surprise, fear, supernatural reassurance, and dawning hope, and of a stretching of the boundaries of normal experience in such a way that it is hardly surprising that the stories they told afterward were not identical.

Historical and Cultural Background

The bodies of those who were crucified were normally left on the crosses or thrown on the ground without ceremony; at best, they were thrown into a common grave. Jews objected to this Roman lack of respect for bodies (especially in the light of Deut. 21:22–23), and where possible, arrangements were made for a more appropriate disposal. But the expense of a new rock-cut tomb (affordable only by the wealthy) goes far beyond any such pious action and marks a remarkable challenge to the norm. Many rock-cut tombs from this period survive around Jerusalem, most of them making provision for a number of bodies (so that a previously unused tomb was unusual), but with a single large stone blocking the low entrance to the complex. Spices were used not to embalm the body but to counter the effects of decomposition in a warm climate.

Jewish convention did not much value the testimony of women (as is reflected in 24:11). The choice of women (exclusively) as the first witnesses of Jesus's resurrection is a striking divine challenge to human prejudice (and also an indication of the authenticity of the accounts, since no Jew would have invented so unconventional a source of evidence).

Interpretive Insights

23:50 *Joseph, a member of the Council.* Either he had been absent from the Sanhedrin when it condemned Jesus, or his dissenting voice was overruled.

23:51 *waiting for the kingdom of God.* This phrase does not necessarily indicate a direct disciple of Jesus, but rather a pious Jew, like Simeon and the others, of whom similar language is used in 2:25, 38. Unlike the rest of his Sanhedrin colleagues, Joseph apparently has responded favorably to Jesus's message. His extravagant gesture, going beyond the call of conventional piety, may indicate a more serious commitment: John calls him a "secret disciple" (John 19:38), Matthew simply "a disciple of Jesus" (Matt. 27:57).

23:52 *he asked for Jesus' body.* This is probably quite a courageous act on Joseph's part, since it associates this prominent Jewish leader with a convicted criminal. But Luke's account of Pilate's belief in Jesus's innocence suggests that he may have been unusually receptive to such a request in this case.

23:53 *a tomb cut in the rock, one in which no one had yet been laid.* For burial

Key Themes of Luke 23:50–24:12

- Joseph, an influential supporter of Jesus, obtains permission to bury him in a new rock tomb.
- The same women who watched Jesus die also see where he is buried, and they are the first to discover that the tomb is empty.
- Two angels declare to the women that Jesus is now alive again.
- The women pass on the message to the apostles, who do not believe them.
- But Peter goes to the tomb and sees for himself that it is empty.

customs, see "Historical and Cultural Background" above. The availability of such a tomb at short notice indicates, as indeed Matthew states explicitly, that it was Joseph's own family tomb. The emphasis on the newness of this tomb (cf. John 19:41) weakens the suggestion that the women made a mistake in identifying the relevant burial space—there were as yet no other occupants.

23:54 *It was Preparation Day.* That is, Friday. The work of burial by Joseph's men had to be completed before the Sabbath began at sunset (cf. John 19:31).

23:55 *The women who had come with Jesus from Galilee.* Three of them will be named in 24:10. The continuity of the same group of witnesses to both the death (23:49) and burial of Jesus (both where and how he was buried) and then also to the absence of his body weakens any suggestion that the women went to the wrong tomb.

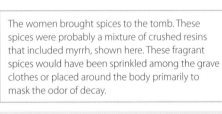

The women brought spices to the tomb. These spices were probably a mixture of crushed resins that included myrrh, shown here. These fragrant spices would have been sprinkled among the grave clothes or placed around the body primarily to mask the odor of decay.

23:56 *prepared spices and perfumes.* These were part of a normally respectful burial, but apparently they had not yet been provided because of the urgency of the burial before sunset. Either Mark and Luke were unaware of the tradition in John 19:39–40 of spices provided by Nicodemus, or they envisaged the women's as an additional contribution. The women's intention shows that they were still expecting Jesus to remain dead.

24:1 *On the first day of the week, very early in the morning.* This gives a period of less than forty hours after Jesus was buried shortly before sunset on the Friday, but in Jewish idiom "the third day" (9:22; 18:33; 24:21) means "the day after tomorrow." None of the Gospels tell us when Jesus left the tomb, only when the tomb was found to be empty.

24:2 *the stone rolled away from the tomb.* Luke has not previously mentioned the stone, which features largely in the accounts of Matthew (27:60, 66; 28:2) and Mark (15:46; 16:3–4). Luke does not indicate how it was removed, or whether it was to let Jesus out or to let the women in.

24:4 *two men in clothes that gleamed like lightning.* Mark speaks of a young man dressed in white, Matthew of an angel of the Lord wearing white, and John of two angels in white. Their sudden appearance, the women's fear, and the imagery of lightning (used also in Matt. 28:3) suggest a supernatural dimension, and in 24:23 these two "men" will be

identified as "angels." Angelic appearances in both the Old and New Testaments are typically in human form.

24:5 *Why do you look for the living among the dead?* Up to this point the women have had no indication that Jesus's death was not final. This challenge therefore completely subverts their natural assumptions and moves the narrative from death to new life. It is a rebuke of their failure, as disciples, to see beyond Jesus's death.

24:6 *He is not here; he has risen!* The implications of the previous rhetorical question are spelled out in terms that rule out any idea of merely spiritual survival. Jesus's body has gone, and he is again one of "the living." "He has risen" could be more literally translated "he has been raised," and the passive form occurs frequently in the New Testament in describing Jesus's resurrection. But it would be pedantic to insist that the passive form makes Jesus purely the object of God's action; compare 24:46, where an active verb is used for Jesus himself "rising." The same two verbs have been used as parallels in 9:22 ("be raised") and 18:33 ("rise").

24:8 *Then they remembered his words.* The angels' words in 24:7 are not an exact quotation, but draw elements from the

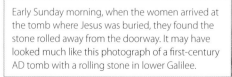

Early Sunday morning, when the women arrived at the tomb where Jesus was buried, they found the stone rolled away from the doorway. It may have looked much like this photograph of a first-century AD tomb with a rolling stone in lower Galilee.

sequence of predictions in 9:22, 44; 18:33. The women have been part of the disciple group, not merely hangers-on, but they, like the rest of the disciples, had hitherto failed to take this element of Jesus's prediction seriously.

24:9 *to the Eleven and to all the others.* For the wider circle of supporters of Jesus at this time, see on 23:49.

24:10 *Mary Magdalene, Joanna, Mary the mother of James, and the others with them.* For the first two names, see on 8:2–3. "Mary" was a common name, but comparison with Matthew 27:56 and Mark 15:40; 16:1 suggests that this "Mary of James" (a literal translation; the phrase more normally would indicate the wife of James) was the mother of one of the two disciples called "James" in 6:14–15. Only Luke indicates the presence of more than the three named women in the group at the tomb.

24:11 *they did not believe the women.* For men who (like the women themselves until they met the angels) as yet had no inkling that Jesus's death was not final, this was hardly a surprising outcome. The term translated "nonsense" suggests a rather contemptuous response to the women's supposedly wishful thinking; it was well known that a woman could not be trusted, still less a whole bunch of them in an emotional state!

24:12 *Peter, however, got up and ran to the tomb.* This verse (absent from some early Western manuscripts but accepted as an original part of Luke by most commentators) seems like a brief reference to the visit spelled out in more detail by John 20:3–10, where the position of the linen wrappings is given some prominence as evidence. Luke's account does not develop this theme, nor does it convey any hint that it was on this occasion that the risen Lord "appeared to Simon" (24:34). He leaves the tomb in amazement, not yet with a firm belief in Jesus's resurrection.

Theological Insights

Luke's relatively spare account of Jesus's burial and of the finding of the empty tomb provides useful material for Christian apologetics in two ways: (1) the reality of Jesus's death is clearly taken for granted by his supporters (Joseph, the women, the disciples) as well as his opponents; (2) a continuity of eyewitness testimony is established with the presence of the same women at the cross, the burial, and the opened tomb. The supernatural explanation for the absence of Jesus's body that is provided by the only nonhuman actors in the scene (24:4–7) is thus established as the only account that fits the narrative data.

The remarkable failure of both the disciples and the women to have anticipated Jesus's resurrection despite his explicit predictions of it may be put down in part to a pessimistic "realism" natural to those who have just witnessed his arrest, trial, and execution, but also perhaps to the unprecedented nature of the idea of individual resurrection. Developing Jewish belief in life after death was focused on the corporate resurrection of the just after the judgment (e.g., Dan. 12:2), while the resuscitation of the widow's son and of Jairus's daughter (7:10–17; 8:49–56), like that of Lazarus in John 11, was simply a temporary restoration of earthly life. What now confronted the disciples was a new phenomenon, since the end-time resurrection had already begun in human history.

Teaching the Text

Teaching on the resurrection commonly focuses on two kinds of questions: (1) historical ones (the historical evidence for the resurrection) and (2) theological ones (the theological significance of the resurrection for faith and practice). Luke's account of the burial and of the discovery of the empty tomb (23:50–24:12) provides a good text for the former. The next two passages (24:13–35; 24:36–53) are well suited for the latter.

Many good books have been written defending the historicity of the resurrection and the teacher may want to consult these during lesson preparation.[1] Consider, for example, these nearly indisputable facts confirming the resurrection: (1) *The reality of Jesus's death*. The Romans were very good at what they did and could not have botched the job. There is no denying that Jesus died on the cross. (2) *The authenticity of the burial account*. The burial of Jesus in the tomb of Joseph of Arimathea is reported by all four Gospels, providing solid evidence that there was in fact a tomb to be discovered empty. It is impossible to imagine that the name of this individual was invented by the church. (3) *The discovery of the tomb by women*. All four Gospels report that the tomb was discovered empty by a group of women on the third day. The church would never have invented these stories, since women were not considered reliable witnesses in first century Judaism. (4) *The witnesses to the resurrected Christ*. Many reliable witnesses claimed to have seen Jesus alive after his death (see 1 Cor. 15:1–11). (5) *The transformed lives of the disciples*. Something radically transformed the lives of Jesus's followers, from fearful cowards to bold witnesses. The resurrection is the only viable explanation for these five facts.[2]

Here are other themes and discussion points that might be developed in a sermon or lesson on this passage:

1. There is no New Testament account of Jesus rising from the dead, only of the discovery of the empty tomb and the meetings with the risen Jesus. Discuss why there is this restraint. What might we have gained, or lost, by the inclusion of a narrative of the resurrection itself?

2. Are the differences between the details of the Gospel accounts troubling? How should they be explained? Is it necessary to try to "harmonize" them?

3. Encourage listeners to put themselves in the place of the women, and to imagine the development of their thought and emotions before and after the angelic message.

4. Discuss the differences and similarities between Jesus's resurrection and the resuscitations of the widow's son and Jairus's daughter.

5. "Christ has been raised from the dead, the firstfruits of those who have fallen asleep" (1 Cor. 15:20). In what ways is our future "resurrection" similar to and different from that of Jesus?

Illustrating the Text

Sometimes, in despair, we fail to remember the hope of what we have been promised.

Christian Living: *Looking to Jesus*, **by Virginia Stem Owens.** Writing about the failure of Christ's followers, men and women, to recognize the event of the resurrection, Owens reflects,

> I'm impressed with the gospel's psychological realism. The movement from despair to hope never appears to happen automatically or instantaneously. Emotional time progresses at a slower pace than our synapses carry simple visual stimuli. Just as it takes a while to absorb the fact of loss, hope takes time to digest. Skeptics are right in observing that we see what we want to see. But the psychological phenomenon works the other way too; sometimes, especially after we've abandoned all hope, we're blind to what we previously longed for.[3]

Literature: *The Silver Chair*, by C. S. Lewis. Lewis has an interesting way of reminding his readers to remember what is true regardless of where they find themselves. In an early scene in this story, one of the Chronicles of Narnia, Aslan tells Jill, one of the main characters, that she must

> remember, remember, remember the Signs. Say them to yourself when you wake in the morning, and when you lie down at night, and when you wake in the middle of the night. . . . And the Signs . . . will not look at all as you expect them to look. . . . That is why it is so important to know them by heart.[4]

The women correctly remember and understand the events and witness to the Eleven in spite of the men's questioning.

Quote: *Are Women Human?* by Dorothy Sayers. Sayers (1893–1957), a renowned English woman of letters, helps us to see why the women were so attentive and why they seemed to understand things better than the men did, why they so quickly

The Holy Women at the Tomb of Christ, 1890 (oil on canvas), by William-Adolphe Bouguereau (1825–1905)

"remembered" his words. In this piece defending women, from an address given to a women's society in 1938, Sayers writes,

> Perhaps it is no wonder that the women were first at the Cradle and last at the Cross. They had never known a man like this Man—there never has been such another. A prophet and teacher who never nagged at them, never flattered or coaxed or patronized, who never made arch jokes about them, never treated them as "The women, God help us!" or "The ladies, God bless them!"; . . . who took their questions and arguments seriously, who never mapped out their sphere for them, never urged them to be feminine or jeered at them for being female; who had no axe to grind and no uneasy male dignity to defend; who took them as he found them and was completely unself-conscious.[5]

The Risen Jesus Revealed

Big Idea *Luke's first record of an appearance by the risen Jesus is to two otherwise unknown disciples outside Jerusalem who do not recognize him until he breaks bread with them.*

Understanding the Text

The Text in Context

Following the discovery of the empty tomb, Luke's Gospel records only two occasions (and hints at another one [24:34]) when the risen Jesus appeared to his disciples, both on the evening of Easter day itself, and chapter 24 taken alone would suggest that Jesus's ascension followed immediately that same night. But Luke will record in Acts 1:3 that in fact Jesus appeared to his disciples frequently over a forty-day period leading up to the ascension, so that the few appearances recorded in his Gospel must be taken as only selected examples. Their interlinking, along with the sequence leading up to the ascension, means that Luke's postresurrection appearances, unlike those in Matthew and John, occur only in the immediate area of Jerusalem. The return to Galilee (Matt. 28:7, 10, 16–20; Mark 16:7; John 21) falls outside Luke's deliberately selective scheme.

Historical and Cultural Background

Luke has already indicated (23:49; 24:9; cf. 24:33) that the circle of Jesus's followers in Jerusalem extended well beyond the twelve (now eleven) apostles from the Galilee period and the group of women who were at the tomb. Here we meet two Judean residents who were fully accepted as part of the group (note the phrases "our women" [24:22] and "our companions" [24:24]), which Luke will reckon a few weeks later as containing 120 members (Acts 1:15).

Hospitality to a passing stranger (especially one with whom they have enjoyed animated conversation) was an expected part of Palestinian culture. What is quite irregular is the assumption by Jesus of the role of host rather than guest at the meal.

Interpretive Insights

24:13 *Emmaus, about seven miles from Jerusalem.* The exact location is debated (and some manuscripts give a distance of nearly twenty miles, not seven) and is not important, but the involvement of residents of a village some distance from Jerusalem indicates the widening impact of Jesus's message. A distance of seven miles allows time for the journey to be made in both directions on the same day.

24:14 *about everything that had happened.* In 24:19–24 we will hear the gist of this conversation. They have perhaps been staying in Jerusalem for the Passover festival, and so they have witnessed the whole sequence up to and including the dramatic announcement by the women.

24:15 *Jesus himself came up and walked along with them.* While there are features of the risen Jesus in the Gospel accounts that differ from normal human experience (notably the ability to appear and disappear suddenly, even through closed doors), the principal impression is of a human body sufficiently unchanged (though restored after the horror of crucifixion) to be perceived as a normal human being (cf. John 20:15; 21:4).

Key Themes of Luke 24:13–35

- The travelers do not recognize Jesus when he walks along with them.
- He rebukes their failure to expect his resurrection and explains to them from Scripture how his mission must be fulfilled, through death to glory.
- It is when Jesus takes the place of host at their meal that they recognize him.
- Then he simply vanishes.
- The disciples in Jerusalem have now also come to believe in his resurrection.

24:16 *they were kept from recognizing him.* Compare Luke's strong statements about the disciples' earlier inability to understand Jesus's words (9:45; 18:34). The language in Greek here is quite forceful: "their eyes were overpowered." As in John 20:16; 21:7, recognition will subsequently follow. In this case, however, it takes longer, and this allows time for the stranger to deliver the remarkable "seminar" that follows before they reach their destination.

24:18 *One of them, named Cleopas.* We know nothing else of this man; it is possible that he is the Clopas of John 19:25, but that is speculation. Nor do we know whether his companion was male or female (Cleopas's wife?). They are simply two among the group of Judean supporters of Jesus from whom, along with the Galilean disciples, the church in Acts will emerge.

There is much discussion about the exact location of the town of Emmaus, to which Cleopas, his companion, and Jesus walked shortly after Jesus's resurrection. Many towns were called by that name, but this map shows three possibilities that have been given consideration because of their location relative to Jerusalem. Emmaus-Nicopolis (modern Khirbet Imwas) was the traditional site for pilgrimages as early as the fourth century AD. Another suggestion is el-Qubeibeh, which was favored by the crusaders. Colonia (modern Qaloniyeh) is another suggestion.

Are you the only one visiting Jerusalem who does not know? From the disciples' point of view, the execution of Jesus dominated their recent experience. Others in the crowded city at festival time may not have been so keenly aware of it. It was the events recorded in Acts 2–5 that would bring Jesus's name more fully into public notice some weeks later.

24:19–21 *a prophet . . . we had hoped that he was the one who was going to redeem Israel.* This poignant description expresses the conflicting attitudes of Jesus's Judean supporters. His prophetic status is not in doubt, but his role as the Messiah remains a frustrated hope in the light of his condemnation by the Jewish authorities and now his decisive execution. The past tense (lit., "we were hoping") conveys a dead aspiration that only Jesus's resurrection will now be able to revive.

24:21 *it is the third day.* Is this simply a note of time, or did they have a vague memory that Jesus was supposed to have said something about what would happen "on the third day" (9:22; 18:33)?

24:22–23 *some of our women amazed us.* These two verses summarize 24:1–9 above, confirming that Luke's description of the "two men" was intended to denote angels. These two travelers are thus to be included in "the Eleven and all the others" mentioned in 24:9.

24:24 *some of our companions.* Only Peter is mentioned in 24:12, but the plural here may reflect Luke's knowledge of the fuller account in John 20:3–10, where Peter was accompanied by another disciple.

24:26 *Did not the Messiah have to suffer these things?* It was "these things" that had finally destroyed these disciples' dawning hope that Jesus was the Messiah (24:20–21). Now they must learn to see things in a quite new light: Jesus's rejection and death were not the end of his messianic claim, but rather the necessary means to its fulfillment. They should have known this, because it was already clear in the Old Testament prophets, as 24:27 will explain (and as he has already taught in 18:31–33).

enter his glory? Jesus's resurrection is the first stage of this "entry," which will be consummated in his ascension to heaven in 24:51. Luke has used "glory" to speak not only of the transfiguration of Jesus during his earthly life (9:31–32) but also of the future exercise of Jesus's messianic authority in 9:26; 21:27. Compare the use of "glorify" in Acts 3:13.

24:27 *what was said in all the Scriptures concerning himself.* The inclusion here of "Moses" and in 24:44 also of "the Psalms" points to a comprehensive hermeneutic of fulfillment that finds in Jesus the endpoint not only of selected prophetic oracles but also of the whole pattern of Scripture, including its nonpredictive as well as predictive parts. This is the basis on which the New Testament writers delighted to explore the links between the Old and New Testaments, including typological correspondence as well as prophetic prediction. The whole exciting project began with this groundbreaking "seminar" delivered by Jesus to two obscure disciples on the Emmaus road.

24:28 *Jesus continued on as if he were going further.* The verb *prospoieō* ("act as if") can denote pretense, but here it indicates Jesus's apparent intention. He politely will not presume on their hospitality until invited.

24:30 *he took bread, gave thanks, broke it and began to give it to them.* This was the host's role, but Jesus naturally assumes that position. The verbs used are virtually the same as in 9:16; 22:19. We do not know whether these two disciples had been present at the Last Supper, but no doubt Jesus had followed the same familiar procedure at any other meal where they had been present with him.

24:31 *Their eyes were opened and they recognized him.* Their previous lack of recognition was described as God's initiative ("they were kept from"), and so its release is also described with a passive verb. However, the sequence from 24:30 indicates (as does 24:35) that Jesus's action in breaking the bread triggered their awareness of who he is. For the possibility that this action revealed the scars of the nails in his hands, see also on 24:39.

he disappeared from their sight. Literally, he "became invisible from them." Several postresurrection stories are of a sudden appearance (e.g., 24:36; and cf. the use of the verb "appear to" in 24:34; 1 Cor. 15:5–8); but this is the only one that describes how such an appearance ended. Jesus's resurrection body apparently could relocate and/or become visible/invisible at will.

24:32 *Were not our hearts burning within us?* Their mounting sense of excitement now made sense. It is surprising that Jesus could explain his own scriptural credentials so fully without their guessing his identity; perhaps the idea of his being alive again was too improbable for them to accept, but 24:16 also indicates a divine purpose to postpone recognition until the climactic moment.

24:33–35 *There they found the Eleven and those with them.* A lot has happened in the five hours or so since the two set off for Emmaus. The original scorn of the male disciples at the women's report has given way to dawning belief. The decisive new event has been the appearance to Peter, which must be presumed to be subsequent to his inconclusive visit to the tomb in 24:12. The Gospels have no other record of this individual appearance, but Paul records it as part of the received tradition in 1 Corinthians 15:5. Now the experience of the two disciples at Emmaus further confirms the reality of Jesus's resurrection.

Theological Insights

This postresurrection-appearance account is unique in the Gospels in its length and detail, in its focus on two otherwise unknown disciples (who seem to be given priority over the Eleven), and in its explicit statement that the risen Jesus could simply disappear at will. The blend of this unique feature with the ordinariness of Jesus's physical appearance, which allowed him to be taken as an unremarkable fellow traveler and guest, neatly sums up the paradox of the Gospel accounts of Jesus's resurrection body.

But the theological importance of the story lies also in its assertion (here and in 24:44–48) that it was Jesus himself who inaugurated the early Christian approach to Scripture, which would go on to discover pointers to Jesus across the whole range of the Old Testament, not only in its explicit messianic prophecies, and not only in its prophetic books, but also in "Moses" and "all the Scriptures." In particular, New Testament typology would soon establish many links between aspects of Old Testament history, persons, and institutions and their "fulfillment" in the coming of the Messiah, who came to fulfill not only the prophets but also "the Law and the Prophets" (see Matt. 5:17; 11:13).

Teaching the Text

As noted above, this account of two disciples on the road to Emmaus is Luke's most distinctive contribution to the Gospel resurrection appearances. Particularly important for these disciples (and for the teacher of this passage) is the surprising revelation that Scripture predicted all along that the Messiah must suffer. While these two disciples recognize that Jesus was a great prophet (24:19), his death negated their hopes that he might be the Messiah, "the one who was going to redeem Israel" (24:21). Jesus opens up their eyes to see that the sufferings of the Messiah were foretold in Scripture. His death does not negate his claims to be the Messiah. It rather confirms them.

When teaching this passage, you might ask listeners to put themselves in the position of these two disciples. What knowledge and/or expectations are they likely to have brought to the encounter? What aspects of Scripture and specific passages would Jesus have focused on in his teaching? What was it about this that would cause them to say, "Were not our hearts burning within us?"

In addition to this central theme, here are two others that could be developed in a sermon or lesson:

1. Discuss the nature of Jesus's postresurrection appearances and how this one fits into the overall pattern. Why has Luke devoted so much space to the experience of two otherwise unknown disciples? What was the nature of a body that could both be mistaken for a fellow traveler and take part in a normal meal, and at the same time be capable of sudden disappearance?

2. An additional angle is to discuss the similarity of 24:30 to the accounts of the Last Supper. Is there a eucharistic element to the story? Why was it "in the breaking of bread" (the term used several times in Acts for the Christian fellowship meal) that Jesus was finally recognized? Is it significant that the disciples recognize Jesus not through the proofs of Scripture (24:27) but at a fellowship meal (24:31)?

Illustrating the Text

The "chance" encounter with Christ turns the disciples' depression to excitement and teaches them to expect the resurrection.

Sermon: "Emmaus Epiphany," by Cindy Holtrop.

The future they thought they had solved is turned on its head with this teacher's words.

Here was a Savior who had saved them not from political enemies but from themselves. The guilt they placed on others was the guilt they found hidden in themselves. And the one whose death they mourned cancels their guilt. A whole new future is opening up for them. Their life compass is pointed in a new direction. They want to drink and eat more and more of what this stranger has to say.

Later they say to each other, "Didn't our hearts burn as he talked with us along the road?"

What does it mean to have a "burning heart"? Your intense longing is finally fulfilled. Your eyes see something as if for the first time. The treasure you've been searching for is here. You realized the good news is really for you. The deliverer you were looking for has come and fills the deep cavity you did not know was there. . . .

Our hearts burn when the words of Scripture meet the horizon of our needs; that is, when the Word comes so close it shouts our name. It confronts our despair, shapes our future, and offers us Easter hope.[1]

We, like the two on the Emmaus road, need Christ to remind us of his power in our generation.

Theology: *The Challenge of Jesus*, **by N. T. Wright.** New Testament scholar N. T. Wright re-creates the Emmaus Road scene for the post-modern reader in a riveting and practical way:

Two unbelievers . . . [are] discussing, animatedly, how these things can be. How can the stories by which so many have lived have let us down? . . .

Into this conversation comes Jesus, incognito. . . . "What are you talking about?" he asks. They stand there looking sad. Then one of them says, "You must be about the only person in town who doesn't know what a traumatic time the twentieth century has been. Nietzsche, Freud, and Marx were quite right. We had a war to end wars, and we've had

Jesus appeared to two of his followers on the road to Emmaus. While walking, Jesus explained the Scriptures that spoke about him. He then revealed himself to the two disciples upon breaking the bread at supper. Rembrandt's first interpretation of this scene, in his 1629 painting *Supper at Emmaus*, highlights the astonishment of one of the travelers when he recognizes Jesus. The other disciple's response is to fall down at Jesus's feet.

nothing but more wars since. We had a sexual revolution, and now we have AIDS and . . . ended up with half the world in crippling debt. . . . Our dreams have gone sour, and we don't even know who "we" are anymore. . . .

"Foolish ones," replies Jesus; "How slow of heart you are to believe all that the Creator God has said! Did you never hear that . . . in his own death he dealt with evil once and for all? . . . and that he is even now at work, by his own Spirit to create a new human family in which repentance and forgiveness of sins are the order of the day, and so to challenge and overturn the rule of war, sex, money and power?"[2]

The Commissioning of the Disciples

Big Idea *The risen Jesus meets with his disciples and commissions them as witnesses of his life, death, and resurrection. Then he leaves them and ascends to heaven.*

Understanding the Text

The Text in Context

This passage not only brings Luke's Gospel narrative, and especially its developing resurrection motif, to a triumphant conclusion, but also prepares for the taking up of the story in Luke's second volume, Acts. The summary of the gospel message in 24:46–48, the cryptic promise of "power from on high" in 24:49, Jesus's ascension in 24:51 (more fully narrated in Acts 1:1–11), and the communal life of the believers in Jerusalem in 24:52–53) will be developed in the early chapters of Acts. The story of Jesus is now becoming the story of the Jesus movement.

The most obvious difference between these verses and Acts is the lack here of any indication of the passage of time (forty days [Acts 1:3]) between Jesus's resurrection and ascension. In bringing his Gospel to an appropriately "orderly" (1:3) literary conclusion, Luke apparently feels no need to be pedantic about the chronological data.

In view of the partial parallels to these verses in John 20 and Acts 1, it is not surprising that there are variations among the manuscripts. The following words in the NIV text of Luke 24 are missing from significant early witnesses:

- "and said to them, 'Peace be with you'" (24:36)
- "When he had said this he showed them his hands and feet" (24:40)
- "and was taken up into heaven" (24:51)
- "worshiped him and" (24:52)

Most interpreters nonetheless now accept these as part of Luke's text,[1] but in any case none of them introduce anything that is not supported in the parallel texts.

Historical and Cultural Background

"Ghost" in 24:37, 39 translates *pneuma*, "a spirit." In most cultures there is a popular belief that dead people can reappear in immaterial form and sometimes return after death to the places where they lived. Jewish theology did not support such beliefs and discouraged attempts to contact the dead (Deut. 18:11; 1 Sam. 28), but the disciples' reaction here (which only Luke mentions) probably owes more to popular superstition than to formal theology. Instead, Jesus emphasizes his physicality, both by offering his body to sight and touch and by eating food, thus differentiating his resurrection body from a mere immaterial survival. He is not a temporary visitor from Sheol.

Interpretive Insights

24:36 *Jesus himself stood among them.* Luke does not specify that Jesus appeared despite locked doors (as in John 20:19, 26), but both the abruptness of the verb and the disciples' reaction in 24:37 indicate a sudden "materialization" among them.

Peace be with you. Compare John 20:19, 21, 26. This is the normal Jewish greeting (cf. 10:5), but in this highly charged context it goes beyond social convention. The presence of the risen Jesus brings reassurance, a sense that after the trauma of the last few days all is now well.

24:37 *They were startled and frightened.* Not only was Jesus's appearance sudden and unexpected, but it also raised questions that they had not yet resolved fully. Despite their declared belief in Jesus's resurrection

(24:34), they had not yet come to terms with what it meant. For the belief in ghosts, see "Historical and Cultural Background" above.

24:39 *Look at my hands and my feet.* The focus on hands and feet (rather than face) reflects the manner of Jesus's death. Only John 20:25 specifically mentions the scars left by the nails, but the marks of crucifixion would be unmistakable, so that this invitation to look and to touch confirms not only his physicality but also his identity. (The scars would also have been visible when Jesus broke the bread at Emmaus; was that why they then recognized him?)

24:41 *they still did not believe it because of joy and amazement.* Joy

While Jesus was alive he had been telling his disciples that the Son of Man would "be delivered over to the Gentiles. They will mock him, insult him, and spit on him; they will flog him and kill him. On the third day he will rise again" (18:32–33). This intricate ivory book binding plate from the ninth century AD tells the story of Jesus's passion, resurrection, and ascension.

seems an incongruous reason for disbelief ("too good to be true"?), but all the postresurrection accounts testify to a heady mix of shock, fear, astonishment, joy, and incredulity that is easier to empathize with than to analyze psychologically.

24:42 *a piece of broiled fish . . . he took it and ate it in their presence.* The point is not necessarily that the risen Jesus needed physical sustenance (though Luke will again mention his eating with the disciples in Acts 1:4; 10:41; see also John 21:10–15), but that only a physical body could consume solid food.

24:44 *Everything must be fulfilled that is written about me.* In 18:31–33 Jesus explained his coming arrest, suffering, death, and resurrection as fulfilling "everything that is written by the prophets about the Son of Man." Now, after the event, the lesson is repeated but in a fuller exposition of Scripture that will also take in the future development of the mission (24:47). Presumably, he goes over again some of the overarching biblical theology that two of the disciples have already heard on the Emmaus road (24:25–27).

the Law of Moses, the Prophets and the Psalms. The Hebrew canon consists of three parts: the Law (Genesis, Exodus, Leviticus, Numbers, Deuteronomy), the Prophets (what we think of as the prophetic books plus the Former Prophets, which are Joshua, Judges, Samuel, Kings), and the Writings, of which Psalms is the first and most prominent constituent. This inclusive listing makes it clear that Jesus's postresurrection teaching found its basis not just in the predictive utterances of the prophets but in the whole gamut of Scripture. See

further on 24:25–27 and "Theological Insights" on 24:13–35.

24:45 *he opened their minds so they could understand the Scriptures.* Early Christian biblical interpretation was distinctive among Jewish hermeneutical approaches, and this consistently christocentric reading is most plausibly traced to Jesus's teaching on this occasion and during the forty days during which he "spoke about the kingdom of God" (Acts 1:3).

24:46–47 *This is what is written.* The teaching begins with the now familiar theme of the scriptural basis of the Easter events (cf. 18:31–33), but then it expands to include the essential gospel message and the mission of the church, which Luke will relate in Acts.

24:47 *repentance for the forgiveness of sins will be preached in his name.* For a similar summary of the gospel message, see Acts 2:38; 3:19; 5:31. Although the word "faith," often linked with "repentance," is not used here, "in his name" makes it clear that it is through a relationship with the risen Jesus that this forgiveness can be achieved.

to all nations, beginning at Jerusalem. The same commission will be repeated in Acts 1:8, and it summarizes the geographical spread of the gospel that Luke will record in Acts. Both halves of the expression are important for Luke's theology: the gospel is universal, and since 2:32 Luke has signaled the inclusion of the Gentiles in God's saving purpose, in fulfillment of Isaiah 49:6; but at the same time Jesus is the Messiah of Israel, and Jerusalem, where the apostles will remain based, will be the headquarters and reference point of the new movement throughout Acts.

24:48 *You are witnesses of these things.* Acts 1:21–22 will underline the importance of eyewitness testimony for the apostles. This commission, however, is apparently wider, addressed to the whole group of disciples. In the early chapters of Acts the focus will be on the apostles, but there will be frequent references to a wider group of disciples involved in the church's mission.

24:49 *I am going to send you what my Father has promised.* If Luke's Gospel is read alone, this statement is strangely cryptic, since Luke has recorded no such promise so far. It is only when we read on to Acts 1:8 and the fulfillment of the promise in Acts 2:1–4 that it becomes clear that the "power from on high" refers to the Holy Spirit, bestowed by the ascended Jesus (Acts 2:33).

24:50 *the vicinity of Bethany.* Acts 1:12 locates the event more broadly on "the Mount of Olives," on the eastern slope of which Bethany is located.

he lifted up his hands and blessed them. Compare the priestly blessing in Leviticus 9:22. This is the only time Jesus is recorded as pronouncing a formal blessing on anyone (cf. Simeon's blessing on Jesus's parents in 2:34); in this setting it is to be understood as a farewell gesture.

24:51 *he left them and was taken up into heaven.* This is a bald summary of what Luke will describe more fully in Acts 1:9–11 (and has already anticipated in 9:51). The visible relocation of Jesus's body makes it clear to the disciples that this is the end of his physical presence on earth. There is a partial parallel in Elijah's departure in 2 Kings 2:10–12, leaving Elisha to continue his ministry, though nothing there corresponds to the death-resurrection-ascension sequence here.

24:53 *they stayed continually at the temple, praising God.* Acts 1:13 will speak of a "room where they were staying," but the reference here is presumably to their daytime location, in the temple courtyard where Jesus had so recently taught. It is there that Luke will locate the life, worship, and public proclamation of the apostles during the early chapters of Acts (Acts 2:46; 3:1, 8; 4:1; 5:20–25, 42). So the story that began in Luke's Gospel with worship in the temple (1:8–25) now concludes in the same place, pointing forward to its dramatic sequel.

Theological Insights

Luke is unusual among the Gospels in the emphasis that he places on the physicality of Jesus's resurrection body and on the proofs whereby Jesus assured his disciples that he was not a ghost. Luke is also the only one of the Gospel

Jesus took his disciples to the Mount of Olives (Acts 1:12) near Bethany where he blessed them and then ascended to heaven. The Chapel of the Ascension, shown here, though part of a mosque complex under Muslim control, has been preserved as a place to commemorate the ascension of Jesus on the Mount of Olives. Its structure is a combination of the remains of several churches that were built and destroyed over the centuries to mark this as a sacred site and renovations made when it was later converted into a mosque.

writers who records the ascension of Jesus's risen body to heaven. It is important for Christian apologetics to be able to establish that what the disciples experienced was not a psychic manifestation but rather a solid, physical presence, and that, after the short post-Easter period, Jesus ascended bodily into heaven. He had told the two disciples on the road to Emmaus that he would "enter his glory" (24:26), and that has now happened; he is "exalted to the right hand of God" (Acts 2:33). It is appropriate, therefore, that here (for the only time) Luke speaks of the disciples worshiping Jesus (24:52).

This passage adds to what we observed in 24:25–27 concerning the scriptural basis of the gospel. In particular, the inclusion of Psalms alongside the Law and the Prophets further demonstrates the holistic approach to the "fulfillment" of the Old Testament that Jesus inaugurated and that the New Testament so fruitfully develops (note especially the importance of the psalms in the typological exegesis practiced in the book of Hebrews).

Teaching the Text

As noted above, this passage represents not only the conclusion to Luke's Gospel but also a transition to Acts, Luke's second volume. The preacher or teacher will want to highlight both. On the one hand, proofs of the resurrection continue as Jesus appears to his disciples, shows them his hands and his feet, and eats in front of them (24:36–43). These are not merely visions, but the real appearance of a flesh-and-bones resurrected Messiah in his glorified body. Jesus also reiterates

the theme that appeared in the account of the Emmaus disciples, that Scripture all along predicted that the Messiah would suffer (24:44–47). All of this proves that everything said about Jesus in the Gospel is true. While these events represent a fitting conclusion to Luke's Gospel, they also introduce key themes of Acts. Jesus predicts the worldwide proclamation of the gospel, identifies his disciples as his witnesses for this mission, promises to pour out the Holy Spirit as empowerment for this task, and then ascends to heaven, from where he will direct this mission (24:47–53). All of these set the stage for Acts and the missionary expansion of the gospel. The story that began in Jesus's ministry continued in the expansion of the early church in Acts. And it endures today as we continue to pursue the mission to take the gospel to the ends of the earth. Be sure in your teaching to stress this continuity: the Gospel of Luke and the book of Acts are the beginning of *our story*, which continues through our bold witness to a lost world.

Here are some other themes that could be developed in a lesson or sermon on this passage:

1. The nature of Jesus's resurrection body (physical but unique, capable of being taken into heaven) and of the disciples' post-Easter experiences (down-to-earth rather than psychic).
2. The ascension of Jesus: an embarrassing extra (why do the other evangelists not narrate it [though there is a hint in John 20:17]?) or a necessary conclusion to Jesus's life on earth? What would be missing from our theology if we had no account of the ascension?

How does modern understanding of the cosmos (is heaven "up"?) affect our reading of the story?

3. Does 24:46–47 give an appropriate summary of the gospel? What else might we have wanted to add? Is it correct to see all this as derived from Scripture (24:44–45)? Discuss what passages from the Old Testament Jesus might have focused on in developing each of these themes.

Illustrating the Text

The resurrection body is substantial and recognizably human, yet redesigned and fit for eternity in a way we cannot fully comprehend.

Visual: Bring in two identical items, one made from iron or mild steel, and the other made from stainless steel. These could be two boat anchors, two tools, and so on. You could also use two pictures, one of an old, corroded item, and the other of a stainless replacement. Explain that the mild-steel version is prone to decay and rot from oxidation. No matter how effectively it performs its assigned task, it will eventually be ruined and discarded. One can't replace it with a plastic copy, a photograph, or a hologram—those things might not rust, but they wouldn't perform the same tasks as steel. The stainless steel item, however, has the same substantial weight and strength of its mild-steel counterpart, but without the tendency to decay—it is

made to endure. In this way, the resurrected body has many of the same characteristics of the earthly body—it can worship, eat, be recognizable, be touched, and so on. Yet, unlike the earthly body, it is not prone to death and decay; it is fit for eternity!

Jesus invites us to understand and interpret his ministry through the lens of the Scriptures, which he came to fulfill.

History: The Rosetta Stone is one of the most significant archaeological finds of modern times. It is a remnant of an Egyptian stone sign constructed in 196 BC that bore a decree on behalf of King Ptolemy V. In order to facilitate communication in his diverse kingdom, the king ordered the decree written in three different scripts: Ancient Egyptian hieroglyphs, demotic script, and ancient Greek. The reason this stone is so important is that it gave archaeologists something they never had before: a decoder that allowed them to connect languages that were still known with ones that were lost. Specifically, it allowed them to connect the dots between ancient Greek (a known language) and ancient Egyptian hieroglyphs (a lost language). The stone's contribution was so significant that its name has become synonymous with any essential clue to understand a new field of knowledge. In a sense, Jesus's ministry and work are the Rosetta Stone of the Old Testament Law and Prophets. When you understand the person and work of Jesus, you have the key to unlocking the direction and intention of the Scriptures.

Notes

Introduction to Luke

1. Luke's historical reliability is usefully discussed in Marshall, *Luke: Historian and Theologian*, 69–76.

2. For an important study of the centrality of eyewitness testimony to early Christian accounts of Jesus, see Bauckham, *Jesus and the Eyewitnesses*.

3. This is the thesis of Marshall, *Luke: Historian and Theologian*, set out in chapter 4 and developed in chapters 5–8.

Luke 1:5–25

1. Frederick Buechner, *Telling the Truth: The Gospel as Tragedy, Comedy, and Fairy Tale* (San Francisco: Harper & Row, 1977), 81, 90.

2. Malcolm Muggeridge, *Christ in the Media* (Grand Rapids: Eerdmans, 1977), 41–42.

3. http://www.poemhunter.com/poem/zacharias-in -advent.

Luke 1:26–38

1. Ilan, "Jewish Women's Names."

2. France, *Gospel of Matthew*, 34n27.

3. *Martin Luther's Christmas Book*, ed. Roland Bainton (Minneapolis: Augsburg, 1997), 13.

Luke 1:39–56

1. A few Latin manuscripts and patristic citations attest to a tradition in some parts of the early church that the Magnificat was the song not of Mary but of Elizabeth, and some modern scholars have defended that reading (see Brown, *Birth of the Messiah* [1977], 334–36). The majority remain convinced that Luke attributed it to Mary, and my exposition assumes that majority view.

2. For a list of links between the Magnificat and its immediate literary context, see Green, *Gospel of Luke*, 98.

3. The parallels are helpfully set out in Brown, *Birth of the Messiah* (1977), 358–60.

4. Gooding (*According to Luke*, 42–45) expounds the Magnificat single-mindedly from this contextual point of view, exploring Mary's own perspective.

Luke 1:57–80

1. The Old Testament echoes are well set out in Brown, *Birth of the Messiah* (1977), 386–89.

2. http://www.biblestudytools.com/bible-study/new -testament/advent-zacharias'-prophetic-song-luke-1-67 -79-11596979.html?p=2.

3. Alan Paton, *Cry, the Beloved Country* (New York: Scribner, 1948), 27.

Luke 2:1–20

1. For a survey of the evidence and the debate about Luke's accuracy, see Brown, *Birth of the Messiah* (1993), 547–56, 666–68; for a cautiously conservative assessment see Marshall, *Gospel of Luke*, 99–104.

2. For a wealth of cultural background supporting this view, see Bailey, *Jesus through Middle Eastern Eyes*, 25–37.

Luke 2:21–40

1. See Aune, *Prophecy in Early Christianity*, 103–52.

2. http://www.christianitytoday.com/ct/2011/julyweb -only/johnstottroundup.html.

3. Billy Graham, *Nearing Home: Life, Faith, and Finishing Well* (Nashville: Thomas Nelson, 2011), ix.

Luke 2:41–52

1. Text in Elliott, *Apocryphal New Testament*, 75–83.

Luke 3:1–20

1. T. S. Eliot, *Murder in the Cathedral*, in *The Complete Poems and Plays, 1909–1950* (New York: Harcourt, Brace & World, 1971), 187.
2. George MacDonald, *Donal Grant* (Philadelphia: David McKay, n.d.), 243–44.

Luke 3:21–38

1. See Brown, *Birth of the Messiah* (1977), 86–88.
2. See France, *Gospel of Matthew*, 32–33.
3. Cited in Alexander, *Zondervan Bible Handbook*, 550.
4. Green, *Gospel of Luke*, 189; emphasis added.

Luke 4:1–13

1. Malcom Muggeridge, *Christ and the Media* (Grand Rapids: Eerdmans, 1977), 41.

Luke 4:14–30

1. Bailey (*Jesus through Middle Eastern Eyes*, 152) argues that Nazareth was a recently founded Jewish settlement intended to reclaim territory in what had become "Galilee of the Gentiles." His study of this passage (pp. 147–69) suggests that it be understood in the light of the ideology and attitudes of Jewish settlers in the West Bank today.
2. http://www.spurgeon.org/~phil/history/95theses.htm.
3. Philip Yancey, *Soul Survivor: How My Faith Survived the Church* (New York: Doubleday, 2001), 150.
4. Leighton Ford, *The Attentive Life* (Downers Grove, IL: InterVarsity, 2008), 131–32.
5. John Killinger, "When We Stop Being Free," *Pulpit Digest* (July/August 1992), 12–13.
6. Tom Hovestol, *Extreme Righteousness: Seeing Ourselves in the Pharisees* (Chicago: Moody, 1997), 57; emphasis in original.

Luke 4:31–44

1. For an exploration of this issue, see Gathercole, *The Preexistent Son*.
2. Cited in Calvin Miller, ed., *The Book of Jesus: A Treasury of the Greatest Stories and Writings about Christ* (New York: Simon & Schuster, 1998), 235.
3. Jim Cymbala, *Fresh Wind, Fresh Fire: What Happens When God's Spirit Invades the Heart of His People* (Grand Rapids: Zondervan, 1997), 109–11.
4. Lyle W. Dorsett, *A Passion for Souls: The Life of D. L. Moody* (Chicago: Moody, 1997), 22–23.

Luke 5:1–11

1. For example, Robinson, *Priority of John*, 119–22.
2. Ruth A. Tucker, *From Jerusalem to Irian Jaya: A Biographical History of Christian Missions* (Grand Rapids: Zondervan, 1983), 261–62.
3. Rebecca Manley Pippert, *Out of the Salt Shaker and Into the World* (Downers Grove, IL: InterVarsity, 1999), 16–17.

Luke 5:12–26

1. Paul Brand and Philip Yancey, *Pain: The Gift Nobody Wants* (New York: HarperCollins, 1993), 9–11.
2. Carolyn Custis-James, *The Gospel of Ruth: Loving God Enough to Break the Rules* (Grand Rapids: Zondervan, 2008), 120.

Luke 5:27–39

1. See Blomberg, *Contagious Holiness*.
2. Green (*Gospel of Luke*, 249–50) makes the unusual suggestion that the "old" throughout 5:36–39 represents the ministry of Jesus in its continuity with the Old Testament, while the "new" represents Pharisaic innovation.
3. Tom Hovestol, *Extreme Righteousness: Seeing Ourselves in the Pharisees* (Chicago: Moody, 1997), 34.

Luke 6:1–16

1. See Carson, *From Sabbath to Lord's Day*.
2. http://en.wikisource.org/wiki/The_War_Prayer.
3. Tom Hovestol, *Extreme Righteousness: Seeing Ourselves in the Pharisees* (Chicago: Moody, 1997), 112.

Luke 6:17–26

1. Cited in Marvin J. Newell, *A Martyr's Grace: Stories of Those Who Gave All for Christ and His Cause* (Chicago: Moody, 2006), 137–42.

Luke 6:27–38

1. Theissen, *Shadow of the Galilean*, chapter 10.
2. Fyodor Dostoevsky, *Crime and Punishment*, ed. George Gibian (New York: W. W. Norton, 1964), 526.
3. Philip Yancey, *Soul Survivor: How My Faith Survived the Church* (New York: Doubleday, 2001), 139.

Luke 6:39–49

1. Bailey, *Jesus through Middle Eastern Eyes*, 322–24.
2. Bailey, *Jesus through Middle Eastern Eyes*, 324.
3. *The Quotable Chesterton*, ed. George J. Marlin, Richard P. Rabatin, and John L. Swan (San Francisco: Ignatius Press, 1986), 79.

Luke 7:1–17

1. It is disputed whether the healing of the son of a "royal official" in Capernaum in John 4:46–54 is a variant version of this story. If it records a separate incident, such an official in the service of the Hellenistic but part-Jewish Antipas might have been either Jew or Gentile.
2. Randy Alcorn, *In Light of Eternity: Perspectives on Heaven* (Colorado Springs: WaterBrook, 1999), 103–7.
3. William Barclay, *The Gospel of Luke*, rev. ed., Daily Study Bible (Philadelphia: Westminster, 1975), 85–86.
4. Charles Haddon Spurgeon, *Choice Sermon Notes* (Grand Rapids: Zondervan, 1952), 63.

Luke 7:18–35

1. William Barclay, *The Gospel of Luke*, rev. ed., Daily Study Bible (Philadelphia: Westminster, 1975), 89.

2. *The Simone Weil Reader*, ed. George A. Panichas (New York: Moyer Bell, 1977), 442.

3. Os Guinness, *Prophetic Untimeliness* (Grand Rapids: Baker Books, 2003), 84–86.

Luke 7:36–8:3

1. Green, *Gospel of Luke*, 307.

2. See Bailey, *Jesus through Middle Eastern Eyes*, 248–50. Bailey (pp. 239–60) gives much additional cultural background to this story.

3. For one useful and brief presentation, see Alexander, *Zondervan Bible Handbook*, 640–41.

4. Alice Walker, "The Welcome Table," in *Listening for God: Contemporary Literature and the Life of Faith*, ed. Paula J. Carson and Peter S. Hawkins (Minneapolis: Augsburg Fortress, 1994), 112–13.

5. http://sheissafe.org.

Luke 8:4–21

1. http://www.sharefaith.com/guide/Christian-Music /hymns-the-songs-and-the-stories/trust-and-obey-the-song -and-the-story.html.

Luke 8:22–39

1. Charles Colson, *Loving God* (Grand Rapids, Zondervan, 1983), 172.

2. Mark I. Bubeck, *The Rise of Fallen Angels: Victory of the Adversary through Spiritual Renewal* (Chicago: Moody, 1995), 62.

3. Tracy Groot, *Madman* (Chicago: Moody, 2006), chapter 19.

Luke 9:1–17

1. C. S. Lewis, *The Lion, the Witch and the Wardrobe* (New York: HarperCollins, 1978), 90–93.

2. Warren Wiersbe, *The Bible Exposition Commentary* (Wheaton: Victor Books, 1989), 1:205–6.

Luke 9:18–36

1. C. S. Lewis, *Till We Have Faces: A Myth Retold* (Grand Rapids: Eerdmans, 1972), 267, 308.

2. William Shakespeare, *King Henry V*, in *The Complete Works of Shakespeare* (New York: Scott, Foresman and Co., 1961), act 4, scene 3, lines 40–67.

Luke 9:37–56

1. Some ancient exorcists used a long list of supposedly authoritative names to gain power over demons. See Barrett, *New Testament Background*, 34–36.

2. Freeman Patterson, *Photography and the Art of Seeing* (Philadelphia: Chilton Books, 1965), 9.

3. Flannery O'Connor, *The Complete Stories* (New York: Farrar, Strauss & Giroux, 1975), 508.

4. Philip Yancey, *The Jesus I Never Knew* (Grand Rapids: Zondervan, 1995), 89.

Luke 9:57–10:12

1. For illuminating cultural comment, see Bailey, *Through Peasant Eyes*, 26–27.

2. But perhaps "say goodbye" involved also asking permission to leave, which might not be granted; in that case, Jesus is setting his demand against the family's expectation. See Bailey, *Through Peasant Eyes*, 27–29.

3. Ruth A. Tucker, *From Jerusalem to Irian Jaya: A Biographical History of Christian Missions* (Grand Rapids: Zondervan, 1983), 289–90.

Luke 10:13–24

1. Alexander Maclaren, *Expositions of Holy Scripture: Luke I to XII* (Grand Rapids: Baker, 1974), 314–15.

2. C. S. Lewis, ed., *George MacDonald: An Anthology; 365 Readings* (San Francisco: HarperSanFrancisco, 2001), xxxvii.

3. Lewis, *George MacDonald*, xxiii.

4. Lewis, *George MacDonald*, xxiii.

Luke 10:25–37

1. Blomberg, *Preaching the Parables*, 58–60.

Luke 10:38–11:13

1. These are listed in Evans, *Saint Luke*, 478.

2. This reading is explained and defended by Gordon Fee in Epp and Fee, *New Testament Textual Criticism*, 61–75.

Luke 11:14–36

1. For this interpretation, see Beasley-Murray, *Jesus and the Kingdom*, 252–57.

2. For an attempt to untangle some of the threads, see France, *Gospel of Matthew*, 260–62.

3. Ruth A. Tucker, *From Jerusalem to Irian Jaya: A Biographical History of Christian Missions* (Grand Rapids: Zondervan, 1983), 237–38.

4. Dick Keyes, *Chameleon Christianity: Moving Beyond Safety and Conformity* (Grand Rapids: Baker Books, 1999), 27.

5. C. S. Lewis, *The World's Last Night: And Other Essays* (Boston: Houghton Mifflin Harcourt, 2002), 9.

Luke 11:37–54

1. John Bunyan, *Pilgrim's Progress*, annotated by Warren W. Wiersbe (Chicago: Moody, 1981), 56.

2. Lundin, *Emily Dickinson*, 38–41.

Luke 12:1–21

1. Roland Bainton, *Here I Stand: A Life of Martin Luther* (Nashville: New American Library, 1950), 134.

2. Arthur Quiller-Couch, ed., *The Oxford Book of English Verse: 1250–1918* (New York: Oxford University Press, 1955), 302.

Luke 12:22–40

1. John Stott, *The Birds Our Teachers: Biblical Lessons from a Lifelong Birdwatcher* (Grand Rapids: Baker Books, 2001), 10.
2. Oswald Chambers, *My Utmost for His Highest* (Westwood, NJ: Barbour, 1963), 89; emphasis in original.

Luke 12:41–59

1. So Gathercole, *The Preexistent Son*, part 2.
2. Elijah P. Brown, *The Real Billy Sunday* (New York: Fleming H. Revell, 1914), 113.
3. David A. Rausch, *A Legacy of Hatred* (Chicago: Moody, 1984), 153.

Luke 13:1–17

1. Walter Lord, *A Night to Remember*, with an introduction by Nathaniel Philbrick (New York: Henry Holt, 2005), 135.
2. Unpublished commentary by Linda Haines, March 25, 2012. Used by permission.
3. Annie Dillard, *Teaching a Stone to Talk* (New York: Harper & Row, 1982), 40–41.

Luke 13:18–35

1. "Desolate" (*erēmos*) is not in the best Greek manuscripts of Luke, and it probably represents scribal assimilation to the text of Matthew 23:38. However, it does appropriately spell out the implication of the house being "left," abandoned.
2. John Bunyan, *The Pilgrim's Progress*, ed. W. R. Owens (New York: Oxford University Press, 2009), 23–24.
3. In Lorraine Eitel et al., comp., *The Treasury of Christian Poetry* (Old Tappan, NJ: Fleming H. Revell, 1982), 86.

Luke 14:1–14

1. For a comprehensive study, see Blomberg, *Contagious Holiness*.
2. Jon Hassler, *Good People: From an Author's Life* (Chicago: Loyola Press, 2001), 42–45.
3. Tom Hovestol, *Extreme Righteousness: Seeing Ourselves in the Pharisees* (Chicago: Moody, 1997), 86–87.

Luke 14:15–35

1. Blomberg, *Preaching the Parables*, 184–87.
2. Timothy Keller, *The Prodigal God: Recovering the Heart of the Christian Faith* (New York: Dutton, 2008), 124.

Luke 15:1–32

1. See Bailey, *Poet and Peasant*, 142–206.
2. Bailey, *Poet and Peasant*, 170–73.
3. http://www.christianitytoday.com/iyf/hottopics/faithvalues/6.42.html?start=3.
4. Philip Yancey, *What's So Amazing about Grace?* (Grand Rapids: Zondervan, 1997), 52.
5. Timothy Keller, *The Prodigal God: Recovering the Heart of the Christian Faith* (New York: Dutton, 2008), 83–84, 82.
6. Keller, *The Prodigal God*, 84–85.

Luke 16:1–18

1. Bailey, *Jesus through Middle Eastern Eyes*, 332–42.
2. Derrett, *Law in the New Testament*, 48–77.
3. John Milton, *Paradise Lost* (New York: Penguin, 2003), 20.
4. Jacques Ellul, *Money and Power*, trans. LaVonne Neff (Downers Grove, IL: InterVarsity, 1984), 76–77.

Luke 16:19–31

1. For the text, see Boring, Berger, and Colpe, *Hellenistic Commentary*, 227–28.
2. http://en.wikipedia.org/wiki/Martin_of_Tours.
3. C. S. Lewis, *Mere Christianity* (New York: Macmillan, 1960), 66.
4. Dante Alighieri, *The Divine Comedy*, trans. Louis Biancolli, vol. 1, *Hell* (New York: Washington Square Press, 1966), canto 3, lines 4–9.

Luke 17:1–19

1. Joseph Bernardin, *The Gift of Peace: Personal Reflections* (Chicago: Loyola, 1997), 34–41.
2. Lewis B. Smedes, "God and a Grateful Old Man," in *The Best Christian Writing 2004*, ed. John Wilson (San Francisco: Wiley, 2004), 147.

Luke 17:20–37

1. C. S. Lewis, *The Weight of Glory and Other Addresses* (New York: Macmillan, 1980), 7–8.

Luke 18:1–14

1. *The Confessions of St. Augustine*, trans. John K. Ryan (New York: Doubleday, 1960), 90–91.
2. Quoted in Dorothy M. Stewart, comp., *The Westminster Collection of Christian Prayers: Over 1,500 Prayers Arranged by Theme* (Louisville: Westminster John Knox, 2002), 359.
3. Flannery O'Connor, "Revelation," in *Everything That Rises Must Converge* (New York: Farrar, Straus & Giroux, 1965), 195.

Luke 18:15–34

1. Garland, *Mark*, 385.
2. Joseph Bernardin, *The Gift of Peace: Personal Reflections* (Chicago: Loyola, 1997), 10.
3. Available to view online at http://topdocumentaryfilms.com/born-rich/.

Luke 18:35–19:10

1. Marshall, *Luke: Historian and Theologian*.
2. Following Bailey, *Jesus through Middle Eastern Eyes*, 170–85.
3. Charles M. Sheldon, *In His Steps: What Would Jesus Do?* (New York: Grosset & Dunlap, 1935), chapter 1.

Luke 19:11–27

1. T. S. Eliot, introduction to *Pascal's Penseés*, by Blaise Pascal (New York: E. P. Dutton, 1958), xii.

2. Pascal, *Pascal's Penseés*, no. 549, p. 147.

3. In Lorraine Eitel et al., comp., *The Treasury of Christian Poetry* (Old Tappan, NJ: Fleming H. Revell, 1982), 134.

Luke 19:28–48

1. William Barclay, *The Gospel of Luke*, rev. ed., Daily Study Bible (Philadelphia: Westminster, 1975), 239.

2. In Benjamin B. Warfield, *The Person and Work of Christ* (Philadelphia: Presbyterian & Reformed, 1950), 120–21.

Luke 20:1–19

1. Bailey, *Jesus through Middle Eastern Eyes*, 418.

Luke 20:20–40

1. http://abacus.bates.edu/admin/offices/dos/mlk/letter.html.

2. Cited in Randy Alcorn, *In Light of Eternity: Perspectives on Heaven* (Colorado Springs: WaterBrook, 1999), 6.

Luke 20:41–21:6

1. Donald McCullough, *The Trivialization of God: The Dangerous Illusion of a Manageable Deity* (Colorado Springs: NavPress, 1995), 46.

2. Charlotte Brontë, *Jane Eyre* (London: Service & Paton, 1897), http://www.gutenberg.org/files/1260/1260-h/1260-h.htm.

Luke 21:7–36

1. I have not published an extended study of this discourse in Luke, but see my longer commentaries on the parallel discourses in Mark 13 and Matthew 24, where many of the same exegetical considerations apply (France, *Gospel of Mark*; idem, *Gospel of Matthew*). See also France, *Divine Government*, 64–84.

2. William Byron Forbush, ed., *Fox's Book of Martyrs* (Philadelphia: The John C. Winston Co., 1926), 331–32.

3. C. S. Lewis, *The Lion, the Witch and the Wardrobe* (New York: HarperCollins, 1978), 144–45.

4. In *The D. L. Moody Collection: The Highlights of His Writings, Sermons, Anecdotes, and Life Story*, ed. and comp. James S. Bell Jr. (Chicago: Moody, 1997), 330.

5. C. S. Lewis, *Mere Christianity* (New York: Macmillan, 1960), 120.

6. Josephus, *The Wars of the Jews*, trans. William Whitson, 6.5.3, http://www.biblestudytools.com/history/flavius-josephus/war-of-the-jews/book-6/chapter-5.html.

Luke 21:37–22:16

1. This is clearly the chronology presupposed in the Fourth Gospel (John 13:1; 18:28; 19:14), and I have argued that it also best fits the wording of the Synoptic accounts. See France, *Gospel of Mark*, 559–62; idem, *Gospel of Matthew*, 981–85; more fully, idem, "Chronological Aspects," 43–54.

Luke 22:17–34

1. For a useful discussion of how far the mishnaic pattern may be assumed to have existed already at the time of Jesus, see Routledge, "Passover and Last Supper."

2. Green, *Gospel of Luke*, 766.

3. http://www.hymnal.net/hymn.php/h/1106.

4. Charles Colson, *Loving God* (Grand Rapids: Zondervan, 1983), 170–71.

5. Alexander Solzhenitsyn, "Matryona's House," in *"We Never Make Mistakes": Two Short Novels*, trans. Paul W. Blackstock (New York: W. W. Norton, 1971), 137–38.

Luke 22:35–53

1. The UBS *Greek New Testament* gives an A rating (very high probability) to the view that 22:43–44 were not part of the original Gospel. Brown (*Death of the Messiah*, 1:180–86), however, is cautiously favorable to their having been written by Luke.

Luke 22:54–71

1. C. S. Lewis, *The Lion, the Witch and the Wardrobe* (New York: HarperCollins, 1978), 156.

2. Harper Lee, *To Kill a Mockingbird*, fiftieth anniversary ed. (1960; New York: HarperCollins, 2010), 339–40.

Luke 23:1–25

1. "A form of plea-bargaining" (Brown, *Death of the Messiah*, 1:793).

Luke 23:26–49

1. For some suggested reasons, and an unusually positive verdict on the likely authenticity of the saying, see Brown, *Death of the Messiah*, 2:975–81.

2. Alan Jones, *A Passion for Pilgrimage* (San Francisco: Harper & Row, 1988), 137.

Luke 23:50–24:12

1. See, for example, Wright, *The Resurrection of the Son of God*; Licona, *Resurrection of Jesus*; and Strobel, *Case for the Resurrection*.

2. These points are taken from Mark L. Strauss, *Four Portraits, One Jesus* (Grand Rapids: Zondervan, 2007), 518–21.

3. Virginia Stem Owens, *Looking to Jesus* (Louisville: Westminster John Knox, 1998), 242.

4. C. S. Lewis, *The Silver Chair* (New York: Collier, 1953), 21.

5. Dorothy Sayers, *Are Women Human? Penetrating, Sensible, and Witty Essays on the Role of Women in Society* (Grand Rapids: Eerdmans, 1971), 47.

Luke 24:13–35

1. Cindy Holtrop, "Emmaus Epiphany," *Christianity and the Arts* 8, no. 1 (Winter 2001): 16–17.

2. N. T. Wright, *The Challenge of Jesus: Rediscovering Who Jesus Was and Is* (Downers Grove, IL: InterVarsity, 1999), 172.

Luke 24:36–53

1. All were omitted from the RSV but are restored in the NRSV.

Bibliography

Recommended Resources

Bailey, Kenneth E. *Poet and Peasant and Through Peasant Eyes: A Literary-Cultural Approach to the Parables of Luke.* Combined edition. Grand Rapids: Eerdmans, 1983.

Bock, Darrell L. *Luke.* Baker Exegetical Commentary on the New Testament. 2 vols. Grand Rapids: Baker, 1994–96.

Boring, M. Eugene, Klaus Berger, and Carsten Colpe, eds. *Hellenistic Commentary to the New Testament.* Nashville: Abingdon, 1995.

Brown, Raymond E. *The Birth of the Messiah: A Commentary on the Infancy Narratives in Matthew and Luke.* Rev. ed. Anchor Bible Reference Library. New York: Doubleday, 1993.

Fitzmyer, Joseph A. *The Gospel according to Luke: A New Translation with Introduction and Commentary.* Anchor Bible 28, 28A. New York: Doubleday, 1981–85.

Green, Joel B. *The Gospel of Luke.* New International Commentary on the New Testament. Grand Rapids: Eerdmans, 1997.

Malina, Bruce J., and Richard L. Rohrbaugh. *Social-Science Commentary on the Synoptic Gospels.* Minneapolis: Fortress, 1992.

Marshall, I. Howard. *The Gospel of Luke: A Commentary on the Greek Text.* New International Greek Testament Commentary. Grand Rapids: Eerdmans, 1978.

Nolland, John L. *Luke.* Word Biblical Commentary 35. 3 vols. Dallas: Word, 1989–93.

Select Bibliography

Alexander, David and Pat, eds. *Zondervan Bible Handbook.* 3rd ed. Grand Rapids: Zondervan, 1999.

Aune, David E. *Prophecy in Early Christianity and the Ancient Mediterranean World.* Grand Rapids: Eerdmans, 1983.

Bailey, Kenneth E. *Jesus through Middle Eastern Eyes: Cultural Studies in the Gospels.* Downers Grove, IL: IVP Academic, 2008.

Barrett, C. K. *The New Testament Background: Selected Documents.* London: SPCK, 1987.

Bauckham, Richard. *Jesus and the Eyewitnesses: The Gospels as Eyewitness Testimony.* Grand Rapids: Eerdmans, 2006.

Beasley-Murray, George R. *Jesus and the Kingdom of God.* Grand Rapids: Eerdmans, 1986.

Blomberg, Craig L. *Contagious Holiness: Jesus' Meals with Sinners.* Downers Grove, IL: InterVarsity, 2005.

———. *Preaching the Parables: From Responsible Interpretation to Powerful Proclamation.* Grand Rapids: Baker Academic, 2004.

Brown, Raymond E. *The Birth of the Messiah: A Commentary on the Infancy Narratives in Matthew and Luke.* Garden City, NY: Doubleday, 1977.

———. *The Death of the Messiah: From Gethsemane to the Grave: A Commentary on the Passion Narratives in the Four Gospels.* 2 vols. Anchor Bible Reference Library. New York: Doubleday, 1994.

Carson, D. A. *From Sabbath to Lord's Day: A Biblical, Historical, and Theological Investigation.* Eugene, OR: Wipf & Stock, 2000. First published in 1982 by Zondervan.

Derrett, J. D. M. *Law in the New Testament.* London: Darton, Longman & Todd, 1970.

Elliott, J. K. *The Apocryphal New Testament: A Collection of Apocryphal Christian Literature in English Translation.* Oxford: Oxford University Press, 1993.

Epp, Eldon Jay, and Gordon D. Fee, eds. *New Testament Textual Criticism: Its Significance for Exegesis.* Oxford: Clarendon, 1981.

Evans, Christopher. *Saint Luke.* TPI New Testament Commentaries. Philadelphia: Trinity Press International, 1990.

France, R. T. "Chronological Aspects of 'Gospel Harmony.'" *Vox evangelica* 16 (1986): 33–60.

———. *Divine Government: God's Kingship in the Gospel of Mark.* London: SPCK, 1990.

———. *The Gospel of Mark: A Commentary on the Greek Text.* New International Greek Testament Commentary. Grand Rapids: Eerdmans, 2002.

———. *The Gospel of Matthew.* New International Commentary on the New Testament. Grand Rapids: Eerdmans, 2007.

Garland, David. *Mark.* NIV Application Commentary. Grand Rapids: Zondervan, 1996.

Gathercole, Simon J. *The Preexistent Son: Recovering the Christologies of Matthew, Mark, and Luke.* Grand Rapids: Eerdmans, 2006.

Gooding, D. W. *According to Luke: A New Exposition of the Third Gospel.* Grand Rapids: Eerdmans, 1987.

Ilan, Tal. "Notes on the Distribution of Jewish Women's Names in Palestine in the Second Temple and Mishnaic Periods." *Journal of Jewish Studies* 40 (1989): 186–200.

Licona, Michael. *The Resurrection of Jesus: A New Historiographical Approach*. Downers Grove, IL: IVP Academic, 2010.

Lundin, Roger. *Emily Dickinson and the Art of Belief*. Grand Rapids: Eerdmans, 1998.

Marshall, I. H. *Luke: Historian and Theologian*. 3rd ed. Exeter: Paternoster, 1988.

Robinson, John A. T. *The Priority of John*. Edited by J. F. Coakley. London: SCM, 1985.

Routledge, Robin. "Passover and Last Supper." *Tyndale Bulletin* 53 (2002): 203–21.

Strobel, Lee, ed. *The Case for the Resurrection: Investigating the Evidence for Belief*. Grand Rapids: Zondervan, 2009.

Theissen, Gerd. *In the Shadow of the Galilean: The Quest of the Historical Jesus in Narrative Form*. Translated by John Bowden. Philadelphia: Fortress, 1987.

Wright, N. T. *The Resurrection of the Son of God*. Vol. 3 of *Christian Origins and the Question of God*. Minneapolis: Fortress, 2003.

Contributors

General Editors
Mark L. Strauss
John H. Walton

Associate Editor, Illustrating the Text
Rosalie de Rosset

Series Development
Jack Kuhatschek
Brian Vos

Project Editor
James Korsmo

Interior Design
Brian Brunsting

Visual Content
Kim Walton

Cover Direction
Paula Gibson
Michael Cook

Image Credits

Unless otherwise indicated, photos, illustrations, and maps are copyright © Baker Photo Archive.

The Baker Photo Archive acknowledges the permission of the following institutions and individuals.

Photo on page 184 © Baker Photo Archive. Courtesy of the Aegyptisches Museum and Papyrussammlung, Berlin, Germany.

Photos on pages 201, 261 © Baker Photo Archive. Courtesy of the Antikensammlung, Berlin, Germany.

Photo on page 256 © Baker Photo Archive. Courtesy of the Art Institute of Chicago.

Photos on pages 5, 27, 204, 136, 222, 248, 253, 310, 362 © Baker Photo Archive. Courtesy of the British Museum, London, England.

Photo on pages 138–39 © Baker Photo Archive. Courtesy of the Eretz Museum, Tel Aviv, Israel.

Photos on pages 214, 277 © Baker Photo Archive. Courtesy of the Greek Ministry of Antiquities and the Archaeological Museum of Ancient Corinth, Greece.

Photo on page 224 © Baker Photo Archive. Courtesy of the Greek Ministry of Antiquities and the Archeological Museum of Thessaloniki, Greece.

Photos on pages 10, 42, 45, 364, 366 © Baker Photo Archive. Courtesy of the Holyland Hotel. Reproduction of the City of Jerusalem at the time of the Second Temple, located on the grounds of the Holyland Hotel, Jerusalem, 2001. Present location: The Israel Museum, Jerusalem.

Photos on pages 207, 345 © Baker Photo Archive. Courtesy of the Masada Museum.

Photo on page 292 © Baker Photo Archive. Courtesy of the museum at Sepphoris.

Photos on pages 33, 294, 334, 387 © Baker Photo Archive. Courtesy of the Musée du Louvre; Autorisation de photographer et de filmer. Louvre, Paris, France.

Photo on page 30 © Baker Photo Archive. Courtesy of the Oriental Institute Museum, Chicago.

Photo on page 27 © Baker Photo Archive. Courtesy of the Papyrussammlung, Berlin, Germany.

Photo on page 330 © Baker Photo Archive. Courtesy of the Skirball Museum, Hebrew Union College–Jewish Institute of Religion, 13 King David Street, Jerusalem 94101.

Photo on page 370 © Baker Photo Archive. Courtesy of the Skulpturensammlung, Germany.

Photo on page 3 © Baker Photo Archive. Courtesy of Sola Scriptura: the Van Kampen Collection on display at the Holy Land Experience, Orlando, Florida.

Illustrations on pages 32, 135, 281 (×2) © Baker Photo Archive / Timothy Ladwig.

Photo on page 2 © Baker Photo Archive. Courtesy of the Turkish Ministry of Antiquities and the Antalya Museum, Turkey.

Photo on page 255 © Baker Photo Archive. Courtesy of the Turkish Ministry of Antiquities and the Istanbul Archaeological Museum.

Photos on pages 153, 175 © Baker Photo Archive. Courtesy of the Vatican Museum.

Photo on page 267 © Baker Photo Archive. Courtesy of the Wohl Archaeological Museum and Burnt House, Jerusalem.

Photo on page 80 © Baker Photo Archive. Courtesy of the Yigal Allon Centre, Kibbutz Ginosar, on the western shore of the Sea of Galilee, Israel.

Additional image credits

Photo on page 389 © Adriatikus / Wikimedia Commons, CC-by-sa-3.0.

Photo on page 115 © Archives Larousse, Paris, France / Giraudon / The Bridgeman Art Library.

Photo on page 298 © Avishai Teicher / Wikimedia Commons.

Illustration on page 314 © Balage Balogh / Archaeology Illustrated (www.archaeologyillustrated.com).

Photo on page 49 © Birmingham Museums and Art Gallery / The Bridgeman Art Library.

Photo on page 100 © Brooklyn Museum of Art, New York, USA / The Bridgeman Art Library.

Photo on page 282 © Darren Swim / Wikimedia Commons, CC-by-sa-3.0.

Photo on page 169 © De Agostini Picture Library / G. Nimatallah / The Bridgeman Art Library.

Photo on page 92 © De Agostini Picture Library / The Bridgeman Art Library.

Photo on page 64 © Deror avi / Wikimedia Commons, CC-by-sa-3.0.

Photo on page 327 © Diego Delso / Wikimedia Commons, CC-by-sa-3.0.

Photo on page 230 © Dr. James C. Martin and the Israel Museum. Collection of the Israel Museum,

Jerusalem, and courtesy of the Israel Antiquities Authority, exhibited at the Israel Museum, Jerusalem.

Photo on page 321 © Dr. James C. Martin and the Israel Museum (Rockefeller Museum). Collection of the Israel Museum, Jerusalem, and courtesy of the Israel Antiquities Authority, exhibited at the Rockefeller Museum, Jerusalem.

Photos on pages 12, 68, 263, 352 © Dr. James C. Martin and the Israel Museum (Shrine of the Book). Collection of the Israel Museum, Jeruslaem, and courtesy of the Israel Antiquities Authority, exhibited at the Shrine of the Book, the Israel Museum, Jerusalem.

Photo on page 186 by English Photographer, (19th century) / Private Collection / © Look and Learn / Peter Jackson Collection / The Bridgeman Art Library.

Photo on page 247 © Fortune Louis Meaulle (1844–1901) / Private Collection / The Bridgeman Art Library.

Photo on page 25 © Frederiksborg Castle, Hillerod, Denmark / The Bridgeman Art Library.

Photo on page 325 from Gemaeldegalerie Alte Meister, Dresden, Germany / © Staatliche Kunstsammlungen Dresden / The Bridgeman Art Library.

Photo on page 111 © Giovanni Dall'Orto courtesy of the National Archaeological Museum of Athens / Wikimedia Commons.

Photo on page 258 © Hermitage, St. Petersburg, Russia / The Bridgeman Art Library.

Photo on page 123 © IKAI courtesy of the Universalmuseum Joanneum, Styria, Austria / Wikimedia Commons, CC-by-sa-2.5.

Photo on page 117 © JoJan courtesy of the Museo della città di Rimini / Wikimedia Commons, CC-by-sa-3.0.

Photos on pages 176, 219, 244, 369, 375 © Kim Walton.

Photos on pages 47, 61, 126, 203 © Kim Walton. Courtesy of the British Museum, London, England.

Photos on pages 59, 90 © Kim Walton. Courtesy of the Chora Museum, Istanbul, Turkey.

Photo on page 38 © Kim Walton. Courtesy of the Israel Museum, Jerusalem, and courtesy of the Israel Antiquities Authority.

Photo on page 304 © Kim Walton. Courtesy of the Museum of the Franciscan Convent, Jerusalem.

Photo on page 358 © Kim Walton. Courtesy of the National Archaeological Museum of Athens.

Photo on page 379 from Koninklijk Museum voor Schone Kunsten, Antwerp, Belgium / © Lukas - Art in Flanders VZW / Photo: Hugo Maertens / The Bridgeman Art Library.

Photo on page 113 © Library of Congress Prints & Photographs Division, [reproduction number, LC-DIG-ppmsca-18419-00055].

Photo on page 120 © Library of Congress Prints & Photographs Division, [reproduction number, LC-DIG-matpc-03036].

Photo on page 140 © Library of Congress Prints & Photographs Division, [reproduction number, LC-DIG-matpc-10616].

Photo on page 181 © Library of Congress Prints & Photographs Division, [reproduction number, LC-DIG-ppmsca-05004].

Photo on page 309 © Library of Congress Prints & Photographs Division, [reproduction number, LC-DIG-matpc-16343].

Photo on page 347 © Library of Congress Prints & Photographs Division, [reproduction number, LC-DIG-matpc-00936].

Photos on pages 57, 228, 291, 306 © Marie-Lan Nguyen / Wikimedia Commons. Courtesy of the Musée du Louvre; Autorisation de photographer et de filmer. Louvre, Paris, France.

Photo on page 159 © Marie-Lan Nguyen courtesy of the Musei Capitolini Centrale Montemartini, Rome / Wikimedia Commons, CC-by-2.5.

Photo on page 55 © Marie-Lan Nguyen courtesy of the Victoria and Albert Museum / Wikimedia Commons, CC-by-2.5.

Photo on page 198 © Mattes / Wikimedia Commons.

Photo on page 178 © Mrbrefast / Wikimedia Commons, CC-by-sa-3.0.

Photo on page 157 © Museum of the Academy of Fine Arts, St Petersburg / The Bridgeman Art Library.

Photo on page 216 © Patrick Denker, CC-by-2.0.

Photo on page 53 from Private Collection / Photo © Zev Radovan / The Bridgeman Art Library.

Photo on page 340 © Tarker / The Bridgeman Art Library

Photos on pages 84, 106 © Sant'Apollinare Nuovo, Ravenna, Italy / Giraudon / The Bridgeman Art Library.

Photo on page 19 © Tate, London 2013.

Photo on page 235 © The Titanic Collection / UIG / The Bridgeman Art Library.

Photo on page 66 © Tretyakov Gallery, Moscow, Russia / RIA Novosti / The Bridgeman Art Library.

Photo on page 192 © Wallace Collection, London, UK / The Bridgeman Art Library.

Photo on page 96 © William Brigham / Hawaii State Archives.

Photo on page 226 © yoel biton / Wikimedia Commons, CC-by-2.5.

Photos on pages 37, 41, 130, 271, 289, 337, 342, 349, 360, 385 © The Yorck Project / Wikimedia Commons.

Photos on pages 251, 302 © Zev Radovan / The Bridgeman Art Library.

Photo on page 88 © Zev Radovan / Private Collection / The Bridgeman Art Library.

Index